Troubadour on the Road to Gold

Troubadour on the Road to Gold

William B. Lorton's 1849 Journal to California

edited by
LeRoy Johnson and Jean Johnson

with a foreword by
Richard Saunders

The University of Utah Press
Salt Lake City

The Defiance House Man colophon is a registered trademark of The University of Utah Press. It is based on a four-foot-tall Ancient Puebloan pictograph (late PIII) near Glen Canyon, Utah.

Library of Congress Cataloging-in-Publication Data for this title available at https://lccn.loc.gov/2020014586

Errata and further information on this and other titles available online at UofUpress.com

Printed and bound in the United States of America.

The diary of William B. Lorton,
[is] the finest Forty-niner diary
I have ever laid eyes on.

—Dale L. Morgan

The diary is superb.

—Merrill Mattes

Contents

Maps

Illustrations

Foreword

The Finest Diary of Its Kind: An Introduction to William B. Lorton and the Southern Route to California

Richard Saunders

Sand and thirst. Distance. Quavering heat. An isolation so complete that it is physically oppressive. Wind-blown silence. The Great Basin was the most terrible stretch of the overland trail across North America, a place without flowing water or the trees that comforted Americans familiar with the humid East. Bands of Goshutes, Paiutes, and Shoshonis eked out a bare subsistence from the Great Basin prior to white encroachment in the 1840s and 1850s. These people lived quietly and self-sufficiently, raising families and traveling perpetually in an endless, cyclical quest for calories. Their very survival and the marvels of basketry they created in one of the least hospitable environments of North America signals a sophistication that outsiders failed to see. When their traditional existence vanished, they left behind little besides the landscape. At the opposite end of their experiential spectrum are those who traverse the Great Basin today. We experience essentially the same landscape though much differently, taking for granted four-wheel drive, air conditioning, bottled water, overnight accommodations, sturdy boots, and paved highways (or at least graded roads).

Between these two groups, culturally at least, are the Euro-Americans who walked the Great Basin during the mid 19th century. They brought expectations and resources to the desert but did not plan to stay. The desert was merely an inconvenient interruption between civilization and California's Eldorado. The very earliest travelers left us few or no firsthand records, except what we may glean by inference. The New World traders traversing the Spanish Trail between New Mexico and California's Franciscan missions, or Jedediah Smith's band of trappers, heading toward destiny on the Mojave, passed through relatively quickly, leaving little besides footprints and place names. Actual records come only from a later generation. The earliest accounts of these crossings are from "civilized" souls who traversed the desert in and after 1849, headed for the rumored riches of Alta California. For them the Great Basin was a *journada*, a waterless waste where their civilized conveniences were nonexistent, and where modern technologies of the day tended to fail on rock and sand. They left, besides the thin trace of wagon wheels and footprints on desert soils, a few accounts written either for themselves or reminiscently for the benefit of others. They are the ones that interest us here. The diary kept by William Birdsall Lorton (1828–1892) is perhaps the best among them.

The Rediscovery

Prior to the preparation of this volume, very few individuals had seen the overland trail diaries of William B. Lorton. Those who knew of them spoke of his record in superlatives. The relevance and story of Lorton's overland diary, now in published form after nearly 70 years, is inextricably tied to the work of four individuals. Two are the editors of this volume. The others are Carl I. Wheat and Dale L. Morgan. To the latter pair belongs the credit for rediscovering and recognizing the value of the documents. To them, too, perhaps, belongs the blame for the overly long story behind the diaries' delayed publication. Their portion of the backstory has been related in detail elsewhere, but there is merit to understanding at least briefly the prehistory of the present volume (Saunders 2016).[1]

Lorton returned to his native Manhattan from California in the 1850s. Prior to his death, in 1896, he had begun preparing an account of his cross-continental travels for publication. It remained incomplete, and Lorton's diaries and his long-neglected account remained in family hands and unknown to historians from his death until the mid-1950s. Carl I. Wheat, a California lawyer and avocational historian of Death Valley, secured a partial typescript of the Lorton diary from Mary Crowell, a contact in Nevada, who had been loaned the diaries by "a friend" some years earlier. Crowell made a partial transcript from the journals. He was highly impressed, but his interests evolved as he pursued a history

1. Wheat introduced Morgan to an extract of the Lorton diary in a May 12, 1958, letter, asking him to keep Lorton confidential, as Morgan was compiling data for the enormous table of 1849 geographic-benchmark information accompanying publication of the James Avery Pritchard diary ("Chart of Travelers Via South Pass in 1849" in Morgan 1959c). Morgan located the diary's owner with a general query to the Chappaqua, New York, postmaster (back in the day, small-town postmasters often knew more about community genealogy than was decent). The resulting correspondence between Valita B. Moran and Morgan is in boxes 14 and 46 of the Morgan papers, Bancroft Library. The publisher's internal documentation on this book and its failed publication is in the Alfred A. Knopf Inc. records, boxes 464, 533, 743, 785, and addendum box 17, Harry Ransom Humanities Research Center, Univ. of Texas, Austin (hereafter Knopf records).

of cartography involving the West (Wheat 1959).[2] In 1958 Wheat handed off his typescript and the task of locating the original Lorton documents to Dale L. Morgan of The Bancroft Library at the University of California–Berkeley. Before the end of the summer, Morgan had tracked down a granddaughter in Chappaqua, New York, Valita B. Moran, who by happy chance was the family custodian of her grandfather's diaries. She loaned the four small volumes to The Bancroft to allow a careful transcription to be made, ultimately donating them to the library for its peerless collection of overland diaries and narratives with the provision that they be published. Morgan was widely regarded as the reigning scholar of the overland trails, but the discovery only began his long and frustrating involvement with the Lorton diaries. He personally made a careful transcription of the miniscule penciled handwriting. By this point Morgan had carefully studied literally hundreds of trail diaries and letters, published and unpublished. Upon showing the Lorton diary typescript to Bancroft director George P. Hammond at its completion in 1960, Morgan was exultant. "Now you can see what the shouting has been about, and why I have abandoned my early caution, which led me to characterize Lorton as 'one of the half dozen best diaries' by a 49er, and now call it straight out, the finest diary of its kind."[3] Over time Morgan's opinion of the diary only grew and his praise increased.[4] Morgan planned to edit and document the diary as the centerpiece in a comprehensive study of the Southern Route in 1849, ultimately tracking down half a dozen other contemporary records from members of Lorton's company.[5] Publication was committed to Alfred A. Knopf, at the time perhaps the nation's preeminent imprint, but the writing project languished for years, crowded aside by Morgan's other commitments, and ultimately wrecked upon his death, in 1971.

Enter the Johnsons. In December 1973, Morgan's former research associate, Lois Stone, mentioned to Knopf the energetic interest in trail research of a young U.S. Forest Service employee—LeRoy Johnson.[6] The fallen torch was taken up by a new generation, and it is in the capable hands of Johnson and his wife, Jean, that the diary's comprehensive, sparkling detail finally comes before students of

2. Morgan to Wheat, May 14, 1958, Accn 1106, box 1, folder 1, Univ. of Utah Manuscripts Division, Salt Lake City (UU-Ms); Dale Morgan papers (microfilm), reel 7 frame 348 (or 7:348).

3. Morgan to George P. Hammond, November 14, 1960, Morgan papers 3:1148.

4. Morgan to Angus Cameron, April 20, 1961, Knopf records 464:5; Morgan papers 2:177; to Fawn Brodie, October 22, 1961, Morgan papers 1:1751; to Fawn Brodie, August 21, 1967, MS 360 7:14, UU-Ms; 1:1759; John Phillip Walker, ed., *Dale Morgan on Early Mormonism* (Salt Lake City: Signature Books, 1986), 205–210.

5. Morgan to Wheat, August 25, 1958, Accn 1106 box 1, folder 1, UU-Ms; Morgan papers 7:362.

6. Lois Stone to Angus Cameron, December 21, 1973, Knopf records 785:5.

westward trails. The editors have spent patient decades tracing virtually every step of Lorton's route, teasing out clues and resolving geographic details that had frustrated Morgan and enticed fellow researcher Todd I. Berens. As a result, the reader can follow Lorton closely as he moves across the continent through the heart of the American West.

The Gold Rush and the Southern Route

The report of gold in California lit bonfires of desire across the eastern United States. Newspapers filled instantly with rumor. One of the earliest confirmations of mineral reality was a sample carried eastward by a Latter-day Saint, a report of which appeared in the *Pittsburgh Gazette*.[7] While rumor flew, the *Gazette*'s story confirmed that the newspaper's editor had handled a sample of California gold. The story, and hundreds like it with less evidence, was picked up immediately by other newspapers. In 1849 tens of thousands of emigrants flooded west by one of three general routes: by sea around the tip of South America and through the Pacific to the California coast; by sea with a land crossing at Panama; or transcontinentally from various Missouri River waypoints to the Pacific Coast. By far, most gold seekers took the quickest and cheapest transcontinental choice, which still offered at least two main geographic options for travel. One was the "Southern Route," which crossed Texas before dissolving into a maze of paths through New Mexico and Arizona deserts roughly paralleling the present-day Mexican border and sometimes dipping into Mexico.[8] The vast majority of gold seekers followed the Oregon-California Trail, a corridor pioneered in the late 1830s and early 1840s from Missouri and Iowa along the southern bank of the Platte River across present-day Nebraska and into Wyoming; the parallel Mormon Trail followed the Platte's northern bank in a conscious effort to remain apart. Once emigrants reached the South Pass, the trail began raveling. Half a dozen "cutoffs," or shortcuts between key points on the trail, purportedly shortened stretches of the safest but longest route. Overlanders necessarily faced decisions, as cutoffs traded certainty and security for time and distance, which translated to speed toward the mines. The trails braided again past City of Rocks in southwestern Idaho and along the Humboldt River, though loose threads,

7. The *Pittsburgh Gazette*'s source, "E. Whipple," was probably but not certainly Edson Whipple (1805–1894), a member of the 1847 Pioneer Company. The *Gazette*'s February 2 account was widely reprinted by eastern newspapers, including the *New York Herald* (morning edition), February 6, 1849, from which this account is taken.

8. This network relied on the geographic knowledge gleaned by American fur trappers based in Taos after 1826. The best overall work on the misnamed "Gila," or Southern Route, is Harland Hague, *The Road to California: The Search for an Overland Route, 1540–1848* (Glendale, CA: Arthur H. Clark Co., 1978). The best treatment of gold rush travel along it is Benjamin Butler Harris, *The Gila Trail: The Texas Argonauts and the California Gold Rush*, ed. Richard H. Dillon (Norman: Univ. of Oklahoma Press, 1960).

like the life-threatening Hastings Cutoff, attracted a few. Once the Humboldt Sink in western Nevada had been reached and travelers approached the Sierra Nevada Range, the trail positively frayed into a dozen possible routes through the steep-sided mountain passes into California's central valley. The California Trail and its cutoffs were fairly well known by 1849. The great challenge of the main California Trail to the gold seekers was that the road across the Sierras was impenetrably blocked during the winter.

Two-thirds of those who raced for California along the main overland trail and cutoffs between 1849 and 1852 took the shortest routes to the goldfields. The remaining third—between 8,000 and 12,000 people in 1849—opted to detour off the main trail and through the Wasatch Mountains to the still-new Mormon settlement at Great Salt Lake City. At least as early as the *Pittsburgh Gazette* article noted, the route west, detouring by way of the new Mormon settlement, "will not take the traveller out of his way more than forty or fifty miles. The Mormons will be able to supply fresh mules and oxen, and, after next harvest, provisions, to those who are emigrating to California." Generally, overland companies or wagons that opted to take the Salt Lake City detour were those needing repairs, or rest, or overloaded with the trappings of civilization they did not need on the trail and which displaced foodstuffs. The Mormon settlement was a welcome bit of civilization and represented an opportunity to rest their livestock and replenish stores. The Gold Rush was just that—a rush.

A fast-moving Argonaut pack train arrived in Salt Lake City as early as June 23, 1849. Dozens of trains and thousands more people followed (Brooks 1964, 1:353). Between 1849 and 1852, Salt Lake City was as busy as a modern-day truck stop. Diaries reveal that many overland travelers departed for the Golden West in haste, overprepared with unnecessary burdens while understocked in perishables. "We were foolish enough to get everything under heaven that we did not want," wrote one traveler wryly, "and nothing that we did" (H. S. Brown in Madsen 1983, 19). By the time gold seekers had completed the arduous trip across the unbroken plains and arrived at South Pass, they had been on the trail two months or more. They were hungry and tired and still had to traverse the Nevada waste. For those who chose the detour to Salt Lake City, the scene of comparative civilization that greeted tired eyes from the mouth of Emigration Canyon was a welcome one. Despite high prices for groceries and livestock, the Mormon capital was a vital resting place for many who chose to risk their fortunes (and lives) pursuing the golden dream. In a letter dated July 8, 1849, one emigrant wrote a firsthand description of the still-new community:

> Descending the table land which bordered the valley, extensive herds of cattle, horses, and sheep, were grazing in every direction.... Passing over some miles of pasture land, we at length found ourselves in a broad

> and fenced street, extending westward in a straight line for several miles. Houses of wood or sun-dried brick were thickly clustered in the vale before us, some thousands in number, and occupying a spot about as large as the city of New York. They were mostly small, one story high, and perhaps not more than one occupying an acre of land. The whole space for miles, excepting the streets and houses, was in a high state of cultivation. Fields of yellow wheat stood waiting for the harvest, and Indian corn, potatoes, oats, flax, and all kinds of garden vegetables were growing in profusion....
>
> At the first sight of all these signs of cultivation in the wilderness, we were transported with wonder and pleasure. Some wept, some gave three cheers, some laughed, and some ran and fairly danced with joy—while all felt inexpressibly happy to find themselves once more amid scenes which mark the progress of an advancing civilization. We passed on amid scenes like these, expecting every moment to come to some commercial centre, some business point in this great metropolis of the mountains; but we were disappointed. No hotel, sign-post, cake and beer-shop, barber pole, market-house, grocery, provision, dry goods, or hardware store distinguished one part of town from another, not even a bakery or mechanic's sign was anywhere discernable.
>
> [On] inquiry, I found that a combination of seemingly unavoidable circumstances had produced this singular state of affairs. There were no hotels, because there had been no travel; no barbers' shops, because every one chose to shave himself, and no one had time to shave his neighbour; no stores, because they had no goods to sell nor time to traffic; no centre of business, because all were too busy to make a centre.
>
> There was an abundance of mechanic shops, of dressmakers, miliners, and tailors, &c.; but they needed no sign, nor had they any time to paint or erect one, for they were crowded with business. Besides their several trades, all must cultivate the land, or die; for the country was new, and no cultivation but their own within a thousand miles.
>
> And the strangest of all was, that this great city, extending over several square miles, had been erected, and every house and fence made, within nine or ten months of the time of our arrival.[9]

Of those who followed the westward route through Salt Lake City, most stayed only a few days or weeks, eventually turning north along the western face of the Wasatch Range to cross the Bear River, angling northwest to pick up the

9. "The Mormon Valley Near the Great Salt Lake," *New York Tribune*, October 9, 1849, as quoted in Sessions 1982, 76–79.

trail again and follow along the Humboldt River, long known as the only reliable watercourse across Nevada's desert—but not all of them left immediately, and that presented the Mormons with a potentially serious problem. Residents of the Salt Lake Valley settlement had put several thousand acres under cultivation and were well on their way to agricultural self-sufficiency, yet Mormon larders in the spring and summer of 1849 were probably as bare as among the overlanders. The winter of 1848–1849 had been a desperate and nearly disastrous one for the Mormons, a struggle against unusually harsh weather, poor housing, and few supplies. Salt Lake City's population had narrowly escaped wholesale starvation only by pooling and strictly rationing resources. Most residents had subsisted on a few ounces of flour or grain daily per person, supplemented by such amenities as half-frozen thistle roots or a thin soup of boiled rawhide (glue, in fact). "It is a hard time for poor folks," wrote one resident to his father in Iowa, "& hungry times for many."[10] They would remain hungry a few months yet, until gardens began to bear. Thus, the laden fields described by the letter writer were still yet to produce any food.

A southern detour was not well known but not completely unknown, either. Lorton himself reports the return of a preliminary exploring party southward in early September (probably the earliest Sanpete Valley exploration; Parley Pratt's Southern Exploring Company would not leave the city until November). John C. Frémont and Miles Goodyear had traveled from the Salt Lake to California, and Frémont's 1845 report and the Frémont-Pruess map documented the geography (but also misdocumented some of it, which members of the 1849 company would greatly regret). Just north of the Virgin River, as travelers crossed the Las Vegas basin and Mojave Desert, the path roughly followed the west leg of the Spanish Trail from Santa Fe, New Mexico, to Los Angeles, a seasonal activity the Mormons may not have known about. Before Frémont, and unknown to the Mormons and many others, fur trader Jedediah Smith made nearly the identical trip beginning from Bear Lake, past the Salt Lake Valley, and along the rim of the Great Basin and Spanish Trail across the Mojave in 1826—and again in 1827.[11] Most importantly, former Mormon Battalion member Jefferson Hunt and a small band had taken a pack train from Salt Lake City to

10. Brigham H. Young to Phineas Young, April 10, 1849, Phineas Howe Young Papers, Church History Library, Salt Lake City.

11. Frémont's report and the invaluable Fremont-Pruess map were published as *Report of the Exploring Expedition to the Rocky Mountains in the Year 1842, and to Oregon and Northern California in the Years 1843–'44* (Washington, DC: Gales & Seaton, 1845), a document widely available and reprinted before 1849. The Mormons used this document specifically in planning their move west. Regrettably, Smith's earlier (and probably better) geographic knowledge largely died with him. The barest record of that accomplishment was not rediscovered until 1953 (Wheat and Morgan 1954).

Pueblo de Los Angeles in 45 days the previous year. In July 1849, Lorton records the news that Hunt pledged to emigrants willing to go with him that he would get them through to California, verbally confident that wagons could make the journey but doubtless neglecting to mention that their smaller company the year before nearly starved on the journey and fairly crawled into San Bernardino. Two of Hunt's sons arrived so weak that they moved forward only by hanging onto the mule's tails for support. In what could be regarded as essentially a population-control measure, Hunt agreed to repeat his trip of the previous year, leading whoever chose to come with him to southern California. Once in the Los Angeles valley, they could eventually travel north again up the broad Central Valley to the gold diggings. It was a risky venture, but then the Gold Rush was fueled by risk.

Lorton went with Hunt, making the trip as part of the first large-scale company to take the Southern Route, in the opposite direction from the northern on-ramp to the main trail. Heading south from Salt Lake City, the single huge company followed the valleys rimming the eastern edge of the Great Basin; they fell onto the general route of the Spanish Trail across present-day southern Nevada, into the Mojave Desert and across Cajon Pass to Pueblo de Los Angeles. Lorton was one of several who left written accounts of the experience, and one of a very small handful to document their travel while on the journey.

The Southern-Branch Trail as Historical Study

"A tendency exists on the part of...western scholars to ask that each overland journal justify its existence—certainly its publication," commented Dale Morgan in 1961, "by reflecting ordinary events in some extraordinary way." The pinnacle of the overland diary, Morgan felt, was Lorton's journal. "There were a few, a very few, born writers of journals, like William B. Lorton, who set down for us history of the most direct and transparent kind, accounts of their experiences so personally detailed and yet so piercingly general that none who read them can ever forget" (Morgan [1962], 29, 30). With this publication, Lorton's journal joins the voluminous record of other trail literature, a collection of experience and excitement which makes the overland experience a study of fascination to present-day readers. The main northern Oregon-California Trail (sometimes called the Humboldt route) has been studied deeply. The Southern Route to California has been less well studied. Partly this has been because a much lower percentage of the emigrants followed this direction, leaving us with fewer primary sources. Virtually all the travelers on the Southern Route in 1849 were those of Lorton's own very large company.

You will see in these pages that Lorton's account is every bit as valuable and insightful an example of overland narrative as it has been advertised, but its greatest significance is as the defining record documenting the awful decisions and regrettable choices of desert travel between Salt Lake City and Los Angeles. Until comparatively recently, most secondary literature on western trails ignored the Southern Route. The route taken southward by Lorton follows approximately the path of U.S. Highway 91 and Interstate 15. Their trail into southern Utah eventually bisected Parowan Valley and clipped the north end of Cedar Valley, passing within sight of what three years later would be Cedar City. Despite being one of the first instructors at the Branch Normal College (today Southern Utah University) and a committed proponent of trail history, Cedar City resident Howard R. Driggs did not address the Southern Route in any of his many works. Stewart Edward White's *The Forty-Niners* (1921) and Archer Butler Hulbert's *Forty-Niners: The Chronicle of the California Trail* (1931) both focus exclusively on the northern or Humboldt route, as do Irene D. Paden's popular renditions in *The Wake of the Prairie Schooner* (1945) and *Prairie Schooner Detours* (1949). Paden's books are informative, readable travelogues about the main, northern routes of the overland trails, wonderful works even a lifetime removed from their writing. These works, together with George R. Stewart's *The California Trail: An Epic with Many Heroes* (1962), completely miss travel south from Salt Lake City.

The history of the trail branching southward from the Salt Lake Valley began emerging almost coincidentally with the discovery of Lorton's journal. The only significant work to discuss the Southern Route prior to the 1960s was LeRoy and Ann Hafen's documentary compilation *Journals of Forty-Niners: Salt Lake to Los Angeles* (1954b). The Hafens' work appeared prior to the Lorton diaries' rediscovery, collating mostly records of the Latter-day Saints who moved down the trail among the various companies. Its contents are arranged by overland company. Two works by Edward Leo Lyman update and expand the Hafens' work, functioning as analysis where the Hafens failed to tread: *The Arduous Road: Salt Lake to Los Angeles, the Most Difficult Wagon Road in American History* (2001), and *The Overland Journey from Utah to California: Wagon Travel from the City of Saints to the City of Angels* (2004). The most valuable recent work about members of this group is an edited compilation by Jean Johnson, *Grit and Gold: The Death Valley Jayhawkers of 1849* (2018).

Our understanding of Lorton and the 1849 company on the route south will profit from the works mentioned above, but other new sources contribute their own perspectives. Dale Morgan eventually omitted Lorton's journal from the massive data table compiled for his *Journal of James A. Pritchard* (1959). Readers of Lorton's diary will still find that book a useful work, however, since it collates data of travels along the first half of Lorton's path. That trail segment is considered in detail as well in Merrill Mattes's *The Great Platte River Road: The Covered Wagon Mainline via Fort Kearny to Fort Laramie* (1969). The central portion of the route between South Pass and either Fort Hall or Salt Lake

City has not been studied in detail, though considerations of individual cutoffs and elements are available. I will mention, however, that Dale Morgan's "Ferries of the Forty-Niners" includes work on this key aspect of movements along the overland trails. Initially this study was to be part of the Pritchard publication, but it was removed from the manuscript to keep the volume costs within bounds. Morgan later noted that he considered Pritchard finally complete when the ferry study was published in *Annals of Wyoming* in 1959 and 1960. Those who study any part of Lorton's journal will certainly want to consult Will Bagley's *So Rugged and Mountainous: Blazing the Trails to Oregon and California, 1812–1848* (2010) and *With Golden Visions Bright Before Them: Trails to the Mining West, 1849–1852* (2012), which are invaluable. As a basis for identifying potential sources on which to base comparative history, there is no finer resource for future students than Bagley's *Across the Plains, Mountains & Deserts: A Bibliography of the Oregon-California Trail, 1812–1912* (2014). Even John Unruh's magisterial social study of overland emigration in *The Plains Across: The Overland Emigrants and the Trans-Mississippi West, 1840–1860* (1979), which allots a mere two-page summary to 1849–1850 travel, must be considered for its value as a broad picture of the overland experience.

The value of Lorton's diary as a documentary source is greatest for the images and details it contributes to two facets of the overland experience: the experience of those passing through early Utah, and travel along the southern branch of the overland trail. Publication puts this resource before scholars for the first time, and the diary rightly takes its place as the foundational document for both facets of trail history. Of course, the journal fits within a context of other diarists, writers, and documents. Nelson Slater overwintered the 1849–1850 season among the Mormons in Weber County. Passing along to California he disparaged his hosts in *The Fruits of Mormonism; or, A Fair and Candid Statement of Facts…* (1851). Most of those who cite Slater take his statements at face value, failing to note that he was a Methodist minister with a professional antipathy to the Mormons.[12] Lorton's experience in Salt Lake City a year earlier provides a stark counterpoint to Slater's account and parallels the generally positive comments in a compilation of contemporary overlander letters from Salt Lake City published by Dale Morgan in "Letters by 49ers" (appearing in the April 1949 issue of *Western Humanities Review*). Contemporary Mormon sources on interactions with emigrants are only slightly less scarce. The key document in this respect is *On the Mormon Frontier: The Diary of Hosea Stout* (1963), in which Stout complains mostly about the upswing of emigrant business before the courts. As good as it is generally, Unruh's *Plains Across* chapter on "The

12. Dale Morgan planned to produce a new edition of Slater's volume for Talisman Press, but the principals ceased publishing and the volume was never completed.

Mormon 'Halfway House'" slants noticeably in the direction of Slater's negative account from a year after Lorton's stay. Lorton records his failed attempt to secure employment with the Howard Stansbury expedition and thus misses being included in Englishman John Hudson's *A Forty-Niner in Utah: With the Stansbury Exploration of Great Salt Lake*, edited by Brigham D. Madsen (1981), which includes a brief account of Salt Lake City during the same season as Lorton was in residence there.

While Lorton's diary is a readable and important record of travel along the main trail along the Platte River, it is merely one of hundreds of accounts, although probably the most detailed. Lorton's chief contribution to trail history is the peerless, complete record it provides documenting experience along the southern branch of the trail. Publication of Lorton's diary now allows his work to assume preeminence as the key documentary record for 1849. As mentioned above, the southern branch has been studied perhaps least of all the major corridors, partly because material is so scarce. Even Dale Morgan opined that documentary material for the Southern Route was positively rare.[13] LeRoy and Ann Hafen collected and republished key documents from the various companies in *Journals of Forty-Niners*, which can be consulted for a score of primary sources (although only for extracted portions relevant to movement south from Salt Lake City and along the Spanish Trail).

As Lorton's prospective editor, Dale Morgan could not abide his work being incomplete and ceaselessly hunted relevant documents. It was during his preparations to edit the journal that contemporary sources unavailable to the Hafens again came to light. The list that follows contains largely documentary discoveries made by Morgan as they are presently available. Morgan himself rediscovered Lorton's three published letters in the *Sun* of New York City. The first two, dated May 9 from St. Joseph, Missouri, appeared in the June 9 issue, and one from Fort Laramie, dated June 30, in the September 7 issue. The last, dated January 20, 1850, was written from the village that was Los Angeles after Lorton's diary concluded; how it was forwarded east no one knows, but it appeared merely five months after being written in the *Sun*'s May 8, 1850, issue. The Zamorano Club of Los Angeles, a society of California book collectors, printed 150 copies of this last letter as a keepsake for members in 1957 (Lorton 1957). The letters contribute experiential details beyond the journal itself, though it is clear that Lorton consulted his diary in writing them. Regrettably, at least two more of Lorton's letters to the *Sun* were lost. One was written in early October 1849 as the company gathered in Utah Valley for their foray southward. The other (cited in his January 20 letter) was written after the disastrous search for the nonexistent shortcut across the Nevada desert. Lorton sent a letter from Beaver

13. Morgan to Floyd Risvold, April 21, 1960, Morgan papers 6:490.

Dam Wash, Utah, on November 26, unadvisedly entrusting it to O.K. Smith, who went to California rather than Salt Lake City and apparently lost the letter.

Letters of Lorton's contemporaries are similarly valuable. Caleb N. Ormsby's (and others) were collected in Russell E. Bidlack's edited compilation *Letters Home: The Story of Ann Arbor's Forty-Niners* (1960). A few years later Theodore C. Ressler published *Trails Divided: A Dissertation on the Overland Journey from Iowa "Forty-Niners" of the "Sacramento Mining Company"* (1964). One of Ressler's key documents was misattributed to a later owner, David Switzer, and the work was cited as the "Switzer log." Morgan secured a photocopy of the original document and later identified the writer as Adonijah S. Welch. The document was used to good effect in Jean Johnson's *Grit and Gold*, cited earlier. Cephas Arms's journal and several letters published in the *Knoxville (IL) Journal* were collected and published by Michigan librarian John Cumming in *The Long Road to California: The Journal of Cephas Arms, Supplemented with Letters Written by Traveling Companions on the Overland Trail in 1849* (1985). And though the Hafens published relevant extracts of the Addison Pratt journals, S. George Ellsworth eventually published the complete Pratt record as *The Journals of Addison Pratt: Being a Narrative of Yankee Whaling in the Eighteen Twenties, A Mormon Missionary to the Society Islands, and of Early California and Utah in the Eighteen Forties and Fifties* (1990).

Unpublished material beyond the Hafens' volume and now available is similarly significant. Morgan intended to include relevant sections of the Vincent A. Hoover diary in conjunction with Lorton's journal when that set of two documents was acquired by the Huntington Library in 1964. The Lorton and Hoover projects were later divided for separate publication. With the participation of Eleanor Towles Harris, the edited Hoover diary was destined for the California Historical Society. This project, like Lorton's diary, remained incomplete at Morgan's death and Harris moved on to other works. Morgan's careful transcript remains among his papers at The Bancroft Library and is yet unpublished. It was used by Leo Lyman for *The Overland Journey from Utah to California*. Morgan's long, patient research through contemporary newspapers yielded dozens of informative letters and references by contemporaries, supplementing extracted notes and transcriptions from trail diaries which still fill his research files.

The southern branch of the overland route was documented in one printed overland guidebook, Joseph Caine and Arieh C. Brower's enormously significant *Mormon Way Bill* (1851). The route text was compiled by Caine, a member of the fast-moving Flake-Rich company, which relied on pack animals rather than risking wagons. Mileages along trails were calculated by a "roadometer"—a primitive but effective odometer—attached to Addison Pratt's wagon in the Jefferson Hunt company. The combined result was published a year later in Salt

Lake City. The guide exists in fewer than half a dozen copies but was reprinted in 1946 by the Daughters of Utah Pioneers; the relevant section south is extracted in *Journals of Forty-Niners* (Hafen and Hafen 1954b, 321–24).

No matter how one looks over the history of emigration westward, the story of the 1849 companies that risked all on the southward route to California is among the most dramatic. That record is now materially enriched by William B. Lorton's diary, which rightfully takes a prominent place in the catalogue to provide a new generation of readers with the basis of their new adventures.

Preface

We have passed through many dizzy scenes....
It would take an abler pen than mine to delineate in their true character, the various vicissitudes, trials, incidents and dangers attending an overland journey across the Continent. Perhaps all the events in the knowledge of civilized man that has ever transpired on these western wilds, will not compete with the present year.

—William B. Lorton, letter to the *Sun*, 1849

Thus William Birdsall Lorton introduced the saga of his trek to the California goldfields to readers of the *New York Sun* in his hometown of New York City. He was a troubadour in the medieval sense: not only was he a fine singer (so-called "Negro melodies" were his specialty) and violinist, but he was an impressive chronicler of what he saw and heard and reported it to his hometown readers—and now to us.

Merrill Mattes, noted western historian, said in his description of Lorton's California Journal: "The diary is superb, but the tiny fuzzy script of the original poses a challenge to the reader" (1969, 183). "Tiny" is an accurate descriptor for Lorton's handwriting. (The height of his capital letters averages three millimeters, the thickness of two pennies, and his lowercase letters average one millimeter.) Another prominent western historian, Dale Lowell Morgan, gave radiant praise for the daily jottings of this young man who was visiting relatives in western Illinois and who began a monumental trip west with people who, until only days before leaving, were strangers to him. Lorton's self-confidence, positive attitude, musical abilities, and willingness to work with others made him a worthy traveling companion.

This is not just another, although very good, gold rush trail journal. It is far longer than most, with almost daily entries, and not only expresses personal observations, but includes objective information as well—some mileages, locations, and occurrences. His wagon train—the Knox County Company—was unusual in that it had no deaths from cholera; sickness from it, yes, and Lorton mentions deaths from cholera in other trains. But his train was unique in that it

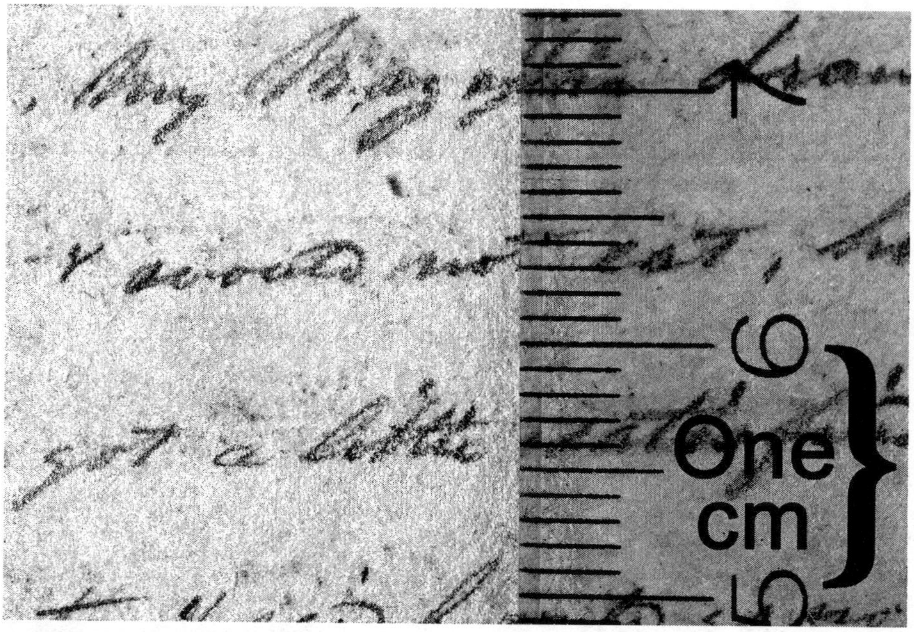

FIGURE 1. Lorton wrote in pencil. His script in these journals is about one millimeter for lowercase letters and about three millimeters for capitals. Courtesy of The Bancroft Library.

suffered from an excessive number of serious cattle stampedes. He says it became notorious as the "stampede train," which caused other travelers to shun them.

Lorton's journal corrects some long-held assumptions about where and when the Knox County Company was formed, and more importantly for Death Valley historians, it provides the preliminary story of the trek of the Death Valley Jayhawkers from western Illinois to southwestern Utah. He provides information that allows us to positively identify Mount Misery, the jumping-off point for the Death Valley '49ers and for the packers who left the wagons at Mount Misery in search of a bogus route toward Walker Pass in the Sierra Nevada. William Lorton becomes one of these packers.

We present information about why the San Joaquin Company formed south of Salt Lake City, why it was so large, and why its detour down Beaver River was disastrous. We analyze Lorton's route through *terra incognita*—the desert in southeastern Nevada that Lorton traversed with other packers, and we present new research on a fragment of the Old Spanish Trail south of today's Resting Spring near Tecopa, California.

Lorton's early notebooks (five sewn into one volume) describe his travels from New York City to western Illinois in the fall of 1848, where he visits his aunt and her husband and his adult cousins on his mother's side, and where he makes the momentous decision to continue his western journey by becoming part of the rush to California for gold. We excerpt these early notebooks and start his California journals, word for word, in early April 1849. Although Mattes and Morgan refer to Lorton's work as "diaries," Lorton uses "journal" on his title pages, so we follow his choice. His journey is one of adventure, physical labor, discouragement, hope, loss, tenacity, and ultimate success—a journey worth taking with him.

Lorton's Journal Notebooks

William Lorton's granddaughter, Mrs. William J. Moran, and her son, Vallandigham B. Nisbeth, donated the original pocket notebooks to The Bancroft Library in 1960 (*Bancroftiana* 1960, 6). Also in The Bancroft is a typescript Morgan made of Lorton's journal plus copies of Lorton's letters.

In 1966, in preparation for publication, Morgan sent a copy of his "edited re-transcript" of Lorton's journals to Alfred A. Knopf, Inc., in which he used conventional spelling and punctuation. But Morgan was unable to finish the introductory text, notes, bibliography, or supporting material before cancer brought an end to his prodigious work on western history (Saunders 2016, 479). We call this the Knopf (or "and") manuscript to differentiate it from Morgan's typescript (the "ampersand" copy), in which he used Lorton's original spellings. Richard Saunders (2016) discusses the convoluted process Morgan navigated for over a decade to get the Knopf manuscript near completion only to have it halted by his untimely death in 1971.

In the early 1970s, we came across the typescript Morgan made of Lorton's journal (or diary) while working on *Escape from Death Valley*, Lewis Manly's serialized articles about the '49ers who made their way into (and out of) Death Valley. Years later, the historian Will Bagley asked us to work on the Lorton journals for publication, and thanks to his inducement and early support, we herein present Lorton's California Journal.

The whole of Lorton's journal from New York to California consists of eight booklets (notebooks), each about six by four inches. The first five are sewn together to make a single, thicker booklet without a leather or leatherette cover. Lorton titled the other three booklets Volumes I, II, and III of his California Journal.

The first five notebooks describe Lorton's travels from New York City to the Monmouth area in western Illinois and his six-month stay with cousins during the winter of 1848–1849. A synopsis of these early notebooks is in chapter 1.

Volume I of Lorton's California Journal (the second separate volume), starts with Lorton impatiently waiting near Monmouth for the other members of his wagon mess. His title page proudly proclaims "Wm B. Lorton A.D. 1848 [1849] California Journal. Vol. I," and on the verso side is the first of several winsome pencil sketches Lorton places at the front and back of his California notebooks. Following are 124 hand-numbered pages of text that becomes smaller and

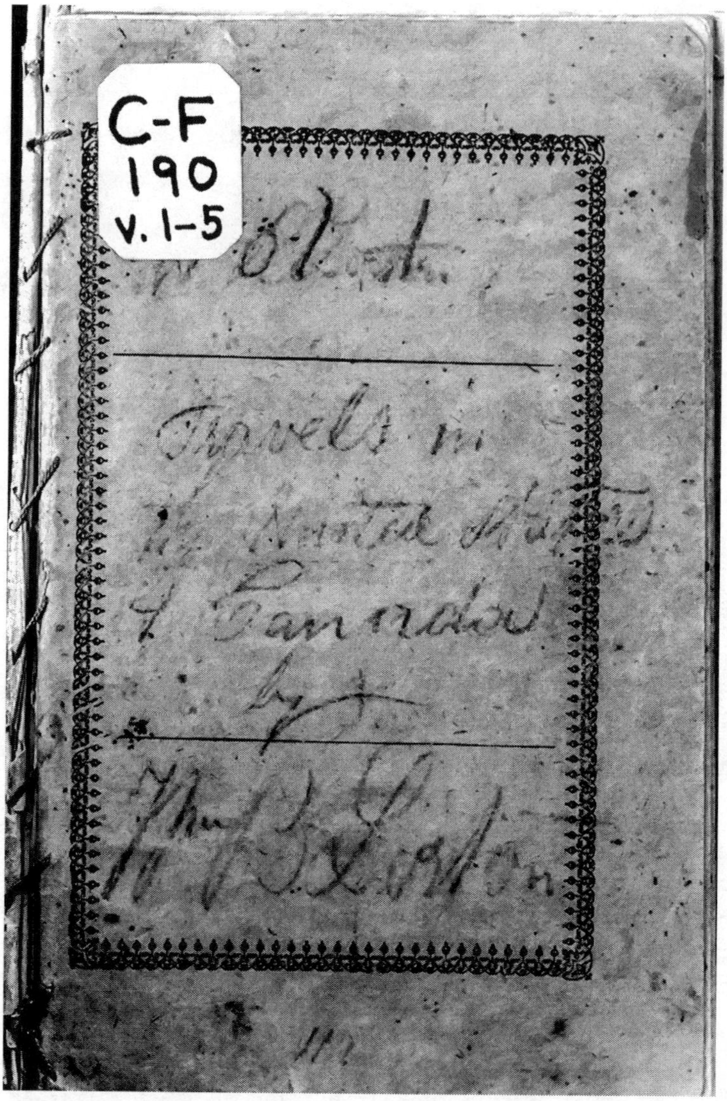

FIGURE 2. Lorton's sewn-together book of the five notebooks preliminary to his California Journal notebooks. It reads: "Wm B Lorton/Travels in the United States & Canada/by/Wm B. Lorton." Courtesy of The Bancroft Library.

harder to read as his journey progressed. The tan leather cover has a loop on the front to hold a back flap that keeps the pocket journal closed.

Volume II of the California Journal is bound with green leatherette and begins with several pencil sketches. The title page, "California Expedition Journal Vol. II," includes a sketch of Laramie Peak and the Black Hills. It starts as the continuation of a stampede on June 4 after crossing the Loup River. Volume III, with a black leatherette cover, is titled "California Journal from Salt Lake Vol. III 1849." It opens with Lorton's own Indian-to-English dictionary and a startling

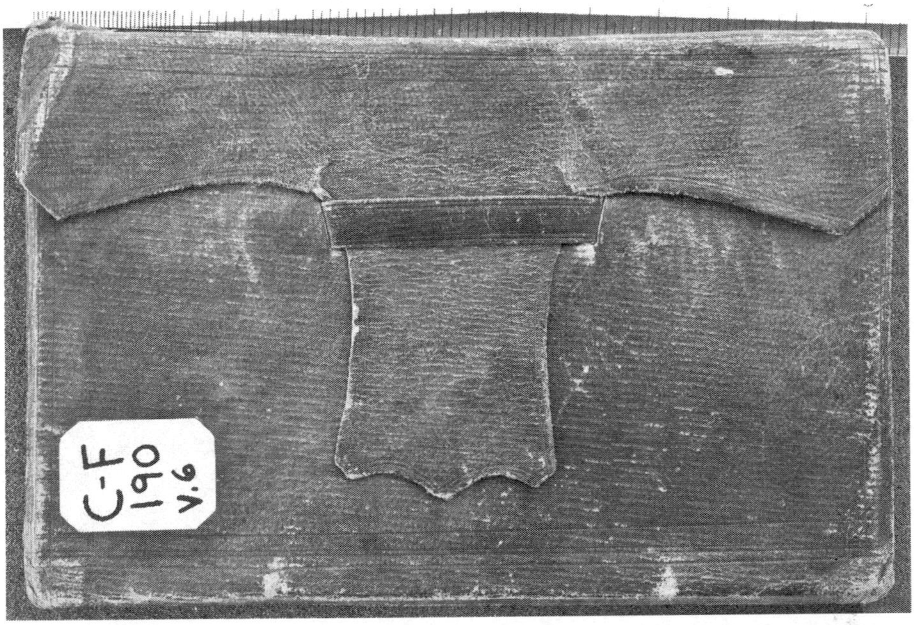

FIGURE 3. First California Journal notebook. Tan leather cover with back flap folded through front loop. Courtesy of The Bancroft Library.

self-portrait (we assume) of what starvation and arduous labor had wrought by the time he arrived in the Sierra Nevada gold camps on the Feather River by April 30, 1850.

In this book, we have divided Lorton's travels into three chronological parts: Part I from New York City to western Illinois; Part II from western Illinois to Salt Lake City; and Part III from Salt Lake City to the Feather River gold diggings via Pueblo de Los Angeles. The chapters within each part have their own introductions, which provide background remarks that touch on historical context, Lorton's locations, and some of the people he meets and travels with on particular sections of his journey.

Lorton also wrote letters to the *New York Sun* during his journey. We insert three of them at appropriate points in this volume to provide additional details.

Lorton's Letters

When Lorton decided to go to California's gold country, he wrote the editor of the *New York Sun,* suggesting he become a correspondent for the newspaper. He subsequently wrote four letters to the *Sun*, but apparently only three of them were published. They are based on his journal but add details, afterthoughts, about what Lorton felt would interest his readers. He wrote his first letter, dated May 9, 1849, from St. Joseph, Missouri, and the next on June 30 from Fort Laramie. They were printed in the *Sun* on June 8 and September 7, 1849, respectively. The third was apparently written from camp at Hobble Creek, Utah, but we have not found a copy of it. Lorton mentions in his journal, on November 26, that he sent still another letter via Captain O. K. Smith to Salt Lake City. This was written just after Lorton's disastrous pack trip into *terra incognita* following a bogus cut-off map to the goldfields. But since much of that part of his journey is covered in his letter of January 20, 1850, it is possible he wrote the November letter to friends or family. This letter was probably lost in transit when men from Smith's company were picked up by two different wagon trains and continued to California instead of returning to Salt Lake City.

Lorton wrote his last letter to the *Sun* while in Los Angeles on January 20, 1850; that letter was published May 8, 1850, under the heading "Terrible Sufferings of the Emigrants—Thrilling Details." The Zamorano Club in Los Angeles reprinted 150 copies of this letter as a keepsake in 1957 (Lorton 1957).

Editorial Procedures

Fortunately, we were able to work with Lorton's original notebooks, the microfilm of them that The Bancroft Library supplied, and our photographs of each page made with a high-resolution lens on a Nikon digital camera. We were able to enlarge and enhance each page on our computer for clarity to corroborate Morgan's typescript. Considering the tiny size of Lorton's handwriting, this was an important advantage Morgan did not have. In only a few instances could we not decipher some of Lorton's words, primarily because of smudges from time (and sweat).

Invaluable to our work was Morgan's typescript of the Lorton journal. Morgan's experience reading well over a hundred diaries in his work at The Bancroft Library eminently qualified him to decipher Lorton's handwriting and to adhere as closely as possible to Lorton's spelling and writing style (Morgan 1959c, 15–16 and chart in back pocket). In his typescript, Morgan's only major change was to put a capital at the beginning and a period at the end of what he judged to be sentences. When a word ended with a squiggle, he wrote out the full word. Again, we call this typescript Morgan's "ampersand" copy, and that is what we use herein.

We keep Lorton's creative and often phonetically logical spelling. Although reading Lorton's spelling may take some adjustment by the reader, we think it adds to the adventure and intimacy of his journey and not only reveals the young man's personality but also opens a window on American language and concepts in 1849.

You'll see Lorton's spelling of soup as *soop*, pretty as *pritty*, route as *rout*, crossed as *crost*, and juicy as *jucy*. He is not always consistent, and you can almost hear him think, "That doesn't look right," so he tries a different spelling. "Though" is almost always contracted to *tho*, and "through" is usually *thro* (both typical of the period). "Company" is shortened to *Comp* or *Compy*, sometimes with a period but most often without.

We also preserve Lorton's oddities of original grammar with the following exceptions: He abbreviates Indians *Inds*, but we spell it out; "negro" is now *Negro*; and we capitalize names of persons and places. We change "½" to *1/2* and use *o'clock* to standardize Lorton's variations.

In the latter part of his journey, Lorton's *c*'s looked more and more like his *s*'s, which became a frustrating transcription problem. We finally chose to use whichever letter the handwriting looked like, not necessarily the conventional spelling.

Lorton sometimes began a sentence with a numeral, which we let stand rather than spelling out the number. At the beginning and middle of the month, we add the year to his date. Many times, Lorton's dates are off a day or so. We put the correct dates in brackets, and when we refer to a day in the text or notes, we use the corrected date, not Lorton's.

We maintain the punctuation (or its absence) in the original, except we add periods to the ends of sentences as did Morgan, and judiciously add or remove commas for clarity. We also add paragraphs for the same reason. In other words, we perform a balancing act between being obsessively true to the author while still providing a smooth and coherent progression for the reader. He often places an apostrophe before a contracted word (e.g., *did'nt*) rather than in place of the missing letter. Sometimes Lorton forgets to use close-quote marks, so we add them silently. He usually uses possessives correctly, but not always.

We rarely correct words silently except to spell out squiggles at the ends. This usually occurs at the inner margin bend of the page, where writing is difficult. Parentheses in Lorton's text are his. We use brackets to enclose added letters, missing words, or conjectural readings (except as noted above). [*Blank*] indicates Lorton left a blank space, while other bracketed comments, such as [*tear*], denote physical defects in the manuscript, and [*illegible*] means we can't decipher the word or it was obliterated in some way. A question mark in brackets [*?*] means we think this is the word but the penmanship cannot be deciphered positively.

From time to time, Lorton inserted what he called "Errata." Usually it was information he forgot to insert a day or so before. We silently insert the information where it belongs.

Years later, while preparing to publish his memoirs, Lorton wrote in pen across some pages, underlined words, and even added words or dates. We do not include these later additions except where they add information. Since Lorton crossed out certain words because he did not want them used, we don't use them either. We drop superscripts (3rd to 3rd) and place interlined information in its logical place in the text. We sometimes add place names [in brackets] to help orient the reader.

Lorton's sketches are done in pencil, and several of them are shaded in both graphite and blue pencil. One unlabeled sketch is graphite, blue, and red pencil with what looks like smudges of charcoal.

The Mormon city west of the Wasatch Range was originally named "Great Salt Lake City," but we use Salt Lake City throughout. In the notes and discussion material, we shorten The Church of Jesus Christ of Latter-day Saints to LDS, LDS Church, or Mormon Church.

We often use the terms *left* and *right* bank (or side) of a river or canyon instead of south side or north side. This is based on nomenclature scientists have used, particularly surveyors, for the last 200 years: *Always face down-river (or down canyon) when describing the river's banks*, i.e., face the same way the water flows.

"Crow-miles" is our more descriptive term for straight-line measurement versus trail miles.

Entries in the References section are alphabetical. There is a separate section for maps, most of which are found online in the David Rumsey Historical Map Collection, but there are sufficient data provided to retrieve them from libraries. We list articles or letters in newspapers by the writer's name when it is available. To reduce the number of footnotes, many of the citations are in the text. We cite unauthored newspaper articles in the text but do not include them in the References. Because there are many editions of William Lewis Manly's *Death Valley in '49*, the page references are, of necessity, to the original edition. Facsimile copies are readily available.

Acknowledgments

This book could not have been completed without the help of many people who possess knowledge and interest in western American history. Our sincerest thanks to all of you. Here we mention a few by name:

First and foremost, Dale Morgan, for his meticulous work transcribing Lorton's journal notebooks while working at The Bancroft Library, Berkeley, California. Then Will Bagley for the impetus, encouragement, wise guidance, and information he provided, which was essential to getting this project both started and completed; Dr. Richard Saunders, whose searching inquiry into the fate of Morgan's Lorton project enabled us to determine that no finished manuscript existed; and the peer reviewers made constructive suggestions that enriched the manuscript; the Eldon Hafen family, who gave us support in so many ways during our Mount Misery research; Tom Sutak for being a wise sounding board and co-investigator along the Southern Route; our son, Mark, who four-wheeled us into *terra incognita* and other research jaunts; Roy Tea, for providing us with Southern Route material in Utah; and Diann Biltz for her expertise in genealogy. The New York Hastings-on-Hudson Historical Society was particularly helpful by providing information on Lorton's life after California.

We could not have done as thorough a job of research without the help of staff at The Bancroft Library, the Library of Congress, The Huntington Library, the Bureau of Land Management, and numerous other historical repositories across the nation. We also extend our appreciation to the Stanford University Library for providing access to the David Rumsey Historical Map Collection, and to those organizations that have provided online access to obscure books otherwise difficult to find.

We particularly appreciate the generous contribution Dr. Saunders made by writing the foreword to this volume—his encouraging interest, extensive time, and depth of knowledge on western American history. And we are indebted to the staff at the University of Utah Press, who have brought this book to completion.

Introduction

The Sirens' Call

The rush for California gold started with one of the great coincidences of timing in United States history—James W. Marshall's discovery of gold on January 14, 1848, in the Sierra Nevada of Alta California, and the signing of the Treaty of Guadalupe Hidalgo only nine days later, ending the Mexican-American War and ceding Alta California (and other Mexican territory) to the United States.[1]

Neither nation was aware that just days before the treaty was signed, Marshall had discovered gold while building a sawmill in a joint venture with John Sutter at today's Coloma, on the South Fork of the American River (about 45 miles east of Sutter's Fort at today's Sacramento).

California newspapers started carrying news of the gold discovery in April 1848, and those newspapers were sent east, but the time delay was generally two or more months. Mentions of California gold started to appear in East Coast newspapers during August 1848—news carried by men such as Kit Carson and Edward Beale (Bieber 1937, 66–67; Brewerton 1930, 14–19; Carter 1968; Sabin 1995, 580).

Official news of Marshall's momentous discovery arrived in Washington, DC, on September 14, 1848, via letters from U.S. Consul Thomas O. Larkin to Secretary of State James Buchanan (Larkin 1848, 53-56; 1960, 301–5). With Larkin's communiqué was a small sample of gold dust highlighting the veracity of his pronouncement. He also sent letters to newspaper editors who spread the word nationwide, often with embellishment. "Your letters & those of others have been running thro' the papers all over the country, creating wonder and amazement in every mind," wrote Ebenezer Childs to Larkin on September 27, 1848.[2]

1. Congress passed the Declaration of War on May 13, 1846, and the war ended February 2, 1848 (*Statutes at Large* 9 Stat. 922, 1848, Treaty of Guadalupe Hidalgo). The United States paid $15 million for just over 545 million acres of Mexican territory (about three cents per acre).

2. Larkin was the United States' Consul to Mexico's Alta California, a nonsalaried position, but he was "entitled to fees and commissions for many of his services" (Childs in Hague and Langum 1990, 105, 169).

Acting Lieutenant Edward Fitzgerald Beale carried Larkin's few flakes of gold plus his report (and those of Commodore Thomas Catesby Jones) to Washington, DC. According to Beale's biographer, Gerald Thompson, Beale "knew the importance of the news of the gold discovery to the residents of the United States and desired to be the messenger who carried back the important information to the East" (G. Thompson 1978, 64; 1983, 30).

Commodore Jones, stationed aboard the USS *Ohio* near the southern tip of Baja California, needed a courier to carry official reports and letters, including the one written by Larkin. Beale volunteered to make the trip and said he would do so at his own expense. He left on July 29, 1848, and after an adventurous, arduous, and dangerous odyssey across Mexico to Veracruz on horseback, then by ship to Mobile, Alabama, he reached the nation's capital on September 14, 1848 (G. Thompson 1978, 64–68; 1983, 30–31).

In addition to Larkin's very small quantity of gold, Beale also carried a sample of his own. "In the Navy the tradition was that Beale secured the treasure from one of the earliest visitors to the mill-race in exchange for one hundred grains of quinine which Beale was too old a traveler ever to be without" (Bonsal 1912, 40).

Beale met with President James K. Polk, but according to Thompson, Polk "brushed aside the story of the gold discovery by suggesting that Beale and his fellow officers were probably speculating in city lots in San Francisco and hoped to induce an immigration" (G. Thompson 1983, 248n5).

The *New York Herald* ran the following tantalizing article on November 28, 1848:

> THE GOLD MINES IN CALIFORNIA
>
> There is little room to doubt that that newly acquired territory of the United States is rich, to an extraordinary and almost unparalleled degree, in mineral resources.... It is beyond all question that gold, in immense quantities, is being found daily in this part of our territory.... As yet, we have received no importation of the gold thus gathered; but this is accounted for by the fact that every vessel which anchors in the neighborhood of California, is immediately deserted by her crew...[the sailors] affected with the mania...of gathering the rich material.

This and similar articles tickled the imaginations of many in the East, hinting that they might obtain wealth by simply walking along a stream and picking up nuggets of gold to fill their pockets. However, these dreamers were still leery, in part because "seeing is believing." Other than the small quantities of gold Beale brought and Larkin sent (too miniscule to be put on public display), no tangible proof had yet reached the Atlantic states to support the fabulous claims of limitless gold. But that oversight was soon rectified.

Col. Richard Barnes Mason, military governor of Alta California, and his staff officer Lt. William Tecumseh Sherman toured the newly discovered gold region of Alta California in July 1848. Mason estimated that 4,000 men were "working in the gold district…[and they extracted] from $30,000 to $50,000 worth of gold" each day (Mason 1848, 57, 59, 60; see also Gudde 1974, 366).

Miners donated and sold specimens of gold dust and nuggets to the military governor, which he sent east in "a tea caddy containing 230 ounces, 15 pennyweights, and 9 grains of gold" (Mason 1848, 64). A tea box three inches cubed inside would have held the 230.769 Troy ounces of gold. Lt. Lucien Loeser, Colonel Mason's special gold courier, hand-carried the samples, plus a report from Mason, via the Isthmus of Panama and New Orleans to Washington, DC (Gay 1967, 208–9; also in Bieber 1937, 125n132). In order to get Mason's report to Washington as quickly as possible, Loeser wired the report on November 24, 1848, using the newly installed telegraph in New Orleans (Bancroft 1888, 115n14). Thus, it arrived in time for President Polk to incorporate parts of Mason's report into his written State of the Union message delivered to Congress on December 5, 1848. He extolled the mineral reserves—mainly gold and quicksilver—recently found as part of the vast spoils of war (Polk 1849). The Mexican-American War was unpopular, and the president used the serendipitous gold discovery and the seemingly unlimited reserves of quicksilver ore (cinnabar) found in Alta California to effectively put an end to criticism.

Meanwhile, Loeser hand-carried Mason's report, the little tea caddy of gold, and 13 additional samples, to Washington, DC, arriving on December 7. After the secretary of war showed the impressive nuggets, dust, and flakes of gold to the president, they were put on public display at the War Department, and the remainder were taken to the U.S. Mint in Philadelphia (Polk 1910, 224 [December 7, 1848]; Bancroft 1888, 115–16).

Seeing is believing, and once the public viewed the compelling contents of the tea caddy, reporters immediately began to extol the golden trove. On December 8, the Washington, DC, *Daily Union* commented: "However skeptical any man may have been, we defy him to doubt that if the quantity of such specimens as these be as great as has been represented, the value of the gold in California must be greater than has been hitherto discovered in the old or new continent…. The heaviest piece brought by Lieutenant Loeser weighs a little more than two ounces" (Bieber 1937, 126–27).

The furor that erupted launched one of the largest voluntary mass movements of people ever witnessed—the California Gold Rush. By the mid-1850s the overland migration to California numbered 153,600 (Unruh 1979, 120, table 2). The rush was on, and William B. Lorton, visiting relatives in western Illinois, was caught up in the torrent.

PART I

Gold Rush Overture

CHAPTER 1

New York City to Monmouth, Illinois, 1848–1849

Lorton liked keeping a diary, and filled his with all those minutiae which bring an age to life. He had a most vivid eye for details, and a quick ear, too; I have seen no diary which in a comparable way evokes for the modern reader the sound of things on the trail in 1849.

—Dale Morgan, March 14, 1961

Background

The diarist, William Birdsall Lorton, was a 20-year-old from New York City on a journey to visit his relatives in western Illinois and to see the country along the way. He was born June 29, 1828, in Peakskill, Westchester County, New York, and by 1840 the family lived in neighboring Corlandt. His father, Louis R. Lorton, had been a prosperous merchant, and his grandfather owned considerable property at one time in New York City. William Lorton acquired the trade of house painter, and because of his fine voice, he had vocal training and specialized in "Negro spirituals."[1] He also had certain skill as a violinist and was a member of a New York Handel and Haydn Society, a group inspired by the longstanding Boston H+H Society (Jesse Levine, pers. comm., May 15, 2019). While visiting his Illinois relatives, he became enamored with the idea of joining the rush for California gold, and this he did.

1. Music of black African descent—ballads, work songs, and Christian revival music—was coming into vogue in the Northeast by 1849. The original Christy Minstrels were performing in New York City in the late 1840s, and Stephen Foster had composed his first black-influenced songs—"Old Uncle Ned" and "Oh, Susanna." In 1848 *The Ethiopian Glee Book: A Collection of Popular Negro Melodies* was published in Boston. The underground railroad had been bringing slaves northward from the South since the 1830s, and they brought their music with them. In 1837, antislavery advocates founded Galesburg, Illinois, and it became the first underground railroad depot in Illinois ("Underground Railroad Freedom Station").

Lorton was congenial with people, pulled his weight, and entertained with his singing and violin playing; and by all accounts he could cook well, a rare trait for a man starting his trek to the California goldfields. He admired attractive young women, smoked cigars, and related well with his elders. He does not mention alcohol in his journals, so we assume it was not a burning need, nor was he traveling to improve his health. Thus, struck with the gold fever raging throughout the country, Lorton suddenly extended his journey into a trip to the distant California goldfields.

Lorton's writings reveal a droll sense of humor and a keen sense of observation and inquisitiveness. Although he writes little about his traveling companions, he talks to everyone he meets to accumulate as much information as possible—a doctor whose house he camps nearby, Mormons in Salt Lake City, five young men who wander out of the Wasatch Mountains. Then he makes sound assumptions based on his observations.

From time to time Lorton rhapsodizes about flowers or a sunset, trees on a hillside, a hole in the ground or a mound on top of it. He even sketches scenes that interest him. He seems ambivalent about slavery, but he speaks with sensitivity about deaths and graves. Lorton is incensed when a Tennessee wagon company keeps lost oxen that belong to his wagon train and makes this heartfelt comment: "To kill our cattle is to take our life" (May 29, 1849). In general, Lorton is cheerful when others are despondent, and he mentions only in passing the injury that keeps him from walking for almost two months. One point that perplexed Dale Morgan, and us as well, is how little Lorton says about the people close to him—those he was related to and those with whom he associated daily on his westward trek. He seems more interested in acquiring knowledge than in developing close relationships with other people.

Since we have no picture or physical description of Lorton, we are free to envision him as handsome or homely, winsome or rugged, tall or short, brunette or blond, as our imaginations choose to conceive him.

Lorton's trip across the plains, mountains, and deserts to the California goldfields began in Monmouth, Illinois. But to set the stage for his momentous trip, we abstract his five preliminary notebooks (stitched into one volume) that cover his trip from New York City through the Great Lakes to western Illinois, and the winter he lived with his mother's Olmsted relatives near Monmouth and Galesburg.

Abstract of Lorton's Journal: New York City to Western Illinois

"New York Sept 20th 1848." With no preamble or comments about leaving friends or family, Lorton departed New York City to travel up the Hudson River to Albany by boat, then by rail to Schenectady, where he boarded the packet *Oregon* to travel the canals to Niagara Falls. The *Oregon* traveled the Mohawk

River along today's route of Interstate 90 at a pace of about four miles an hour. On the Erie Canal, a horse pulled the boat while walking on the towpath.

As Lorton played his violin on the boat, a "baby [joined] in the last note of singing." In Rochester, the packet passed under about 50 bridges, and at Lockport they passed through a number of locks. Along the way Lorton described the towns, the weather, and the crops.

On September 24, Lorton waxed rhapsodic about the view of Niagara Falls at the Table Rock viewing area:

> The craggy grotto shakeing & thundering like some mighty earthquake, where the demonic laugh of combating waters send their sepulchral tones of bitter anguish through the deep caverns and recesses.... Here where ripple leaps the limped stream in extacies of delight & fancies it has wings to soar awhile, then drounds itself in foam or else more thoughtful than the rest takes pinions of the wind, & dances through the air on misty sails.

He describes the suspension bridge crossing to Canada, visits Benders Cave (Devils Hole), and comments on the Canadian houses and what the children are wearing. Here he sees a house with a decorated frontispiece depicting Mazeppa on the wild steed. Lorton apparently read Lord Byron's epic poem about the young man who, as punishment for seducing a countess, was tied to the back of a wild horse that ran for days through brambles, rivers, and forests before the horse died from exhaustion. The young man survived. About a year later, in Utah, Lorton barters with an Indian for a white stallion and names it Mazeppa, a prophetic choice (October 11). He talks to Canadians about the possibility of the United States annexing Canada (they are not impressed with the idea), and after dinner at his hotel, he writes letters home by candlelight.

From Niagara, Lorton takes railcars to Buffalo, New York, where he books a cabin on the splendid lake steamer *Niagara*. He comments on hearing "Negro melodies in the barber shop" and enjoys dancing at the ball in the evening. He describes the fancy breakfasts and the profusion of culinary offerings, a logical interest for a young man.

The steamer travels down Lake Erie, enters the Detroit River, then heads north through Lake St. Clair into Lake Huron. At the top of the Michigan mitten, it passes through the Mackinac straits to enter Lake Michigan. The lake is rough, but they finally dock at Milwaukee, where Lorton describes the town with its two lighthouses and blocks of brick buildings. The boat passes Racine and arrives in Chicago, where Lorton boards a Michigan and Illinois canal boat that travels parallel to the Des Plaines River and connects to the Illinois River.

The boat passes under a number of bridges as it floats past Joliet and Utica to arrive at Lasalle on October 2, 1848, where Lorton describes the hotel as a rough-board shanty and a log cabin tavern that also serves as church, courthouse, lock-up, theater and place for political meetings. He recognizes the irony of two tons of powder being loaded into the bow of the boat with the mouth of the furnace nearby.

Beyond Peru, both the Illinois River and the canal turn south, where Lorton indulges in shooting ducks, eagles, and cranes from the bow of the boat. After disembarking at Peoria, he takes a stage to his destination—the mill and farms of his cousins and his aunt and uncle near Monmouth in western Illinois. On the way he comments on a notice for the upcoming U.S. presidential election that would transfer the country's leadership from James K. Polk to Zachary Taylor.

The stage stops at Knoxville—"3 log cabins called a town"—where Lorton has supper and lodging for 40 cents. Although he is not particularly impressed by the town, he appreciates the Knox County courthouse made of bricks and mortar, fronted with four Ionic columns, and crowned with a steeple. He is more impressed with Galesburg, with its two "pritty churches, white & clean"—the prettiest town he had seen in Illinois.

The stage driver drops Lorton off at the farm of his Uncle Lewis and Aunt Jane Olmsted on October 4, 1848. The next evening, they go to his cousin Silas Jr.'s mill, and though it has been years since they had seen one another Silas recognizes Lorton immediately.

Lorton was related to the Olmsteds through his mother, Sarah Westervelt Lorton. One of Sarah's sisters was Jane Westervelt Olmsted (Lorton's Aunt Jane), and Silas and George's mother, Nancy Westervelt Olmsted, was an older sister. Uncle Lewis, Aunt Jane, and their several children had moved to the Monmouth area in 1836, and by 1848 they had a prosperous farm. Lorton and Silas had known each other in New York, where Silas was a member of the same music society as Lorton. Silas was also a fine singer and for many years was the lead tenor (his wife, Emily, was lead soprano) at the Congregational Church in Galesburg (Olmsted 1912, 276). While in New York Silas also played both flute and cello. Fourteen years Lorton's senior, Silas settled in the Monmouth area in 1835 and established a flour mill. Charles Olmsted, an older brother of Silas, and Lewis Olmsted (uncle to Charles, Silas, and Lorton) had farms not far from Monmouth, which was about 16 miles west of Galesburg and 30 miles east of Burlington, Iowa (on the other side of the Mississippi River).

On October 8, 1848, Lorton sends a letter to his mother in New York City. On November 1, he writes a letter to Mary Ellis, possibly a girlfriend, and he sends several letters "to society," which may have been the Handel and Haydn Society. He makes no other reference to writing family or friends while on his journey. Lorton makes arrangements to paint cousin Silas's mill ("for $20. dolls—2 coats, put extra coat, only dry paint") and cousin Charles's barn, plus a good deal of interior house painting.

On November 16, 1848, Lorton and Silas head west to the metropolis of Burlington, Iowa, for supplies. When they arrive "in sight of the gran dady of all rivers," they board a ferry where six horses turned the two paddles. A man keeps whipping them until "the poor thing[s] are nearly killed." Horses propel the ferry by walking on a treadwheel on the deck. Gears transfer the treadwheel's rotary energy to paddlewheels that move the ferry (Crisman and Cohn 1998, 31–37, 91, 136, 148, and fig. 18; Shomette 1998).

At night at the Western Hotel, they could hear violin and accordion music through the stovepipe hole. For privacy they set a trunk in front of the door and snugged a jack knife into the windowsill so it could not be opened. Among their purchases was house paint, apparently dry so Lorton could mix it with oil or another liquid to paint the interior of Silas's house and Charles's barn.

On a Sunday, Lorton goes to Galesburg where he comments on the "fine society at this place"—the academy, the college, and the schools—and he views the buildings through the eyes of a painter: "Fine church, beautiful finish.... Academy brick, paint cream color. Cupalo on top." After dinner at a tavern, Lorton's party takes Mr. Abner C. Hardings's daughters to a meeting, then spends the night with that family. This is where we discover that Lorton smokes cigars.

A new fall of snow at Thanksgiving entices the young men to rig up a jumper—a small, one- or two-horse sleigh with hickory runners and short, wooden posts attaching them to a buckboard.[2] A couple days later they rig a horse to the sleigh and set out for Lewis Olmsted's, eight miles from Silas's flour mill. On December 23, eight inches of snow fell, making a firm 28 inches, the deepest snow even the oldest settler had ever witnessed. "You can katch rabbits with your hands the snow is so deep," Lorton observed. Even the Mississippi River freezes over. Lorton writes a letter to David Cairnes, another cousin, who lives in Como, Illinois, about 100 miles northeast of Monmouth, on the Rock River. David is the son of Elizabeth Westervelt Cairnes, the fourth sister of Lorton's mother (Westervelt 1905, 65).

The night before Christmas Eve, Lorton entertains by singing his specialty, "Negro melodies." A couple days later he goes to spelling school, and the following day he attends a singing school that he finds pleasing. About this time, he hears talk of the gold regions and of men going to California.

While Lorton was visiting his Olmsted relatives, the small tea box, or caddy, containing California gold dust and nuggets arrived in Washington, D.C. The world went wild when the samples of gold were put on public display in December 1848. It was indeed a tempest in a tea caddy.

2. In the mid-1800s, Thanksgiving Day was not a federal holiday, but many states celebrated it on the last Thursday in November, the last day of the month in 1848 (Stathis 1999, 6–7; Hatch 1978, 1053–57).

Dr. Ormsby, whom Lorton mentions on the Southern Route from Salt Lake City to Los Angeles, summed up the western movement:

> This emigration may be regarded as one of the greatest anomalies in the history of man. In enterprise and daring, it surpasses the crusades, Alexander's expedition to India, or Napoleon's to Russia. These originated with Potentates and religious enthusiasts—were supported by the combined wealth of nations, and urged forward by the power of Kings, Emperors, Pontiffs.... This is the spontaneous exhibition of the enterprise and daring of the American character.... Acting on obedience to no political power—urged on by no religious zeal, he is actuated solely by his love of adventure, and his love of gold. (Ormsby 1850; Bidlack 1960, 37)

The torrent of humanity started west when men from every hamlet, from Maine to Iowa, reacted to the news of easy wealth. Two months after Lorton decided to go, the *Oquawka (IL) Spectator* emphasized this westward tide:

> Nearly every steamer passing Cairo [Illinois] bound to the South, seems to have on board more or less persons on their way to the gold regions. The fever is decidedly on the increase. Almost every town in the country will be represented in California. We scarcely know a person entirely free from the fever. Lawyers, doctors, editors, preachers, painters, mechanics of all kinds and farmers, alike are pondering over the matter, and some of them packing up their duds for a start. ("Going to California," March 14, 1849)

The frenzy was fueled by newspaper articles: "The great attraction, however, of late weeks has been California. This is the El Dorado of avaricious expectation. The news comes that $40,000 are taken out daily from the gold washings there. Such tidings turn some heads hitherto reported sound," announced the *Oquawka Spectator* ("Golden Region," February 7, 1849).

North American culture was ready for the burst of movement, change, and adventure that transpired in the mid-1800s. The nation had just acquired over 545 million acres of land from Mexico, explorers had mapped routes to the west, mountain men had probed these wild lands, and early emigrants had successfully settled in distant Oregon. A fusion of nature (genes) and nurture (culture) was ignited by a little tea caddy full of gold.[3]

3. Scientists call this ignition the "genotype–environment interaction." The gene DRD4–7R (7R=7 repeat variant) *may* be tied to "curiosity and restlessness" and *may* assist a propensity for people to "take risks; explore new places...and generally embrace movement, change, and adventure" (Dobbs 2013, 44, 45, 50). Some researchers have investigated the link of dopamine receptor D4 (D4DR or DRD4) to the personality trait of "novelty seeking" (Ebstein and Belmaker 1997, 381–84). Other scientists use the term "response ready"

On January 10, 1849, Lorton decides "on going to California, every body talking of going, gold feever rages through out the Country. Commence buying thing[s] such as: spades, shovels, & tinware." He notes his momentous decision as briefly as he does a rabbit hunt.

On a trip to Galesburg on January 23, he goes to an exhibition at the Knox College academic department, and has tea with Abner C. Harding, during which he has a conversation about slavery. This is what Lorton records:

> [Harding has] been among them a good deal. Masters child whips the little Negroes. Use the slaves better in the northern [and] western states. If they do wrong they threaten to take them down to N[ew] O[rleans] & sell, which they hate as they do death. They [the sellers] have to give a warrentee or writings, as they do for a horse or any animal. The Negros word is not to be taken. Exhibition [of the slaves] 3 nights, exam'n 3 days.

To include this discussion about slavery in his journal implies the information is new to Lorton, but it was a subject he was curious about, possibly because of his musical interest in "Negro melodies" or because he knew little about slavery.

At the end of January 1849, Lorton arranges to buy two oxen for his trip west from John Vestal for $50. Lorton wants a written contract, but "Old Man" Vestal said his word was good enough. On this excursion Lorton stays with the John Strode family and gives a vivid description of western living arrangements:

> Drive up to yard, 3 log cabins. Horses put out. Take dinner—short cake & no butter, pork & homony. Hungry, & it goes well. Large fire in house, & back log as big around as a barrel. Storm does not abate, but, rather increases. Bed time, same room, 4 beds in it, cheap dresser. Ladder to go up in loft which was constructed of slab boards set apart & a bed up thare. Undress before all the folks, no curtains to beds. Old man & his wife, oh! dear me, on one side of us & his son Levi & his wife, lately married, on the other, & how many in the trundle bed I cant say. (Lorton, January 30, 1849)

When Lorton returned to Silas's, he found some Galesburg folks visiting, including five ladies. Lorton described them as "very pritty, neat & tidey, sensible, have pattent leather belts." He was pleased they admired the painting and varnishing he had done to the interior of the house and added there was "plenty of singing in the parlor I painted" including a request for him to sing some of his "Negro melodies." Later that day he went to singing school and got home late.

---

for a person (or mouse) with the variant DRD4–7R (Wang et al. 2004, 931–44; see also Mukherjee 2016, 386).

Lorton made the acquaintance of Henry J. Ward, who worked at Silas Olmsted's mill. Ward was brother to Silas's wife, Emily. One clear, cold day these two young men headed out for Henderson, about 20 miles away, and came upon frozen Henderson Creek, where the ice was pretty weak. After deliberation they decided to unhitch the horses from the jumper and lead them across the creek, but the ice cracked and one of the horses went through. The bottomland was a quarter-mile away, but they finally got across the creek safely.

On February 7, Lorton and Ward attend a meeting at the Oquawka Courthouse to discuss forming a wagon train to the goldfields. Although they sign up to go in William Findley's Oquawka train, the young men's plans are changed at the last minute. However, at the meeting Lorton makes note of Findley's comments about the problems of leadership in a wagon train. Dissension among people, especially under stress, is natural, and it became particularly evident in many wagon trains. Lorton's budding awareness of this human foible is revealed when he quotes Findley extensively:

> "As soon as a comp[any] gets beyond the settlements [said Findley], no law to guide them but the law of the strongest, every person was as if he was let loose. They choose a leader at St Joseph, & before they have traveled 2 weeks, they become dissatisfied with him & complain & if he be a man of spirit, he will throw up the office." So they have to choose another [says Lorton].... [Findley continues] "They complain to him of his conduct, & he curses & quits. Then they have to choose another commander forthwith...till at last they are displeased with him.... So that when they arrive at their place of destination, every man has been a captain." (Lorton, February 7, 1849)

William Ritchey Findley was already an experienced guide, having traveled to Oregon via routes on both the north and south banks of the Platte River. On March 14, 1849, the *Oquawka Spectator* announced: "All persons belonging to Capt. Findley's company are hereby notified to be in readiness to start for California by the 26th of this month."

For those who doubted they were making the right decision, the *Spectator* included this titillating article the same day: "One man dug twelve thousand dollars in six days and three others obtained in one day thirty-six pounds of the pure metal. Two months ago, these stories would have been looked upon as ludicrous, but they are now common occurrences."

By March 20, Lorton had his two oxen and was prepared for his departure, but the Kelloggs, with whom he and Ward were to travel, kept them waiting. March 26 was the appointed day for the William R. Findley train to start, but still the Kellogg wagon had not arrived. Ward was Edward Kellogg's son-in-law.

Henry's wife, Esther (Edward's daughter), had died two years before, and Edward's wife had died just seven months before they left for California.

Edward Kellogg, age 50, was older than most who left for the goldfields. His son, William, born July 27, 1829 (Illinois, Cook County Deaths 1878–1994), was about a year younger than Lorton. He had completed a year at the Galesburg Seminary. With them was Frederick Saxton Kellogg, Edward's cousin, age 39, who had 160 acres just north of Elmwood, Peoria County, in 1840. When the Knox County Company was later formed, Frederick was assigned to the Committee of Inspection to check the wagons and equipment. These five men made up the Kellogg-Lorton "mess" (several people who eat together).

Only after William Kellogg drives into Silas's yard two days after the Findley train had assembled to depart do we learn Lorton will be traveling with a completely different train that never catches up to the Findley train. This last-minute change of plans surprises Lorton, but he has the resilience to adapt quickly to sudden setbacks. This change turns out to be an unfortunate one; Findley's train was exceptionally swift, and they had few mishaps. It became known as the "Telegraph company" (W. [Wood] 1849) and "Findley's lightning train from Oquawka" (Seymour 1849) because of its rapid pace. "It is said to be the quickest trip ever made by ox teams" to Fort Laramie, boasted H. M. Seymour in the *Oquawka Spectator*, July 18, 1849. They "left Iowa Point [above St. Joseph] on the 6th day of May, 1849...[and] on the 12th day of August arrived at the Gold Diggings in California" (Findley 1849).

Others who signed up for Findley's company but did not go with him became part of the Knox County group (not yet a formal train), which left a week or so later: Alexander Ewing, John Ewing, E. Norman Taylor, Robert Kimble, Cephas Arms, Alexander Palmer, Aaron Larkin, and Leander Woolsey. These men are mentioned throughout Lorton's journal.

Between the inception of the Findley train and Lorton's departure with the Kelloggs, a difference of opinion apparently arose about the route to be taken—the Oregon-California Trail on the south (right) side of the Platte River (when facing *downstream*) versus the Council Bluffs Road on the river's north (left) side, the same road the Mormons used to migrate to Salt Lake Valley in 1847 and 1848. This prompted the formation of the train Lorton and the Kelloggs ultimately joined that chose the Council Bluffs Road. It entered Indian country west of the Missouri River in the Council Bluffs area. Its center was the small Mormon village of Kanesville, Iowa.[4] Lorton, Ward, and the Kelloggs traveled

4. Kanesville was officially named Council Bluffs in 1853 (Federal Writers' Project 1986, 204) although the general area around Kanesville had been called Council Bluffs since the 1820s.

with the Knoxville-Galesburg crowd and were closely associated with them in the months to come.

The start of Lorton's momentous trek in search of gold was not propitious—mud, rain, swollen streams, and slow progress—"bad going," as Lorton said. To add to the gloomy mood were reports about John Frémont's disastrous expedition. "News of Frémont's comp[an]y's suffering in the mountains. 250 mules lost in 1 night."[5] During Frémont's Fourth Expedition (winter 1848–1849), 10 of 33 members died from starvation and exposure in the San Juan Mountains, Colorado (Kern in Hafen and Hafen 1960, 133; Frémont in Hafen and Hafen 1960, 208 and 208n14; Frémont 1984, 52, 54n13, 81, 89n20). A few of the expedition members resorted to cannibalism in order to survive, which was widely reported in the nation's newspapers (Frémont 1984, 83).

The lurid stories of cannibalism suffered by both the Donner Party (winter 1846–1847) and the Frémont expedition made argonauts leery of crossing the Sierra Nevada, the mighty barrier on California's eastern border, late in the season. The possibility of experiencing such a catastrophe was always lurking in the emigrants' minds. It caused a mood of anxiety to beat the winter season, which in turn was responsible for some trains to travel on the Sabbath, others to deny their oxen needed rest, and many to dump valuable goods along the trail to lighten their loads.

According to reminiscences of Asa Haynes, the wagon teams from Knox and surrounding counties "were to meet at Monmouth, Ill. where the company was to form some sort of an organization, hire a pilot, and choose a Captain, but for some reason this was not done and on the morning of the 7th [of April] we left Monmouth, then a small village, and started westward" (Haynes n.d., 1).[6] Lorton's frustration is mounting: "April 7th. Not out [of Monmouth] yet. Bot box cigars [for] 2 dolls."

The Kellogg-Lorton wagon stood out among those of their fellow travelers. Lorton gives snippets of information throughout his journal that suggest "Noah's Ark," was a Conestoga wagon. A Conestoga bed-box had curved floors and was about fourteen feet long and three and a half feet wide. The tires on each axle were about five feet apart (Shumway, Durell, and Frey 1964, 170, 177–78). However, the typical prairie schooner, or covered wagon, was shorter—nine to ten feet long—with a flat interior bed of the same width and wheelbase width

5. Lorton, April 3, 1849. Frémont had between 100 and 130 mules and horses. Senator Thomas Hart Benton (Frémont's father-in-law) claimed 100 mules froze to death in one night (Hafen and Hafen 1960, 200, 306).

6. Asa Haynes was later voted captain of the Knox County Company and still later became a Death Valley Jayhawker (Jean Johnson 2018). He is buried in the Haynes Cemetery, DeLong, Illinois, about six miles south of Knoxville.

as a Conestoga. On June 15, the Lorton mess sawed four feet off the Ark to reduce its length.

The *Oquawka Spectator* reported on April 4 the departure of the company piloted by William Findley, with which Lorton had originally signed up to travel. The following week the *Oquawka Spectator* published another report that mentioned the ownership of some of the teams in the large contingent that stretched from Monmouth to Galesburg, which now included the Kellogg-Lorton wagon ("For California," April 11, 1849):

> On Monday last [April 9], there were fourteen wagons passed through this place from Knox and Warren counties [Illinois]—having camped a few miles from the town on Saturday last. This company have commenced their long journey by "keeping the Sabbath day."—May prosperity attend them.
>
> *Henderson.*—Nelson D. Mor[s]e, Orrin Clark, James E. Hale—One Wagon.
>
> *Knoxville.*—Alexander Ewing, Jno. Ewing, L. Dow Montgomery, Robt. Rice [Price?], A. M. Richards, Edward McGowan—Three Wagons.
>
> Josephus [Cephas] Arms, E. [Norman] Taylor—One Wagon.
>
> J[ohn] L[ewis] West, J[ohn] W. Plummer, A[sa] Haynes, Thomas McGrew, George Allen—One Wagon [probably two].
>
> Robt. Kimball [Kimble], D. C. Norton, Nathaniel Hulbert [Hurlbut], Wilson Temple, Leander Woolsey—Two Wagons.
>
> Alex. Palmer, Aaron Larkin, Thomas Shannon—One Wagon.

The *Spectator* lists only nine of the 14 wagons they say came through on that date. Others may have been the Colton wagon (John Colton, Sidney P. Edgerton, and John Cole); the Clay wagon (Alonzo Clay, Luther Richards, Charles Mecum, and Marshall G. Edgerton); the Frans wagon (Harrison Frans and John Groscup); the Kellogg wagon (William Lorton, Henry Ward, and Edward, Bill, and Frederick Kellogg); and the Thompson wagon (Jno. D. Thompson and maybe J. Mackey). There are a number of men still not counted but who were soon included in the train—the Bartholomew brothers, Bill Rude, and others. A list of the men is given in Appendix A.

PART II

On the Trail

Western Illinois to Salt Lake City

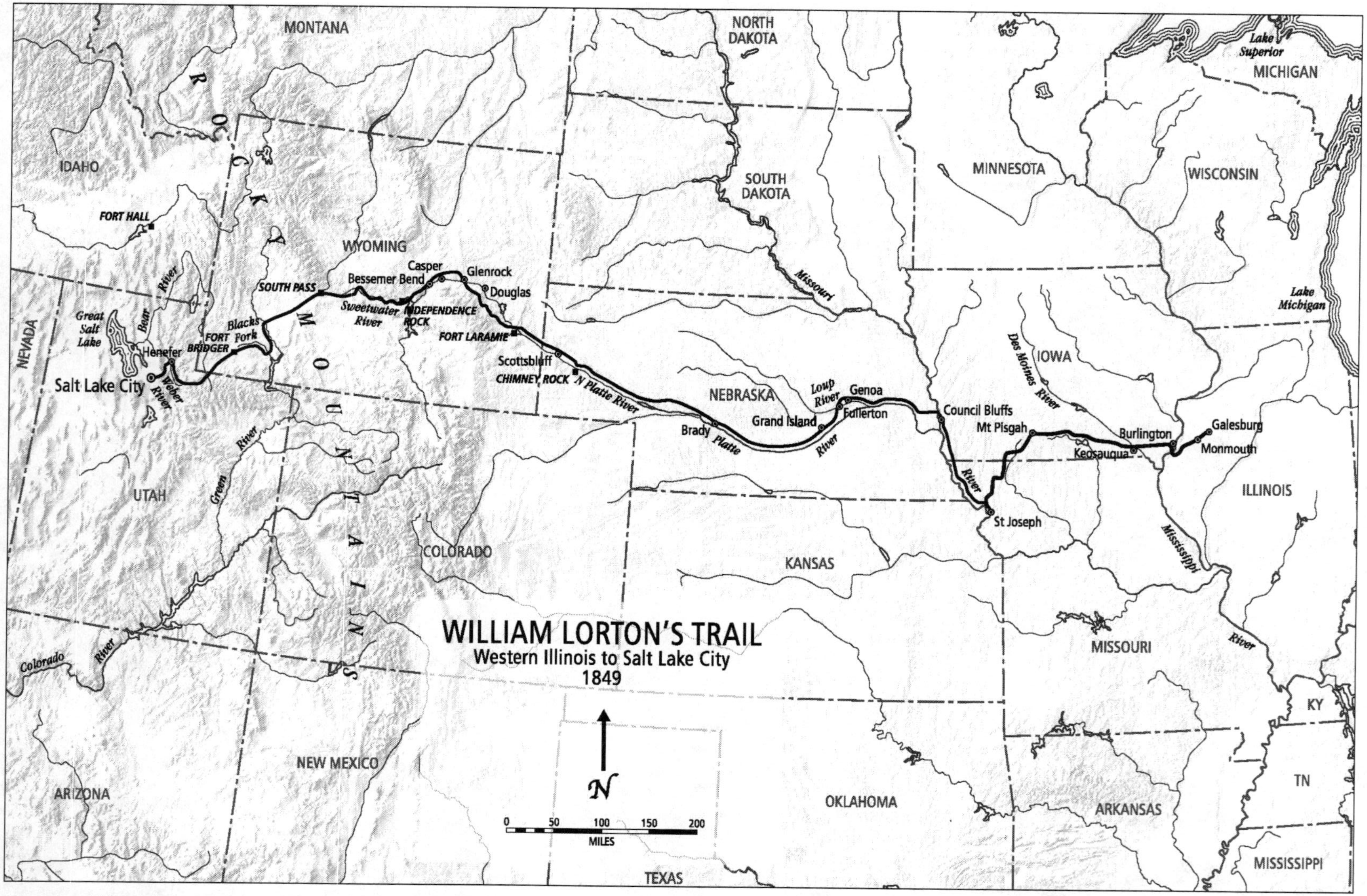

MAP 1. William Lorton's Trail: Western Illinois to Salt Lake City, 1849. Map drawn by Eureka Cartography based on editors' trail analysis.

CHAPTER 2

Across Iowa to St. Joseph, Missouri

Background

Before leaving Monmouth in western Illinois, the Knox County gold seekers had decided to take the Council Bluffs Road as they entered the flow of "Californians" rushing to the Golden State. The road entered Indian country after crossing the Missouri River near Kanesville (Council Bluffs) on the western border of Iowa. As their guide, they selected a Mormon who had been over the route. "The pilot, [Ira] Miles, from Salt Lake City, had crossed the plains many times," Asa Haynes said (n.d., 3). On July 4, 1849, Israel Lord said, "Miles, a Salt Lake man, brother in law of W. E. Bent, pilots them through."[1] Haynes told his daughter each person was to pay the pilot one dollar for his services (Haynes n.d., 3; Lord 1999, 48; Wiley n.d., 2).

The train of about 14 to 20 wagons planned to ferry the Mississippi River from Shokokon, Illinois, to Burlington, Iowa, then to travel the primitive government and Mormon roads across southern Iowa to Kanesville. At Burlington, the men shipped most of their heavy gear down the Mississippi River and up the Missouri to reduce the weight the oxen would have to pull over the 300 miles across Iowa. This was seemingly a smart decision owing to the muddy roads the heavy spring rains created.

As the wagon train (not yet a formal company with a name and constitution) from Knox and nearby counties rolled into Iowa, the towns they entered manifested signs of hysteria because of cholera, a scourge that was sweeping congested cities and ultimately dogged the western trails. New York and New Orleans were primary ports of entry where European emigrants carried Asiatic cholera to America in late 1848. Many emigrants became infected at the crowded

1. Ira Simonds Miles, born 1808 (sources differ) in Rutland County, Vermont, accompanied Brigham Young to Salt Lake Valley in 1847. He married Mary Kilburn Bent, sister of William Erving Bent, in Nauvoo, Illinois, in 1846 (Family Search.org/family tree; Membership of LDS, 1830–1848—Ancestry.com; Bent Family, 65, Ancestry.com—North America, Family Histories, 1500–2000).

staging areas along the Missouri River (Blair 1997, 55–57, 59; see also Snow 1849, 22, 30; and Milikien 1996, 4–11). No one knew what caused it since they had no knowledge of germs and microbes. No one knew how cholera was transmitted—from person to person, by clothing, by water, by air, by animals? Not knowing who, when, or where it might strike contributed to the fear and hysteria.

In 1849 Dr. Snow—a medical doctor in London, England—proved that well water contaminated by effluent from cesspools was responsible for deaths from cholera among persons using the well water. The solution was "for all persons attending or waiting on the patient to wash their hands carefully and frequently... [to never use] water into which drains and sewers empty themselves; or, if that cannot be accomplished, to have the water filtered and well boiled before it is used" (Snow 1849, 10, 21, 30). This communicable disease originates mainly from polluted water, tainted milk, or food prepared with contaminated water, but along the Oregon-California Trail, family members and mess-mates readily came in contact with contaminated clothing or bedding while nursing the sick or preparing the deceased for burial. Vomiting and diarrhea from cholera brought on severe dehydration and shock, and if the infected person was not properly treated, death followed rapidly. In 1849 alone, an estimated 2,000 emigrants died along the trails from cholera (Milikien 1996, 9).

Early in his trek, William Lorton began to see another dreaded malady then called "fever and ague" or "intermittent fever"—now called malaria. It could have been cured if "fever tree" bark, which contains quinine, had been used. It comes from trees in the *Cinchona* genus native to eastern slopes of the Andes. In the 1880s *Cinchona* bark became the "first effective 'magic bullet' in medical history" (Snowden 2006, 45; see also Honigsbaum 2002).

In Iowa the wagon trains followed roads "citizen labor gangs" first built in 1838. Iowa Territory enacted a law requiring "every male between the ages of twenty-one and fifty" to spend three days building public roads. Before long the legislators realized they could tap federal funds because "national defense [was] an avowed purpose of road building," and the secretary of war administered the road-building program. Two types of federal roads crossed Iowa: Indian agency and military (W. Jackson 1949, 15, 17, 20; see also *Statutes at Large* 5 Stat. 352).

West of Keosauqua, Lorton's train traveled a branch of the Mormon Trail that became a well-beaten road in 1846 when the vanguard of Mormons were forced out of Nauvoo, Illinois, and crossed Iowa to the Council Bluffs area (Van der Zee 1914; Hartley in Black and Hartley 1997, map, xiv). Lorton mentions both Garden Grove and Pisgah (today's Mount Pisgah), way stations where Mormons could rest and resupply during the trek to their new Zion. Orson Pratt wrote about Pisgah on May 19, 1846: "We concluded to form another settlement here, for the benefit of the poor, and such as were unable, for the want of teams, to proceed further." They immediately plowed, fenced, and planted over a thousand acres of prairie land, and by fall they harvested peas, cucumbers, beans, corn, buckwheat, pumpkins, and squash. Today, the old way station is a nine-acre park on private land containing a cemetery, interpretive exhibits, historical markers, and a reconstructed log cabin (O. Pratt 1947, 26; Gentry 1981, 445–61; Hartley and Anderson 2006, 86–90).

On April 30, the day before Lorton visited today's Mount Pisgah in south-central Iowa, a courier from St. Joseph, Missouri, intercepted them with bad news: the boat carrying their goods was stuck on a sandbar in the Missouri River below St. Joseph, and the water was too low to transport the cargo above St. Joseph. They were forced to change their course from going straight across Iowa to turning southwesterly toward St. Joseph, thus adding about 160 miles to their journey. In addition, the added miles from St. Joseph north to Kanesville (Council Bluffs) would be with heavily loaded wagons.

The stock emigrants used to pull their wagons were as varied as the men who drove them. Some were smart, some sensitive, others lazy or high-strung; some dull-witted, cantankerous, badly treated, or poorly trained. Merrill Mattes (1969, 37) said 60 percent of the teams used on the overland trails were oxen (castrated male bovines), the rest, mules or horses.

Oxen were stronger than horses or mules and generally more docile (although not in the Knox County train). Oxen were willing to face a threat rather than run from it (a river crossing, for instance), and they were cheaper to feed. They rarely needed blinders or restraining tack as did horses and mules. An oxen's working gait was a walk that covered two to two and a half miles per hour, and they could pull for seven or eight hours at a time. Oxen could pull a wagon out of mud when horses or mules could not do so. "An ox was not broken; rather it was induced to co-operate" (Watts 1999, 19). Driving oxen took strength; just lifting a yoke was often hefting 50 pounds or more. If an emigrant were lucky, he procured a pair of four-year-old working oxen that had been trained together from an early age.

For cross-country trail travel, all stock needed metal shoes to protect their hooves. Since oxen are cloven-hoofed, they needed a metal shoe nailed to each of the two "claws" on each foot.

Three yoke of oxen were best for pulling a sturdy wagon capable of hauling 7,000 pounds of goods. The ox driver walked next to the nigh (near or left) ox looking forward, and used a stick (goad) and voice commands to guide his team. Oxen could be particular about which side they were hitched on or even where in the team they were placed. If a pair of oxen were trained together, the near ox was often given a one-syllable name (Dan, Nig), and the off (right side) ox given a multisyllable name (Brigham, Balley).

Lorton was fortunate to buy a working pair for 50 dollars several months before he left for California. The Kellogg–Lorton team had three yoke of oxen and one yoke of cows, but which pair of oxen Lorton provided is not clear. Near as we can figure, the oxen names were Ben, Brin (Brindle?), Balley, Dick, Duke, Giraff, Nig, and Tom.

Trained, well-bred, and sensitively handled mules were better than horses for pulling, but the emigrants had a hard time finding such animals (and experienced drovers). After the Revolutionary War, bigger, stronger jackasses were imported from Europe, and men such as George Washington started breeding them with large horses to increase the size and strength of their working mules. They have a higher strength-to-weight ratio and greater agility than horses. Mules endure heat better, can travel longer distances without water, require half the feed, have stronger legs and hooves, travel better on rocky ground, and have a longer working life than horses. They are more sure-footed because their eyes are set back farther on the head, giving them better peripheral vision that allows them to readily see their hind feet. Mules have a larger brain cavity and are more intelligent and judgmental than horses and have a better sense of self-preservation. They halt to figure out a route or situation before plowing ahead, which is often construed as stubbornness. Mules have a keen sense of smell and excellent hearing, so a smart drover heeds the alertness and forward direction of a mule's ears (Buck 2015, 36).

Many wagon trains recognized the Sabbath as a day for religious services, rest, and catching up on needed camp work. But as the trip progressed and travelers did not keep to their planned schedules, many of them felt pressure to travel on the Sabbath. This caused dissension to the extent that some trains broke up over it.

Lorton's Journal Resumes as He Waits to Leave for California

Sunday night, Mar 20th [1849]. My yoke [of] oxen run off. Paid [Levi?] Strode $1 to get them. Found them 15 miles N. E. in a slew feeding on grass. Near their former home.

Got things as near ready as posible, but still kept waiting for the Kelloggs, the 26th March being first app[ointe]d time for starting by Capt Finley [William R. Findley] of our comp[an]y. While waiting several parties retired—the Paxtons &c. News pritty discouraging.

On Thursday [March] 28th, Wm K [William Kellogg] arrived about 9 in the eve'g. We then had to get the [wagon] tongue altered &c.

Taking aim at a mark over a broom stick, the gun fell, boared [into] the ground & blew the tube in the air. I had loaded it for deer. Saw 12 deer, [then] saw 8 deer, 2 deer stood looking at me in the road 200 yds off. Went to Uncle

FIGURE 4. Conestoga wagon at Scotts Bluff Interpretive Center. Note higher back wheels, as well as longer box and cover, than on a typical emigrant wagon. Photo by LeRoy Johnson.

Lewis's bid them good bye. Lewis gave me [a] Mackinaw blanket, Mary gave me stockings & mittens. See him in town after wards. Settled up ac/ts with Silas, rec'd on my order on Charles O[lmsted] 100 dols, paint bill 64 dolls.[2] Put in my equal 4th share in teem & out fit, $110.63. Give due bill to [Henry] Ward for 14 dolls. Went to Monmouth to Church on Sabbath, April 1st for the last time, to say nothing of the concert a few day[s] previous.

[April 2.] Haveing every thing all packed on Saturday nearly. Set out from Milford 1 o'clock, Monday, Ap 2, 1849, for California. Hard parting, good deal of crying. I stood it without a tear, hard hearted, I suppose. Our team consists of 4 yoke oxen & 1 [yoke] cows (non milch). I paid 50 dolls for large yoke oxen & if I had not paid $1 to bind the bargain, the man [John] Vestal up on the Henderson would not have let them go. Fine teem altogether. Kelloggs put in 2 yoke good oxen & cows, about 2500 [pounds] on board the wagon, 1000 flour & meel (kill dryed), 350 Bacon, Teas, sugars, Coffee, Lemon syrup, medicines, dryed fruit, nearly all the provisions in bags, [and] bed quilts. Wagon box 14 feet long, long

2. Charles Olmsted, also a cousin of Lorton, was an older brother of Silas.

FIGURE 5. Typical emigrant wagon at Scotts Bluff Interpretive Center. Photo by LeRoy Johnson.

coupled [a Conestoga wagon]. Got as far as Monmouth April 2, staied all night at Grants. Taylor, White, E. Ward & Jo accomp'd us to town. Attended sing in the eve.

Erata; every boat that comes down the river has wagons on board & teams for Cal[iforni]a. Strings of teems constantly coming through town on their way to Cal'a. We wait for the Knoxville croud & Jno. Thomp[son].[3]

[April 3.] Stay in Monmouth all day Apl 3d. Rainey & mud[dy]. Rec'd a letter from M.Y. Beach [editor of the *New York Sun*] requesting a correspondence from me & placeing me on the free list. Think something of shipping our provisions & plunder to Counsel Bluffs by way [of] St Louis. News of Fremonts compy's suffering in the mountains. 250 mules lost in 1 night.[4] Get my rifle repaired. Dull day, feel drouzy.

April 4. Not out of Monmouth yet. Rains hard. Cold & chilly. 20 teems camped between here & Galesburg. Camped. Bad going.

3. Lorton's errata are written as continuous text, not a later addition.

4. Senator Thomas Benton claimed 100 mules froze to death in one night (Hafen and Hafen 1960, 200, 306).

April 5. Muddy & clear. Lots of teems going through town [Monmouth].

April 6. Still at Grants. Rains pitch forks, thunder & lightning. Dispose of half our flour. Knoxville teams arrived last night. They camped south of Monmouth. We visited their tents, all struck, camp fires & stoves all burning. 1 marque tent, table set, stools &c. With pistols in belts, knives &c. & dresses, looked like a scene in theatre. Saw a man from Wis. [who] said the road is literally lined for 200 miles back. O's [Olmsted] cousins came in town. We make a large tent, set up till midnight sewing.

April 7th. Not out yet. Bot box cigars 2 dolls. Soon after writing the above, word comes that Knox C comp had struck tents & started.[5] Feed the cattle. More mud to start with than I ever see before. As the teams pass through, the mud roled like the waves in the sea. Break a hook. Struck north near Lewis O[lmsted]'s, kill two snakes, the 1st of the season. Come up to K[noxville] teams at Cecedar Turnbulls. Feed [stock, have] lunch on fried cake. All [the] croud [went] gunning. Shoot 3 c's [prairie chickens], 1 duck & snipe. Arrive west of Stringtown, 5 o'clock, travelled 15 miles. Strike tents. We make fire in stove & cook for the 1st time, good. Tents all in row, & wagons. Have dancing in eve'g, violin & singing. Lot of boys come from Monmouth to see us take supper. Stay all night. Go to bed 10 1/2 o'clock, sleep for the first time [in wagon], 1 blanket on. Tie up & go to sleep. Hear some noise in night. Cattle in the pails laping. Quiet [quite] a racket. Go to sleep some. The moon shineing through the tall trees as bright as day. Get up [at] 5 in morn'g.

Sunday, April 8th. Lay too all day.[6] Rains some & then clears a little. Our visitors bid us good bye. Here we are camped in an enclosure of a farmer 4 1/2 miles [east] from Oquawka [Illinois, near the Mississippi River], plenty of fodder for cattle. Make tent on Sunday.

[April 9.] Monday morn, 9th. Got up at day break, cloudy. Got up [earlier when] I thought it was morn'g. Went to bed again. Ate breakfast of boiled eggs, ham & buiscuit, coffee, &c. Fed [and] hiched up oxen & started [at] 7 for Oquawka.

5. Asa Haynes says, "S[aturday] the 7 we all rolled out [of Monmouth] to gether numbering 33 men & 12 waggons." (Haynes n.d., 2; see also Ellenbecker 1938, 125–27).

6. In the Hebrew Bible the seventh day (Sabbath) was deemed a day of rest (Genesis 2–3). Thus, many wagon trains halted on Sundays for rest and worship. The day was also used to catch up on work not done—repairing harness and wagons, cleaning guns and clothing, and doing some trail baking (such as in a frying pan or Dutch oven). Rest for the animals was a major benefit from these halts. As time went on, many trains decided to continue travel on the Sabbath.

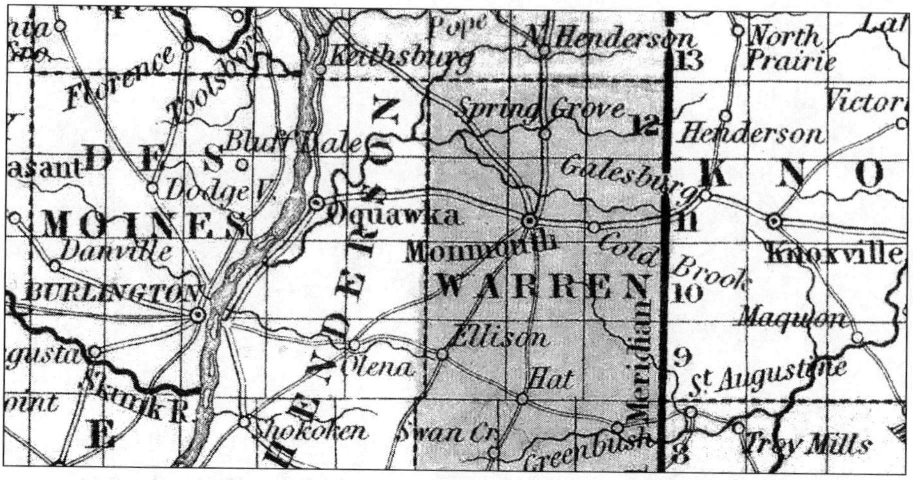

MAP 2. Detail, Mitchell's 1853 map of Illinois depicting Lorton's environs—Monmouth, Galesburg, Knoxville, Oquawka, Olena, and Shokoken, Illinois; and Burlington, Iowa, with the Mississippi River. Courtesy of David Rumsey Historical Map Collection.

Hooked [Hook] slipped out, brought up all standing. Arrived in town 9 1/2 o'clock. Shot 1 gray squerrel on the way. Editor of the *Oquawka Spectator* took our names to publish ["For California," April 11, 1849].

Road sandy nearly all the way. Went on till noon, crossed a creek running swift, fed [cattle] & got our corn at an old cabin. Forlorn looking boy, nees all out of pants. Little girl said her father had gone to Skink Creek & expected he would come back as high as a cats back. [We] take the wrong road to the ferry—steam ferry—7 miles below Burlington [Iowa]. Cross the plain & intersect the other teems. Talk of trading for a horse. Saw Mrs Hopper & her daughter.[7] Mend bridge, wander off, follow creek, see ducks—chickens & rabbit dead. Send on a man ahead to procure fodder 4 miles ahead. Man swore he would'nt sell any to a Californian. Some of them had shot his turkeys, thought they were wild. Said they abused him & then give him a bad name. Part go there. We put up on the prarie bottom [and] buy the man out, 4 teams of us. I have the dizzentary [dysentery], take [cayenne] pepper tea,[8] go to roost [at] 10. The other teams tells the man they will have feed any how. He finally gives in.

[April 10.] Wake up next morn'g. A strong S-east wind had broke the ropes of our curtain & blew its cold breath in on us. A beeting sleety rain acompany it. Get up all hands as quick as possible, & with out break fast make for a port in

7. Lambert Hopper (a merchant, 40), Mary (his wife, 40), John W. (a clerk, 18), and Lula C. (15) are listed in the 1850 census (Richard 1977, 132).

8. This was a blend of tea and ground cayenne pepper (*Capsicum fastigiatum*). In the early 1800s, a noted herbalist claimed this combination would cure ague (S. Thomson 1835, 39; 1849, 53).

the timber. Just see the white tents in the distanse along the bluffs. Cross slew by riding the oxen on their back & so whipping them. Lusern [Luzerne Bartholomew] gets his boots full waiding.[9] Stop at edge of timber, strike fire in little stove as soon as the boys came up, who had been left in the rear gunning [shooting]. Boil the kettle, fry ham, [make] coffee &c. Get water from Missisippi River to cook with & drink. Not long after, the K[noxville] Comp send their horses ahead to engage passage. Swallow our vituals as soon as possable & put for the river, for the white toped wagons were gaining on us, & we were bound not to be beat to the boat.

Met man on horse back, addressed us as stranger as do all the westerners. As we turn we see the steam ferry boat through the trees. This place is called Shawmung town.[10] Large citty, 1 log cabbin & a hog pen besides a lot of logs to build another with.[11] Flat bottom land all round. Put 14 teams on bourd.

We sail up the river to Burlington, 7 miles in 1 hour.[12] Plenty of islands about this distance. River, including around the islands, 3 or 4 miles [a]crost. Pritty prospect of Burlington as you approach it from below being a gradual assent from the father of waters. Building[s] nearly all brick, 1 Beautiful store & 2 dwellings & church. In particular, I noticed the private houses with fluted collums in front. See Californians camped near the shore. See 6 mule team bou[n]d for El Darado. Loose tongue bolt overboard. Deck hands call our craft Noas Ark, & other remarks.[13] Buy numerous articles in town. Oxen come up in the next boat. Pack our ham, Bacon, beens, coffee, sugar, utensels &c for shipping. See our men we sent ahead to overtake Capt Finley [Findley]. He still continued his course for St Jo & was 25 miles ahead. Make for a camp ground in a hollow west of Burlington 2 miles. No feed for cattle, but get a man to cart some, 27 cts [per] Bu [bushel].[14] Devel in the cattle, like to broke my neck runing after them. An ox gets staled & comes near getting his neck broke. Chain them to logs & trees.

9. There were two Bartholomew brothers in the train: Luzerne (37) and Edward F. (21).

10. Shawmung is likely a corruption of Shokokon (Shokoquon), Illinois, an unincorporated village on the left bank of the Mississippi River. By 1911 the site was "only a river landing" (Gordon 1911, 633).

11. This is an example of Lorton's droll humor.

12. About five miles south of Burlington, Iowa, near the left bank of the Mississippi River, is a seven-mile-long island. They steamed three miles upriver (northward) from Shokokon in the eastern channel before reaching the Mississippi River's main channel. If Lorton's seven-mile distance is correct, the Burlington landing was at least a mile north of the city (Map 1876, Union Atlas Co.).

13. Hints throughout Lorton's journal indicate the "Ark" was a Conestoga wagon, seldom used in the western migration because they were long and heavy. Their slightly downward-arching floor gave them the superficial appearance of an ark.

14. They traveled across Iowa before there was sufficient forage; thus, they purchased corn to feed the animals.

After hearing the bugel play, go to bed [at] 11. Till then I set up writing this. One man said as he looked over his yard rails, that we were like locuses where we went. Said 250 wagons had passed. Poke it on to the Californians in price all over you go [meaning stick it to those heading for California].

April 11th. Get up [at] day light. Assemble Counsel in morn'g after breakfast, in relation to shipping goods & getting fodder. Agree to send 2 men in advance all the way to Counsel Bluffs & 2 men around with the goods. Send H[enry] J. Ward & Mr [Robert] Price, leave our team in camp.[15] Old man [Edward] Kellogg stays in camp. The Camp at present [is] between 2 high streeps with a small stream within 4 rods [66 feet] of us.[16] Cattle get loose during the day & break 1 chain. I go to town 1 mile east, get Rifle tube, cillinder &c. Get table made for tent. The rest work on the tent. Set it up not finished & eat supper for the first time in it. Have butter milk to day. Let our milk set over night, then put it [the cream] in churn & the motion of the wagon churns it to butter. Talk of buying horse. Man asked $35 [for] saddle, &c. mess. [I] back out [of] the bargain. Man said he was short of change. Though[t] he was a little stiff in his hind legs, did'nt buy.

April 12. Get up [as] the sun is just making its appearance over the bluff below. Strike tents & get under way 7 o'clock on the road towards Lowell [Iowa]. This is a road made by Government, when Iowa was a Territory, it being an old Indian agency trail. The road is bridged in a firm & substantial manner, the [a]butments of nearly all being made of masonry. Travel on through some very good roads & others very muddy, down steap ravines, slews &c. till near noon [when] we haull up at a gentlemans country seat. He had a fine large barn, dwelling, out houses, fields &c. He was dressed up like a gent & had men to perform the labor. The country thus far is undilating & roleing, groves of timber being dispersed intermediatily along the rout. As you pass, neat Brick, stone & woden dwellings & substantial out houses adds to the scene & indicates the good circumstances of their owners. I my self like it far better than the military tract [in] Ill.[17] (That is all lying between the Ill & Miss sis-pi rivers.) It was once dowered by Con[gress]

15. Henry Ward was from Lorton's mess and Robert Price was with the Ewing mess.
16. A rod equals 16.5 feet with 320 rods to a mile (5,280 feet). A "rod" is a survey term commonly used in the 1800s but rarely used today.
17. Charles O. Paullin (1932, 31) wrote, "The practice of granting public lands to soldiers as bounties or as rewards for service" was first adopted during the Revolutionary War. Later, Congress set aside two million acres of land in Illinois Territory for the men who served in the War of 1812 (Paullin 1932, 31–32 and plate 45B; *Statutes at Large* 2 Stat. 728). Most soldiers who served twelve months or more in the Mexican War were entitled to a bounty land warrant for 160 acres "upon any of the public lands" (*Statutes at Large* 9 Stat. 123). There being no draft, these warrants were a strong inducement to serve their country (see also Oberly 1982 and 1990, 3–12, 95).

to solgers, which mak[e]s titles rather dubious. Iowa appears to be settled up by men of cappital.

Start on [at] 2. Crossing prarie (some sport) dog after hare at full speed, overtake[s] it & as he crabs [grabs], they both roll over together. That is a rabbit dog costom. Stop for the night about 12 miles from Burlington, strike tent in a meddow turn our cattle loose. The man is an Englishman & appeared to be thriving. His house built of brick. Charges 20 cts [per] Bu for corn. Just before comeing to this, we cross a large, substantial bridge. This has splendid scenery all around it.

Commences raining hard. Put on my oil cloth coat & feed cattle 1/2 mile east with oats. Lay straw in our tent for floor. The rains sits us all afloat. The rain is now pouring down on our wagon cover as I write & will probably hold up all night. It dont leak a darn'd bit, through 2 thicknesses. Bake buiscuit with cream, first rate. Dont see any difference in cooking [between ours and that at home?], without [question] ours is better. I have a ravinish appetite, as have all the crew. Shoot more game to day. Let the cook sleep with me to night [in the wagon]. Talk about the privilege of kissing the cook. It is 8 1/2 o'clock so I blow out the candle for it is dark as pitch outdoors.

[April 13.] Get up, eat breakfast. Next morning herd our oxen up to camp. Early morn was hazy but at length the sun shed forth her rays upon the wet ground, a fresh breeze blowing strong from the N. E. Get under way 9 o'clock. Decend & [an] awful deep rutted steep into a bottom which came nearly upsetting our wagon. At the Bottom a large streem runs into Skunk River on the left. The scrubbery on this extensive bottom is far in advance of the upland, haveing put forth her green foliage, while above only buds appear. Over this stream Uncle Sam has a bridge built of firm oak, studded & braced with cross timbers ironed & bolted. In turning to cross this, one wheel of our Noah's Ark came in contact with a tall monarch of its native bottom, from which we had to back out quickly. On the other side, in assending the hill, was another exciting time, so steep, & to keep clear of stumps & trees, ruts &c., made us keep our top eyes open. Lot of deer off in the timber, men after them.

About 2 miles a head, you get in sight of the town of Lowell. This you approach by assending a hill of the muddiest kind for the time [?]. Lowell is situated on the bank of Skunk River. The principal part is facing the river on its west Banks. Here we meet Norman Talor who had been sent ahead to overtake Capt Finley [Findley], & stayed here till we came up.[18] This river Uncle Sam has not bridged so we have to ferry it in a flat boat. This boat is propelled acrost by

18. Findley sent word back that he would not wait for the Knox train to catch up nor would he change his route from the Oregon-California Trail (south of the Platte) to the Council Bluffs Road (north of the Platte).

means of a rope, which is suspended to trees, one on eather side, the middle not touching the water, with the near end up stream so as to let the loaded boat float down a little. The stern is kept from floating down by a roap & pulley that plays upon the main rope. The boat holds 1 wagon & 3 yoke oxen. It took, to get 18 teams over, from 1 to 5 o'clock P.M. Man with buggy tryes to rush in ahead of us, but we threaten the ferryman if he lets him, & thus bluff him off.

Lowell a neat place, not very large. It has a flour & saw mill, 1 on each side the river, & a dam clear crost that falls 3 feet. Caugh[t] several fish while waiting, 1 pike shot weighing 40 lbs.[19] Assend a high but gradual assending hill & move off westward. Camp on a prarie, turn our cattle in a field just opposite. Bake bread, &c. & retire to bed at a seasonable hour, with a good breeze. Saw some California gold that was brot round by the Isthmus [of Panama]. This night is full[y] as cold or colder than last night. We have our wagons all arranged, standing obliquely aside of each other so as to cut the wind & keep our tents from blowing down. I'm bound not to sleep so cold tonight by poking on all the bed clothes I have.[20]

[April 14.] Errata Have a hard mudey road all day, mud at times up to the hubs. Cross Little Cedar Creek by bridge, made in a substantial manner. There is something singular about this creek. It rises near the mouth of Skunk River & runs a north westerly course (a contrary direction to the Skunk) & emties into it near its source. Pass thro' Salem, a small town, & at length arrive in Washington, a town of some note in this cou[n]try.[21] Two tavern in it. The buildings are mostly frame & log cabins. Man who had kept a/c [account] said 150 teems had [passed] enrout for California. Talking with a farmer, said he came 12 years ago when it was a territory, did'nt like it, to[o] cold. See scarcely any plowing along the rout, season rather late. Said sometimes he had enough to last them over. Little girls come down to the train to sell eggs & butter, eggs 5 cts doz., Butter 10¢.

The houses so far generally better built than those of the Mil[itar]y tract [in Illinois]. All the log cabbins look snug & neat. Saw 1 with porch through the middle. Kimble, one of the Comp. breakes his wagon tongue. I tried to roll mine up a tree but could'nt make it out. In milking the white faced cow, she jumped

19. This was a huge fish. The current International Game Fish Association record for northern pike caught with tackle is 55 lbs. 10 oz.

20. After this sentence Lorton wrote his Sunday, April 15 section. Then he added an "Errata" that appears to be April 14 material. We place his "Errata" (April 14) section before his Sunday, April 15 entry for continuity.

21. Lorton's Washington is today's Hillsboro, Iowa. It was laid out in 1840, but when it got a post office, it was renamed Hillsborough since there was another Washington, the seat of Washington County (*History of Henry County* 1879, 555, 568). Lorton's Washington is shown on Mitchell's 1846(b) Iowa map.

a 5 rail fence, I [chased] after her like a dog after a buffalo, & brot her back. She tried to jump an 8 rail, but I cut her on the head so that she stood. Corn 15 cts a bu. Tortured all night by the sharp edge of a box that boared in my side. Cover gets off & I get cold.

[April 15, 1849.] Next morning was the Sabbeth, the sun was shining splendidly as I awoke. Kellogg said he wanted the flowr, & I was laying on it. He wanted to make short cake. Roused up, but lay down again to sleep. Get Breakfast 8 o'clock. Lay still all day Sunday. Herd our cattle on the prarie. Place pickets to prevent their running off. We try to milk the white faced cow, but she kicked over the pale & douces the milk over us & runs off. We will fix her next time. Eat dinner & tea to gether. Have custard of our own make (superfine) & bird & rabbit. Wash my self, grease boots & put on clean shirt after smoking a cigar. Kemble [Robert Kimble] offers us 6 soverigns for our cows, temptingly shows the gold (no go).[22]

[April 16.] As I lay in bed of the morn'g of the 16th I hear someboddy say there had been a horse stole out of Kembles te[a]m during the night. Kembles horse eather stole or run away. He borrows a horse & puts back in serch. During our march there has been several things stolen. During the day a great deal of excitement prevailed during the day in regard to the thief in the camp. We yoke up our oxen & get ready to start out first in our turn, but find 1 chain gone. In [On?] the way we pass over 2 of the boggyest praries extant. The day is dark & hazy & we have a snow storm. The fine flakes fall, the air is chilley & every thing has the appearance of approaching winter. It melts upon our clothing & wets us thro.

17 miles from Wash'g'n a hansome brick house makes its appearance on the edge of a pritty timber. It has green blinds, frontispiece, dooryard in a tasty stile. Here the road takes a turn off short to the south & then takes its usual course. Men burning brush in piles. Scarcely no game through [here]. People come down to meet teems & sell produce. See a wagon standing in the road. The fellow had his wife with him. His teem had give out. He wanted to sell his pistols. Some Californians go in sunchsly [sumptuously] furnishing teem & as we stop to feed we see the wagon coming, the woman on foot. About 5 o'clock, 2 miles from the Des Moines River, we turn of[f] the main road & camp in the midst of brush & timber all round. Fodder our [oxen] in a stalk field 1/4 mile east. Procure water in a slew near by &c. After setting by the fire out in the open air till it went out, telling stories, we turned in. Slept tolerable comfortable all night.

22. A sovereign, a British gold coin, was legal tender in the United States in the 1800s. It was about the size of today's nickel and had an 1849 gold value of $4.31; thus, Kimble offered about $26 for the cows.

[April 17.] After breakfast we went in the stalk field to harness up, cattle all there. Duke takes a notion to devil a little, & not be yoked. Jumpes a rail fence & disappears in the thicket. We however yoke him. Our white faced bitch gets the same freak & tries our very souls. Strike our tents & make for town, & arrive there after 1/2 hours drive. We enter the town of Kesouqua [Keosauqua, Iowa] on the East. Here are a few straggling houses of not much note. On the west of a slew appears the Court house. Standing on a high hill as it does it can be seen a great ways where there is no timber to obscure. It has a cupalo on top. It is square built (brick) & with the exception of the quantity of pains broke out of the windows, & want of paint, it was a pritty fair house for a western county seat.

Kesouqua is the county seat for the county of Van Buren. It is situated on the banks of the Des Moines River. East of the C[ourt] House there is a tavern kept by F. L. [*blank*]. It is a curious affair haveing round collums its whole length, which must be 100 feet. To the bottom of the hill is the County Jaol [Jail]. It is built on the plan of the western jaols. They are built of hughen [hewn] logs placed close to gether & iron barred windows. To its right is another tavern whose sign post must have got drunk for it appeared on the point of falling down. Take this rode & the Des Moines appears to the ox drivers view. Stores of different kinds string pritty thick above the shore, some of them grog & gambling holes. These western rivers are celebrated for gambling. On the other side of the river is timber. Occasionaly a house appeares to the eye.

The river here is about 1/4 mile wide & runs pritty swift. Here they have a flat boat ferry. They have block pulleys on the rope, & by placing the scow in a diagonal position, it is propelled from one side to the other with out any exertion. This boat had just come over, & a host of ox teems [were] waiting to go over. A steam boat lay by the levee puffing away. The boat being bound up the river, the capt beckoned them to lower the cross rope. The wheel of the boat was on behind, & as the boat moved over the roap it caught in the wheel & being carried above, the capt. knowing how it was going had a man stationed to cut it with a broad axe, & he did so with a blow. This produced a great deal of excitement amonge the towns people, & a number of bets taken in regard to cutting it, but this was finally settled by halling in the rope. Cutting it prevented any ferriage to our teems for the pressent, so we camped near timber n'east [of] the town & turned our cattle out in the yoke. Pay 1 bit [per] Bu for corn, 4 dolls [per] ton for hay.[23] There is something strange that the farther we go west we hear of corn being dearer & instead of that we find it cheaper.

23. A "bit" is one-eighth of a Spanish 8 Reales silver coin that was equivalent to one U.S. dollar. To make change, an 8 Reales coin was cut into eight equal, pie-shaped parts; thus, a "bit" was 12 1/2 cents and two bits was a quarter. These Spanish coins and their "bit" parts were legal tender in the U.S. until 1857 (*Statutes at Large* 1 Stat. 300 and 11 Stat. 163). The jingle "two bits, four bits, six bits, a dollar" is a lasting memorial to Spanish pieces of eight.

A number of teems in town bound for Cal. Keosauqua is 55 miles from Burlington, measured dist[ance]. Today we have more snow & as cold as thunder. Kemble [Robert Kimble] returns to camp with out his horse but has since rec'd some tidings of him (supposed to be him). Offers $25 to any one to get him. Steam boat bound for the Raccoon Forks. The greatest place for emigration at the present moment is to the 3 rivers below the fort.[24] See rafts float down the river. A drunken fellow that brings corn to camp wants to fight 1 of our men. [Alexander] Ewin[g] parts them. [They] go down to town & have it out. Plenty of feever & ague on this river.[25]

April 18. Cold as the devel. Go up in stalk field after wild geese. Go down from camp to the river. Our men with a lot [of] others, man the scow, holding the rope, row out in the stream & after numerous dificulties succeed in crossing the river & raising the rope in a tree & tightening it with a windlass. After 6 hours hard labor, race betwen 2 canoes. Our mess goes to work on tent, & after working all day we nearly finish it. We get other poles, & raise it for the night. Now our tent is the largest & most convenient in camp. It is so allowed by the comp generally. After we raise it, set the stove in it & get the supper ready. Visitors come in from the other tent[s]. They say we beare off the palm in shape of a house. To day we suffered considerable from cold, working out doors all day, but now feel quiet [quite] comfortable. The devel in the white faced cow again.

[April 19 Thursday.] Hear the men yoking the cattle & get up. It was 19th Apl. As soon as prepared we make for the ferry [on Des Moines River]. We put 4 yoke on the first lode, & the wagon & Dick & Tom [two oxen] the next lode including our selves. The river at this time is falling & as the noble sun assends the east glittering on the rappid stream, the numerous objects floating on its surface becomes brilliant particularly on such a beautiful spring morn as the present. This river never overflows its banks at this place. A person to look at this river from a distance would not believe it as large as it [is], & even to look from 1 side to the other, but as you cross, you just realize its width, & as the current propells the scow acrost, & the bubling of the water as it gushes past, the oxen become frightened.

After landing we pass up thro a number of deep ravines, with dark overhanging rocks. One place we decend, we unhitch 4 yoke & lock both wheels on account of the steepness of the place, & even then it was like descending a precipiece as you pass over. To hear the noise of the many teemsters bawling

24. Old Fort Des Moines (1843–1846) was built at the confluence of the Des Moines and Raccoon Rivers. This military post grew into the city of Des Moines.

25. "Fever and ague," now called malaria, is not a communicable disease. An infected person can have repeated bouts of chills, fever, and sweating (Boyd 1975, 135; 1999, 84).

to their cattle, the lashing of whips & the greating of the tires over the stones & grit, it presents a scene beyond description, unique & imposing. To see the b[r]awny arm repeating stroke upon stroke to fell the noble forrest oak who has conquered every other foe, to make room for his train to pass is also picturesque. Some fellow during the day through [threw] his lighted cigar ashes in his wagon. It ignited with some combustibles & set his wagon on fire. Under the fire sat a keg of powder, which miraculously escaped. The fire was subdued by soom [some] mud & water being thrown on.

We stop at Dr. [*blank*, John D. Elbert's], a man of enormous proportions. He appears to be a fine man, & the size & resemblance of Father Longstreet. He said 10,000 Mormons passed his residence in 1 day [huge exaggeration], & several hundred teems of Cal. & among the whole of the Cals. he says he never see a better regulated & orderly set of men in an army, & in all no accidents of any a/c, & more over, he said he never found a rascal amongst them but 1 & he was drunk & cheated his [the Doctor's] boy out of some corn.

Ben & Balley runs of[f] & after searching the woods I find them browsing in a thicket. The Dr lends me the U.S. doc[ument] of the gold regions. Have a concert in the eve in our tent. Call council around the campfires & decide to lay still till Monday [April 23]. Our Mormon guide is expected daily. Some of the R[oc]k Island comp. talks of joining us. Corn [sells for] 15¢, hay 30¢ cwt. [per hundredweight]. A great number of large squarrels & doves killed to day, & a lot of wild turkeys seen. In the eve'g I give a Negro melody concert in our marque [tent].

April 20th. [Lay by] 1 man got killed in our rear by his comrades rifle. He was in the brush & the first thing he knew a ball passed through him. I have just rec'd news of another man ahead being killed in a similar manner. I presume it is true. While I write a gun goes off & if it had'nt been for a heavy post it would have shot an ox in the head. Pass rules not to have any shooting near the camp. Nearly all the comp. are out gunning. Bill [Kellogg] brings in 10 gray & fox squrrels which we have for supper. I make camp stool. Nearly every tent has some game to eat. Some of the men cuts down a bee tree & collects lots of honey from it. Get some fine shirts washed in a cabin. Great fears entertained of the cholera in Keosauqua, on a/c of a man being taken with the cramp [and] cholic & produced quite [a] sensation in town. People crossing the river to escape. Three boats arrived up in 1 day.

April 21. [Lay by] About daylight, a warm easterly wind, the sun bursts out from beneath the haze hot & sultry, making it almost sufficating in the tents on a/c of the sudden change in climate. I never see a more close day for the time of year in my life. Dr Elbert relates his experience amonge the Indians to us. After taking a nap in the after noon supper was announced, [at] which squirrels were served up in Ed's [Edward Kellogg's] own manner, & after supper we had a concert in our tent in the eve'g, & to help the base [bass], roleing thunder joins the chorus, while clashing through mid air. The rain, in meanwhile, decending in large drops.

April 22d was the Sabbath, the day pleasent & warm tho a little hazy. What a difference a few hours will make in vegetation. The woods of yesterday whose limbs were full of buds have bursted their wintery locks & gaze once more on spring. This is encourageing, & if the weather continues warm we may expect grass in a few days, & then we can persue our jorney. Had conver[sation] with a settler in his cabin about the Mormons in Arkansun, as he calls Arkansas, & the country of Iowa.

The dispute about the boundary line between Iowa & Mo has been finaly settled in favor of Iowa.[26] Mo. contended for the Des Moines line & collected [taxes]. While the suit was pending, Mo continued to collect, & Iowa, to oppose what she thought injustice, armed her citizens. But I must go & look for our Duke ox, who is lost since last night. It showers a little so I put on my oils. I hunt the brush for 3 miles & over, & on my return find him home. The Dr invites us into his dwelling to sing. His house is furnished beautiful, has 2 handsome daughters. All the boys try to run their shape. The old man is very rich & a free mason. He has 300 acres under cultivation. I forgot to mention the sermon preached to us Californiens expressly, it was good & solid. All the crowd listened very attentively as they set in their check shirt sleves. The Dr came in tent & asked if 1/2 hour would do to get our supper, & then the sermon would commence 4 o'clock. The old man was not eloquent but his charge to us was pointed. He said our guns, our knives of defense would not protect us from injury if God did not protect us. He affectionately implored us not to put our hearts to[o] much on the treasures of California, but assemble our meditations on things above where thiefs do not break in & steal.

April 23. [At] dawn of day, I am awakened by Dick the Dutchman who always says, (its myself that knows how to do it.) I get up, get corn to feed, & take 1 feed in waggon. As quick as we can harness up & milk the cows, we strike tent & depart amid the best wishes of the Dr & his lovely daughters. After travelling over a roleing, well fenced & splendid farming country, we come to a little

26. In handing down its decision on April 6, 1849, the U.S. Supreme Court concluded: "We are, therefore, of opinion, that the northern boundary of Missouri is the Osage line, as run by [surveyor] Sullivan in 1816" (Catron 1849, 660–81). It was called the "Honey War" when a Missourian cut down several hollow trees the Iowa settlers used as beehives (*History of Johnson County* 1883, 55–56; Kraus 1969, 91–94; Everett 2008, 283–84; see also Spencer 2008, 22–40).

town called Dover.[27] He[re] there is a way post, with this inscription, 260 ms to Council Bluffs, 140 ms to Jefferson City, 90 ms to Iowa City. Here we bought some provisions, of which we had run out. Thence taking over a large prarie, we struck a little northwesterly course along the ridge rode, & camped in a large lot of a farmer. This rode to the [Council] Bluffs is called the ridge rode, & is the dividing ridge between the tributaries of the Des Moines & the Missouri rivers, & thus we avoid nearly all the streams.

When we were at Keosauqua we made arangements with a Mormon [Ira Simonds Miles] to act as our guide to Salt Lake. To day he overtook us. His family lives there at Salt Lake. He emegrated with the Mormons & helped build bridges, cut away woods, & make roads. They then averaged 10 miles a day. On his way back which was in the winter of 1848, he froze 1 leg up to his thigh, & has sence been in poor health. I talked to him upon subjects connected with his trip & Salt Lake. He said Buffalo & antelope were plenty, in places. He said he saw the Sauxs [Sioux] kill 200 [buffalo]. There were about 200 hundred Indians. They killed them in 2 hours & dress them for their hides.

[April 24.] At the dawn of day of the 24 Apl it was a little chilly & all night it was extremely cold. The sun rose from our camp amonge the forrest trees as red & [as] blood. After traveling a little we strike north of west. While rideing in Ewins [Alexander Ewing's] mule carriage, we came to a bad mud hole which came near upsetting the vehicle. The mules, being snagged, laid down helpless. We unhiched & by the [help] of the Comp, a rail & an ox teem, we halled it out high & dry. About 12 we lay up for dinner in Drakesvill a fronteer town.[28] After travelling thro' numerous places where the trees had been cut down & the stumps left high enough to touch the axel tree, it takes as skillful a driver as it does a pilot to run a steamer up the Missouri, & look out for snags.

At night we pitched [camp] on the edge of a woods & turned out oxen in a stalk field. Here we bought 10 Bus. of corn to carry us acrost the unsettled country between Soap Creek & Garden Grove. I was taken sick to day, & after taking a remedy went to bed. Here we had scarcely any water & what we had the cattle would not drink. We drank it.

Ap[ri]l 25. We arrose with the sun & after completing our work, started, as we were 2 miles from Soap Creek, & that we made [by] 1 o'clock. Bot some maple

27. Dover no longer exists. It was first called Harpersville, then Dover, then Stringtown, and was located about one and a half miles south of today's Troy and about 15 miles due west of Keosauqua (*History of Davis County* 1882, 603).

28. Drakesville was surveyed in 1847, and in 1850 had 108 inhabitants (*History of Davis County* 1882, 589).

sugar of a woman. Along this road there is considerable travelling, & a no. of log cabins going up of considerable size, showing the march of improvement westward. On each side of the ridge road, slues & ravines slope off north & south from it. These bottoms are well timbered & fine lawns in front, & on these bottoms the grass is green with flowers of various hews & tints, the lilley, the blue bell, the joney jumper &c reign on here. After passing through a woods of some extent, we commence decending the steep & rugged hills that leads to Soap Creek. It is so steep that after locking both wheels the wagon slips & slides, nearly upsetting against the trees as you decend. The bottom presents a pritty appearance, the green grass, the serpentine course of the creek, the log cabin, & wild flowers. The reason for calling this Soap Creek I have not learned. But I know 1 thing, that its banks are as clayey & as soft as soft soap.

From here we proceeded through timber for a few miles & then launched out on a huge prarie that extended as far as the eye could reach, & up on this prarie no house of any kind could be seen. We see several spots on the horrison which must have been men on horses. This prarie conveys to mind immediately a scene at sea, & the white covers of our wagons, a fleet of sails following in each others wake.

According to the instructions of our guide we have to travel 13 miles from Soap Creek to reach timber & water. On, on, we went & if ever a jorney seemed tedious, this did. The farther we went, the farther the timber appeared to retreat from us. Along the rout we see a deer skin laying [to] one side. Some boddy had killed a buck & left the skin. At length, tired & wearried, night came on & the timber yet in the dist.

At length a light appeared on our left, be[ing] made for us. The light directed by the Mormon [guide], & as we went, the top of timber shows. The light proved to issue from a cabin, inhabited. I do think, any person that would live here in the wilderness must be fond of solitude. There had been a piece of ground fenced in but the fence was broke down. This spring is called Lone Spring. Part of our comp. is on behind & probably had to camp out on the prarie, & if it had not been for our guide we would had to have done the same. I turned in tireder than I had ever been in my life before.

[April 26.] On the morning of the 26th April the horn blew its blasts upon the morning air, & the usual cry of up here, everyboddy, there is a woman a drounding. Oh yes. Oh yes. Now I had been sick yesterday & not much better to day. It comme[n]ced raining as we started out [from] camp. We soon regained the road, & travelled 5 miles & then on a/c of the hard rain pitched [tents] & laid up for the day in a woods, during which the ballance of our comp. came up. On the edge of this timber, in a log cabin, died 1 of the men that was accidentally shot.

Another man is staying in a house near by waiting for his wounds to heal, which were nearly well enough to proceed to Cal.

[April] 27. Started out early, heard the wild turkeys gobble befor day break. [By] dinner time we had come 10 miles. Killed 5 rattle snakes,[29] found 2 elk horns. Our pilot & a lot of horsemen went ahead 8 miles with spades to bridge a bad slew. When we arrived it was all finished. They had arched it with sod. Going along, [we heard] the cry of a wolf, a wolf, & sure enough, some 20 of us on horses went after him full jump, but he escaped. He was a large grey wolf.

Came within 1 [*blank*] of setting our tent on fire by the leaves. At night camp on the banks of the Chariton River near its head. Graze our cattle, unyoke & leave them out all night for the 1st time. This river is fordable at this place, but ferried down below. Beautiful flowers of fragrince grow all along its bottom & banks while its green folliage sets it off. To day we made a 20 mile drive. Call council in eve'g, appt. wagon master &c. I have a bad cough yet. The air chilly nights & mornings.

Ap[ri]l 28th. Cloudy, chilly, raw & cold as snow. Near where we camped is a log cabin. This is the county seat of the new co. of Lucas. A couple of boys going out to cut wood barefooted & shivering with cold. You frequently see a log cabin about the size of a hog pen with out any inhabitant upon a piece of land, think[ing] to make a (Bonna fide) claim, & sometimes they plow around it the size of a town lot.[30] Start 7 o'clock in morning, pass over a marshey bottom of the Sherridan [Chariton], decend a deep ravine called the Grave. There is a Mormon woman who fell out the wagon when going down this steep [who is] burried there. See prarie wolf. Bill [Kellogg] shoots 2 bald headed eagles. Travel 21 miles, [to] head the Chariton River. Form our wagons into an enclosure for yoking. Turn our cattle out to graze out on a beautiful lawn with a fine bubbling brook running thro a fine grove of timber. 2 of our men started out hunting this morning & have not returned. Blow horns & make fires to signal them, & set the praries on fire near us in spots, round rings, there being no danger to us because where we are it had been burnt. Our brown cow comes up to our tent in the middle of the night bellowing, knows our tent.

29. Lorton does not mention eating the rattlesnakes they killed. One of this book's editors (LeRoy), in his thoughtless youth, killed every rattler he encountered, but they did not go to waste. He recalls that "each skinned carcass was coiled (back-strap down) in a cast-iron skillet, fried in butter, and eaten with great satisfaction."

30. To raise money and to encourage settlement of the western states, the federal government offered up to 160 acres of land at $1.25 per acre to persons willing to settle on the land. These hog-pen sized farmhouses were likely shams plunked on the land to satisfy the loose "proof of settlement" requirements of the 1841 Preemption Act (*Statutes at Large* 5 Stat. 453, Sec. 12).

Apl 29th, the Sabbeth. The wind blows a hurricane, some rain & a little sun. Our lost men return—some ponies lost but get them. Get slippery elm bark.[31] Find 2 elks horns. Cattle all there. The lower part of Iowa was lately the country of the Sacs [Sauk] & Foxs Indians.[32] The western part [inhabited] by the Pottowatomies.[33] Observe the Sabbith as usual today. Bill [Kellogg] had the fever & ague last night, & is very sick today.

Ap[ri]l 30th. We have a wind storm, a pampero, a torpedo, a whirlwind, any thing you are a mind to call it. When you have to shovel the dirt out of your eyes, a day when the d[evil] is in the cattle, when the roaring whirlwind & the flakes of sand cuts your eyes nearly out, when you have to pilot & cant see, when every boddy is cross & ready to fight, imagine this & multiply it by 20 & you may get a faint idea of this day. We make bed in wagon to carry our sick in. All in a hurry this morning. Find elk horns [on] side of the rode marked: For California 1849, Apl 20.

Decend a ravine. Egerts [Marshall G. or Sidney P. Edgerton] gets his stove &c. lost [?] off. Another ravine. It was so steep it was nearly up & down. In going down we stove in the front of our wagon, so the old Ark stove her bow in. I sink in the mud above my boot top in the fray, [a] pritty fix. Pass similar ones thro out the day.

About 3 o'clock as we cross an almost endless prarie, a man appears flying thro our lines upon a black glossy charger, crying, stop! stop! You are on the wrong road. He did not stop till he reached the head of the line. He proved to be a brother of one of the members of our comp. & bore letters to them & Ewin[g]. [Alexander] Ewin[g] & the guide were off some miles ahead so we immediately dispatched a messenger on horse[back] to overtake him while we waited doubtful whether to proceed for this reason. He said our goods was now on a sand bar below St Jo, & that the water was so low in the Missouri that they could'nt get up to Kanesville [Council Bluffs, Iowa]. Thus we were snaged on the middle of a prarie. He was just from St Jo 4 days agoe. At length our guide arrives. He said if we had kept on we would have been right. We turn off to the south & at length the tops of some scrubary appears in a ravine, & cotton wood. Here we have

31. Singers routinely used slippery elm (*Ulmus rubra*) to sooth their vocal cords—the reason Lorton added it to his medicine chest. It is so named because its inner bark is slippery. It was "well known to the early pioneer woodsmen on account of its mucilaginous inner bark...when steeped in water [it] produced a common remedy for throat inflammations and fever" (Harlow and Harrar 1968, 347–48).

32. The territory of the Sauk and Fox Indians, as delineated on Tanner's Iowa map (Map 1845, Tanner), lay between the so-called "Neutral Ground" to the north and the "Iowas" tribal lands to the south.

33. The Pottawatomi (numerous spelling variations) Indian territory is shown on the southwest corner of Tanner's Iowa map (Map 1845, Tanner).

scarcely any grass on a/c of the prarie being burnt so lately. They however snoop arround & bellow for food. We had two Bs corn but did'nt like to feed it all out for fear of necessity—& cattle will hardly touch corn after tasting grass. The letter said that our goods were on a sandbar 300 miles below St Jo. The boat had broke a shaft but expected it up in a few days. The water so low in the Missouri that the boats could'nt get up to the Bluffs as advertised, & that we must not put any confidence in any thing we heard on the road.

May 1st, [1849]. Cold morn'g. Cattle found after looking till 9 clock, ponies & all, quite discourageing. Bill sick yet. We perpose taking a short cut to intersect the road [to St. Joseph]. We cut down a mammoth cotton wood tree & with its branches make a bridge acrost the creek. We see the prints of old Mormon trail. Windy all day & the dust blows terribly thro the air. Go down terrable steep places, almost perpendicular. Make for Pisga [Mount Pisgah, Iowa] 15 miles dist.[34] See 4 elk horns with names on them. Get near Pisga & have to turn of[f] in an easterly direction. Some of us went to the settlement. Some of the men had 3 spiritual wives.[35] About 100 families in this place & is some times called Mount Pisga—all Mormons.

5 miles east we camp on the middle fork of the Grand River.[36] This we ford thro the rappids. [Have a] great time [at] the place where we decend [to] the stream. It is very steep with stumps on its banks, 1 wagon came very near upsetting. We get acrost by clinging to the back of the wagon & the last men get over by means of horses. There is some grass on the Bottom & quite a grove of trees nearby. This is a beautiful stream abounding with fish, grub, trout, &c. The road we are on now is a new one & some 25 miles to St Jo. The guide says its 100 miles to St Jo from here.[37] We lay to till 10 o'clock & then start out with our oxen full of grass. In expectation of camping on the prarie to night we put in a supply of wood. 12 o'clock we turn out our cattle on a bottom of the south [east?] fork of the Grand River. There were wagons with families bound for some part of Iowa.

We crossed another stream as large, south of that, & I cling to the hoops

34. The *15* is written over a *25* to correct the mileage.

35. In 1868, William Dixon said, "The theory of Spiritual Wives, as it appears to the carnal mind, may be stated in a few words; since to the carnal mind this mystical doctrine is but a religious and romantic disguise for an abomination known…under the name of Free Love.… No one can deny that the advocates of Spiritual wifehood are, and have been, for the most part ministers of the gospel" (1868, 88–89). "The term 'spiritual wifery' was generally a derogatory one" and not to be confused with plural marriages, according to the Mormons in the mid-1800s (Grow et al. 2016, 530n16). For the "theological justification" of plural wives, see Brodie 1960, 297–308.

36. Lorton's middle fork is today's Grand River and the "W. Fk of Grand River" on the 1851 Henn Williams map (Map 1851, Henn, Williams & Co.).

37. The guide's mileage is nearly correct.

& covers [of the wagon]. One wagon run against a tree, & they had to cut the tree down. The families were from St Jo. They had cattle, yearlings, & calves. 1 man had a little baby on the horse when he drove the cattle, the woman helped drive.[38] All thro this country you see small mounds with a stick stuck in it—a mark of the surveyor. Luzern[e] [Bartholomew] shot a deer & broke its leg but it got away. Six turkeys fired at but none killed. It is 50 miles to a house on this road.

[May 2nd.] It was very rainy & cold this morn'g but it has sence cleared off warm, & the barn swallows commence flying east. To day we travel 14 miles & camp in the middle of the prarie. While I write the wolves keep up a terrible noise out side. I presume we are now in Missouri, Pisga being near the line.[39] Pisga is a poor settlement, being principally composed of log cabins.

May 3d. We start out early & find the cattle some 4 miles off. We travel all day over 1 roleing prarrie with out the least timber in sight, with the exception of a little on a stream where we stoped [at] 11 o'clock to graze. Here we had to unhich our forward cattle.[40] We had to decend a steep embankment on one side & in assending the opposite diagonally, the wheels roled along on the top [of] a log, & if it had slipped it would have precippitated it sideways over the precipiece into the water. This I waded 3 times. 1 wagon driven by [James Ellery] Hale upset to day hurting a man in side the wagon, nothing broke. On the banks of this stream we see the remnants of an Indian wigwam with a fire [?] for cooking. They bend over a sapling & then suspend a croch [crotched] stick tied on with bark. Here they hang on their game & broil it. I take a nap in the afternoon. We travel 20 miles today & camp near timber. The west is constantly lightening as with heavens electric fluid, & the rain leaks thro our tent cloth it rains so hard. Ate a hearty supper & now I'll retire to the wagon. Got quiet [quite] discouraged today, but feel better. The stream near us is the west fork of the Grand River. Down on the bottom near its banks is an Indian camp ground. We found arrows, an Indian pack saddle, & two snow shoes.

38. Hollywood, fiction writers, and many western artists often portray women and children riding in covered wagons, a generally false portrayal of their role in the western migration. Children who were old enough walked, and women walked most of the time. On the plains they foraged for buffalo chips and wood for cooking fires. Prairie schooners lacked springs, so when a sick or injured person had to ride, they spent a miserable day being jarred and tossed around.

39. Mount Pisgah is about 37 crow-miles north of today's Iowa-Missouri boundary.

40. They left the wheelers attached to the wagon tongue for steering to let them hold the wagon back when going down hill. Often the back wheels were chained to prevent their turning.

[May] 4th. We strike down the bottom about 11. Did none [nothing] out[side] on a/c of the rain. About 4 o'clock we reached a settlement of 1 log cabin. Here was western pioneer life in true stile. Spot fenced in. The man said that was Iowa & the line run south of his cabin. In getting thro this timber that covers its banks, we had to turn & twist—up & down, & then assend a steep hill, muddy & soft. With great difficulty guiding our Ark thro the stump[s] & trees at the bottom of this hill, we cross the west fork of the said Grand River. Our Ark goes in up to the box. We cling to it & over she goes. The next teem gets stuck. The drivers get douced in the river. They pull of[f] their pants & [*illegible* swim?] in their S— t— [Shirts?]. We camp for the night for the first time in Miss[ouri]. A man just from St Jo, horseback, builds a fire, puts his horse out to feed, & eats from his pocket. He had a blanket & expected to stay here in the woods to night. This is a western traveller. It has now commenced raining. The disputed territory [between Iowa and Missouri] is 12 miles wide.[41]

[May] 5th. We start out 8 o'clock & follow the bottom for a number of miles. As we passed thro a little grove on the banks of a stream, we discov'd the remnants of 4 huts that Indians had lately occupied. The manner of constructing their houses is this: hoop poles are placed & bound in the form of a sugar lofe with bark & then they lay their cloth over that which they purchase of the whites. Strewed arround about the huts were deer skins, legs, jaws, Buckskin &c., turkey & chicken bones & feathers, pieces of blankets, burnt wood. They must have had horses to[o], for the prints of their hoofs [can be seen], & where they had gnawed the bark of the saplings. The owner of a log cabin said it was no use of hunting where the Indians had been. See 3 deer, 5 elks & deer horns. Our road now is the old Indian trade [route] to Fort Levenworth [in Kansas]. We travel all day with out watering our cattle, such a scarcity. We send men out a head to prospect & we finally haul up on the [Little] Plat[t]e River.[42] Here there is quite a settlement, 3 log cabins & land under cultivation. We passed in sight of 2 to day. Saw lot of men on horseback hunting with 5 Blood hounds. We travel to day about 18 miles. Fine groves of timber all round us. Water, like all the Missouri water [is] riley, & bottom[s] of grass to feed our cattle on. Our course to day is south west, nearly.

41. The disputed land was a strip of land "about 10 miles wide and 200 miles long, north of the present" Iowa–Missouri boundary (Van Zandt 1966, 213).
42. The headwaters of the [Little] Platte River is in Iowa and flows southward into Missouri where it debouches in the Missouri River. The [Little] Platte is about 170 miles long and is now channelized throughout much of its course. The river's official name is "Platte River," which is at variance to the "Little River Platte" name shown on the Lewis and Clark map (Map 1814, Allen).

May 6th was the sabbath. Got up rather late, washed myself, & after a considerable variety of opinions in regard to travelling on the sabbath it was finally decided to push on. 10 1/2 we pushed out [of] camp & followed the Little Platt[e] down. Old Ball liked to killed him self pulling. Nig would'nt pull but hung back.[43] In some places you look off the high bluffs & look upon the winding river runing thro a fine [valley] till it is lost in groves of trees, while numerous ponds dot the low bottom. Enter in thick settlements today. The boys buy provishions in a large log cabin, cheese &c. Fine roleing prarie & woodland & fine farms, a great many of them cleared wood land. Meet stranger just from St Jo, said there was plent[y] of Cal[ifornians] there, & cholera there. It showered a little in the morn'g but the sun now shines splendidly thro the trees where we are camped near a small tributary of the Little Platt. It is said to be 30 miles to St Jo from here. We are a going to have some potatoes for supper.

This is the first day we have travelled on Sunday. There is a mill (flour) down the river a little ways. Hear the owls screaching out doors & wolves barking. Man comes along with a lot of large fish slung acrost his horse, caught at the mill dam on the Little Platt. One man they thought died of the cholera. They after wards found where he had been stabed in the abdomen. Good market at Savanah, 13 miles [south], & at St Jo. Sell any thing that is eatable. See a mammoth wench as black as the ace of spades. Diarreah comes on me some.[44] I take cayane pepper tea.

[May 7th.] All hands up before day light after cattle. Set down on the Banks of the L. Platt River, full of snags & about 50 ft acrost, full of snags, muddy & not navigable. Fine woods on each bank. Banks caved in. See squirrels frisk about the branches of trees. Lot of cattle not to be found. Out looking after them. Lay in 6 Bus. corn at a cabin up on the hills. The old mans son had been out to within 100 miles of Santa Fee [New Mexico] for Uncle Sam. They carried out provisions for the troops stationed there. They carried 60/100 lbs [to] the teem acrost the plains, 3 mo there & back. He liked it well he said.

Got off 9 o'clock & traveled thro a variety of scenery, mostly woodland & some plaines. Stoped to feed our cattle & ourselves on the banks of the Little Platt River where we ford. This is a fine park, a perfect parridise. The river here is about 100 feet wide where we ford. Beautiful scrubbery line its edges & trees of mighty & tender groth mingle together. Birds of a variety of plumage warble on their branches, doves, blue jays, bobalinks, &c. Upon the level ground,

43. The oxen Lorton calls by name are Tom, Dick, Nig, Balley (or Ball), Duke, Ben, and Giraffe Ox, which might refer to the color of one of the others.

44. Diarrhea can be a harbinger of cholera, which apparently Lorton did not have.

eddies & little lakes, with their green moss edges, while tender leaves droop in the smooth water. On these ducks & geese float & dip their bills under the surface, & nurse their young. I saw & chased some ducks with their little ones with my ox gad [goad]. The old one tried to protect her little ones which were no biger than a hens egg. We finally scattered them & the old one hid herself under the roots of a tree. Deers run throu this grove. We saw 2 while we stoped. If I was going to locate in the Puke state, I would select this spot.[45] We cross this river by fording. Here the water runs rappid over stones &c. With the ponies we guide the oxen a crost while others ride. Pass this thick settlement, fine log cabins & 2 Brick houses. Stop & get water from a well at one, & eggs from another. He had emegrated from N Carolina to Ohio & from O[hio] to Mis[souri].

Up hill & down dale all day, steep, deep ravines, high & mighty, so that it tried the cattle. This is the state road. See a great many people on horse back, men & women. Guess they had been to market, from the new things they had. Come to the river called 102.[46] This is truly beautiful in the extreme, the banks rugged & broken in places & in others bluffs rise out [of] the river, & the [tree] roots project out. Uncovered log cabins appear on the west side in profusion & farms fenced in of moderate size. A little above, there is a mill [and] a dam that reaches across, made of brush & stone. All around there the stumps of trees bare marks of the woodmans axe. We see a man & woman cross this ford on horse back. We go up to the mill, decend a steep bank & then ford down to the road about a 1/4 mile down amonge the rocks & stones, rakeing the wagon & cattles feet. We use ponies to guide the teems. The hollowing of men to the oxen, & the teems continually arriving makes it picturesque in the extreme—the rushing of the water, the spattering of water, the rushing among the stones. This is a fine river of about 100 feet wide, & the water comes up to the box. We float over the old Ark, wh[ile] we sing a "Life on the ocean wave" & finally asend a steep acclivity to the top of the Bluff. There is plenty of fish in this river (102). We hear numerous stories from travelers about murders, cholera, small pox, & the numbers of teems.

We camp about dusk at a spring 2 miles from Savanna[h, Missouri], turn our cattle out in a lot, & eat a hearty supper. I feel fine to day [good as] a new pin, take corn along. Hearty as ever, dont think so much about pestering. The camp fires are burning, & the bright moon is just rising so as to see it from the ravine in which we are camped. This must be rippervice hollow, from the noise these pip[p]eds keep up.

45. "Puke State" was a pejorative or slang name for Missouri, thought by some to be a corruption of Pike for people coming from Pike County, Missouri.
46. The One Hundred and Two River originates in Iowa, flows southward, and joins the [Little] Platte River in Missouri.

May 8, 1849. After a few miles drive we come to the town of Savannah. Just as you aproach the town on the north side near the bridge, you see all in 1 view. It is the most florishing plase I have seen for 2 weeks, a court house of Brick, stone collumns, & stairs that assend from the out side.[47] This stands in the middle of the square, & has a cupalo on top. In the main st[reet] stores appear on either side the str[eet]. Log cabins deck the subberbs & stand on fine roleing hills & bluffs. Green fields of wheat looks fine on every [side]. Every common log cabin has its Negro slaves while the inmates look as if they never done a days work, pale & sickly [Missouri was a slave state; Iowa was not]. I stoped at a comon log hut, & asked if I could get some shirts washed. Under a bonnet appeared a lady like countenance. She done nothing while the wench done the work. She said in reply that I might get some Blacks to do it some wheres in town. Pass a carding machine propelled by oxen (wheel). Number of teems comeing up to Savannah & [Old] Fort Ke[a]rny to cross the Missouri [River]. Come along a man enquireing for Lorton, & who in the world should it be but David Cairnes [Lorton's cousin]. I gave a hearty shake & rec'd [the same] in return, passed conversations in regard to friends in N. Y. We sit down on the trunk of an old tree in the woods for some time. He may joine our comp.

It is one continual succession of hills & dales, & nearly all timber. We get into the subberb of the town of St. Jo, & see the blue tops of the hills & trees.

47. In May 1844, the Andrew County, Missouri, court "ordered that a courthouse of brick be built on the public square in Savannah, the same to be forty by fifty feet, two stories high, and finished in a workmanlike manner." By December 17, 1845, it was completed (*History of Andrew and DeKalb Counties* 1888, 31). In 1899, this courthouse was condemned and the current one stands in its place.

CHAPTER 3

St. Joseph to Kanesville, Iowa

Background

Two major events occurred on the road between St. Joseph and Kanesville: the formal creation of the Knox County Company, and the recommitment to continue north 145 miles to Kanesville to follow the Council Bluffs Road west into Indian country. Merrill Mattes said the following about the Council Bluffs Road (which many referred to as the Mormon Pioneer Trail):

> This trail was actually blazed by fur traders in the 1830s. Thousands of non-Mormons, or "Gentiles," used this north route during the California and Montana gold rushes, and they probably outnumbered the Mormons in 1849.... Thus, in contemporary usage there really was no distinct Mormon Trail from Council Bluffs to Fort Laramie. It was, instead, the Council Bluffs Road. (Mattes 1969, 7, 129)

We use Mattes's nomenclature.

The Knox County Company was formalized with a constitution and by-laws on May 12, 1849, almost three weeks before it arrived at Kanesville. The train halted to "form a more perfect organization" on a pleasant bottom near the Missouri River north of the Nodaway River while still in Missouri, after retrieving their goods at St. Joseph from the stalled riverboat. Four days later, on May 16, on the lower Nishnabotna River, the men signed the roster.

They had chosen Asa Haynes as their leader in Monmouth, Illinois, and from this time forward he was known as Captain Haynes. At age 45, he was older than most men in the wagon train and was a prosperous businessman. He and his wife, Mary Gaddis Haynes, had moved to Knox County in 1836, where Asa purchased 300 acres of farmland. He built a large brick house (and an even larger barn) for his seven children (and an even larger barn) and started a brickyard and sawmill near Knoxville. Asa spelled his name Haines until the early 1880s, when he changed it to Haynes.

Lorton begins to know other men in the train: he mentions the two Bartholomew brothers, Luzerne (age 37) and his much younger brother, Edward Franklin (age 21). The Bartholomew family had settled in Elmwood Township, midway between Peoria and Knoxville (Runner 1995, 1; see also Bartholomew Jr. 1885). Edward was closer in age to Lorton and to several of the young men who initiated themselves as Jayhawkers in the Platte River Valley. One of Edward's descendants is the actor Clint Eastwood (McGilligan 1999, 14). Luzerne and Edward are listed together in Salt Lake City's Emigrant Rosters for 1849 (see also Cannon 1999, 146). But they separated, and Luzerne took the wagon and entered California via the Lassen Cutoff, arriving in Sacramento on November 3, 1849. Edward remained with his younger Jayhawker friends and became one of the Death Valley '49ers.

The Jayhawkers included about two dozen young men from Knox County who pledged support for one another and later named a division in the San Joaquin Company after themselves. One of them said they called themselves Jayhawkers because it was "about the most devilish name that could be fished up" (Colton 1895). Most of them also became Death Valley Jayhawkers, part of the emigrants who continued west from southwestern Utah toward Walker Pass in the Sierra Nevada (Jean Johnson 2018; Manly 1894; L. and J. Johnson 1987). These Jayhakwers of 1849 preceded the abolitionist Kansas Jayhakwers by about 10 years and are in no way associated with them. The Jayhawkers of '49 emerged, destitute, from the western deserts into coastal southern California on February 4, 1850, three months after Luzerne Bartholomew arrived in the goldfields.

Alexander (age 43) and John Ewing (age 17) were father and son. Lorton calls Alexander "Judge." He moved to Knoxville in 1835, fathered three children, and opened the first general store in town. He returned to his family after his trip to California. The Ewings continued down the Southern Route to Los Angeles as did Lorton, Cephas Arms, and the Taylors.

While in Missouri, Lorton appears to have had his first look at slavery. When speaking of black people he almost always uses the term *Negros*, and only rarely does he use the more pejorative *nigger* Lorton shows his contempt for slave owners when he refers to them as "inmates," while showing respect for the "blacks" who did the work (as we've already seen in some of his diary entries). He takes pride in his repertoire of "Negro melodies," and throughout his journey he is called upon to sing them. Later, south of Salt Lake City, he travels with "a tall Negro," and at Mount Misery (southwestern Utah) he helps bury a black man and defends his property. On Cajon Pass, California, he sleeps under the same buffalo robe as a slave, presumably a black man. But Lorton also participates in an incident that today would be viewed as racist, albeit one that can also be interpreted as a case a racist incident. In an ill-chosen attempt to become one of the boys, Lorton uses the N-word when playing a joke on a black man, imitating an example set by the Knox County young men. In another case, Lorton is asked by someone to sing "nigger songs." We assume he did not put the object of this request in quotation marks because he rarely used them.

In the 1800s, all classes of white people used the N-word as a pejorative to express either implicit or explicit antiblack bias. Black people had (and have) a wider range of use for the N-word: either to disparage other blacks or sometimes as a term of affection (Parks and Jones 2008, 1306, 1345). Reverend Hosea Easton (1837, 40–47), who called himself "a colored man," described how white children grew up with disparaging terms all around them—systemic racism—that fostered bias toward blacks: "nigger lips," "nigger toes," "black as a nigger," even "nigger chair" at school, a chair of punishment placed near the segregated black students. Racism was encouraged by separation—whites traveled in railroad coaches; blacks sat apart in public meeting rooms; whites attended mainstream churches where blacks could attend if they sat in designated "negro pews." However, most "free colored Christians" worshipped the same God in their own churches (Price 2002, 200). Emigrants on the western trails brought their preconceived attitudes and prejudices with them, including their societal presumption of white male superiority that included varying degrees of antiblack bias or racism, of which use of the N-word was evidence. Their anti-Indian bias was based on the same fallacious assumption of white superiority—with a dose of fear and misunderstanding added to it.

In the jumping-off town of St. Joseph, Lorton is introduced to "seeing the elephant," a phrase common to the gold rush era. In *Law for the Elephant* John Reid writes that the term meant "to face a particularly severe ordeal, to gain experience by undergoing hardship, to learn the realities of a situation first hand, or to encounter the unbelievable" (Reid 1980, ix; see also Bagley 2012, 31–35).

As his train passes through Savannah, Missouri, Lorton meets his cousin David Cairnes, who lived about 100 miles north of Galesburg, Illinois. Although they do not travel together in the same wagon train, they do meet again in the goldfields of California, and it is thanks to the diary of a friend of Cairnes that we can follow some of Lorton's journey after he leaves Los Angeles, where his last extant journal ends—midsentence. There may have been more journal notebooks, but they have not come to light and may no longer exist.

After traveling north from St. Joseph about 145 miles along the bottoms and bluffs of the Missouri River, the Knox County Company arrives at Kanesville. The town was built on a site called "Miller's Hollow," located below the Missouri River bluffs in the middle of today's Council Bluffs (Hartley 2002, 14, 16). In late 1847, Brigham Young proposed the Mormons build a tabernacle in the hollow, and Miller was foreman for the project. On April 6, 1848, the new town was given the name Kanesville to honor Thomas L. Kane, a non-Mormon emissary of President James K. Polk (Hartley 2002, 17–18; Jenson 1886, 32). Kane helped negotiate federal permission for the Mormons to use Indian land for their winter encampment of 1846–1847 (Bennett 1992; Jenson 1886, 32).

Kanesville became the main outfitting point for the Mormon Exodus as well as for the gold seekers traveling the Council Bluffs Road. A boon to the town was this wave of non-Mormons who bought supplies and thus provided cash to the temporary residents. In 1853 the town was renamed Council Bluffs in memory of Lewis and Clark's council meeting with the Indians in 1804, north of the town on the opposite side of the river (Federal Writers' Project 1986, 203–4). Explorers and early travelers often called the area on both sides of the Missouri River "Council Bluffs."

Father Pierre-Jean De Smet arrived at Council Bluffs on May 31, 1838, "to found a mission among the Potawatomies" (Laveille 1915, 82; Chittenden and Richardson 1905, 149). Fortuitously, Col. Stephen W. Kearny, U.S. Army, was vacating a temporary fort that had a single-story blockhouse that he turned over to Father De Smet, who converted it into a church (Lorton's "Roman Catholic cathedral"). Father De Smet used "Council Bluffs" as his return address on letters sent to his superiors (Chittenden and Richardson 1905, 149, 158, 160n1; Babbitt 1916, 53).

In the Council Bluffs area, Lorton begins to see more Indians and writes about several of the tribes. Instead of giving just a token comment, however, he tries to learn something about them. The Pottawatomies were originally in the Lake States, centered in the upper portion of Michigan's Lower Peninsula. When Anglo-Americans confiscated their ancestral lands, the Indians were removed to Indian country, west of the Mississippi River.[1] The Otoe and Missouria tribes are often mentioned together: "These tribes, about 1,500 souls [in 1820], dwell together in one village on the south east side of the Platte river, forty miles above its junction with the Missouri, near the mouth of the Elkhorn. In their character and customs, they resemble their neighbors, the Pawnees" (Morse 1822, 251).

We fortunately know more about who was in the Knox County Company from an article published May 30, 1849, in the Kanesville *Frontier Guardian* that included the constitution, by-laws, and membership roster of the Knox County Company after smaller companies joined them at Kanesville (Appendix A; Jean Johnson 2018, 197–200). These additions more than doubled the number of wagons to "42 teams each averaging 4 yoke oxen" (Lorton, May 22, 1849). On May 22, the company took in teams from Canton (Fulton County, Illinois) and

1. "Indian country" was already reduced to the unorganized remnant of the 1803 Louisiana Purchase west of Iowa Territory and the states of Missouri and Arkansas (Map 1836, U.S. Topographic Bureau; Paullin 1932, maps 46C, 61G, 63B).

the "Rovers" from Fayette Township, southern Michigan. The Fayette Rovers, a cohesive group of twelve men, already had been in Kanesville for a couple of weeks. A few months later their captain, Henry Baxter, became colonel of the San Joaquin Company of 107 wagons on the Southern Route from Salt Lake City to Pueblo de Los Angeles, and the men became part of its Buckskin division. The Canton wagons belonged to about 16 men from Canton Township, located about 40 miles southeast of Galesburg, with J. R. Parker as their leader (Rasmussen 1994, 58, 68; see also Wheat 1940, 103–8).

We hope Lorton later got a copy of the glowing editorial send-off printed in the *Frontier Guardian* on May 30: "The Knoxville Company, taking in several other small companies and increasing their own, left this town to cross the Missouri River on Tuesday the 22d inst. This is a very fine company. The members of it appear to be honorable, whole souled men." The by-laws contained items dealing with the use of firearms, "spirituous liquors," provisions to call meetings, providing a horse for the guide, and punishment for willful violation of the by-laws. The list of company members was not complete. One hundred four men are listed, but at least two women, a child, the guide Ira Miles, and at least three other men are not included.

In Kanesville the train waited four days to cross the Missouri River via the upper ferry located near vacated Mormon Winter Quarters. After the Mormons were driven from Nauvoo, Illinois, in 1846, they began a westward migration hoping to find their new Zion somewhere in the Great Basin, which was then part of Mexico. But first they were forced to overwinter near the Missouri River. They selected a spot just north of today's Omaha, Nebraska, in "Indian country," on lands the Otoe and Omaha Indians occupied (*Statutes at Large* 4 Stat. 729). Although the Mormons had no legal authority to build this small but temporary city, they erected 538 log and 83 sod houses (dugouts) that sheltered about 3,500 people by spring 1847 (Bennett 1987, 81; Hartley and Anderson 2006, 214; for in-depth discussions of Winter Quarters, see Trennert 1972 and Coates 1984). By 1849 it was a ghost town.

Lorton's Journal Continues at St. Joseph, Missouri

[May 8, 1849, continued] St. Jo lies partly behind the bluff so that scarcely any houses appear. As you enter, the river Mis[souri] strikes your eye. Here the river bends, & is very narrow. You approach thro a chain of bluffs. Out in the country, the people are affraid to venture in on a/c of the cholera & small pox raging here (so reported). We find on entering that only 2 or 3 cases have occurred atal. On the right of the main road, perched up on a very high eminence is the court house, & at the foot of which, a Catholic church with a cross on it, & the priests dwelling attached to the church. On the left is a level bottom. It is dry & settling up. The major part of St Jo is 50 ft above the water, so they have a natural dock. Most of the stores are brick, & the principal st. is one block from the river. Take it altogether the ground all around is abrupt, caving & crumbling.

You see the Indian territory on the opposite side. Woods cover a low flat sandy bottom. This is green with foliage. To this point the ferry boats cross, & a road leaves back. This road Cal[ifornians] take that cross here. In a town like St. Jo at the present time, [there is] every thing to attract the eye. Boats are now going up to the [Council] bluffs. Our goods are here, & as we have come 100 miles out of our way, wagons are perfectly ram[ed], jamed, cramed, in among the cattle & mules that croud its st[reet]s. Teems are formed in a line by the hundreds, numbered, awaiting their turns to cross the ferry. There is only 2 flat boats, crossing night & day. These are rowed acrost by the persons owning the teems. Some have waited 3 weeks their turn, others have went out on the suburbs & camped almost discouraged. Corn is selling at 50 cts. A great many persons are out of funds, & have to let their cattle nearly starve. To prevent some of the cattle from falling apart, I surjest [suggest] a visit [?]. The stores are croud[ed] with purchasers. The store keepers are independent. The grog shops & gambling houses are full. The hotels are crouded to excess, & steam boats are constantly arriving up the river with teems & Cal[ifornians]. There are a great many with mules & carriages, horses, & a great many packed mules, & to all appearance some expect to run express right thro. Nearly all the wagons are heavy & clumsy.

There is a variety of classes, the gent & Blackleg [gambler or crook] all bound for El Darado. Scenes like brakeing oxen, mules &c. appear in the st[reet]s. Nearly all that come up the river are green as to the knowledge of oxen or mules. One fellow agreed to brake a yoke who said he was [an] experienced hand. [He] agreed to take $10 to break a mule. He had never seen one, hardly, & so [it] showed him the elephent. Speaking of the elephant, 1 wagon reads thus, "Traveling Edition of Pilgrims Progress" & then elephants, buffalo, & animals appear on their way to Cal. in carricature. A great many teams are now making for [Old] Fort Kearny & Council Bluffs [up the Missouri]. The merchants sell just as much as they want to. We load up our wagon before dark, & camp on a high bluff overlooking the river & town. There has been considerable skirmishing in town in consequence of every person being armed to the teeth with pistols, bowie knives &c. See a squaw straddle [a] hourse from over the river, dressed in gaudy col[or]s.[2] Write a letter till 1/2 past 2 in the morn'g to *N. Y. Sun* in the waggon.

2. "Squaw," in Algonquian dialects, means North American Indian woman. Recently it has become a pejorative. "Papoose" (North American Indian child or baby, or the carrying pouch for such a baby) has the same origin but has not suffered the same degradation as "squaw."

Lorton's Letter from St. Joseph, Missouri

Below is Lorton's first letter as a correspondent for the *New York Sun*. It appeared June 8, 1849, a month after Lorton penned it. Although portions of his journal are in the letter, Lorton adds interesting details he thought the folks back home might want to hear.

FROM THE CALIFORNIA ADVENTURERS

St. Joseph, Mo. May 9th, 1849.
Messrs. Beach, Brothers: — Dear Sirs: I now devote my first leisure moments in penning a few lines for the perusal of the numerous readers of your valuable journal. About 3,000 teams are here waiting to cross the ferry, and more are constantly arriving. The average estimate of the number of teams that have passed through the streets of St. Joseph on their way to different points on the river is 15,000. Incredible as it may appear it is nearly correct. This being one of the principal crossing places, the mass has centered here, but there are two ferry boats (or flat boats) propelled by oars, worked by persons owning the teams. These flats are not capable of carrying more than 1 waggon and 5 yoke of oxen at a time. Teams commenced crossing about 4 weeks ago and since that, the ferry has been worked day and night.

The streets are all blocked with wagons and carts. Those who have shipped goods to the warehouses along the levees, with difficulty, gain access. Those crossing first are formed in a line on the road reaching to the ferry, each numbered in turns. Others getting tired of waiting, have gone out on the suburbs of the town and encamped, almost discouraged. Several told us they had been waiting 2 weeks. Large India Rubber boats, or pontoon trains if we had them here now, would be worth their weight in gold.

Feed is selling at exorbitant prices, and those not having the necessary funds are forced to let their cattle nearly starve. The grass is all eaten off for miles around, and nothing now remains for such, but to sell out (if they should be so fortunate as to find a customer), and take the back track. There has been considerable skirmishing about the ferries and houses of entertainment. Pistol balls were exchanged between two men at the ferry yesterday, and report says they both died.

Nearly every man you meet is armed. Some with revolvers, horse pistols, bowie knives, and some with all three stuck in their belts. We have an endless variety of specimens of human nature, from the affluent gentleman, who rides in [a] mule carriage, with a numerous retinue to obey his call, down to the coarsest scrapings on God's earth. Several hundreds of very rich merchants have passed through here within a few days, on their way to the Sacramento valley. Many of these take their families out with them. They carry out large capitals to speculate on, and all have mule carriages of the most splendid workmanship, wagons to draw their provisions, cooks, teamsters, &c. Some say they go for their *health*!

From what I have been told by several trappers, and from what I have seen with my own eyes, I am convinced that ox teams are far preferable to mules for this lengthy trip. For a few hundred miles the mules go ahead, but the oxen overtake them in the long-run. I have seen a light mule carriage so set in the mire that ox teams had to be resorted to. Oxen pull slow and steady, while the mule gets tired and lays down discouraged. There is much drunkenness and debauchery among the lower classes here. These people neglect their teams, and most of them will not go 200 miles from the States.

A great deal of the emigration is aiming for Fort Leavenworth or [Old] Fort Kearney, Kanesvill, and different points along Council Bluffs, and near the mouth of the Platt. Those coming from the upper countries, follow the old St. Augusta Indian agency road to the Des Moines [River in Iowa] and from there strike the old Mormon trail. This follows the dividing ridge between the Des Moines and the Missouri rivers. By taking this trail they head all the tributaries of those streams. From the Bluffs they follow the Mormon trail as far as Salt Lake, where they expect to replenish. According to the account of some Mormons just from the Lake, the Mormon settlement has now on hand 50,000 bushels of surplus wheat.

The cholera has appeared at nearly all the towns along the river. Some are entirely deserted, stores closed, &c. The country people around have reported that all in the towns are dying with cholera and small pox. So great is the panic among the farmers, that they dare not venture in with produce. Only four cases of actual cholera have taken place, and no smallpox up to this time. One who was thought to have died with the fatal scourge was afterwards found to have been killed by a stab inflicted in the abdomen. If a man gets drunk and falls in the mud, the report of cholera flies from tongue to lip like wild fire, and in 30 minutes it multiplies into 20 cases of real Asiatic.

We have encamped upon a high bluff, and look in any direction the white carts and wagon covers meet your eye. Bluffs, fields, streets, and dales, are literally covered with canvas. Away out on the rolling prairie, long lines of white topped vehicles are seen rapidly advancing, and as you gaze steadfastly upon them, it calls vividly to the imagination the clean sails of an approaching fleet, floating before the breeze, while upon the green grass fanned gently in the wind it appears like the heaving ocean. I will merely add in conclusion, in regard to the imposition practiced at the frontier settlements, that you have only to let it be known you are a Californian, to have the tariff raised 100 per cent higher than that charged to any other person.

Yours truly,
W. B. L.

Lorton's Journal Continues in St. Joseph, Missouri

[May 9, 1849.] On the 9th write home & mail them. A great many pestering here today. See creolds & half breeds, foreigners & picpockets, about town. Every store & house has its slaves. Buy bran at mill for cattle. Walk & stay arou[n]d town all the morn'g. Eat & drink good things & then put out to catch up our team. After traveling a hard days march we camp in a fine open woods about 2 miles from Savannah. The weather to day has been hot but the atmosphere smokey. You see little boys with pistols as large as themselves stuck in their belt, & knives 3 ft long all bound for Cal. I get my shirts from washing today.

The 10th May, we reenter Savannah on one of the coolest, sun shiniest days extant. After staying in Savannah a little while, we drove out 6 miles & camped on a small praririe. Put our cattle in a farmers field to graze while we kept them off the timothy [grass], put things to rights in our wagons, aired our bed clothes, &c.[3]

[May] 11th. Made for Smiths Ferry on the Nodaway River.[4] Between the camp & this river there is some of the greatest farming land in the world. One succession of beautiful farms, cottages with the ivy twineing its branches around their door posts, some with large sycamores casting its huge branches over the small but neat hamlet. The buisey bee huming around the garden hive, the rose just bordering the wild lilac in full bloom, the crab apple in blossom, & the wild plum bursting from the shoot. The strawberry with its white flower, the sweet smell of the early flowers & freshness of the new green leaves, above the grassey carpet, the cooing of the ringneck & turtle dove, the chirps of the robbin & molking bird, the Cookies hollow [Cuckoos' call], hundreds of Black birds swarming the bushes, the noise of the wood peckers upon the trunks of trees, the gray squirrel chattering & skipping among the branches, all this added to the beautiful scenery contributes to inspire the heart.

Bill [Kellogg] & my self goes ahead of the team hunting. Come to the river Nodaway. This is about 50 feet wide & as crooked as can be, a fine bottom of green grass & trees & bushes dropping their branches in the gentle river. We come up to the river a few hours after leaving the team, & find the flat boat laying to on the near side, reaching 1/3 way acrost. I set on a stump to rest & while resting we see a wild turkey acrost the river, strutting about, & hideing its[elf] under the small bushes, when observed. Bill went up to get the ferry man to take

3. Since Timothy grass is desirable forage for horses and cattle, we assume the farmer did not want emigrant cattle chomping all the young Timothy before it developed into useful hay. Thus, the cattle were put into a field, probably with corn stalks to feed on.

4. The 120-mile-long Nodaway River originates in Iowa, flows across the northwest corner of Missouri, and empties into the Missouri River eight miles west-southwest of Savannah, Missouri.

him crost, while I watched the turkey. While he was gone I fell asleep, elevated 3 ft on a stump & when he returned he found me catching fish instead of catching game. So he crossed & I took up on the other side of the river, & [while I was] getting ready, it flew acrost on my side, but it hid & I could'nt find it.

We cross our teams about 2 o'clock & pitch our tent, & feed our cattle amid a few streaks of thunder & lightning, & a little rain, in a fine grove. Coming along, [we met] a little nigar on horse back. One of our men asked where he lived & who owned him. He answered very politely Mr Lamors. Take off your hat & make a bow. Off it went in the best nature. I told him [one of our men] I would beat that on the next nigar. So the next we met, I says, You see that nigh ox? Yes, massa, answered he. Well, he is the great Sultan of Muscat, make your bow. Off it [his hat] went on the little niggars knee like a thousand [pounds] of brick. Amid the roars of laughter, he chuckled & went on. See a dead ox in the road. He belonged to some Cal[ifornian]. Lot of our men went in swiming in the Nodaway.

[May] 12th. Passed up the bottom & intersected the lower ferry road. Meet a few farms & see the river running down the prairie & the blue mountains in the dist. Cross a green roleing prairie without any settlements. Come to a brook with a mirey bottom, bridge partly carried away. 1 team gets stuck, we go over like grease. 1 mule team of 6 mules & 2 ox teams that we passed some ways [back] comes up when at dinner. In crossing the mule wagons, 1 mule strains its leg. We sholder the wheels & help them out. They then put 8 yoke on each wagon, & after hard work up she comes. These teams are in charge of an app'ted gov't officer. He was dressed very fancy & rode a fine black horse with two silver mounted pistols (revol's) in the holsters. They are bou[n]d for Fort Kearney. From there they are escorted by U.S. troops as far as Bear River at the junction of the Oregon & Cal. roads [in southwestern Wyoming]. They are going to build a fort here & send out troops & mechanics. They get 40 dolls a month. They sell to the U.S. solgers. Catch a live crow, knock him on the head. 12 o'clock have meeting of comp. Elect Asa Haynes, Cap.; C[ephas] Arms, Lieut.; [Thomas?] Shannon, sarg. 1st.; & 3 others for the trip. Pass constitution & by laws.

There is we hear trouble amonge the Indians in Indian Territory. Some Pitsburg Cal[ifornians] fired at a monument erected to an Indian chief. This caused trouble, & the Cal. killed 2 Indians. They say they [the Indians] stole their mules. Report says that gov't sent out troops from the fort [Kearny] to bring the comp back, & settle it & also that crossing at Gr[and] Is[land] is stoped till settled, in consequence of the certainty of Indian revenge. It must be settled by govt.

Go on after dinner till we come to bad slue. There we find our govt officers team stalled up to the hub & unloading. Their principal cargo was whiskey. In that wagon they had 40 hundred [4,000 lbs.] on board, & 5 yoke small oxen to it. The other had 35 [3,500 lbs.] & 4 yoke, & 1 bull tied behind. The mate they turned off on the prairie, lame. Jno. [John] Thompson [one of Lorton's train] gets stalled, 8 yoke pulls him out. See a large dead wolf in the road. I go on ahead some 5 miles with Judge [Alexander] Ewing in mule carriage to hunt camp ground. Find Capitan & Pilot at the Doct[or's] on the hill. Collect firewood & have it cut by the time the wagons come up. Camp by the side of a brook on the Missouri bottom.

This bottom is most splendid to gaze upon. Reaching for miles, it presents at one vision one vast, level, green surface. A line of fine bluffs run in a southeasterly direction. Towards the river these are pointed like snow peeks, substituting green & blue in the place of white. On the south & west runs groves of fine trees & on the opposite side of the river chains of blue bluffs. On the north you perceive a straight line of drooping willows & bushes, indicating that a stream of water here forms its banks. There is a bridge that crosses it near by. Near where we are camp[ed] on the bottom is about 50 acres of land under cultivation. Over the creek a lot of Strikes are camped.[5] To look upon this lovely scene just as the sun is sinking behind the western hills, the rosey clouds tinged with the violet almost following the fierey ord [orb] with its own bed chamber, while it rests a shadow upon the dist[ant] objects in view & sheds a healthy hue upon retiring day. Our cattle by hundreds roming over this vast plain, contented with their transient home. In the evening a lot of men from the neighborhood comes down to hear some music, having heard we were players. As many as could croud in assembled in our markee. After hearing some airs from violins, flutes, &c., I was called on to sing nigger songs, which I did, & [at] 11 o'clock I retired to the waggon, the ground being damp.

[May] 13th. The sunshiney sabbath. Slept rather late on a/c of our not going on today. The Lord that made all must be hon[ore]d while I write this. Fred [Kellogg] is in the tent picking beans. Bill [Kellogg] is reading the *Hist of Cal* near the stove.[6] [Henry] Ward is of[f] somewhere, the old man [Edward Kellogg] taking a walk up the creek, & I writing in the open air. Got a shot at a wolf, see 3 rattle snakes, 1 4 ft long, 2 joint snakes, see gofer. We slept in the wagon, & in the night comes up a tearing shower. Winds blew, the storm beet thro the tent on the beds & set them all afloat. To day we had baked beens, custard, hot biscuit, & apple sauce.

[May] 14th. Started 11 o'clock, & followed road over bottom & bluffs. See 2 snakes, 1 blue snake that spits its poison.[7] There is a post office up on the hill &

5. "Strikes" may refer to the contractors who are going west to build the fort on Bear River in southwestern Wyoming.

6. Possibly this is *A Natural and Civil History of California* by Miguel Venegas, the two-volume English edition published in London in 1759.

7. Likely this was a yellow-bellied racer (*Coluber constrictor flaviventris*), commonly called

FIGURE 6. Detail, James Wilkins sketch. "Crossing a Creek." Emigrant wagons did not have brakes. Here, many men hold back the wagon on a down-grade before crossing a log pontoon bridge. WHI Image ID 31443.

called the Bluff P.O. & the stream Davises Creek. Kill a large white crane 5 feet high, & 6 from tip to tip. Mail a letter to uncle Lewis [Olmsted]. Meet several Mormons comeing down. Went 14 miles to day & camped on the river Big Tarcio [still in Missouri]. The roads are all bridged. Where we took dinner was Little Tarcio.

[May] 15th, [1849]. Passed over a bottom where the wheels sunk in to the hub, & ours went thro easy. Way mostly over the bluffs. Crossed over several streams. One had a mill on it. Canton teams gets stuck & 9 yoke of oxen could just pull it out after breaking 3 chains. Near night camp near Mormon town. Guide went up to [Old] Fort Kearney. Meet plenty of Mormons.

[May] 16th. Up 5 o'clock. All sign the constitution. Pass thro Linden [Missouri].[8] This is some punkins [first rate], I tell ye, composed principally of log cabins, & some of these very good ones. There is 2 taverns in town, one the Frontier House, a log cabin. It is situated on an eminence & commands a tolerable pritty aspect. The residents are Mormons, generaly, & is a pritty frontier

blue racer. This snake is not poisonous but when confronted it mimics a rattler by vibrating its tail. It moves fast, as its name implies, and adult length ranges from two to six feet (Wright and Allen 1957, 1:138–42).

8. This Linden was a small community about six miles south of the Iowa-Missouri state line.

town. During the day as we made along the bluffs we come in sight of Missouri River. I read the *Hist of Oregon*. See an old man with his hair & beard as white as snow. [He] tells us about the Indians, he had been among them. Dont stop at dinner time. One of our men tries to hit a Quinzy [Quincy, Illinois] man on the head for rushing ahead of him. They afterward armed with their revolvers & bowie knives. Come to the Nishnabottona River. This is 25 ft deep at this time. It is within its banks. It is so crooked that birds try to fly over & get on the same side. It runs thro some timber, prairie, &c. Its banks in some places are very abrupt. Cross the Nishnabottona on flat boat. Take 1 yoke & wagon at a time. Ferriage 65 cts. About 100 ft wide. We camp over on the west side, being first, & the other teams still crossing. It is 80 feet deep [below the prevailing landscape], a little lake above us. Lot of our men go spearing fish. Indians throw clumps in the river to scare the fish. They were camped on the other side.

[May] 17th. Call the roll 4 o'clock in morn'g. Hold counsil. The majority for the Bluffs [in preference to crossing the Missouri at Old Fort Kearny]. Traverse nearly all day [on] the prairie. Travel 18 miles & camp a little off the road on the prairie with a little stream nearby. I go 1 mile after wood. Kemble [Robert Kimble] gets lost in chaseing cow over the prairie which ran off with yoke on. Blow horns & put light in tent for signal.

[May] 18th. Roll called, in bed. 3 cows & the ponies gone. They [the men who went after ponies] overtake us about noon. Take dinner on Keg Creek on cold beans. A man from Cal. visited us on a large black horse. [He had] a Spanish saddle made of a frame & buffalo skin over it, twisted strands of horse hair girths, the stirups made of wood with leather toeings. A dispute arrose bet'n him & our pilot as to the Bluff & Kearney routs.[9] He is going to Salt Lake with a comp. He said Kearney was 100 miles nearer for us, but [and?] he was going that way. He also said we would not get to Cal this year, & we would all have to come to [eat] dog, mule meat, &c. He became quite excited when we laughed & he talked as if the Mormons would rob us on the way. The principal dispute was about Loup Fork & the [Elk]Horn, tributaries of the Platt. He jumped on his horse & rode off quite vexed with us bidding us mark the truth of his words. His object was to send us off his track. Our rout for 12 miles today lay over prairie, & in the afternoon for 6 miles thro timber & brush on a new rout to Cainsville. Leading to all these groves of timber, you see Indian trails or footpaths. The water gets in these paths & gullies them out deep. Some sittlements. Met a young fellow, he said he had been to Salt Lake & back in 6 mos. See several large snakes

9. The Bluff route is the Council Bluffs Road on the left (north) bank of the Platte River. The Old Fort Kearny route leads to the Oregon-California Trail, which is on the right (south) bank of the Platte River (Mattes 1988, map nos. 14–15).

4 ft long. Camp in the edge of timber 6 miles from Keg Creek, in a valley. Good treat, like to founder my self on butter milk. I drive all day.

[May] 19th. Very showery till 9 o'clock, roads muddy. Pilot gets drunk, quarrels with a man about the roads. We get on the wrong road. Road over prairie mostly, no settlements. See several picket railings indicating a grave of some cheif or white person, tho it seams to[o] far from any dwelling for white person. We cut down tree, build bridge acrost stream. Here 3 roads intersect, 1 from Pisga, & about 25 teams bring up our rear, a long string with our own. 5 miles from Kainsville, see a Cal. ox dead. Not long after this we enter a narrow long valley. On each side one continued succession of cabins & hovels appear. Many of these are rough logs thrown up in the rudest stile, about the size of a large hog pen, built in the flats [?] with sod roofs & vegetation growing on top. Out of all I see only one with window glass, & those were 2 8x10s. Some used muslin for glass & others had no windows not even a hole. As you pass along, you see women & children peeping through the crack[s] & crevices, bet'n the logs. The doors are made of oak staves, those that had doors. The ground serves for the floor. You see women with 8 or 9 children clinging to their mother while the father lays up on the bed asleep. Some have a few cows, & have a little butter & eggs to sell to emegrants. This place is called Cartrevil[l]e or Carter Town.[10] Its inhabitants are all Mormons, & have located here, it is said, temporarily till they can raise the means to get to Salt Lake. They will do any thing for money, & an honest old woman said she wished they would all go, for it was no place to raise children, for they set such bad examples, & they were as common as the beasts. The chiminies are composed of split sticks put acrost each other & then plastered with mud & clay. The report is that the Mormons are as bad as the Indians to steal. We were considerably delayed at this [place] on a/c of the mud. In 1 place our Brin ox sliped some, & in another, we had to [use] double teams to get thro. Some 25 teams from Oscaloosa came in here & our ranks were broken till near dark. We went back of the bluffs & camped in a valley & drove our cattle of[f] on the Mis[souri] bottom 4 miles. We had wood but no water near by & that we carried from a spring down on the bottom. This made supper late, which we ate with a keen appetite [New] Yorkers know not of. A comp. camps near us, which had a most splendid violinist.

[May] 20th. Awakened by the bugle [at] day light, but no roll called. It was Sunday, & we had several applications to join ou[r] comp. The day was cloudy but we went after & could not find our Duke ox. Several went in search on horse[s], & we met him & all hands. We entered Cainsvill, I having rode Nig [ox]

10. Cartersville, which no longer exists, was three miles east-southeast of Kanesville (Map 1856, Chapman).

horseback. As for Cainsvill, it is some[thing], for there is not a dwelling, store or church in it that is not a log cabin. Near the entrance, standing on the top of a tall bluff in a very conspicuous position, a Roman Catholic cathedral strikes your eye the first thing.[11] This costly structure is also built of hewen logs. It is about 25 ft to the peek, & on the off peek stands a cross, in front of a rude, shacking [shaking] cupalo or rather a belfrey, if it were strong enough. I ascended this hill which was just off the road, to take a birds eye squint. As I assended I see a lot of hogs & poultry scratchin & rooting the soil up under it, for it set on high blocks. So creeping around a little farther, I discovered the ingress, which was reached by some rails laid from the bank to an extension in a log cabin next to it. I suppose the rev[erend] prelate lived in this way. The papel see has sent his church up the western water. After entering Kainsvill, you ask where the town is, for you cant see it for so many dam'd log cabins. There is several stores of not much consequence, & pie & beer shops. I see 1 house that was only partially built of shingles. One side of the roof was on & part of the side [had] shingles. Under this roof was two bed[s] & a little furniture. When the rain comes from the south it is tollerable, but from the north they must be inundated.

We camped on the bottom west of the town, & 4 miles from the river on the edge of a creek. There are now Indians in town from acrost the [Missouri] river, some squaws making mockasins for the most limited compensation. See a couple of Indians skin a hog that had lain in the mud 4 days, it haveing died from some cause not known. After gutting it they cut it up in q[uarte]rs, a portion of which they thrust in a large iron pot which they carried with them, made a fire, & not waiting till it was done they devoured it like wolves, half starved beings. They put it in as if they knew no fire [?]. After eating this boiled pork up clean, & all most licking the pot, the tallest of the 2 tied a piece of string to half [of] what was left. He stuck his head thro the string, letting the pork hang over his back. This one had on a U.S. [Army] jacket with 3 marks on the arm. With the exception of this & his mockasins, a buffalo robe was the only clothing on their person. Being now ready to depart with his load, he picked up his bow & arrows, & opened his robe to gather it close to his naked limbs. Just now a fresh wind was blowing from the direction of the river. The thunder spoke and lightnings flashed amid the dark clouds that hovered above the forrest trees on the neighboring shore, & amid the houling of the elements you could hear him say to us, as he pushed forward, "squaw" "pappoose" & then he pointed to old Missouri, almost breaking into a run. The other still continued sitting huddled up by the rail fence with his robe close around him. He had a large piece of the

11. This "cathedral," known as St. Joseph Mission, was Father De Smet's "fine little chapel, twenty-four feet square, surmounted with a little belfry" (Chittenden and Richardson 1905, 168).

pork laying on the bars but did not attempt to carry it away. I supposed that he was awaiting the others return, as there was a large pot to carry besides the pork. In reply to my interogations, he would point to his game & then acrost the river, saying, "squaw" "pappoose." This one was apparently 40 or 50 years in age & with the exception of the robe & mockasins he was naked. They belonged to the Ottoes tribe. They were both tall & muscular, their looks were fierce, at times breaking in a smile. I have since learned that this old Indian was waiting for his squaw to come & carry the pork, who was some 4 miles from the place, across the river. Thus they make the squaw carry home the game & do all the laborious work. So indolent is the tribe that they will not work, but begs & steals, there being not much game on the Mis[souri], & to go very far back in the territory would be certain death, as the other tribes shoot them down when ever they meet. This Indian set some hours in the sun waiting for his squaw. Another wanted to sell me his squaw for a plug [of] tobacco. Some of these Indians are Omehaus, & when they come around town to beg, the men sometimes club them away which they bear like a beast. They come scouting around watching an opportunity to pilfer. One came in our camp, entirely naked with the exception of a robe. He said he would'nt sell it for then he would be naked.

I assended the top of a tremendious high bluff, & while there I see 3 Indians peeping down on our camp from the top of another bluff opposite. Thus they watch your movemts from hill & thicket. I assended by way of a road, a very tall projecting bluff, some hundreds feet high, to see the Pottawatomies graves which lay on top. Of these there were some 6. 1 of these appeared to have been an infants grave. It had a stone both head & foot. 4 others were Indians, & the 6th appeared to have been a chief, for in addition to the logs that lay criss X each other, there had been pickets around the grave & a larg[e] pole at the foot. The others had logs some 7 ft long & 2 wide laid up like a pig pen notched, & the bodies were only laid under a thin cover of earth, as the bones show of 1 that had been exhumed, & a couple of Mormon boys sitting with their feet in the grave were amuseing themselves with playing with the bones of this red man. For amusement they had broken the skull to pieces & were now trying to drive some splintered leg bones into rotton logs that had served as his coffin, using the thigh bone for the hammar.[12] It is a well known fact that Indians nearly always burry facing the west. Some burry in a crooked "zig'zag" position. On the top of a bluff on the opposite side of the valley there is similar graves.

I have learned that the Catholic cabin at the entrance of the town was built for a fort, & commands a very conspicuous position. Down near the square

12. Grave desecration was one of a multitude of factors that created a rift between Indians and Euro-Americans.

is the Mormon counsil house. It is some 100 ft long built of logs & sod roof.[13] The Mormons of this place first located on the other side of the river at a place called Winter Qrs. Here they lived 2 years, & built several hundred log cabins, but gov't said it was Indian Territory & they must move. A great many of these cabins have been burnt, some by emegrants & other[s] by the Indians. 1 of the 2 ferries are at that place.

[May] 21st. I with a man from each team go down on the bottom to see if our cattle was all there, which was found to be all safe. Down near the timber we see an Indian, & on his discovery he stooped behind some brush. Some times cattle stray in the timber on the edge of the river, most generally in the day. Indians seeing this shoot them down, weather [whether] fat or lean, & takes the meat over in their canoes. Others wait for an opportunity to steal horses, which they swim acrost. They carry this on most effectually when leaves are on the trees, for they steal whole droves, & then conceal themselves & animals in thickets [where] they are beyond persuit, & others go that dare, off to the buffalo country. The last winter has been so long & hard on them that could it be known hundreds if not thousands must have perished. Very few of these have any wigwams, using their robe for the double purpose of remnent [raiment] & house. They appear to have no ingenuity whatever, except it be in cutting long slits in their ears & hanging brass rings & pieces of wire press[ed] together about the size of a log chain, & hanging in holes 1 above another.

Today I wash a lot of shirts for the first time. A Mormon shoe maker here says he see 2 men who dug several thousand doll[ars] of gold out of Sutters mill-race. He wayed 40 ozs for 1 man.[14] The men arrived here on mules & said they would have stayed to get more, but for food. They lived on mule meat, mule guts & leather boiled down into soup. When they arrived, they were dressed in skin clothes & rode on Spanish saddles.

[May] 22d. Still camped. We only had 5 hun[dred] breadstuff in the wagon,[15] flour selling at 7 & 8 dolls. [per] hund, corn $1 bu, bacon 10¢. [Henry] Ward

13. This was the Kanesville Tabernacle, built of logs, 60 feet long and 40 feet wide (Bennett 1992, 206, 212–14; Hartley and Anderson 2006, 126–28). Here, Brigham Young became president of the Church of Jesus Christ of Latter-day Saints on December 27, 1847 (Bennett 1987, 199; Bennett 1997, 292).

14. The man had $640 in gold based on the 1849 price of $16 per troy ounce. Based on the November 2018 price of gold of about $1,210 per ounce, he had about $48,400.

15. The "breadstuff" was likely hard bread—a small biscuit about the size of a hockey puck also called "sheet iron crackers," "teeth dullers," or "worm castles," the latter name connoting the weevils and "maggots" often found in barrels of hard bread (L. Johnson 2005a, 269–70).

buys some. [Alexander] Ewing gives me a piece of gold to buy more flour for myself, & asked me if that was enough. Said he was bound to see me thro, & I was 1 of his children. I caught a man that wanted to go out of town & got it [100 pounds] for $6. I put it on board of Kembles [Robert Kimble's] wagon to bring up, & take lodgings, Supper & breakfast. They haveing [trouble] with a Canton team, had to stay back & hunt up some stray cattle. We had a meeting today & took in some Canton teams, Quincy [teams], & Wiss. [Wisconsin] teams called the Rovers.[16] In all we have 42 teams each averaging 4 yoke oxen.

Meet fellow that used to live in Marietta St, N.Y. He slept on the ground without any blanket. Visit the inside of the Mormon counsil house. It looks very large inside with a fireplace, 20 ft long collums being tree trunks.

16. The Rovers were from Fayette Township, Michigan, not Wisconsin.

CHAPTER 4

Kanesville to Fort Laramie, Wyoming

Background

To cross the Missouri River, the Knox County Company used the Mormon Ferry (Upper Ferry) about 10 miles upriver from Kanesville, which landed just south of Winter Quarters in "Indian country." Thus, it avoided "the long and hazardous journey up steep bluffs that had always characterized the original" ferry south of Kanesville (Bennett 1987, 48 map, 49, 265n21). Cephas Arms reported about half the teams in the train crossed on May 23 (Arms in Cumming 1985, 1). Lorton helped shepherd the company's oxen across the Missouri River the following day.

From the river, emigrants used the Council Bluffs Road to cross the plains to the Platte River, where they followed it westward to its confluence with the Loup River at today's Columbus, Nebraska. The Loup River was too dangerous to ford here, so the road continued up the north side of the Loup River to the vicinity of today's Fullerton, Nebraska, where emigrants used several fords. After crossing, they continued along the Loup's south bank several miles, then turned south to the Platte River in the vicinity of Chapman (about 12 miles northeast of Grand Island, Nebraska), and followed it and its north fork to Fort Laramie, in eastern Wyoming.

Now that the emigrants were in Indian country, Lorton expressed the apprehensions of most who ventured west in the quest for gold: fear of death by scalping knife, tomahawk, or arrow, or freezing and starving in the snows of the Sierra Nevada. This angst was fed by fearmongers who regaled wide-eyed greenhorns with tall tales that sent imaginations into flights of dread and alarm. True, there were scattered murders of emigrants by Indians, but they were few and far between in 1849. There had been the widespread stories of cannibalism in the Donner Party, trapped by deep snow in the Sierra Nevada (winter 1846–1847), and among some of Frémont's men in the Rocky Mountains (winter 1848–1849). But Lorton left the destiny of "our little band" in the hands of "a High Omnipotent Being." He maintained an objective but wary attitude toward

Indians. He was entering a land where two cultures were bound to clash. An act the emigrants interpreted as stealing, the Indians saw as an opportunity for needed sustenance. The Indians had lost much of their wealth (horses), during the particularly hard winter of 1848–1849, and many of them suffered severely or died from starvation. Slaughtering oxen was a means to feed their families, but the loss was extremely serious for the emigrants. Cattle were their source of locomotion, their means of carrying possessions, and ultimately a source of food. Their goal of finding gold in California was a long way off, and they needed those oxen to get there.

Along the Loup River Lorton sketched what was left of one of the vacant Pawnee villages. In spring 1841 Presbyterian missionaries attempted to establish a permanent mission on Plum Creek. Pawnees built a village near the mission, but a Yankton Dakota (Sioux) war party raided the village on June 27, 1843, killing 67 Pawnees and burning most of their lodges. Another attack in 1846 drove the missionaries away (Jensen 1994, 305–8; Morgan 1963, 1:220–23; Hyde 1974, 216–18).

In the 1830s the Pawnee Nation had a population of 10,000 to 12,500, but a combination of factors, including Euro-American diseases (notably smallpox and cholera) and almost incessant war with other tribes, significantly reduced their number. In 1849 an Indian agent reported their population had diminished to 5,000 men, women, and children. Then, during 1849, emigrants carried Asiatic cholera along the trails, where hundreds died east of Fort Kearny. Pawnees who visited the emigrant camps contracted the disease, and the agent recorded that 1,234 Pawnees had died of cholera in 1849 (Capace 1999, 32–33; Hyde 1974, 229, 364; Blaine 1996, 472–74).

Lorton commented on two deaths inflicted by Indians—one near the upper Loup River ford west of Fullerton. Adonijah Strong Welch, one of the Rovers, copied a report of this murder after he "observed a small, white paper on the end of a stick, standing near the road, half a mile from the river." Upon reading it, Welch quoted:

> "Examine the flag on the eminence opposite, and you will find an account of the death of Harrison Rowe, merchant at Plattsville, Iowa, who was murdered by the Sioux Indians, May 23, 1849."
>
> Looking up, we saw on the mound described, a newly-made grave, by the side of which was a pole, bearing a white flag. —Ascending the mound some thirty feet, we found in the folds of the flag the following letter:
>
> Rowe's Bluff. May 23, 1849.
>
> This friend whom we have left, was one of the Mutual Protection Company, starting from St. Francis, Iowa. We were in camp to-day searching

> for a ford, when about a hundred Indians appeared on the opposite shore, and riding into the river, began to cross. Presuming their intentions to be hostile, we retreated to the camp, and had our cattle brought to the corral. The supposed enemy approached. The chief came to us and shook hands, saying that they were Sioux. They passed up the bluff, meeting three of our men who were up the creek; they shook hands with the first, received a handkerchief as a present, and passed on toward the others. One hid—overtaking the other, they killed him, taking his arms, watch and money. The secreted man brought the unwelcome news. We sent after and bro't the mangled corpse, which now lies here, far from the abodes of civilization or friends, to bedew with tears his rude grave. This sad transaction is sufficient warning to private individuals from leaving their train. When necessary, go in large numbers. H. W. McMillen. (Welch 1849a; also in Cumming 1985, 17)

Curious Indians later carried off the document left at Rowe's grave and handed it to a Mr. Reed, who was hunting with them, so he might tell them what it said. Reed subsequently gave the original document to the Kanesville *Frontier Guardian*, which printed it September 19, 1849, word for word as Welch wrote it.

After crossing the Loup River, the Knox County Company headed southwest to intercept the Platte River and follow it westward. It is the main artery draining the central section of the Rocky Mountains and plains of Nebraska, Colorado, and Wyoming. Thus, it had become a natural human migratory pathway from the Missouri River almost to South Pass in the Rocky Mountains. Through Nebraska, the 300-mile-long Platte is a braided river—broad and fairly shallow with many islands and sand bars. Native Americans, stock, buffalo, and emigrants swam or waded across the river when need arose, but there were no established fords or ferries in 1849. From the headwaters of its North Platte fork, the Platte flows about 1,050 miles to the Missouri River. The North Platte heads in northern Colorado and flows northward about 200 miles to Casper, Wyoming, where it turns southeast to join the South Platte River at the town of North Platte, Nebraska. From here the emigrants traveled up the angled North Platte toward Fort Laramie.

The major causes of trouble and loss of time for the Knox County Company were cattle stampedes. It had so many the company became known as the "stampede train" and was shunned by other companies. The consequences of their numerous stampedes were injury to man and beast, loss of time and oxen, destruction of supplies, damage to wagons and equipment, and worn-out oxen. Some were stolen and others were lost due to these stampedes. Still other oxen were so weakened or injured they had to be left along the road. On May 29 Lorton succinctly stated a cardinal dictum of the trail: "To kill our cattle is to take our life." The initiating factors of the stampedes were varied—a barking dog, a loose pony, thunder and lightning, wolves, a dead carcass, the oxens' imaginations, and occasionally an Indian. Regardless of the cause, as herd instinct took over, blind hysteria spread instantly, and the cattle ran in all directions.

Lorton was run over by oxen during a stampede and his foot badly injured on June 9. He was unable to walk for several days and had to ride in a wagon or on a horse. Later he used a cane for assistance until he crossed South Pass.

A few landmarks along the Loup and Platte Rivers help us navigate Lorton's journal—streams, Pawnee villages, sand hills, Grand Island. We add some references to today's towns to help orient his location.

Sand was a continuing landmark. Lorton also mentions bluffs and rock formations, but most particularly he describes the difficulty of traveling through sand. The toll it took on oxen pulling heavily laden wagons was considerable (though it did not tire them enough to keep them from stampeding). Lorton's repetition of the word "sand" imprints the problem.

Along the North Platte Valley, Lorton mentions the picturesque stone formations on both sides of the river. These sedimentary layers are "ground-up debris of the Rocky Mountains. Ancient rivers swept this debris east out of the mountains and spread it as layers across the plains" (Meldahl 2007, 63). Then about five million years ago the landscape tilted eastward and the ancestral rivers of today's Platte River drainage system began to carve through the layers, leaving "today's dissected landscape of towering rock monuments, ridges, and bluffs" (ibid.).

The most famous formation was Chimney Rock, which Merrill Mattes points out "was no ordinary landmark. More enthusiasm and more diary space was devoted to this particular landmark than to any other of the covered wagon migration" (Mattes 1969, 378). Four miles west of today's Bayard, Nebraska, it pierces the sky 470 feet above the river, looking like an upside-down funnel as it rises 325 feet from its base (ibid., 380, 397).

Fort Laramie was a major stop on the trails to Oregon, California, and Salt Lake City. Two days after Lorton lost sight of Chimney Rock, he arrived at the ferry that crosses the North Platte about one and a half miles from Fort Laramie.

The U.S. government purchased Fort Laramie from Pierre Chouteau Jr. and Company (the American Fur Company) for $4,000 on June 26, 1849, just two days before Lorton visited the fort (Mattes 1969, 464, 494; McChristian 2008, 39–40, 40n11; Sanderson in Hafen and Young 1984, 141–42). This included only the fort, not the land, which was part of Indian country.[1]

1. The 1834 act "to regulate trade and intercourse with the Indian tribes, and to preserve peace on the frontiers" deemed this land where Fort Laramie stood "Indian country" (*Statutes at Large* 4 Stat. 729; see also McChristian 2008, 38–40, 40n11; Hafen and Young 1984, 142n253). It was the third western fort established under the congressional act "for establishing military Stations on the Route to Oregon" after [Old] Fort Kearny (1846–1848) and Fort Childs, which was later renamed [New] Fort Kearny (1848–1871).

FIGURE 7. Detail, James Wilkins sketch. Fort Laramie, June 24, 1849, with Laramie River in the middle ground. WHI Image ID 3935.

In the early 1830s William Sublette and Robert Campbell built a log fort on the left bank of the Laramie River, not far from its confluence with the North Platte, and named it Fort Williams. In 1835 Sublette and Campbell sold the fort to Jim Bridger, William Fitzpatrick, and some other mountain men who, in turn, sold it to the American Fur Company in 1836. That year Narcissa Whitman and Elizabeth Spaulding visited Fort Williams, the first white women to pass that way (Mattes 1969, 481, 482). In 1841 the American Fur Company had to update their fort when a rival, Fort Platte, was built nearby. They upgraded with adobe walls and renamed it Fort John. The rising tide of the western movement stopped at Fort John/Fort Laramie over the years—the Bidwell-Bartelson party, Lieutenant Frémont, the first Oregon emigrants, Colonel Kearny, the Donner Party, Brigham Young, the Mormon migrations, and the gold seekers. Over time, common parlance shifted the fort's name to Fort Laramie (McChristian 2008, 23n1, 28; Lavender 1983, 27, 35; Hafen and Young 1984, 60n88, 70; Morgan 1959a, 7).

Lorton's Journal Continues as He Prepares to Cross the Missouri River

[May 23, 1849] Our comp. arrang[emen]ts were pub[lishe]d together with our names in the *Frontier Guardian* [May 30]. I order a paper [sent] to Jas. R. Hill [at the *New York Sun*]. As I am in the office, a severe hurrycan passes over prostrating & tearing our tent in its way, amonge other things.

[May] 23d [continued]. I walk from Kainsvill to the ferry 9 miles north. The first part of this road is on a ridge. 1 of our teams up set yesterday. To day I see a Mormons wagon turned over loaded with tea & other goods. In the turn it broke the top clean off.

These bluffs I should think run on both sides of the river some 30 or 40 miles. It is for the whole dist a contin[ue]d pitch & fall mounting to the sugar loaf form & sinking far below. As you follow the various Indian paths along these peeks you look down on the river tho some dist from it. Some of them are 4 or 5 hun[dred] ft high, nearly purpendicular on the sides. At last you turn the bluffs at the left & travel 4 miles over the bottom till you arrive at the ferry.

The Missouri River here is not over 200 ft wide in its low stage, & they row the flats [flat boats] acrost by hand only averaging 30 teams a day. At this place there is several log huts, & the people verey poor, little girls selling cakes & beer, & women doing washin & sewing. Acrost the river is a cabin town belonging to the Mormons called once Winter Qrs., but is now deserted as I spoke of before.[2] The river is now in its lowest stage but rose 1 ft in the last 24 hours.

This water here is very riley, very near the collor of its bed which is a sort of a sandy yellow clay. The water is used by the inhabitants along its shores, & by steamboats navigating its waters, tho by standing it becomes clear. A little milk or Indian meal clarifies it readily & the mixture settles to the bottom of the vessel. We used it for camping purposes, & the inhabitants say it is healthy. Here the water runs 5 miles an hour. By jumping in a canoe it has been tried.

The river all the way is filled with Islands & sand bars, & the channel can never be determined with the least certainty for it may change in 24 hours. Its shores & the upper ends of the bars & islands are filled up with driftwood for 20 ft, to say nothing of the snags. Boats will not traverse it without a heavy insurance, which makes transportation high. Even down at the mouth of the river where it emties in the Miss[issippi] it seams loft [loath] to mingle with the clear water of the Miss. & shows a dividing line for several miles below its mouth.

A man of some wealth went out on Sarpys Pt to swim his oxen acrost. The ferryman told him how far to go, but not heading [heeding], he steped of[f] the bank hid beneath the water & went under. As he tried to stem the current, they called on him to swim the other way, but he went under & was drowned. There has been no [steam] boats up the river as far as our ferry. There were 8 up last summer as far as the Yellow Stone River. They were atacked by the Indians & 1 man killed. They were promised powder but [boats] did not bring it. The American Fur Comp. will probably send up after the June rise which has

2. By spring 1848, the Mormons had vacated Winter Quarters. Some Mormons returned east and located in Iowa, but most trekked to the eastern edge of the Great Salt Lake—their new Zion (Babbitt 1916, 89; Bennett 1987, 110).

comm[ence]d.[3] Our wagon was taken over after dark with Brin & Bell & on a/c [account] of the darkness of the night & the wind springing up from the east they did not make another trip. So I got lodgings in a cabin near the ferry in front of a fire. There was to have been a shin dig, but did not come off.

[May] 24th. We cross our cattle over [at] sunrise, & for the 2d time find my self out of the U.S. & in Indian terri'y, & the sensations produced by leaving a civelized country for a wild wilderness, by leaving a Christian land for a barbarous country, one inhabited by the savage & unprincipaled red skin, launching out as we do upon hardships & troubles, dangers & perhaps death by a savage foe, a victim of the scalping knife, the tomehalk, or the arrow from a high strung bow, perhaps starvation, or wild beasts of prey may yet hold a caucus meeting over our tenements. We may have to encounter the eternal snows of the mountains & perish in the high hills of Cal. These are the sensations produced by entering the western wilderness as the wayfarer puts his face westward, but a High Omnipotent Being, who holds the thunder bolt in his right hand & the pampero in His nostles [nostrils] knows the destany of our little band, & He & He alone will direct our movements.

Today as we are camped every body is fixing there fire arms, loading their revolvers & rifles, sharpening their bowie knives & daggers, & preparing for service should it be required. So about noon we start on for a better camp ground 5 miles dist. Part of our teams haveing not yet come over [the Missouri River]. As we proceed every boddy is on the look out for Indians. All in fine spirits. At length we see something off in the dist. upon a high bluff, moveing. We loose sight of the moving object for some time. Again it makes its appearance with the adition of 2 other objects. We get out the telescope, & find them to be 2 Indians & 1 on horse back, making off from us. 1 other Indian was met by a couple of our men in the rear. He pretended to be looking for the foot prints of 3 ponies he had lost. He was well dressed & a fine looking personage. Hundreds of their ponies died in the winter, the bones of which can be seen lying in the hollows.

The wind has been blowing a gale all day & towards night large black clouds commence rising in the north east, so we dig trench around tent in anticipation of rain. The capt. comes around & orders all fire arms to be loaded & ready for action. Our orderly comes around soon after & details me with 3 others in our mess to stand guard in the after part of the night. About then the storm commences, the wind blowing high & the large drop[s] rattling upon our canvass

3. The American Fur Company—founded by John Jacob Astor in 1808—relied heavily on Indians providing beaver and buffalo pelts. These were bartered for "whatever the white man brought into their country." Sadly, much of the "whatever" was alcohol, which gave the white man a trading advantage and virtually destroyed Native American social-economic cultures (Chittenden 1986, 11, 21–30, 313).

roof. I am awakened about midnight. Having my rifle & belt in readiness I was not long in sliping on my oils, & getting to my station.[4] By this time the storm had arose in all its fury. The very elements seamed to be at war with each other. The winds swept over the plains with nothing to obstruct its passage, moaning & whistling in its course. The windows of heaven seamed let open as if to deluge the earth. The Egypt darkness encircled us on every side yet you could almost see the large black clouds touch the wagon top.[5] Occasionally a light spot would make its appearance on the horrison but it was soon covered with midnight gloom, & the storm deamon raved with redoubled fury. Now & then a flash of lightning streaked acrost the west but it was very faint, tending to make it still more gloomy, as even quick glimmers ceased to act [?]. The cattle all stood with their backs towards the storm in perfect stillness, & nothing disturbed the wind in its noisy revels save the occasional shudder of the guards, the chatter of the teeth, the rattle of a chain, or the restless bark of some noisy cur chained up to the wagons.

Now there was some 50 ft on our side of the "caral" open,[6] & up & down here we paced with our rifles sholdered except when we took shelter behind a wagon tho it shield us [little] from the sweeping wind. The watch fires cinders being caught in the wind were swept over the bluffs. Wagons rattled on their wheels, & canvass flaped till near day break when the rain ceased. The cattle became restless & with difficulty we kept them in. 4 o'clock we blew the horn & others came to our relief. During the night my poney got loose & ran for the prairie.[7] Stormy nights are the times for Indians to atack or in the gray of the morning, but we see none all night, tho the Omahas are pritty thick. Thus ended the first night's standing guard.

[May 25th.] Stay still all day waiting for about 30 [20?] of our teams. Their wagons had crossed but not their cattle, & the winds are blowing & the water so rough they could't cross. I rec'd 110 lbs. flour on board of 1 wagon. We send the Fayette Rovers with our pilot ahead to the Horn [Elkhorn River]. We are camped near a ravine with only water for cooking purposes, except in puddles.

[May] 26th. We sent a deputation of 3 horse men well armed, back to Winter Qrs. to hurry up the Comp. The mail contractor for taking the mail thro to Salt

4. "Oils" were semiwaterproof garments made from oilcloth. Heavy cloth was stretched on a wooden frame and several coats of oil—typically linseed oil—was painted on it, then it was made into rain garments.
5. Moses's "thick darkness in all the land of Egypt" (Exodus 10:22).
6. *Corral* had a dual meaning throughout the trek: an enclosure made by circling the wagons in which the livestock were confined, and the act of bringing the livestock together in an enclosure.
7. This is the first mention that Lorton had a pony, but it was probably his on loan.

Lake passed here. He had the wagon he Bot from [Alexander] Ewing, 4 mules before it, 3 other men with packed mules. About 9 o'clock, we move on 12 miles to Pap'pee [Papillion Creek] & there camp [still in today's Omaha suburbs]. During the day we see several Indians at a dist. Meet 2 men on horses just from the Horn. They said our Comp had crossed on raft. These men had squashed a wheel & were going back after another. They were hungry as wolves & we give them something to eat. There is a small grove of trees near our camp, with scrubbary, gooseberry bushes & under brush. "Pap'pee" creek runs at the bottom of a deep ravine. Its banks are composed of the blackest mole [mold?] I ever see [soil rich in organic matter]. The wind went down with the sun & now the air is sarene & mild. The moon peeps thro the green branches on the west, & the stars shine brightly.

The prairie is burning on our east, which I set fire, & the wolves howl, bark, yell & appear to be reveling over some carcase. Our deputation has just returned & say the men left behind are as mad as thunder, so that they would not give them any thing to eat.

[May] 27th. Sunday, splendid day. The birds sing in the grove near us, the prairie or meadow lark chirps & twitters as it mounts the air, the green leaves rustle as they are moved by gentle zephyrs, while the resplendent sun beams forth from deep blue sky. No church bells tole forth their joyous sounds upon the mornings air but still their seems to be something about this day that would tell us it was the sabath, did we not already know it.

We start on for the Elk horn river 6 miles ahead. To gain this, we cross a large roling prairie. In our course we meet various objects that attract our attention. In the dist., aided by the telescope we see 4 Indian ponies grazing, & 2 Indians near them watching. We also put after 6 or 7 wolves during the day.

We arrive at the Horn (the general name for Elkhorn River) about 12 o'clock.[8] As we descend the hill we see some 50 teams off on the wide & extensive bottom that stretches out before us. Capt Parker's Canton T[ownship] comp having streched a rope a cross, and the raft being in readiness, we prepared to cross. I drove the cattle to a point below, & swam them acrost, and with the raft we transported 1 wagon at a time. Some of the wagons heavy loaded sunk it 18 in[ches] below water. Our Dick & Tom [oxen] drew 20 wagons over with a long rope, while some 20 of us pulled the raft back in the same manner. We were just 5 hours in crossing 30 teams. This stream is dreaded next to Loop [Loup] Fork by emegrants. It runs very swift, but haveing every thing requisite for crossing, we had not much trouble. It[s] banks are well timbered & presents a very curious appearance. The sand upon its banks is nearly as white as Rockaway &

8. Lorton later says the Elkhorn River is 26 miles from the Missouri.

much finer, forming a beach.[9] As we crossed over the [Elkhorn] on the western side I fell over board, as did others (all sport). We find the [Canton] T. & Rovers comp. 1/2 mile up on the river. This river at this point is 26 miles west of the Mis[souri River] & emties in the Platte. The water is as clear as christal & abounds with fish & feather'd game.

This river is also celebrated for being the haunt of red skins. At the entrance to our caral is a pole 50 ft high with pins about 18 in. a part from the bottom to the top. This was erected in memory of Frank Weatherly who was killed by the Indians in 1847. A raise of earth & a board on the right marks the spot where his murdered remains are deposited. There is also 3 [2?] other graves aside of him. These are Mormons. On the board at the head of Frank Weatherly's grave, the following simple inscription appears, cut on with a knife, "Here lies the murdered remains of Frank Weatherly who was killed by the Indians [*blank*] 1847."[10] We find several things thrown a way to lighten, such as irons, plows &c.[11] At night word comes that [Robert] Kimbles teams were on the way.

[May 28th.] In the mornings watch, they fire signals to let us know they had arrived. We hear it 2 miles dist. from ferry & with our rifles on sholder go down to cross. This eve learn that F. [Harrison Frans?] had broke a wagon tire. Word is forwarded, & immediately Capt. [John R.] Parker with other blacksmiths burn a coal pit, melt the iron in a twinkle,[12] & move on, driving on down to the ferry to bring up the rope. Other comp. wants our ropes to ferry [the Elkhorn] but we only lend ours to assist them in crossing their line. Dissension seams to have entered in the heart of the comp. Some are for proceeding & leaving those behind, & others to the contrary. After we had crossed Dr Wells wagon, he looking [on], & not touching a hand, he had made up his mind to join that company.[13] So they

9. Rockaway Peninsula, on the south shore of Long Island, New York, was noted for its white, sandy beach.

10. The grave was that of Jacob (not Frank) Wetherbee, who was mortally wounded by an Omaha Indian on June 19, 1847. He died the next morning and was interred next to the Liberty Pole that the Mormons had erected before his death. His surname was variously spelled Weatherbee, Wetherby, and Weatherby (Bennett, 1987, 98–99, 261n82). William Clayton places the pole near the Platte River 39 miles from Winter Quarters (Clayton 1983, 41). Clayton's 1848 *Latterday Saints' Emigrants' Guide* became a standard text for trail emigrants for many years.

11. Many emigrants "soon realized that the basic question was what they could do without, since their draft animals could never survive pulling such heavy loads" (Unruh 1979, 149).

12. The broken metal tire was forge-welded together. The broken ends were heated to red-hot, overlapped, and hammered together on an anvil. High temperature and pressure from hammering makes a strong weld.

13. Ira R. Wells, M.D., from Rock Island County, Illinois, apparently signed on as doctor for the train. Luke and Alexander Wells (his cousins?) were traveling with him. Lorton

elected him capt. on the spot, & he said we were a d—d pack of S—ts. We act as an escort up to [the] teams. Stop & lunch at a beautiful creek called Lorton's Creek. It is lined with see grass & full of fish. 1 mile bad bottom to cross, wheels sink in hub deep, have to double teams. Bottom lays full of drift wood. The Platt overflous the bottom at times which is several miles wide. See smoke along the Platt proceeding from Indian wigwams.

After walking 14 miles from the Horn we strike the Platt. Here we meet 2 Indians. They are friendly & we make them presents of pipes, tobacco, pork, bread, &c. All the teams give something & load them down with presents. They are naked with the exception of the blanket, which they thro of[f] when they fire at a dime.[14] We see their brush arbor. There is about 100 [*written over 200*] ruined wigwams here, w[h]ere they campd all winter. They said all their ponies died & a great many Indians. 2 miles from here we campd. These Indians soon follow with a dozen others. When they came, the Chief of the Paunies [Pawnees] shook hands with me & so did the rest. The chief had a boy 10 years old. He had a fine tomehawk made into a pipe. The chief had on a fine cloth coat & pants, a fine, manly looking fellow. He asked for our cheif. We took him to the capt's. [Asa Haynes's] markee. He made tea for them all, which they ate hearty. The head chief took all it would hold on his plate, & distributed the vituals to suit himself. They use the Knife, fork, spoon, & plate well. They say they have drove off all the Omehas. The chief & under chief had flint lock guns.[15] The chief showed numerous scars upon his person, marking him as a brave. He showed how he was pierced with the arrow & how he killed his enemy with his tomehawk. Scarcely any have fire arms except the chiefs. We fired a revolver. This they thought curious, thinking it will keep on firing if you let [it] all the time, & then he showed how quick he could throw his arrows. All the arrows around here have steel points, very sharp.[16] We played the violin for them as they set by the table. They thought it made a curious noise, but did not indicate suprize. The chiefs had quite a bundle of papers. Recommendations from

---

mentions Dr. Wells's train from time to time. These men returned home in 1850 (Roots-Web: Wells-Rock-Island).

14. This refers to a shooting contest in which a dime was put on a stump or thrown into the air. The Indians threw off their blankets when they shot.

15. Many Native peoples preferred flintlock rifles to the more modern percussion-cap rifles. The latter required a manufactured percussion cap not readily available in remote areas, whereas flint, or a flint-like rock, was somewhat easy to find or to secure through trade with other Indians or trappers (Russell 1996, 219, 242–43).

16. These metal arrowheads were probably manufactured locally. In the 1833 treaty with the "four confederated bands of Pawnees" the U.S. pledged (via Art. 6) to provide each of the four Pawnee bands "two blacksmiths and two strikers [smithy helpers who wielded the sledges], with shop, tools and iron" for 10 years (*Statutes at Large* 7 Stat. 448).

Missionaries, traders, &c., with which they were very careful. They say the buffalo are 3 days from here, & the Paunees 2 days (the way they count dist). They want corn very bad, for they are planting over the river. After night-fall they went away saying they would come again [at] sunrise.

[May 29th.] Shure enough, just as the sun peeped up over the eastern bluffs they made their appearance. The chief ate breakfast in our markee. A piece [gun] went off accidentally & the ball grazed the hair of a person nearby, a[s] one of the comp was handling it.[17] Several little lakes near our camp. We bought a buffalo robe of the Indian for a bu. [of] corn.

We start 7 o'clock & as we come in sight of the Platt again, 2 men came riding on horse back & said the Indians had drove off their cattle & had them now down to the river. The 2 men approached to within a few rod[s] when a leveled rifle appeard above the bank. Thinking it not safe to approach nearer, they retreated, 1 getting strayed off from his comrade. 3 Indians approached him & wanted to get him off the horse, but he threatening to shoot if they did'nt desist, [so] they left.

Just then they see some of our horsemen back in the distance, but did not know whether they were Indians or not but waited the result, determined to fight till they died, & finding us to be whites, they related their tale. Just then our teams emerged from behind some river timber, & immediately capt Parker & the capt of the Fayette Rovers [Henry Baxter] ordered every man to be prepared. Altogether 60 men of us armed to the teeth, 20 of which were on horse[back], made hast[e] to reach the rivers bank to stop the work of death. With impetiouosity every man made for the brink expecting to meet opposition [from] Indians concealed beneath the bank. Orders were given not to fire till the word should be given. They, seeing us, jumped in the river & swam acrost. We discharged our guns at them, but they were to[o] far off.

When we arrived there, we found the cattle, 14 in all weltering in their blood. As we approached, one was yet standing, & others yet moved. Nearly half were shot with bullets in the forehead, & they held the muzzle so close that the powder burnt the hair off. The rest were killed with the arrow behind the fore shoulder. There they were huddled up together as no white man could do it, all in their yokes & chains. Horrible sight to gaze upon. Some were partly skined, being cut down the back to the tail. Their they lay in every position just as they died, fat creaters. I cut a large piece off the side of 1 with my bouie knife. Some were for dumping their carcases off in the water, others for poisoning the meat, but the conclusion was that they would follow us up, commit simular outrage

17. "After drownings the commonest cause of fatal accidents was careless handling of the fantastic arsenal of firearms the overlanders carried west with them" (Unruh 1979, 410).

on the next carravan, or something worse, & those cattle would pacify them for some time. We picked up 1 yoke out [of] the water & took 3 yokes off the cattles necks & 2 chains, which we put on board of our wagons.

The [Platte] river here is 100 rod[s] wide [1,650 feet] with timber on the other side, but on this side one level plain with the exception of a little timber & brush, from behind which Indians were peeping as we left. The whole story is this: The Mich[igan] comp. 35 wagons in all, camped on Shell Creek 12 miles from the scene of slaughter. In the night the guard was alarmed by the falling of a wagon tongue, & the cattle became frightened & broke out. They were however secured, & all still again for some time, till at length they again frightened & broke out, but with difficulty [men] secured them again within the "caral." Every man was now on guard. Pickets were stationed at a dist from the wagons, & searches made for Indians. The cattle were all yoked & chained to wheels & stakes, & in spite of all this caution, the cattle broke the fastenings, leaped ropes, chains, wagons, men, & in fact every thing that came in their way. Chains rattled, hoofs claped, whips snaped & in fact a bable scene ensued, & the cattle made their egress & ran acrost the plains in great confusion, & in spite of some 80 persons, they made their way off.

Some say Indians were conceiled under the wagons, others that their arrows were shot in them from the thicket, & others that the dogs caused it all. However, all their dogs were taken out & shot this night, the 29th May. The capt of the guard says no Indians were near. One thing is certain, that they drove 7 yoke 10 miles, & butchered them as aforesaid.

They entertained Indians on the previous eve'g the same as we did, giving them all their fill & at night fall sent them all away. This affair created considerable sensation in both comp., for to kill our cattle is to take our life, & it proved conclusively that we were no cowards, & yet not impetious or hotheaded.

We dine at a point where the road joins the river. Lat. 41°27'5".[18] This is a point where a branch runs around an island. To this island the Indians tried to swim the cattle, but could not make it out. There is plenty of timber on it. We see an Indians grave 80 yds north of the rode. This is a large pile of earth. Road again joins the river, splendid sight. See 500 Indians on the opposite bluffs at a new Indian village. Plenty of sand hill crane on its banks. We come to a sandy road, as white as ever bleached on the shores of Rockaway [on Long Island]. After traveling 20 miles we camp on Shell Creek, opposite to the Mich. comp. This creek is 12 ft wide, 3 ft deep, & has a poor bridge.[19] Plenty of small timber on its banks. A squaw was here just now & when she told about the cattle being

18. Based on Lorton's latitude, this slaughter was likely two miles east of North Bend, Nebraska, 12 miles from camp on Shell Creek where there is a convenient island in the river. This is the only latitude Lorton gives during his trip.

19. Camp is a couple miles west of today's Rogers, Nebraska, about 60 miles west of the Missouri River.

killed, she cried. Killed 1 wolf, chased 1 elk, 1 antelope, & some see three more. Double our guard to night. I stand guard.

[May] 30th. Pass over Shell Creek by bridge made of brush, very crooked road here. Pass Mich. comp. camp & see quite a pile of dead dogs. Meet some Otto Indians, well dressed. Pass long lake formed by the Platt when high.[20] Very rainey to day, get wet to the skin. Road to day over sand principally. Camp at Loop Fork.[21] Lake & timber close by the river, 24 miles from Shell Creek. Here Loop Fork is about 300 yds wide & filled with sand bars & islands. Its banks abrupt & the water pritty low & the scene looks dreary. Near its shore in the woods are 2 log houses formerly occupied by traders or missionaries. Near here is the lake. It is very long, follows the river, & the water very clear.

[May] 31st. Follow the river & see an elks head, lately killed, in the road. [At] noon we pass Mich. comp. Some 20 families with them. See no Indians all day. We ford Beaver River. Water comes up to box. The banks are very precipitous, but are diged away.[22] Great & exciting time in crossing. Ponies are all calld into requisition to guide the oxen. Some oxen got wound up in the chains. Men wade up to their breasts in water. We camp on other side. This river is filled with fish, such as cat, bullheads, trout. We caught bullheads weighing 6 lbs.

June 1st [1849]. Early start. Pass a supposed to be missionary station. It is situated on the edge of a ravine at the bottom of which runs a stream.[23] There are 3 or 4 log dwellings, ash houses, pig pens, barracks, "carals" for enclosing cattle in. 3 or 4 deep holes plainly shows by the burnt timber laying in them & blackened sides that cabins once rested over them. At the bottom of one lay a broken cast iron rotary stone. Corn cobs lay in piles strewn around. Some 100 acres of ground has been cultivated with corn & potatoes, but the fences are now burnt & broke down, & the whole is entirely deserted. 1 mile west appears 2 high log houses, built in a substantial manner. They stand as they were built never haveing been finished. Around these forts stands part of a "caral" part burnt down, & timber intended for the same. Around lays timber for various purposes of red

20. One of the numerous oxbow lakes (from older riverbeds) found in this area.
21. This is the confluence of the Loup and Platte Rivers near today's Columbus, Nebraska. The emigrant road follows the north bank of the Loup for almost 40 miles as it somewhat parallels the Platte.
22. The ford of Beaver Creek was south of today's Genoa, Nebraska, about 25 miles from the confluence of the Loup and Platte Rivers. On April 22, 1847, the Mormons "went to fix the fording place a little, the banks are steep on each side and the water a little over two feet deep" (Clayton 1973, 89).
23. Today's Plum Creek is east of the lower ford of Loup River, which is east of Fullerton, Nebraska. Clayton called it Plumb Creek in 1847.

cedar, grindstones, doors, window sashes, &c. This was built by government for the benefit of the Indians, surrounded by some 100 acres of cultivated land. There has been 1 crop or more raised here, as will be seen by the stalks. This was to instruct the Pawnees in agriculture, but the Soixs [Sioux] came & burnt the bulwark & drove of[f] their foe, the Pawnees, so this righteous undert[ak]ing had to be abandoned in the fall of 1847.[24]

At noon we halt at a small creek. Its banks are steep & very difficult to get at the water. The soil her[e] is 4 ft thick & [Henry] Ward, in watering the cattle, drove them down in. In attempting to get out, our Dick ox, who had came unyoked by the breaking of a bow pin, got entangled in the deep mold up to their bellies. The cow got out but Dick, in trying to turn to go up the opposite side, sank in the mud in a helpless state, & the water being deep, his head was under water, & I instantly see he was drounding. I just arrived at this crisis & sprang in up to my waiscoat pockets in mud & water, & with difficulty held his mouth & nose out till he could recover, & then he arrived on the opposite side in safety. It was a narrow escape & the best ox in the team.

At length we came to the old Pawnee village, distroyed by the Souixe [Sioux] in 1846. The site chosen for this village is on one of the most beautiful & most level plains in the world.[25] It overlooks the river Loop Fork on the south west. The bank is a steep precipice about 70 ft high & on a point that projects in the river. The water here surrounds an island & arround the front is a mud wall partly down & a ditch on the out side. Tho this is not a formidable bullwork it is nevertheless a hindrance to an enemy, forming a breastwork to the village. There is about 100 wigwams, lodges &c. Some of these are built in a circular form of poles braded together with grass & sod, forming a barrier against the weather. The roofs incline to the centre, there being a round hole at the top for the smoke to go out. The fire being placed in the middle on the ground floor. Arround the sides appear banks made of poles & the remnants of mats yet thereon. The largest are some 25 ft in diameter & 18 ft to the top. An entrance constructed of the same material leads to these vast huts so low that you have to stoop to enter. Nearly all of these have barrels, mats, buffalo heads, &c in them. Some are broken in from the weight of the roof material & inhabited only by wild animals. Each house has a hole made simular to a cistern, used formerly for a reception of provisions or a place of conceilment from the enemy, & a person has to be pritty careful how he walks or he may find himself down in one of these suteraneous [subterraneous] passages. There are several that seams to

24. Lorton was looking at the last vestige of the Presbyterian Mission to Pawnees, an ill-conceived plan to "civilize" and convert the Pawnee Nation to Christianity and to a ranching society.

25. This site is listed on the National Register of Historic Places as 25–NC–07. See also Whitney 2018, 205–6.

FIGURE 8. Lorton sketch. Pawnee village. Although this sketch is labeled "on the Platte," Lorton's description of Pawnee villages took place on the Loup River. Writes Lorton: "PAWNEE Village on the Platte, Distroyed by the Sioux Indians 1836 [1846]." Courtesy of The Bancroft Library.

have never been finished. To visit these specimens of Indian ingenuity is truly worth a great deal. The position chosen on the banks of the river, a precepice an enemy would never approach, & then the fine level, well situated plain shows taste not to be excelled by the pale face.[26] Off to the right is a corn patch with passages underground near it. On this plain I see hundreds buffalo heads & 2 human skulls but whether Indian or white, it is not known. The Pawnees have only 9 thousand warriors, while the Souixs [Sioux] have 30 [thousand], & each is the others most deadly foe.

We ford Cedar Creek & have to wade in with our clothes on.[27] As the wagon crosses, the quicksand underneath constantly gives & produces a constant settling, & the longer a wagon stands in 1 place the more it settles. Our oxen stop[p]ed in the middle, but our [wagon] box did not ship any water. The water is clear & deep. Our road today lay over some of the most level plains I ever witnessed, as [s]treight as a die, & as level as a ten pin alley. It was princip[ally] a sort of table land to the bottom of Loop Fork. Along the whole rout we find

26. Pawnees built this village in 1842, but the Sioux destroyed it four years later. Clayton described it in his 1847 journal: "The Sioux succeeded in burning this village last summer during the absence of the Pawnees when on their [buffalo] hunt. They rebuilt most of it again, but last fall the Sioux made another attack and burned the whole village except one dwelling or lodge, which is not harmed.... The village is composed of about 200 houses or lodges varying in size" (Clayton 1973, 95, 97; Fullerton Archeological Site 1974; see also Bennett 1997, 126).

27. Cedar River enters the Loup just east of today's Fullerton, Nebraska.

buffalo heads, some of them of enormous size. Today we find (& heretofore) [a] board stuck upon the side of the road with writing thereon, addressed to friends behind. Here we see plenty of buffalo dung, & 2 black objects ran off to the westward supposed to be buffalo. Today there was 2 deer killed. Some 7 or 8 antelope seen & shot at. We run past the Mich teams. They break a wheel all to pieces. Like to have been a fight bet'n [between] 1 of their men & ours. We see a grave on a bluff near our camp of some white person. Camp on the second bottom of the Loop & near the lower ford [just east of Fullerton]. In the night wolves set up their howl & yell, & from the many noises it would seam as if there was enough to cover a 10 acre lot.

June 2d. Early start over a good road & fresh breeze from the Swest, like unto the breeze of Rockaway. Some are out on the distant bluffs chasing the antelope & elk, & others in the dry ravines hunting the deer. At 10 o'clock we arrive at that much dreaded river, Loop Fork. But see! On the right as you decend its sandy banks, elevated upon a fine shelving bluff a grave ti[m]bered as if by human hands, a fit sepulcher for the reception of the dead in a wilderness like this. You assend some 20 ft & then read that a man named Harrison Rowe [was] killed, nay, basely murdered by the hands of 100 Cowardly red skins only 3 days agoe.[28] It appears that the Dubuque Mining Comp. had came to the banks for the purpose of crossing this streem. Soon after they arrived & while some were wading the river to find the best place to ford, above 100 Indians reporting themselves as Souix appeared on the opposite side, mounted. They immediately crossed on their horses & pretended to be friendly & in chase of another tribe of Indians. In the mene time the comp gathered their cattle in the "Caral" and after receiving presents the Indians made up the river. 3 of the comp. who had went off from the body to hunt, came in contact with the Indians. The first [emigrant] they shook hands with and asked for presents. He gave them a hand[kerchie]f & he was allowed to pass. The 2d conceiled himself in the brush & was passed unnoticed. The 3[d] they shot & rob[b]ed him of his rifle, knife, & pistols & every thing on his person. The 2d who lay conceiled see all & was left to tell the murderous, cowardly tale. Harrison Rowe was a merchant of Wis.[29] They burried him on this hilloc, & a warning to others written over his head, a timely warning to others straying of[f] from the main body. They warn persons never to go off unless in large parties.

Loop Fork the stream we are about to cross is dreaded by all going this rout. It is not fit to raft on account of its width, & dangerous to ford on account of its quicksand bottom. It is at this place 300 yds wide, & deep in spots & in others

28. This gravesite was about 12 miles west of Fullerton. The date of Rowe's murder was May 23, 1849, 10 days before the Knox train arrived (Welch 1849a).
29. Rowe was from Plattsville, Iowa, not Wisconsin (Welch 1849a, June 12).

FIGURE 9. Lorton sketch. Crossing Loup River west of Fullerton, Nebraska. "CROSSING LOOP FORK, JUNE 2d 1849 W. B. LORTON." Note the grave of Harrison Rowe on the hill in the foreground, killed by Indians three days before Lorton arrived. The serpentine route was necessary to find the firmest footing in the quicksand bottom. Courtesy of The Bancroft Library.

knee deep. To cross effectually you have to follow bars, a mile upstream, double your teams, raise the wagon boxes, & when once you get agoing, keep moving, for the minute you stop the sand washes from beneath the wheels, from under the cattles feet & you are lost. Also the streem is swift in the channel, & as the wagon moves along it grates & jars as if you were running over stones. As soon as the [Iowa] Rangers cross, we commence, 20 teams crossing at a time.[30] The shores of this river are composed of what we would call Rockaway [sand], with bright stones intermixed.

Seven persons in our comp. pledged themselves, on hearing the a/c of Rowe's death, & also of 1 of our men being shot at five times, that if any 1 of our men should be killed by the murderous devels, to shoot down every Indian they should gain an opportunity to kill.[31] We squash a wagon wheel in our comp., lend 1 of our wheels to cross the river with. Take off false tongues & make spokes, & the old wheel is made whole in the twinkling of a bed post. A lot of packed mules & horses cross the river. They say 1 of there men lay in the mule

30. This is the upper ford, about 12 miles west of Fullerton.

31. Over time this attitude unfortunately evolved into pervasive disdain for American Indians. James Michael Cavanaugh, congressional delegate, Montana Territory, boasted on the floor of the U.S. Congress on May 28, 1868, that he liked "an Indian better dead than living" (Cavanaugh 1868).

carriage under the wounds rec'd from a revolver [discharged] accidentally. They also report 100 Indians on the opposite side. 2 other comp cross to day.

Thro some oversight we camped near the edge of the brush & within 300 yds of the river, a bad place for us. 'Twas dark before it was tho off [thought of] & the Indians [*illegible*] over the river. There was a probability of an attact, & the place as well selected as if they had chosen it themselves, for just on the edge of the brush, the ground fell abrupt, making a natural breast work for the skulking thieves. They could just peep up their heads & level their deadly shooting irons upon the guard passing up & down. In the tall brush lay a swamp so that no white man could pierce this dense thicket & the probability is if they attack they would rake us all to pieces. The capt now see this & ordered every man to load & be prepared for action as if the enemy now lay conceiled in the bushes. The usual guard now turned out, & it being my night I stood. It was thought expedient to place pickets down on the river's bank, to listen & watch the movements of the Indians & see if any should attempt to cross the river. This was thought to be a crittical position on account of the dist from the comp., which was [*illegible*], a q[uarte]r of a mile to the east, & 1 felt a fraid & another hung back. Finally a man, Douglass, & my self volunteered to go any wheres the serjent should place us, & we were accordingly placed there. Others paced up & down the edge of the bushes, that point being doubly guarded. Several volunteered to stand extra & so we had a double guard. The night was beautiful with a fine breeze from the south. The moon peeped down upon our camp as if to say, I'll serve as a candle in case of danger. I stood till 12, & arose again a little after 3 to bate [bait] the cattle just in the gray of the morning, & no attact from Indians.[32] [They] probaly meditated [an attack], but relinquished on a/c of there being 3 other comp[s] camped on the same prairie.

June 3. Sunday. Lay still all day & rest our cattle.[33] Have church in the other camp. Have business meeting in ours for the better organization of the guard, during which time we elect 4 capt. & make our present capt. Colonel, there being 40 wagons, 1 capt to every ten. During the meeting we hear a good speach from prof. [A. S. Welch] of Jonesvill, Mich, & now of the Fayette Rovers. To our ten we elect Mr [Alexander] Ewin[g].[34]

32. To "bait" is to take a brief halt for refreshment or to feed animals on a journey.
33. They camped on the right (south) bank of Loup River near the ford. From here they traveled south to get closer to the Platte River.
34. One of the divisions appears to have been called Knoxville (vs. Knox County). Another, possibly called the Rovers, included the Fayette Rovers from Michigan and maybe the Canton, Illinois, men. Lorton was in a third division captained by Alexander Ewing. Ewing and Henry Baxter, both highly regarded, were each nominated to be colonel of the San Joaquin Company on the Southern Route from Salt Lake City; Baxter won. At one point,

About 11 o'clock at night lights begin to flitter amonge the willows, their flashing lights reflecting in the water. This looking rather susp[icious], we sent up word to the other comp, & they sent an armed force down to the ford to watch their movements & prevent any landing.[35]

June 4th. The 2 comp start to gether. The 2 capt flip up a doll[ar] to see which should take the road [first]. Other comp beats. Travel over a heavy sandy road in the morning. See several killed prairie dogs, see no timber all day. Carry brush 24 miles, the dist we travel today, to mend a bad slue or creek.[36] 3 o'clock P.M., as I am standing or walking by the side of the wagon the cry of men, the noise of prancing cattle meets our startled ears. You turn & look & lo & behold the hind teams running towards us like magic & as quick as lightning the spirit of "stampede" runs along the whole train. You turn startled by the confusion of you know not what. I turn as quick as possible & find 4 teams within a few rods of me with scarcely room to escape. I pulled off my hat & succeeded in turning a team coming full split on our near side. They geeed off & come in contact with the hind part of our Ark, & [it] knocked them all down in a heap. Had they kept that course they would undoubtedly have run over Bill Kellogg who was knocked down by the oxen, & like wise [would have] broke our wagon to pieces. The whole train has now the epedemic, & like a mighty whirlwind they fly towards us. One team stumbles down & the next are thrown on top of that. Did ever man see a comparison. Did ever man think cattle could make such spead. All still a minute before & now all confusion, & none can give the cause.

End of Volume I of Lorton's California Journal. Volume II, below, Continues the Stampede.

Volume II of the California Journal

On they come like a mighty avalanch toward us, chains rattling, wheels grating, Wagons cracking, piles of oxen upon oxen, Men thrown down, cattle run over, & all in the utmost confusion. Our oxen [are] not backward in the chase. Takes it [the wagon] as quick as [a] wink, & the first thing known, they are off. We all run after it, but we might as well stop! for the fleetest steed could not out run

---

Lorton calls Ewing "Judge." A fourth division, captained by Edward Doty, called themselves the Jayhawkers (initiation rites in Manly 1949, 25; Mecum and Manly in J. Johnson 2018, 27–28). Charles Mecum (1878) remembered they were "a large party of young robust men...a goodly company to behold: with our buckskin pants and bald heads. We needed no mirror to tell us we were handsome—we *just knew* it."

35. These flashing lights were likely fireflies (lightning bugs).

36. Scouts had warned the drivers they would be crossing a marshy area, so they carried brush to make a firmer roadbed. They also carried brush for campfires.

these terrified animals. And when they all stop [they are] entangled & whirling upon the ground. Women were in Some of the wagons & what must have been their feelings.

After assisting the falling cattle & summing up the broken wagons, we found as luck would have it that not much damage was done to the wagons, & only 1 cow seriously injured. This belonged to Capt [E. N.] Taylor, & his wife nearly cryed her eyes out. The cow was run over, & in the act got her foot torn off. She followed us a little ways & there [we] shot her. Capt [Asa] Haynes [now colonel of the train] was knocked down & hurt, one mans leg strained, & out of all the persons knocked down, none was very seriously injured. The "stampeed" took place on an extensive prairie. A horse that had broke loose ran past, & a dog ran out after the animal which caused the stampeed. Well has it been said the devil is in every thing upon the Platt. In the eve'g we call a dog meeting for the better security of dogs. Many say they will shoot the dogs, & the owners swear to shoot the executioner. However, there being several valuable dogs in the Comp., it was passed that every dog be placed in a tent, or staked at the dist. of 100 paces from the "Caral," & if they barked or were found loose in the night or day the 5 Capts. order them out to be shot.

We cross Prairie Creek & camp on the west side on the broad prairie. We brot wood from Loop Fork to burn.[37]

June 5th. See some 20 antelope in droves of 2 & 3. Dinner at Wood River.[38] Here we find lots of articles, such as hats, irons, cowbells, salt thrown away to lighten the load. Here we see a paper stuck up notifying us of the attack on 1 of the Rangers by the Indians on the preceeding night. They were chased into camp. Opposite Grand Island the straight line of timber on our right, denoting the Platt. We travel several miles along a level plain with the Platt timber on one side & Wood River on the other. More antelope. Make a 25 mile drive & camp on the Platt. Stand guard till 11, & feed our cattle by Pale Cyntha's modest light.[39] See several Indian lodges during the day but no Indians. The water here dont need any milk, for its so white & wont settle, like the Missouri.

During the day a dog belonging to the Canton T[ownship] comp. got loose. Several men prepared to shoot it, but its owners secured it & tied it, saying they would shoot any person that should [shoot] their dog, & called the Knoxville comp. a d—d pack of house theives, upon which Capt [Edward] Doty took it

37. From Prairie Creek they continue southward to Wood Creek near the Platte.

38. Wood Creek (or River) parallels the Platte for many miles before they join about three miles south of Chapman. Welch (1849a) says they traveled 26 miles on June 5.

39. "Cyntha" is Lorton's spelling of Cynthia, meaning moon.

up, & was agoing to knock the asserter flat. An Eng boxer steped up & pacified the parties, upon condition that the cur should be shot immediately. He was accordingly taken out & shot. Another man followed suit & so two dogs died on the spot.

June 6th. In the morning road rather bad. On the Platt lower bottom we pass over a prairie noted for being the rendezvous for numerous kinds of animals. The ground is litterally undermined by these creatures, such as wolf, prairie dogs, gophers, &c.[40] We run some wolves into their holes, shoot several prairie dogs. They are small, & bark like a dog tho their claws are like a squerral's. These are eaten by many & they say they are excelent food.

In the afternoon [the road] rises to higher ground & we litterally wade up to our knees in beds of flowers, flowers of all traits, shades, & hues, fragrant as the rose, & [as] you pass, the fresh southern breeze causes you to inhale their sweet perfume with your nostles. Neither of these flowers have I ever seen before except it be 1 looking similar to the Blue bells of Scotland. At last we come in sight of Grand Island, it having been sheltered by trees most of the way. It is said to be 100 miles long.[41] Here the western horrison assumes a dark gray appearance, which soon covers the whole heavens, & old thunder with a hollow rattling noise, follows the sharp flashes of lightning as they flitter along the sky. Suddently large hail stones decend & we have to seek shelter from the pending storm. In the mene time we had formed with a "caral" in anticipation of a storm, & our cattle were driven by the hail some dist. acrost the plains. After a while, the sun breaks thro & the clouds dispel.

June 7th. A great deal of dew on the grass, fine day for travelling. Catch a young antelope, see a great many Elks & antelope of[f] on the fields. Pass an innumerable number of [prairie] dog citys, shoot any quantity of these animals as they set in the mouth of their caves suning themselves. These animals live on grass, & you find the grass around their cells knawed off short. There is something mechanical about these dogs cells. The houses all connect by avenues that lead underground, in nearly right angles.

40. These were the black-tailed prairie dogs (*Cynomys ludovicianus*), so named because the tip of the tail is black.

41. In the 1800s the Platte River flowed on both sides of Grand Island. Frémont said it was "fifty-two miles long, with an average breadth of one mile and three quarters" (Frémont 1970a, 283). Grand Island has morphed into at least three islands—Shoemaker, Mormon, and Indian Islands. Today's town of Grand Island is about six miles north of what was once the eastern tip of Lorton's Grand Island. The Pawnees relied on the island as a major grazing area for their horses (R. White 1988, 180–84).

Dinner at pritty little creek.[42] Here we take in a keg of water for night. Catch a lot of fish here. Here we see notice stuck up of the Buckeyes being attacked by the Indians June 5th, no men killed. To day we have a sick man & expected to lay up as soon as we arrive to timber. He has been failing every day. Another man sick. Kill 2 very large rattlesnakes.

June 8th. See lots of antelope & 18 deer & a number of Elk. 4 wolves. See dark object of[f] in the dist. on the Bluffs. Get the telescope but on a/c of the dist. cannot tell distinctly whether it was an ox or a buffalo. We go, some 5 persons on mules & ponies, to chase it & if an ox drive it in camp. Upon close inspection it proves to be a buffalo bull, probably driven away from the herd by the young ones. A number will attack 1 old bull & so cripple him that the wolves worry them down & devour them.[43] There is a species of wolf that follows this for a buisness, called the buffalo ranger.[44] We see a number of buffalo carcases partly devoured & heads & bones without number. Shot a wolf who was partly inside a carcase & broke his leg.

We are now passing thro the saleraetus country.[45] The article appears in places where the ground is destitute of vegetation, so thick that you can scrape it up. Our Brin ox is very tender footed & has been 3 days. We see a number of teams on the other side of the Platt in the dist. in the afternoon & follow it a ways. Here it is 1 1/2 miles wide & falling fast. We camp 3 o'clock to accommodate our sick man. On the Platt opposite us on the other side, a comp formed a "Caral." Between us & them is a number of small islands covered with vegetation. We wade to the islands to get brush to burn. Near us is 3 wells 5 ft deep dug by the Mormons.[46]

42. This is probably Elm Creek, mentioned by Welch (1849a; also in Cumming 1985, 30–35). It flows parallel to the Platte past today's town of Elm Creek, some 16 miles west of Kearney, Nebraska. "Dinner" was often a midday stop, rather than a camp, and it could have occurred anywhere along this creek.

43. An American buffalo (bison) bull weighed between 1,800 and 2,000 pounds, and cows were half that weight. The wolf's "technique of first wounding an animal and then attacking it again sometime, perhaps even days later, may be used commonly with bison" (Mech 1970, 241).

44. Here Lorton most likely encountered what is called the Great Plains wolf (*Canis lupus nubilus*). Since coyotes and wolves will feed on carrion, the emigrants made every effort to bury their dead in such a way these scavengers could not exhume the corpses.

45. Saleratus: sodium or potassium bicarbonate (baking soda) used as a leavening agent. Water from springs and seeps infused with these compounds would dry, thus becoming evaporites. The compounds are also absorbed and translocated to plant leaves, where they give the plants a dusty-white appearance.

46. Rather than drinking the murky river water during the migration to their new Zion (Salt Lake City), the Mormons dug numerous wells in 1847 and 1848, many five to six feet deep (Bullock 1997, 134, 137, 153, 156, 157, 168, 172).

June 9th. To day we see lots of game, form comp & go out shooting. Out of some 5 Buffalo, 20 deer & 30 antelopes we only shot 2 antelopes. One of these was a cow antelope, & had a very large bag. 1 shot went through the bag. We see as we follow the river buffalo paths, foot prints, hair &c., in abundance but very few buffalo. Buffalo make streight paths up from the [river] & to all appearance follow these in Indian file down to the water.

The Oscaloosa comp which is behind us, burried a lady day before yesterday, & this morning intered a man. The woman on the preceding day, said she felt as good as she ever felt in her life & walked 15 miles. At night she felt chilly & layed down & the next morning she was a corpse. This woman's husband's partner helped get out the stuff for her coffin & the rising of the next sun beheld him dead. He was attacked by the diarreah sickness, & cramps. The physicians call it cholera. They are both burried by the rode side. There are others sick now in that comp with similar attacks, a minister & his daughter amonge others.

Dinner at Willow Lake.[47] Off from the road near the rivers bank, we see 2 Am. hyenas on a grave. We go to the paper & read that the Hawkeyes had burried 1 of their number the day before, fallen by a similar disease. The Oscaloosa comp overtakes us & camps near us, just on the other side of a slue. Their phycisians consult on our sick men.

I am on guard the first watch. We drive the cattle into the "caral" & so did the other comp'y, but with difficulty for they tryed to "stampeed" over an old carcase as they are always want to do. I was one of the cattle guard on the south opening. I had just been getting a camp stool & had just been conversing with the capt of the O's [Oskaloosa company],[48] when all of a suddent the cattle started to their feet. I took my whip which I held in my hand & tried to force them back. By this time they began to rush out & I started to run but had not taken many steps before I was knocked down by them on my face, & then they all rushed on like a mighty torrent. The next moment I expected to be crushed to pieces by the terrified animals. After a few had passed, a faint ray of hope glided acrost me. I thro up a leg to screen them from my head, & there lay in breathless anxiety almost counting them as they passed over my prostrate boddy. What a moment of agony is it as you lay beneath the trampling feet of hundreds of infuriated beasts, expecting every moment to be your last. At last as I thought they had all passed I made an effort to rise, but a steer behind me sprang over my head & just carried my hat off with his foot. I felt my leg hurt but picked up my hat that lay off a ways, & the whip stock served as a cane till I could get the sholder of an individual to aid me in getting to the tent bed. The first inquiry was whether any

47. This lake was one of many formed and reformed by the fickle meanderings of the Platte River (Kimball in Clayton 1983, 51). There is no longer a Willow Lake in this area along the Platte. The old Willow Lake was somewhere between Cozad and Gothenburg, Nebraska.
48. Oskaloosa, Iowa, is southeast of Des Moines toward Ottumwa.

person was hurt. Judge [Alexander] Ewing came in with a lantern & cut my boot to get it off. Upon examination, no bone was found to be broken. We bathed it with liniment & I went to bed in the wagon but I am now laying, as I write, with my leg [elevated?]. It took place 1/2 past 10 in the eve'g. 2 others were with me & got hurt less than I did. My nose blead, & [I have] a large bruze on my right forhead. Orders were immediately given to get up the ponies & surround the cattle.

Such another noise as they made, like roleing thunder. Onward they went. The cattle in the other "caral" caught the infection & burst out in an instant, & all to gether about a thousand head scattered in every direction.[49] Such a bellowing & bewildering sounds I never before conceived of. Every boddy goes out, hollows & tries to pacify them with salt, &c., & after several hours they get quiet. [*Illegible*] leave them all night. The next morning they are scattered for miles over the vast plain but they are finally collected together & left to herd on the plain. The 2 other unfortunates, or rather fortunates, were steped on but not hurt badly. As soon as they see them coming they ran. They were knocked down as fast as they attempted to rise. They hollowed at the top of their voices while I lay still. The night was dark & had just comm[ence]d sprinkling, & the no. of cattle around us made it as dark as Egypt. It is said by Deacon [Cephas] Arms who was on the opposite side that a mule jumped up of a suddent & snorted & soon after he heard the prancing of hoofs.

[June] 10th was the Sabbath. The day was one of those days we read of, sometimes following after a battle & indeed it appeared so to me. I was wounded, & lay on my bed unable to get up, the least twich appeared like amputation, & [I] had made an attempt to get out to breakfast but failed, so I ate my coffee, ham & cakes where I were. The scene of the preceeding night appeared to me like a dream, like an ugly vision, & I tryed to banish it from thought. Even now I hate to relate the reallity which I now write. What a narrow escape!

To day they collected a party in our tent & had a sing. The cattle were tollerable still all day on a/c of their not being able to find any excuse to be frightened at, tho they made an attempt several times. At twilight however the northern bluffs were covered by thick black clouds, & the slow flashes of lightning thro' forth in reddish hue & tended to increase the timidity of these foolish oxen. Soon twilight darkened down into night & with its first shades a steer happened to rise suddently, & again the whole drove was in motion. However they were pacified in a measure & surrounded by a guard.

I was awakened in the night by a general alarm being sounded. All hands were ordered up, ponies order[ed] out & every possible movement made to check the cattle who were again in motion, as could [be] heard mingling with

49. Cephas Arms said there were 320 cattle in the corral on June 9 (in Cumming 1985, 12).

pealing thunder their footsteps upon the ground. I lay in bed, the lightning flashed sharp & quick piercing thro' the thicknesses that sheltered me from the storm all except the pouring on the roof. Another loud peal & then another prance. Every clap served [to] increase the excitement & cause a new "stampeed." At length the storm grew more tempestuous, & seamed to center in one place to form a compleat termination of the conflicting elements, & the storm. This was done by a more than terrific blaze of the whole heavens & the clanking of ten thousand roaring thunders.

At this the cattle took 1 general flight scattering in every direction over the plains, leaving the pursuing horsemen far in the rear, & the fleetest steed far behind. The men put on to guard them had to escape for their lives.[50]

[June 11.] At the rising of the sun not a createur in sight. A few were found some 10 miles dist & are now coming in in droves of 40 & from that down to 3. A party out over the bluffs thought they see a lot [but] when on approaching proved to be buffalo. The bluffs are covered with buffalo & it is feared the cattle have joined them as wild as themselves.[51] To comment is useless, for it is well known that cattle become as wild as the beasts of the chase. The devel is in the cattle as Adams said & everything else on the Platt. A new party is now just going out, taking provisions with them & intend not to return with out them if they can help it.[52] Other parties have not yet returned, & the country has been scoured for 17 miles around. 1 horseman see 17 wolves this morn'g. A wolf just shot upon the fresh grave nearby. Stragling cattle coming in. 2 men saw 2 Indians off on the bluffs. They acted curious—1 lay down & another beckoned for more Indians. They fled to camp & related their story that they had seen Indians. This was bad news & we feared for our cattle, if they got hold of them. Not long after

50. The whole train was stalled for six days while men searched for the missing cattle. The stampede occurred several miles east of North Platte, Nebraska, in the Maxwell or Brady area.

51. Concerning the number of buffalo on the plains, William Hornaday (1889, 387) said, "It would have been as easy to count or to estimate the number of leaves in a forest as to calculate the number of buffaloes living at any given time during the history of the species previous to 1870." The data used to come up with estimates would not "remotely meet the standards of modern biological sciences" (Shaw 1995, 150). There are unsubstantiated estimates of 60 to 100 million buffalo around 1800, dropping to 15 million by 1860 (Neiburger, 1986, 140, 142; see also Shaw 1995, 148). Neiburger makes a case for numbers fluctuating by the tens of millions due to weather—dry spells (1830–1850) or cooler temperatures (1850s). He says, "buffalo inhabited less than 1/3 their former range" by 1850 (1986, 143).

52. Cephas Arms (in Cumming 1985, 13–14) relates that on June 11 they found 127 oxen as far away as 15 miles. On the twelfth they learned that a Tennessee company traveling on the opposite side of the river (the right bank) had driven 78 of the 126 missing oxen from the north side to the south side and yoked them to their wagons. Lorton's division found all but two of their oxen (Welch 1849a, June 28; Arms in Cumming 1985, 25–29).

capt Doty & another person came in camp & said they beckoned for those 2 persons that saw the Indians & they ran from them. One lay down because he was tired, & there was quite a laugh over the narrow escape from the Indians, for the captain, seeing them run, ran after them to get them to stop but that only increased their speed. It was quite a chase. A party went out in the direction of these Indians & have not yet returned.

Kemble [Kimble] chased a herd of buffalo & thought they were oxen. Amonge this herd 1 ox was following. He aproached a[s] near a[s] 40 ft & killed 1 buffalo & broke anothers leg. Some others aproach the camp but an antelope & deer, a wolf or an elk which are as thick on these plains as the hair on a dogs back, running past starts them off again. There has been several animals killed this day. There has been no Indians seen by us west of Loup Fork.

We drink water out of the Nebraska.[53] It is very white. Settles on standing but not as good as the Mis[souri] water, but is far better than slue water for the health, & less liable to produce diareah. This eve'g a party started out for the bluffs & there camp so as to be off early in the morning. They packed provision enough for 2 or 3 days on their ponies & with their blanket[s] & shooting irons is all they carried. Ward & several others returned at nightfall. They had been some 30 miles north & had seen no cattle, tho' they had seen herd after [herd] of buffalo, "thousands!" laying down on the hills. They could ride with in a hundred yds, but they had nothing but pocket pistols. They see 1 bull crippled in his fore leg, probably the one Kemble crippled in the morning. He put a doz pistol balls in him, but on a/c of the smallness of the weapon it did not take any deadly effect. However, it made him sick & he gave them chase, but soon relinquished his design & they left him pawing in a puddle, venting his rage upon the ground. While out they see myrids of game of every description. More horsemen out so we highst [hoist] 2 lanterns on a pole as a signal. [James Ellery] Hale & [John L.] West arrive 2 in morning. Another party is still out on the 11th June. 4 of ours found & 2 cows. 125 cattle lost yet.

[June 12.] More parties pack provisions & start for Loop Fork in search, & others scatter in all directions [see Welch, June 12, 1849a]. During the night the cattle tryed very hard to "stampeed" but were flumuxed because we had them tied down with ropes to stakes drove firmly in the ground. A party has just come back & say they have seen some hundred head of cattle following a train unyoked, acrost the river. These may be ours, but we wait [*illegible*].

[H. D.] Walker who went away [hunting cattle] last night met a comp. of 13 wagons. They said they see a drove of cattle that they took for ours 39 miles from

53. Frémont said "the Nebraska, or Shallow river" is the name given to the Platte River by the Indians (Frémont 1970a, 283). His 1846 map designates the waterway "Nebraska or Platte River" (Map 1846, Frémont).

camp with 7 large white wolves after them. This was Sunday when they were seen & Sunday morn'g they fled, so they must have traveled it in 4 hours. Soon after, 2 men crossed over from the other side & swam them [the cattle] acrost. This comp. [of 13 wagons] asked if they [the cattle] did'nt belong to the Knoxville comp., for they thought they recognized a number of our comp. [company's cattle], but the [2] men told them that the cattle belonged to their comp. from Tennesee on the other side & had stampeed[ed]. "A blackened lie! Dareing robers! Worse than murder!" to thus jeperdize the lives of they knew not who!

Our men as they passed, looked thro the glass & recognized some of their cattle in the drove behind the [Tennessee] train & hollowed to them but they turned a deaf ear & passed on thinking our men could not cross, for a swift current sped between the shore & the island on which our men stood. At length an old man sent his son out to wade in the water aways to tell us that our cattle were in their teams & beconed & pointed with his coat which he held in his hand (this man belonged not to the train that had just passed). It was a good 1/2 mile from the island to shore, but 2 [of our party] said they would reach the shore or perrish in the attempt. This they did & the rest followed, tho they did not swim all the way on a/c of shoals & bars. This train furnished them with dry clothes, & told them if they wanted help they would assist. By this time the Tenn[essee] robers, who had had the major part of our oxen yoked up formed a "caral" & com[mence]d unyoking & substituting their own again, for they had been driving theirs behind. The owners went up & claimed their cattle. To this they [the Tennesseans] objected & said they did not belong to 'em, but our men swore peremtorially if they did'nt give up the cattle there would be blood shed. This had somewhat of an effect on them & they give up all they [our men] could swear to which amounted [to] 81 & had the audacity to take them [our men] to a team where there was none of our oxen & ask if any was theirs. [Later,] "What the devel are you doing with my off ox on the near side," said he [one of our men] to one teamster.[54] He let him [our man] have both which he took, [the] other [ox], of which he did not recognize, but thought it must certainly wouldnt be theirs. All the owners not being there, for they could not all swim the river which is 1 mile wide, there is consequently 40 head gone some wheres. Out of the no. we have 3 [missing]. The others they sent acrost 1 mile above camp. Here the bottom is curious & a person not aquainted with it would little think of crossing it. Some times you are over your head & then not above your ankles & [it is] unlike the other crossing.

A larg party our capt sent out to night in pursuit. Our oxen brought back are run down very much. Our men who were in search of cattle on the bluffs see a splendid horse but he was so wild they could not catch him on account of his

54. The "off" ox is on the right side in the yoke. The near, or nigh, ox is on the left side of the yoke, closest to the left front wheel from the driver's perspective.

swiftness, but might with a "lassoe." There is a number of ridges of bluffs towering from 100 to 200 ft above each other. They are singularly level on the top & fall abruptly into deep ravines on either side.

The ravines or glens are inhabited by the fiercest of wolves. Here they lay secluded till an opportunity offers to spring upon their prey. Here is also the home of the buffalo ranger, & the glens are litterally filled with carcases of buffalo with hair, bones & teath. Upon these bluffs buffalo are principally to be seen. The number of teams constantly passing on the bottoms keep them from the river. Here they lay when the sun shines, halting in its rays. Here they have their calves. Some yearlings pawing the ground. Rain falls into their beats [beds] & then they wallow in the mud. When persued they lumber off but not at great speed. The calves are most spry. A small comp. camped near us to night.

June 13th 1849. We borrow 2 cows for our waggon & set out late in the morning, expecting to meet our men who had went in pursuit acrost the river. They were to hoist a red handkerchief & we a flag, so we hoisted upon a 4 pronged pitch fork the cooks apron, dirty as dishwater, truly emblematical of our late occurances that the devel is on the Platt for theres his pitch fork.

Our comp threw away a [few] things such as iron stoves &c. See flocks of pelicans fly along the rive[r]s edge. I ride horse back unable to walk yet. Road sandy all day & wet after the hard rain. After going 10 miles we have to put up on a/c of the shower. Have turtle soup & turtle eggs for supper. Camp without any timber.

June 14th. Determine that one half the train go on to meet the boys on the other side & the rest remain behind, rather than have delay.

Bart[holomew] volunteered to go alone & take provisions to the boys that had went to Loop Fork, on whose a/c they were agoing to wait, for fear of their starving. So taking a buffalo robe & the required provisions he set out immediately. [We] leave the river & take it again amonge some sandy bluffs. This same chain of bluffs has not reached the river sence we took up the bottom, it haveing been from 5 to 20 miles off but allways in view, tho' sometimes faint. Today I rode horse back all day & consequently I mounted these high bluffs (100 ft) that form a steep on the river edge & commands a picturesque view down on the numerous islands that dot the stream at this point, & [see a] cove, green with foliage & also of the still higher ragged & peeked bluffs on the other side, that seam in their ambision to aspire to reach the clouds but unfortunte for them I fear they never can for they are too sandy.

Here I stood gazing upon the fine scenery, the buffalo reclining on the neighboring hills, the light & elastic antelope skipping about, the astonished elk as he elevates his tall antlers & gazes in astonishment at the passing train, or the wolf who is trying to escape. The hunters [*illegible*] do not perceive. I turn my eyes again down in to the river & there floating majestically up the bossom of old Nebraska [Platte River] appears an enormous flock of "pelicans." "Fine shot," but no gun. But see! The capt. is crossing along the ridge under shelter of some bushes. He aims for the flock, the ball whizzes, [and] up flies the birds with the exception of 3 which were floating downstream. These mamoth birds 3 times as large as a goose fly over & frightens my horse with their large wings, making the most horrible noise & fly round as if waiting for their companions. Others waided out & got them.

Road mostly today over sand. Shot 4 antelopes. Shot 2 buffalo 1 1/2 miles back of camp in the bluffs. We camp on Cold Spring.[55] It is very large & clear, & cold as ice. At nightfall our men returns from over the river, almost dead, hungry, fatigued & worn out. After taking some norishment they felt better & related what they had to say in relation to their expedition. They over took the comp. in which they were in chase, inspected all their cattle but could not learn any thing in regard to ours. They might have drove them on several miles ahead, but 2 comp lay ahead which they did not pass. After eating up the raw bacon & crackers which they carried in their pockets, they fell in with the Pioneer train, the passenger train from St. Louis via Independence which carry out passengers for 200 dolls & 100 [pounds] of baggage. These passengers cook their own vituals, & collect their own wood. A great many have ponies. Each carriage has 2 mules, & a lot of extra ones behind the train.[56]

A young man asked [our men who had crossed the river] if we had had any trouble with the Indians. They related the circumstance of Harrison Rowe on Loop Fork, when [a] man exclaimed, he's my brother! & true, to[o] true, it was. There has been several "stampeeds" on the other side but mostly caused by dogs. 1 comp of 19 wagons had some cattle drove off by the Indians. When they came on the Indians, they were skinning them. As soon as they see this, they fired on the red skins & killed 5. Sence that the comps on the other side make a practice of killing all [Indians] they see.

There has been from all a/c's a great deal of stuff thrown away & indeed the boys see piles of bacon laying by the road side, casks of liquor let off upon the ground & the barrels left. Every thing has been done to lighten loads. At night the boys [were] put up in another comp tent. Some had ox yokes, & others sod for pillows. They [the train across the river] entertained them as hospitable as

55. Likely this is the "Good spring of cold water" mentioned in Clayton's 1848 emigrant guide (1983, 50). It is near Maxwell, Nebraska, east of today's community of North Platte.

56. Dale Morgan (1959b, 175) said the Pioneer Line was "an unlucky commercial undertaking of Turner & Allen to deliver Forty-niners in California as if by stage" and was "a catalogue of mismanagement and misfortune."

possible & made no charges. They say that scarcely a day elapses without passing a grave. Dozens of persons have died along the way & 2 in this comp. They were taken with a diareah & without the least pain carried off in 48 hours. They call it Cholera.

They crossed the river at the bluff where the pelicans were killed (1 1/2 miles wide). Here they undressed & put the clothes on their backs. Some places they had to swim 500 yds with a heavy current, & then land on an island. One nearly gave out, & would [have] had they [not] floated out an Indian [rubber] bladder, which saved him. Some of the rest were nearly exhausted. However, they arived on this beach & were going down to where we camped the previous eve'g but they see the prints of horses shoes going downstream which they knew to be the pilots. They also found a buffalos head with Cephas Arms name on it, which proved that we had passed on, & [they] arrived in camp after travelling 40 miles that day, & the way they went into hot tea & cold antelope wasnt slow. We have antelope for supper, threw pellicans away. Hoist a light as signal. At 10 eve'g 2 of our hunters arive. Killed a buffalo on the hill, so we cut off steaks for breakfast.

June 15th, [1849]. Conclude to wait for our Loop Fork men & so lay up.[57] In the meantime, we overhall our waggon as well as all the rest. We take the barrel off the crackers & put them in bags, tie up the bacon in a canvas bale, compres our best clothes in 1 box or trunk & put the residue in sacks, & throw away 1 trunk & put the rest in a bag, as did others. We then sawed off 4 ft of our box & coupled up the ark shorter. Here every thing thought not necessary & bulky they disposed of on the ground. Amonge the rest was 40 lb. Keg of powder. This they took to a wolfs den, fixed a train [trail of powder] & then set fire to it. A great many took off their [wagon] projections.

Killed 2 buffalo today. Found a curious plant resembling in shape a beet tho' white & scarcely any teast [taste], a flower growing on sand banks of a reddish & yellow flower, leaves like a winter green & the flower as large as your fist. Boys return from search down the river. They found 2 cattle & they were yoked up in a train.[58] When Bart[holomew] over took them they were out of provision[s] having ate the last 1/2 cracker allowance [that] morn'g.[59] He gave them

57. These men were Halstead, Baker, Gale, and Welch from the Rovers, who volunteered to backtrack as far as the Loup River if necessary (over 170 miles away) to look for more cattle. As it turns out, they did not go that far.

58. The two oxen belonged to the Canton boys, whose two wagons were part of the ten in the Rover division. The oxen were found east of Dry Creek, likely somewhere near Grand Island about 40 miles away (Welch 1849a; also in Cumming 1985, 30–35). Clayton mentions three dry creeks in his guide. Lorton does not use a name for the camping spot, so we do not know which Dry Creek Welch is referring to on June 12.

59. This was probably Luzerne Bartholomew.

eatables which they ate with extremely good gusto. They left 1 horse on the road, worn out.

June 16th. Called a meeting to dicide whether to start on or farther search. It was decided unanimously that we go on. Bad road all day, sandy bluffs to cross. Plenty of lizards, toads with horns & tails in profusion, perfectly harmless. See plenty of buffalo off on the bluffs all day. Met a man with a wagon load of buffalo he had killed & was taken it into camp. They were pitched as we passed with a large American flag & penant flying.

Grave near where we eat dinner. It was the grave of W. Williams who died June 10th 1849 of the cholera in the 23d year of his age.[60] He came from Detroit, Mich[igan], & belonged to the "Badgers." The grave was well sodded, with a head board at his head, & situated on the banks of the river, 1/2 mile above where South Fork [of the Platte River] comes in. There is directly opposite the grave, in the middle of the river, a fine little island, with fine bushey toped trees & under scrubbary.

[June] 17th Sunday. While in camp [at] sunrise we see buffalo looking down on camp from the neighboring hills. Travel thro' sand & sand bluffs all day, some times 1/2 way up to the hubs. See plenty of buffalo. Some shot but none brought in to camp. [I am] Still laid up. Go 20 miles, & camp in sand bluffs, after crossing north bluff fork.[61] While I write, I am called to look at a herd of buffalo fording the river 1 mile above. They cross over from our side.

June 18th. Think we see our cattle over the river [lower North Platte], but on swimming over find we are mistaken. Get large chunks of salt peeter, as clear as crystal.[62] Air in places smells like sulphyr & salt peter. The cattle will not touch salt in this country. Find some little particles of gold on Carrion Creek which we cross, but not worth bothering with. One of the Badger comp's men drowned in the Platt in swimming after a piece of driftwood out in the stream, which they

60. Arms relates their train nooned near this grave, adding, "His clothes and bed were lying around, thrown away for fear of infection" (Arms in Cumming 1985, 36).
61. This is today's Birdwood Creek, about 18 miles northwest of the town of North Platte, Nebraska (Kimball in Clayton 1983, 53). Because the sand bluffs came all the way down to the river, the road was forced northward over the sand hills. A swale, part of the wagon road, is still visible over the highlands north of the North Platte River.
62. Lorton does not differentiate the North Platte, which he is now following, from the main Platte River. Potassium nitrate and sodium nitrate are both called saltpeter. It is unclear if Lorton is just collecting specimens of the mineral or if he is planning to use it for curing meat or softening beans or tough meat.

wanted to get for an axle.[63] He went down & did not rise again. His hat & coat lay on the shore where he went in, & a Dutchman in the employ of Ewing recognized the coat as the 1 he gave him. Sand bluffs & sand road all day.

June 19th. During the night a hurrycane springs up & slits our tent. At sun rise next morning (being camped on a marsh) millions of musquitoes make their appearance to the great anoyance of all hands, but a wind rising soon dispelled them. Buffalo came down off the bluffs & feed with our cattle, & in our men trying to get near them they made for the river. The boys in chase & they full jump dashing thro' the water on the bars, then swimming in deep water, but a train passing on the other side drove them over on our side again. Being fenced in, they were soon dispatched by bullets. Cut off some steaks for supper, & tenderl[o]ines.

Boyd, while sitting on the [wagon] tongue, fell off & both wheels run over his back & leg—very badly hurt.[64] See Indian village on the south side the river, about 24 wigwams made of sticks & skins, very peeking & round. Around these they had several 100 ponies grazing & running & jumping. Very few Indians at home—out on the chase. These are the 1st Indians we see sence we left Loop Fork. These are Siouxs & every man has 2 or 3 ponies.

The rode on the other side is gravelly & every opportunity that offers they strike down on the bottom. The edge of the Bluffs are lime stone. About 4 o'clock a white squall made its appearance in the west, & we put up in a "caral" for the night. The very sky looks a greenish hue. For fear of the storm driving our cattle off we tie them up till its over. We have a vilent tornado, rain, hail, thunder & lightning.

[June] 20th. See grave opposite Ash Hollow & clothes of the dead man lying near.[65] He died 2 days before with the cholera. One of capt Wells men. Cross several creeks, & [*blank*] river.[66] Pioneer train opposite us. They have 8 & 10 mules to a waggon, & Spanards that throw the "lassoe."[67] Just above here 3 buffalo tries

63. The Badger Company that Alexander Combs Erkson helped organize left Kanesville May 29, 1849 (Erkson in Munro-Fraser 1881, 709; Manly 1894, 367; Rasmussen 1994, 67). Several of the company took the Southern Route, and the Bennett family, and possibly William Abbott, became Death Valley '49ers.

64. This is probably Thomas Gordon. Boyd may have been a middle or nickname.

65. Ash Hollow is on the south (right) side of the North Platte River, two miles southeast of today's Lewellen, in western Nebraska. Its name comes from the prevalent green ash (*Fraxinus pennsylvanica*) in the area. The grave is on the north (left) side of the river, same side as Lorton's trail.

66. This is Blue Creek, which is the biggest creek in the area. It debouches west of Lewellen.

67. Throughout his diary to Salt Lake, Lorton mentions the Pioneer Line traveling on the other side of the river. Merrill Mattes (1988, 207) commented that its grim "reality

to cross the river but are intercepted in their retreat. They made tracks back & as they land ahead of the train, they [the men] might have driven them in home but for fear of frightening the cattle. They fire a volley in broadsides but it makes them lumber off faster to wards a craggy bluff which they could not assend. With fast horses they pen them in & fire & wound 1. The others go faster, while they continue [to] pelt it into him. By this time, the footmen come & after a great many shots he finally falls like a log. This I witnessed from the waggon in which I am confined. The Pioneer men stood on the other side [of the North Platte] witnessing the sight. We camp opposite the Pioneers. They [are] just under the shade of a high, precipitous lime stone bluff, we [are] in a wet spot alive with musquitoes.

[June] 21st. Plenty of salsodo on the ground today, road gravelly.[68] Camp on a small creek of clear cold water. Cook supper with buffalo chips, in a fire place made of sods.[69]

June 22d. Start 6 o'clock. Up early & make moccosens for lame ox out of green buffalo skin. Road laid today thro' miles of flowers, the major part being a yellow flower groing on a slender stem & resembling the small sun flower, wild pinks, 5 or 6 species of "cactus," blue bells, some resembling roses but smell like a holly hawk, several kinds of flowers resembling poppies, besides scarlet, red, pink, flesh collor, purple, blue, all natives of this bottom. It is strange, the farther you ascend the river new kinds appear & the others vanish.

Road to day more roleing. Pass several dry rivers, beds dry, sand & gravel & have the appearance of haveing been rushing streems. The bluffs to day are rockey & singularly formed. Some peek in form of a cone up towards the sky to a prodigious hight. You can take a horse to the top & observe. Other[s] present to the eye a long chain of broken down walls, fortifications, ramparts, decaying castles, moss covered turets, rewined [ruined] cittadels, fallen spires, & others yet standing, & an observer can scarcely convince himself that these are not real ruins.[70] A person standing on top looks as small as a mouse, & there appears as

---

was rebellious mules, overloaded wagons, inadequate provisions, disease, and death of at least twenty of the party, . . . the harrowing experiences of emaciated, hollow-eyed men who straggled into Sacramento. . . . Cholera deaths began five days out" of Independence, Missouri.

68. Sal soda, or sodium carbonate, is a white crystalline compound used to wash fabric.

69. Cephas Arms said, "We have had no timber since Saturday morning. Buffalo chips [dried dung] do first rate as a substitute" (in Cumming 1985, 37). This creek might be Coldwater Creek at Lisco, Nebraska.

70. The Ancient Bluff Ruins are along the north side of the North Platte River just east of Broadwater, or about 25 miles west of Oshkosh, Nebraska. Clayton (1983, 56) described them as "resembling the ruins of ancient castles, fortifications, &c."

FIGURE 10. Lorton notes a single spire near the Ancient Bluff Ruins in the North Platte River Valley, looking north. Lorton writes on June 22: "I see 1 spire 50 ft high standing alone.... These are composed of a petrified soft rock & looks as if it washed with the rain." Photo by LeRoy Johnson.

you proceed walls as if enclosing cities with now & then tall chimnies peeking up above. I see 1 spire 50 ft high standing alone, & another a tall slim sugar loaf.

These are composed of a petrified soft rock & looks as if it washed with the rain.[71] Dry ravines proceed from some & in these you find huge rocks hurled hundreds of feet from their beds as if by a mighty torent. On the top of these you find bones petrified with stone. These bluffs continue for miles but are not so striking.

Iron[ing] bord, fine stoves, boxes of soap, carpets, locks, nails, and boxes lay by the way, thrown out. Assend high bluffs & decend on bottom again. Day pritty hot & hard on cattle. Meat wont spoil in the hottest weather owing to the [dry] atmosphere. [Make a] 20 mile drive & camp on the Platt right in the sand. Chimney Rock on in the distance, & opposite us standing on the level plain a huge pile of stone resembling a rewined [ruined] castle [Courthouse Rock], with a chiminy detached [Jail Rock].[72]

71. The picturesque formations along the North Platte are "made of stacked layers of sandstone, siltstone, mudstone, and volcanic ash. Differential erosion of these layers—some soft, some hard—gives each monolith a distinct shape" (Meldahl 2007, 59).

72. Courthouse and Jail Rocks rise about 400 feet above the valley floor five miles southeast of Bridgeport. Courthouse is also called the Castle or the Capitol.

FIGURE 11. Jail and Courthouse Rocks with North Platte in foreground, looking south, as Lorton would have seen them. Writes Lorton on June 22: "Opposite us standing on the level plain [is] a huge pile of stone resembling a rewined [ruined] castle, with a chiminy detached." Photo by LeRoy Johnson.

[June] 23d. Road roleing & scarcely any bluffs on the north. Pass an extraordinary sand bluff or drift. It runs up from the river about 40 ft above the water. It is entirely destitute of vegetation while at its base grass grows very luxuriously. It assumes a brilliant & flesh collored & finest graned sand.

Camp opposite Chiminey Rock on the opposite side. This rock is situated on the top of a rock of the species resembling a mound that is probaby 100 ft & the Chiminy Rock reaches above 140 ft more making it 240 ft high & about 30 ft acrost the top. It can be seen at the dist. of 50 miles & is the most deceiving thing in the world as for dist. It seems to receed as you approach. Halks have made nests in the top. Tried to shoot. Standing alone as it does it calls forth wonder & amazement. There are some strange looking rocks at a dist. from it, 1 in form of a cone & another representing a large square building & a mamoth dome on the top. I turn cook to day. Have a pampero that came near carrying away our main sheet, but lasted only a few minutes.

[June] 24th Sunday. Early start. Fill our canteens from the wells. Read Sears *Wonders of the World*, & read during [convalescence with] my lame leg: *Haunted Oak*, *Simon the Radical*, *A. Whim*, *Belle of the Bowery*, *Harry Martingale*. Have a visit from over the river. They had 4 cases of Cholera.

FIGURE 12. Lorton sketch. Chimney Rock and what Lorton thinks is Scotts Bluff. Lorton writes: "W.L./J.23"; "SCOTS/BLUFF 200 ft high composed/of hard clay"; and "Scotts Bluff is/about 5 miles above/chiminey Rock." Lorton's lower description says "CHIMINEY/ROCK. 250 ft from its/base to summit"; "top is 30 ft in diameter/the rock was 3 yrs agoe 200 ft but/has washed away 50 ft." He camped across the river from Chimney Rock on June 23, 1849. Courtesy of The Bancroft Library.

FIGURE 13. Chimney Rock is a slender spire rising 120 feet atop a 205-foot, cone-shaped mound on the south bank of the North Platte River in western Nebraska. It is composed of layers of volcanic ash and Brule clay dating back to the Oligocene epoch (34 million to 23 million years ago). Merrill Mattes (1969, 378) pointed out that "more enthusiasm and more diary space was devoted to this particular landmark than to any other of the covered wagon migration." Based on early drawings, the spire was some 30 feet taller in 1849 than it is today. Photo by LeRoy Johnson.

[June] 25th. Start daylight without breakfast & go seven miles to Trout creek & lay there all day to overhall wagons. Tear off projections, throw away unescessary articles, &c. Threw away enough in camp to load 5 yoke. Mess does washing. I write 3 letters.

[June] 26th. Nothing of importance. Plenty of wolves. 27th [*sic*] Came 17 miles. Camp near a small creek, catch salmon & perch for breakfast. Comes up a heavy shower that wets thro' tent. Loose sight of Chiminey Rock. Black Hills in the dist. I cook up lots of things.[73]

[June 27] 28th. Rovers find some gold ore. Scenery barren, but plenty of cactus. See the remnants of Indian lodges on island &c. Camp on river. Plenty of dead trees on shores & islands.

73. These Black Hills are the eastern foothills of the Laramie Mountains, not the Black Hills of South Dakota, 170 miles north-northeast, that contain Mount Rushmore. The blackness is the dark hue of conifers scattered over the hills: ponderosa pine (*Pinus ponderosa*), Utah juniper (*Juniperus osteosperma*), and Rocky Mountain juniper (*Juniperus scopulorum*). Seventeen days previous, on June 9, Lorton's foot was injured in a stampede, but now he is able to hobble around the camp and make himself useful by cooking.

[June] 28th. We arrive at the ferry opposite Fort Larimie or rather opposite Fort John [Fort Platte]. Fort John is built of dark brick, & is now deserted & partly going to ruin.[74] Fort Larimie is situated 1 1/2 miles from here. Around here can be seen wagons, wagon wheels, tires, kingbolts, stoves, bus[hels] of beans scattered around. 17 good rifles were bent & thrown in the river. Saddles lay arround, trunks, chests, bacon, &c. Canisters of powder were sold to the Am[erican] Fur Comp to [for] 5 cts. Flour can be bot there for 1 dol. a hund. [pounds], & other articles in comparison. Our men we find here with the exception of Capt Baxter who has gone in chase of a comp that is said to have left here 5 days ago in great haste, 10 wagons & extra cattle with which they kept changing. Here the Black Hills commence. Talk of no grass for 100 miles. 3 [of our] comp took up the river in search of a new rout.[75] Talk of throwing away part of our goods. The gen[tlemen] at the Fort says there has been another rout explored that leaves Salt Lake to the right & cuts off 400 miles.[76] Mules went through last year, & they think they can get wagons over. The greatest difficulty is one mountain. If that is passed, he says there is no difficulty.

The river is deep here & we ferry on an old scow, 1 wagon at a time, swim our cattle. Pay $3.00 & ferry ourselves. We swim our cattle over just [at] dusk. Ferry till 12 o'clock at night. 6 wagons next morn'g.

Lorton's Letter from Fort Laramie

The *New York Sun* published Lorton's letter on Friday morning, September 7, 1849, over two months after he wrote it. Lorton gave his readers what they wanted to hear: the "shock and awe" of crossing the plains with titillating emphasis on predation from Indians and death from cholera. After his general comment about the "vicissitudes, trials, incidents and dangers" of wagon travel, he did not dwell on the everyday joys and frustrations of wagon travel—the brilliant sunrises and fields of colorful wildflowers, the mosquitos, blisters, sunburn, dust, and diarrhea. Because his paper and time were limited, he carefully selected what to tell his readers.

74. This was the short-lived, adobe-walled Fort Platte built in 1840–1841, not Fort John (Hafen and Young 1984, 69–70; Mattes 1969, 489, map after 492). For more information see the introduction to this chapter.

75. These three men may have hoped to avoid the two ferry crossings. We found no evidence of a wagon train traversing the north (left) side of the river in 1849. The next year, on June 22, a train pioneered a new route up the north bank of the river, and Andrew Child, a member of the train, wrote a trail guide that detailed what is today called the Child's Cutoff. "The route we followed from this point [opposite Fort Laramie], was still upon the *north side* of the river, which route was then (June 1850) untraveled and unknown" (Child 1946, 20; see also R. Brown 1987, 17–21; Bagley 2012, 261–68; McKinstry 1975, 129–34).

76. Hastings Cutoff, named for Lansford W. Hastings, is the only route that leaves the Salt Lake route on the right (north of the trail). However, it did not cut off 400 miles.

Correspondence New York Sun: From the Overland Emigrants

Fort Larimie, June 30th, 1849.
Messrs. Beach. — Dear Sirs: — Since leaving Council Bluffs, we have passed through many dizzy scenes, some of which I shall hereafter take notice of. It would take an abler pen than mine to delineate in their true character, the various vicissitudes, trials, incidents and dangers attending an overland journey across the Continent. Perhaps all the events in the knowledge of civilized man that has ever transpired on these western wilds, will not compete with the present year.

We had just struck the Platt[e] bottom on the 29th May, when we discovered two men riding hastily toward us. Upon coming up, they said that they [the Oskaloosa Company] had entertained some Pawnee Indians on the preceding evening, and when night fell, they suggested to them the propriety of retiring, which they did with reluctance, some 300 yards, and there encamped. During the night they threw their arrows into "caral" which caused the cattle to break out and scatter in every direction over the vast plains, the Indians making good their escape under shelter of the bushes that fringed the neighboring stream. At day break a sufficient number of horsemen were appointed to search for the lost cattle. These two forming part of that number, in their eagerness strayed off from the party, and suddenly came upon a collection of red skins who had some two dozen oxen upon the river's brinck, but could not with all their hideous yells compel them [the oxen] to swim the river. An Indian immediately seized one of their horses reins. Having a bowie knife handy he [the emigrant] cut the bridle and impelled his horse to speed. This called forth a shower of arrows and musket balls from the crowd. Expecting to meet some company, they made the back tract, and meeting us, solicited our assistance in reclaiming their property. With 75 well armed men we proceeded to the place. The Indians still retained their former position, and their movements indicated that they intended to act on the defensive. As we approached, they advanced towards us and fired a volley of arrows and lead, but the distance was so great, they did not take effect. They then turned, gave a hideous yell, and plunged into the river, carrying their arms with them. On reaching the bank we found all the cattle stretched in death. Some were pierced with arrows behind the fore shoulder, and others pierced with bullets in the forehead. The major part had undergone the operation of skinning. We, not intending to kill, but to save property, urgently solicited the party not to fire unless occasion required, yet the impetuosity on beholding the bloody sight, caused some to give way to their feeling, in the shape of a rifle ball thrown at the retreating forms of these carnivorous savages. In all, there were probably 100 Indians, all naked. They say they had a hard winter of it, they lost all their ponies, and appear half starved. We left the meat, to be disposed of as they thought proper.

A company named the Backwoodsmen had a herd of cattle driven off in a similar manner. They came suddenly on the Indians as they were engaged in the occupation of skinning them, and without any ceremony, shot 5 down dead.

On the 1st of June, the Dubuque Mining Company arrived at Loup Fork, and had sent men out to sound the bars and find out the most feasible ford of this dangerous river. While performing this, there appeared about 100 Indians on the opposite shore. They were mounted on mules and ponies and soon after commenced crossing. Fearing the issue, the company placed their cattle within a "Caral," and prepared for defense. They, however, showed peaceable inclinations and said they were Sioux Indians, and were in chase of some "Bad Pawnees."[77] They asked for presents as usual, which were given, and soon after left, expressing ardent satisfaction. It appears that three of the Dubuque's number were out, up the river hunting, the rout these Indians took. The first one they met and asked for a present. He gave a silk pocket handkerchief to the chief, and he was allowed to pass. The second was armed with a splendid rifle, revolvers, and bowie knife, him they shot through the heart on the spot, and robbed him of everything he possessed. The third concealed himself in the bushes, and was an eye witness of the murderous deed [see Lorton, June 2, 1849]. As soon as they were gone, he hastened to relate the sad tale. The unfortunates name was Harrison Rowe, a merchant of Platsville, Wis. [Iowa]. They interred his murdered remains upon the top of a conspicuous mount, and on the grave may be seen a written warning against leaving the main body of the company in the Indian country.

The cholera has been making fearful ravages along the route. The Pioneer's company (of St. Louis), reported up to the 10th June, 10 cases, and you scarcely pass a mile without seeing a fresh grave. The Oscaloosa company buried 4 since crossing Loup Fork. Other parties are losing to an alarming extent. Yet, it is stated that a great many go off [die] in 24 hours without the least pain.

A great many, anticipating a speedy journey across the plains, have failed in their expectations, and have commenced lightening their loads. Every thing that is not absolutely necessary is thrown away. The roadside is literally lined with goods of all kinds, such as boxes, stoves, beds, barrels, crowbars, piles of casks of rum poured out on the ground, cooking utensils, books, papers, tools of various descriptions, and chests, carpets, chairs, camp tables, stools, salt, kegs of powder, and in reality every thing is dispensed with that will help them

77. From the Sioux's perspective, all Pawnees were "Bad Pawnees." The Sioux were bent on eradicating them (for insight into the Sioux–Pawnee conflict, see Hyde 1974, 187–218, and R. White 1988, 147–211).

forward with greater rapidity.[78] Fears are now entertained that the hindermost parties will have to winter in the mountains, which, if the snows fall early, will be the case.

I commit this missive to the hands of some trappers and traders, which with their kindness will reach your office in due season.

Yours truly,
W. B. [Lorton]

78. Andrew Child (1946, 56) estimated "the value of property *left* on the California route in the season of 1850, was double that of the amount carried through."

CHAPTER 5

Fort Laramie to Independence Rock, Utah

Background

Beyond Fort Laramie, Lorton could see the Wyoming Black Hills with Laramie Peak in the distance, a granite, pyramidal massif that heralded the emigrants' approach to the Rocky Mountains. The Oregon-California Trail approached the Rockies by crossing the Wyoming Basin, then it crossed the Continental Divide via South Pass.

About six and a half miles beyond Fort Laramie, Lorton descended the notorious downgrade now called Mexican Hill (origin of the name is unknown) (Haines 1981, 143). Thomas Bullock had descended the same steep hill on June 4, 1847, during the Mormon migration, and noted: "We not only locked Wheels, but had attached ropes to the hind end of the Wagons the brethren holding back the same time" (Bullock 1997, 181; Clayton 1983, 60; for hill location see Franzwa 1982, 109, and Berrett and Anderson 2006, 22–23).

About five miles west of Mexican Hill and across the North Platte from Guernsey, Wyoming, are "the most fantastic ruts on the entire overland trail. Here the California, Oregon, and Mormon trails are the same, thus the great depth of the ruts in the stone" (Berrett and Anderson 2006, 24–25). The steel tires of countless wagons pulled over a knoll of soft sandstone incised ruts as deep as five feet (Haines 1981, 147–49).

Two miles northwest of the deep ruts, Lorton arrived at Warm Spring, where he may have soaked his injured foot before the train continued on to pass Porter Rock. The "Portor's Rock," which Lorton sketched and vividly described, has no resemblance to today's Porter Rock. Although his sketches could be fanciful, his written descriptions have been quite accurate. Thus, we conclude Lorton's Portor's Rock is different from today's Porter Rock, which Milliken and others have carefully documented (L. Johnson 2010, 46–47; R. Brown 2010, 95–96; 1987, 17–21).

A few miles past Porter Rock, Lorton comments on a steep hill from which he has a grand view. William Clayton concurred: "From the top of this hill we

FIGURE 14. Lorton sketch. "PORTOR'S ROCK." "On the PRAIRIE BASE of/BLACK HILLS." We suspect Lorton was looking at a different formation from the rock currently called Porter Rock. Courtesy of The Bancroft Library.

FIGURE 15. Porter Rock in 2009, about seven crow-miles west-northwest of Guernsey, Wyoming. Photo by LeRoy Johnson.

had as pleasant a view of the surrounding country as I have ever witnessed. Laramie peak appears only a few miles to the southwest, and from that around to the west, north, and northeast, a very extensive view" (Clayton 1973, 221). Lorton is about 15 miles south of today's Glendo Reservoir, near today's Interstate 25.

About five miles beyond the hill, Lorton descended to today's Horseshoe Creek, southwest of Glendo, Wyoming. Frémont camped here July 22, 1842, on his first expedition: "We reached our proposed encampment on the *Fer*-à-Cheval, or Horse Shoe creek. Here we found good grass" (Frémont 1970a, 235). Thomas Bullock camped here June 7, 1847, and said they found the "most Excellent Grass [and] the most beautiful Spring of Water yet seen on this route." However, when Bullock returned to Winter Quarters three months later, on September 22, "Heber's Spring," was "nearly dry, full of large frogs and covered with scum" (Bullock 1997, 184, 291).

As summer wore on, the fabric of the Knox County Company began to abrade and unravel, just as William Findley had warned his listeners (and as Lorton quoted) back in February. But on July 4, the divisions of the Knox County Company reassembled at Deer Creek to ferry the North Platte. They were more loosely connected now and had less allegiance to the original company's constitution. Injuries, sickness, and stampedes were wearing bodies and emotions thin.

About 110 miles northwest of Fort Laramie, the company ferried the North Platte July 5, after a rousing Fourth of July celebration. They did not cross on the famous Mormon ferry three and a half miles east of today's Casper, Wyoming. Instead, they crossed about 25 miles downriver near today's Glenrock where Deer Creek empties into the North Platte. History of the ferries across the upper North Platte is carefully researched and succinctly told by Dale Morgan in three articles in *Annals of Wyoming*. We use "The Ferries of the Forty-Niners," Part II, as the basis for the following information.

Mormons came back from Salt Lake City on May 27, 1849, to set up a ferry for crossing the North Platte, and the commercial ferries quit operating about July 31, when the river became low enough to ford. But during June, the crush of emigrants arriving hourly created pressure to build more ferries to provide quicker crossing, and this soon encouraged self-reliance and entrepreneurship among the emigrants. They felled the readily available old-growth cottonwood along the riverbank and built their own ferries. Only a month later, ferries were dotted downriver 25 miles from the Mormon ferry "at every place practicable" (Searls in Morgan 1959b, 175). Prices varied from 50 cents to four dollars per wagon depending on the demand, location, and quality of the ferry. As early as June 16, George Burrall "found so many encamped that he had to travel 3 miles up the [Deer] creek to find good feed" (in Morgan 1959b, 155).

The busiest time seems to have been about the third week of June. On June 23 there was "an Encampment of 5000 on fish creek [Deer Creek]" (Farnham in Morgan 1959b, 164).

William Findley was one of the first to build a ferry for the exclusive use of his train (Tinker in Morgan 1959b, 150–51). He permitted one other train to use it as thanks for their saving two members of his train from drowning, but arranged to have it destroyed after he left. The usual procedure was: a company built or bought a ferry, then after using it, sold it to another company which in turn sold it to still another company. Findley was roundly vilified for his action, and rumors of his poisoning springs and burning grass were unfairly heaped on him. From Findley's point of view, he was doing his job to guide his train safely and swiftly to the goldfields. His oxen were tired, and if he gave (or sold) his ferry to others with fresher oxen, they would pass him, and their animals would eat the convenient grass—first there, first fed. In addition, by not using the Mormon ferry, he felt his train was giving its place in line to those behind.

It is hard to envision the crush of people collecting at these ferries. Niles Searls arrived at Deer Creek on July 3—a day ahead of Lorton. He records that "emigrants are crossing from a short distance below us, to a point 30 miles above.... The number of which within 30 miles is estimated even as high as 2000 wagons. The Oregon battalion [Regiment of Mounted Riflemen] with a train of 400 wagons is encamped seven miles above us" (in Morgan 1959b, 175). One of the latecomers (July 31) was Charles Dallas, who had in his employ William Lewis Manly and John Haney Rogers of Death Valley fame.

FIGURE 16. Detail, James Wilkins sketch. "Ferrying wagons at [North] Platte. July 3d." WHI Image ID 31287.

The ferries were of three basic types: (1) well-caulked wagon beds used as a barge to float wagon parts and baggage across, (2) cottonwood logs hewn with hand axes into log canoes attached in some way to form a raft, and (3) simple log rafts made from up to 15 logs lashed together. The locomotion was either via a rope across the river to haul the ferry back and forth with man- or oxen-power or oars and sweeps to propel the ferry across. A skillfully caulked wagon bed could float after the wheel carriage was removed. A hollowed-out cottonwood log, much like a canoe, would float even with a load on top. Several logs, usually three to eight of them, were pegged, chained, or roped together to make a ferry. Hewn planks were attached across the logs like a railroad track for the wagon wheels to roll on. Small rafts carried one wagon; larger ones could take two.

For those who used oars and sweeps, the ferry drifted downcurrent before reaching the north shore, where oxen (or men) hauled the ferry upriver well above the launching place. Then the oarsmen pulled to the south shore while the current carried them, they hoped, to the original landing.

The animals were driven into the river with the hope they would swim to the other side. They were already old hands at crossing rivers and streams. Charles Gould said that "the river is about 800 feet wide here [at Deer Creek] with a swift current" (Gould in Morgan 1959b, 175).

Lorton said his train ferried to an island. Alonzo Delano described such a crossing on June 19, two weeks before Lorton: "[The rope] was stretched to an island, from which to the main shore was a ford that could be passed without much difficulty" (Delano 1966, 90). Lorton does not mention the ford, but we assume his procedure was similar.

The dangers of ferrying were injuries, drownings, and loss of wagons and supplies from toppled rafts. Wind and broken ropes were the most devilish culprits. A canvas wagon cover could act as a sail and tip over an already unwieldy craft. A broken rope allowed a ferry to chart its own course downriver to deal

FIGURE 17. Avenue of Rocks. Writes Lorton on July 12: "The rocks form a complete wall, or passage running on both sides of the road tho' the south wall is not so perfect." Photo by LeRoy Johnson.

with rocks, snags, and sandbars in its path. Dale Morgan (1959b, 188–89) catalogued 45 drownings mentioned in various diaries in 1849.

Before crossing the river, Lorton commented on meeting wagons that were returning to the States. William White (1927, 205), who started over the Oregon-California Trail on May 28, said he "frequently met parties returning to the States, discouraged by the hardships and dangers of the journey, and reporting Indian hostilities and other frightful obstructions along the way." There are no accurate records documenting the number of "turn-arounds" or "gobacks," but Unruh (1979, 123–24) suggests there were "certainly hundreds."

After crossing the North Platte, the road headed west along the river past today's Casper, Wyoming. Although the main trail went to Emigrant Gap, about 10 miles west of Casper, then headed southwest, some trains veered south nearer the river to Bessemer Bend. From Lorton's description, that is what the Knox County Company did. From there they headed due west to pick up the trail before arriving at another unusual formation Lorton called "Rockey Passage," about 25 miles southwest of Casper. Others christened today's Rock Avenue with names such as Devil's Backbone and Avenue of Rocks (Bullock 1997, 197n69, 285n50). William Clayton (1983, 66) called the formation "high rocks, forming a kind of avenue or gateway, for a quarter of a mile." But on July 12, Lorton gives

FIGURE 18. Detail, James Wilkins sketch of Independence Rock, July 10, 1849. This anomalous granite formation rises 130 feet above the desert floor and is 1,900 feet long and 700 feet wide. It is also known as the Great Register of the Desert because of the large number of emigrant names chipped in and painted on its surface. WHI Image ID 31290.

the best description of this "curious freak in nature." Passage through this once rough corridor is now over the well-maintained, gravel County Road 319.

After miles of alkali and creeks with names like Poison Spider Creek, Poison Springs Creek, and Iron Creek, one of the most welcome campsites was Willow Spring, about 10 miles southwest of the Avenue of Rocks. Here was fine water, and for early emigrants there was plenty of grass for their livestock. West of the spring was today's Ryan Hill, from which the emigrants could see a great distance. Sage hens became a welcome change of diet from salt pork—they still abound in this area.

The camp between Willow Springs and Independence Rock was near the junction of today's Fish and Horse Creeks, where the large sagebrush Lorton describes still thrive.

Independence Rock was also known as the Great Register of the Desert. This landmark was the psychological halfway point of their journey to the goldfields (although short of the actual distance), and a goal for many wagon trains was to reach it by July 4 so as not to be caught in the deadly snows of the Sierra Nevada. No one knows the total number of names, initials, and dates inscribed or painted on this anomalous granite monolith, but in 1999 Levida Hileman inventoried "2,056 entries." Three monumental works document the history of the Great Register, and the authors summarize the surviving discernable entries (Ellison 1930; Hileman 2001; R. Brown 2004).

The reddish-brown granite hump rises 130 feet above the sage and alkali valley north of the Sweetwater River about 52 miles west of Casper, Wyoming.

It has been compared to half an apple or a large turtle about 1,900 feet long and 700 feet wide.

Lorton mentions his cousin David Cairnes's inscription and that of "L. S. [L. W.] Hastings 1842," who added his name to the monolith during his trek to Oregon. Hastings and Lovejoy "having provided ourselves with material for lettering" painted their names on the monolith (Hastings 1994, 11). Ellison, however, made no mention of either inscription in his 1930 inventory. Hastings published the popular *The Emigrants' Guide to Oregon and California* in 1845 to attract emigrants to California and to publicize his cutoff from Salt Lake City to the Humboldt River.

Lorton's dates are screwed up in this part of his journal. He has two July 13s and rewrites several dates following, which puts him off a day for most of chapter 5. We correct them in brackets. His composite sketch of Independence Rock shows Lorton's own name with the date July 13, but he draws the "Knox co comp passes July 14th." This appears to be correct. Lorton was a day ahead of the Arms-Taylor-Jayhawker-Canton part of the train that had a bad stampede near the Rock on the 14th (Arms in Cumming 1985, 56).

Lorton's Journal Continues at Fort Laramie

[June 1849] 29th. My birth day [he turned 21]. Fort Larimie is situated on Larimie River, & the fort has just been bot of [from] the Am[erican] fur comp. & taken possession of this day by the troops who have enlisted for 3 years. 3 of them run away & 1 brot back & is now chained up. Major Sanders[on] is commander.[1] 3 of their heavy wagons crossed the ferry, with mules. Many wounded men [from emigrant companies] were left at the Fort in care of the troop[s]. Our comp. talked of leaving [Thomas] Gordon, that got run over with the wagon [on June 19].[2] Fort is built of burnt clay & 4 or 5 other buildings. This [adobe] brick is stone col [color] but they have white washed it, & a flag staff stuck up. The fur comp is making their fortune buying up articles & provisions a[t] low prices. Pionier train here. They say that the graves will average 1 to the mile all the way [back] to St. Jo, & where the roads meet 1 to every few hundred yds but think it [cholera] is on the decrease, & some call it the camp diareah. The Tennesee robbers that had our cattle, 2 of the No. had a quarrel & one was found shot & laying over the wagon tongue.

We started towards noon, left our table, keg, stools, &c., & just rounding the bluffs on the river road when a person getting water out of the river rose up suddenly which frightened the cattle, & in 1 min. the whole were again in

1. Major Winslow F. Sanderson, of the Mounted Riflemen, was the first commanding officer at the fort. He served from June 26, 1849, to September 4, 1850.

2. Thomas Gordon, from Mercer County (adjoining Knox County), was part of the Knox County Company from the beginning (Appendix A; Rasmussen 1994, 65).

FIGURE 19. Lorton sketch. Lorton writes: "LARIMIE PEAK/the Black hills/40 miles west of Fort LARIMIE of a clear day it can be seen 100 miles." Courtesy of The Bancroft Library.

FIGURE 20. Laramie Peak, with the Black Hills in the middle ground and grassy plains in the foreground. Photo by LeRoy Johnson.

motion, scattering. I was in the wagon, & was a fraid to jump out on a/c of my leg. Our team made for the river. A soft place to jump, I thought. We got so used to stampeeds that I took it cool by catching the oxs tail & holding on the tail, but they stoped soon after, & they all held up. They trembled like a leaf. One ox got hurt on the foot, no other damage & we went on.

Thousands of pounds of bacon by the rode side. $12 trunks, plenty of wagons & flour to sell at $2. 1 grave. Stop [after] a few miles [and camp] on the bottom all day. Bake bread, apple sause & bacon. River water like soap suds, & wont settle any. Tennesee robbers camp near us to let their oxen rest for the Black Hill[s] which tower in the dist up to the clouds on the west. Three buffalo on the bluffs on the other side [of the North Platte]. Start our letters by paying 10 cts. Larimie Peek in sight [at 10,274 feet the highest in the Laramie Range]. Catch some fine fish in the river. Send men ahead to clear stones off a bad hill.

[June] 30th. Road over gravel, thro' deep ravines with pine trees, some of which are perched on the tops. Rocks 150 [feet] high. Pass down a steep hill. Have to lock all the wheels [Mexican Hill, about five miles east-southeast of Guernsey, Wyoming]. [The road] full of stones. Stop at noon at Warm Spring.[3] Runs thro' lime stone & [is] very large. Get on a prairie. Black Hills looks as if we were on top nearly but we loose sight of them again. Pass many small mountain streams, finally camp on Platt bottom. Canton boys takes the wrong road. Meet an old trapper said he had been [over] it 50 times. Said it had not been travelled for a number of years, but Gov't trains now went that way. Pass 4 graves, 1 said to have died with feever & the others not men'd [mentioned]. Some cattle gets the scours [a foul-smelling diarrhea] eating beans thrown away. Plenty of articles along the road. No feed till now, go 20 miles [this day]. Shower in the eve'g. Pass Porters rock on the prairie. A small nole rises, & on this stands the rock, & look[s] like an altar. A huge piece stands on 2 collums of stone, & is about 12 ft high. It has several large holes in it.[4]

July 1st [1849]. Road gravel, hard, & hilly. We assend a tremendeous high hill. It commands a view over the surrounding country for 100 miles to the north, & to the west [southwest] rises tall Larimie Peek, black & blue. Some discussion about the white spots seen on it looking like snow, between one elevation & the

3. Warm Spring is often mentioned in overland diaries as a bathing spot. The descriptor "warm" (ca. 70° F) is relative to the frigid water in the nearby North Platte River. The spring is about two and a half miles west of Guernsey.

4. The rock designated Porter's Rock today is about seven crow-miles west-northwest of Guernsey on private land. It bears no resemblance to Lorton's description or sketch of the rock (see L. Johnson 2010, 46–47), but it does bear 17-inch tall, deeply incised *P* and *R* presumably standing for Porter Rockwell.

peek. Rode a continual succession of hill[s]. The peak apparently touching the clouds. [View to] the north shows the chain of Black Hills as they run. The bed of Nebraska [North Platte] slopes down in bet'n bluffs, & the bright sun shining on their submits [summits] gives a fine view.[5]

We again decend as if in a deep abbys [abyss], but gradual to a small creek running over gravel. This is the first water for our cattle sence morn'g & no feed. Quarrel between the officers, capt. & pilot. Dissatisfaction about the camp'g & with the pilot. 1 grave on this creek. We put on ahead & wont go back, so 5 waggons of us camps on a little rivilet. Good springs but little grass [Heber's Spring in Clayton 1983, 60, 62]. We put in Mrs Taylor as capt.[6] Walk some over sandy places & up high hills. Pine. Plenty of pieces of "quartz." Some has the appearance of gold in it.

Talk of a split in the comp. Talk of leaving [Thomas] Gordon on the prairie by his mess.[7] Rovers take it up & the greatest part of the comp. agree to take him a long for his 3 oxen. There is a lot of base unfeeling wreaches in the comp'y. Some [others] are against going on Sunday.

2 dead oxen on the road. Saddles, stoves, bacon, & trumpery by the rode side. Plenty of rain where we camp. We have a shower nearly every night on the Black Hills & hardly any dew. Plenty of ravens where we camp. Grave near where we camp.

July 2d. Us 3 wagons start alone 1 hour before the rest. Assend a very high hill which commands a fine view.[8] Rode gravelly, wears the tires near thro'.[9] Intersect the other road [river route variation on the right (south) bank of the North Platte [Franzwa 1999, maps C31, C37]. A man on ahead sick with the cholera. See 2 graves. Find stuck up on boards all along the names & dates of other comp [that have] passed. Pioneers [company] passed today. Finleys [Findley's] Oquawka comp passed June 7th.[10] Oscaloosa & Dr Wells comp passed. We find these beautiful lines adressed to the Dr [Ira Wells] who was behind & in the hot

5. *Nebraska* is an Otoe Indian word for "flat water" and was used on early maps for the Platte River. French trappers called it *Platte*, or "plate."
6. Twice Lorton says Mrs. Taylor, not Mr. Taylor, is captain of their five-wagon subdivision, indicating this is probably not a mistake.
7. On June 19, Lorton recorded that someone named "Boyd" fell off his wagon tongue and "both wheels run over his back & leg—very badly hurt." Boyd may have been Thomas Gordon's middle name or nickname.
8. The grade up the Horseshoe Creek bluffs was grueling: Thomas Bullock (June 8) said it was "the steepest and most difficult hill yet seen on our route" (1997, 184, 184n37).
9. The "tire" of a wagon wheel is the metal running surface. Locking the rear wheels on steep grades abraded the tires, thus wearing them thin.
10. This was the train Lorton had signed up to travel with in February. It arrived in the "Gold Diggings" August 12 (*Oquawka [IL] Spectator*, October 31, 1849). Lorton arrived six *months* later! Dr. Wells's wagon had left the train at the Elkhorn River.

days had to turn out some of his oxen. "The Dr gave to[o] big a pill, & run his train against the hill. The Oscaloosa "sorked [corked?] his tail & far ahead of him doth sail."

Find the name of a Como man on [a] board. I walk up all the steap hills today.[11] Put our cattle out in a low valley near a good spring. Rovers comes up to us & we give them a rich repast on bread & milk. We leave on a board: "The celebrated comp. of Own-hookers ate bread & milk here, accompynied by a numerous retinue of visitors. Mrs Taylor, Capt."[12]

We go off the road 2 miles & camp on La Bonte River [about 7 miles due south of Douglas, Wyoming]. This river is small, fringed by tall brush, & cedar box trees.[13] On each side tall hills slope up, all destitute of grass & covered with wild sage. 4 persons sick with the diareah. Think it is the milk that is injurious. Leave the cattle out all night.

July 3d. Road very dusty. Pass thro' hills of red sand & Red Ochre, hills of plaster & chalk, pile of stones & rock in a pyramidical form 100 ft high. Lots of elk horns fastened to heads. Some were 4 feet from head to tip. Up rocks, steep gravel hills, down vallies, ravines, & decent[s]. Hard day on cattle. Every thing covered with dust. No graves to day. 4 dead oxen, & 1 lame, 1 by the road. 5 mule packers pass us, 5 mules apiece. Large packs on their backs, buffalo robes [for] blankets. Run part [of] the time. Climb up steeps very readily, & frighten Capt Haynes teams. They [the packers?] have goggles on their eyes & green gause, to guard against [dust].

Several alkali holes. Our wagon runs into a tree. Have to hitch them [the oxen] to the hind axel. Cattles feet tender. [I] walk up all the steep hills, leg getting quite smart. Chase a buffalo out of a ravine close by the road. Lumbers up the ravine & over the hills. Boys after him & shoot him. See 3 large black bears, a mountain goat upon a steep precipice. Fire once & shoot him in the hind Qr. Fire a 2d & carry away his lower jaw. Fire a 3d to his fore sholder & down he tumbles to your feet. Bring 2 Qrs into camp. It is as large as an elk. Get in camp with it after dark.

11. Lorton's cousin David Cairnes was in the Como, Illinois, Company about two weeks ahead of Lorton. Finally, Lorton's foot (injured June 9) was healing. His walking may have been necessary to lighten the wagon on hills.

12. The "Own-hookers" name appears to have belonged to the small subdivision Lorton finds himself in. They were fortunate to still have a cow producing milk.

13. Junipers were commonly, but incorrectly, called cedars. The "cedar box" trees were either Utah juniper (*Juniperus osteosperma*) or Rocky Mountain juniper (*Juniperus scopulorum*). Lorton probably equated the aroma properties of this juniper with eastern red cedar (*Juniperus virginiana*), whose aromatic property ostensibly protected woolen garments from wool-eating moth larvae. Actually, the cedar box's tight construction prevented moths from getting in to lay their eggs.

FIGURE 21. Ayres Bridge. Cephas Arms named this natural stone bridge in honor of A. S. Welch in 1849. It is on La Prele Creek southwest of Douglas, Wyoming, in Ayres Natural Bridge Park. Photo by LeRoy Johnson.

Camp on La Parele River [La Prele Creek]. In the night have a grand jubele. Fire 2 rounds of Fu de joy [a rifle salute], & 1 grand volley of rifle[s], revolvers, & musketry. Load an old musket heavy. Set a slow match & burst her.[14] Beautiful moonlight night. Think of N. Y. & the preparation there about this time.

The La Parele River empties in to the Platte & is a right smart stream for a small one. Some parts are fringed with tall scrubbery & underbrush & runs thro' deep ravines till it ends on bottom land on the north where we camp in a valley, & [it has] black berries. Bluffs rise very roleing on the south & assending on the north. Drive the cattle 2 miles on[to] scant feed. Have guard all night. [They] take their buffalo skins & lie down on the ground to sleep while the relief watches. Party of black snake Indians camped up in the hills. Indians keep away from the road, afraid of the cholera. Cold night—almost friezes. No frost on a/c of no dews. There is some large trees on the La Parele. Just above, it passes under a bluff, forming a subteraneous passage.[15]

14. The men began their Fourth of July celebration early. The "old musket" was likely a blunderbuss—a large-bore firearm with a flared muzzle, highly effective when fired at point-blank range. A slow match is "a cord of combustible material (saltpeter, lead acetate, and lye)" (Russell 1957, 355).

15. Cephas Arms described today's Ayers Bridge as "a natural curiosity in the shape of a natural bridge.... We have christened it Welch's Bridge in honor of one of our company," Adonijah Strong Welch (in Cumming 1985, 49–50). Welch was one of the Rovers from Michigan (for more on Welch, see Johnson and Johnson 2017, 22–30). It has a 100-foot span with the opening about 50 feet wide by 30 feet high. Lorton did not hike upstream to see this wonder since he was still convalescing from his foot injury.

July 4th. The birth day of our American independence. Start late on account of our cattle grazing 3 miles off & very poor feed at that. I walk on ahead 2 miles limping along & by that time get tired & wait for the team. Road tremendous dusty up hill & down dale, round bluffs, hills &c. The dust has a curious & obnoxious smell made still more so by the mixture of manure. At dinner time we stop on a creek of clear water.[16] A few comp. lay camped along the stream, having driven their cattle off dozens of miles to pick up some grass & recruit. So our cattle has to make a meal on water as usual. Several teams going back on a/c of the scarcity of grass. Pritty gloomey prospects, but we are determined to go on till we cant go any further.

Near night we strike the Platte after an absence of 80 miles [five miles southeast of present Glenrock, Wyoming], & we find ourselves over the Black Hills.[17] Over the whole dist' it is destitute of grass with the exception of little spots found between the tops of the hills, tho' nearly all of the surface is covered with wild sage. It grows in thick bunches about the size of a potato hill. It grows to the hight of 18 in. or 2 ft. Its branches which are bushey, serve as first rate fuel, they being woody & dry. Its leaves are a light sage col [color], & are tollerable dry. Cactus grows pritty plentiful here, & the flowers peculiar to these hills are the larkspur, a tall, ult[r]a blue flower that strings along a jucy stem, all on the out side & would make a great & rare garden plant. Pinks of a singular ragged form abounds, & pink flowers of the same discription as the blue ones above.

Tho' the hills cover a wide surface, yet a chain high & peeked, runs as far as the Platte in the same direction as the Rockey Mountains. These are black, with here & there white spots which I think are plaster or white sand stone, similar to what I have seen below. A constant fogy blue hugs the mountains.[18] These hills must form part of the Gt. Am. Desert. The animals found here are the mountain goat, the [bighorn] sheep, the black tail deer, the buffalo, & the black bear. Some antelope, 1 bear, 2 buffalo, 2 goats, 4 sheep was killed today. This is a barren district & the gravel is injurious to cattle's feet. As we decend to the bottom we meet a small comp. going back discouraged, selling some oxen & provisions &c. They had only been to Deer Creek [near today's Glenrock].

On the river we see a No. [number] of ferries. These are mostly owned by the Mormons. The govt. train built a raft of hollow logs & sold it to the next comp. for 30 dol. & by that means it is transferred from 1 to the other. Yet the Mormons

16. Today's Box Elder Creek. On July 26, 1842, Frémont (1970a, 238) said this spot was "a handsome stream, called *La Fourche Boisée*.... Five miles further we made our noon halt, on the banks of the Platte" (see also Clayton 1983, 64).
17. At Deer Creek the train reassembled, after splits along the way, and ferried the North Platte together. On July 4, Israel Lord (1999, 48) says, the "Knoxville company came in; forty wagons and one hundred twenty seven men."
18. The "fogy blue" is photochemical smog converted from ponderosa pine and Utah juniper hydrocarbons by sunshine and ozone (Manahan 2000, 355–56, 384).

will soon buy that to[o] & charge 3 dolls a team as usual. The train taking the back track will take all letters for 10 cts.

24 of the govt. troops have deserted & are now up on a high mountain bidding defiance to the whole train. We observed a smoke up on that mountain for 2 or 3 days, & did not know what to make of it. Some thought it a new volcano. They [the deserters] keep this smoke [so] that other[s] that are agoing to desert may know they are there.[19] Several of them have gone on a head to the gold diggings. The officers use them ha[r]d & they wont stand it. They enlisted for 3 years & say they did'nt agree to build forts. 3 of the troop in attempting to swim their horses acrost got drownded with their riders in the swift current. 1 man doing the same thing to day came near getting drowned, & was nearly gone when they got him on the flat [boat] which was crossing at the time. A Mormon that owns 1 of the ferries says he has crossed 16,00 [1,600] teams sence May at $3.00 a team, & he has bot $900.00 worth of provisions for the Mormons from emegrants. He came from Salt Lake this spring & now wants to sell out. He says grass is scarce but he can find enough in places. There has been 9 men drowned at this ferry this season. They cross here on a/c of grass on the other side, & above cross back. We camp on Deer Creek on some fine grass that had been eaten off close.[20] This is a most beautiful place, a clear pure water murmuring over the fine gravel bed, the tall & stately trees, the green bushes, the birds singing sweetly, the numerous comp. camped in the vicinity, the white tents, the curling smoke as it assends amonge the branches from the campfires. We drive our cattle up stream 10 miles to feed. Men take buffalo [robes] on horse[s] & stay till morning when they are releived by others. The Pioneer mule train have their mules feeding 5 miles up & others with out number, all waiting to recruit, & cross the ferries, of which there are 2 near.

In the eve'g of 4th the Pioneers are heard blazing away for dear life, & numerous other comp. A man that has served in Brittan, Cuba & Cannada mustered us all out with our firearms upon the laun & delivered a 4th July adress. He said he felt proud to find Am. cittizens celebrating the glorious birth day of independence, even here in the wild desert. Says he, you have heard of the elephant, you may see it on your jorney to Cal. but when he throws out his trunk tell him you have thro' [thrown] out a great many trunks since you started. We then fired a feu de joy by the whole comp.

19. The deserters knew the army would pursue them; thus, it is unlikely they maintained a smoke signal pinpointing their location. This was probably a smoldering snag (dead tree) ignited by lightning.

20. Frémont camped here the night of July 26, 1842, and favorably described the locality where Deer Creek empties into the North Platte River: "Here was an abundance of rich grass" and the stream was "well timbered with cottonwood of an uncommon size" (Frémont 1970a, 238). Many of these large cottonwoods were felled to make barges to ferry emigrant wagons across the river.

Then we had a speach by prof. Welch. He stood on a box & addressed us in a very eloquent manner & when he had done [we gave] 3 chears & another fue. All the while the welkin rang with the shout of musketry from the other camps. We then loaded & fired a volley. The [Iowa] Rangers then marched up, & turning an angle near us fired as they turned sepparately. We were then collected in a circle & saluted them with 3 hearty cheers & fired a salute. We then went into a committee of the whole to invite the Rangers to join in the eve'g jollification. Our commander pro tem addressed [them] & recd a reply with 3 deafening cheers & swinging of hats. Our bugle then sounded forth with spirit, when we all formed in one line & fired. We then proceeded to the Oscaloosa & Batavia comp. & were joined by them. In all we had several hundred all in our lines, fireing round after round, with a sentiment in between. One was, "Washington! It shall be a pass word even in the wilderness." 3 cheers for Old Zach—President of the U. S.[21] For our sweet hearts & wives. 2 chears for the Knox Comp. We then fired a gun for every state in the union & a volley for Cal. & the gold diggings. In this salute one of the Rovers [Peter P. Acker] got a thumb shot off, [his gun firing] premature. The fireing kept up till a late hour, & then the violin was brot out & a cotillion commenced on the green. We smoked cigars & drank lemon syrup & [ate] antelope meat. Our fourth [of July] dinner was rice & milk.

July 5th. Lay up all day to recruit. Teams all the time crossing. I do my washing down at the creek, a romantic place. All along you see men & women washing, & the bushes covered with clothes. On the west is a beautiful coal grove [groove?]. Here we bot a blacksmith forge [and] anvil & dig plenty of coal over the creek.[22] We also burn charcoal [in a] pit. Here we have to have tires set on a/c of the heated sand acted on the iron & timber. Here they shoe oxen, make nails, spikes, bolts & refit wagons. Charge 3 doll for shoeing oxen, & for setting tire. Captain [John R.] Parker is our blacksmith. He was appointed to go to Nauvoo to settle [anti-Mormon] difficulties, & turned jack Mormon.[23]

The Canton boys split from us. We find on the ground first rate pickle pork, & use some. The Tennesee robbers camp near us. Capt. Baxter returns from

21. President Zachary Taylor was inaugurated March 5, 1849, and died in office the following year on July 9, 1850. He had two nicknames: "Old Zac" and "Old Rough and Ready."
22. These coal beds were mentioned by Mormons immigrating to Great Salt Lake Basin (Bullock 1997, 188). The surface veins are the antecedents of the present strip mines in the Glenrock area. A few miles north, the PacifiCorp energy company closed the Dave Johnson Mine in 2000 after 42 years of strip-mining. During the life of the mine, they extracted "104 million tons of coal used to generate electricity" (PacifiCorp 2010).
23. In the 1800s, the term *Jack-Mormon* was used by residents of Jackson County, Missouri, to describe nonmembers of the Mormon Church in Clay County who sympathized with the plight of the saints. Today, the term describes members of the LDS Church who are lukewarm in their commitment to living by their gospel principles (Garr, Cannon, and Cowan 2000, 563; see also Morgan 1947, 401).

cattle search after an absence of 2 weeks, with out any knowledge of their whereabouts. They are gone. Poor feed ahead, teams small & run down, no feed, necks sore, feet tender, & loads heavy, late in the season, great croud of emegration, high mountains to pass at an early season or winter in the mountains. Great many get discouraged & think we can't go thro'. Some think of wintering at Salt Lake. Report says they [the Mormons] have no more [food] than they want them selves. Things look rather black, & stout hearts fail. Still, I think we can go it & mean to keep on till we cannot go any further & then go down in some valley, kill bear & other animals, or else if our cattle can find no feed, kill them, & foot it thro' in the spring.

[July] 6th. Take our wagons down to the ferry by hand & ferry to an island.[24] Our cattle are 12 miles off. Buy lame ox for 12 doll to match our Brin. Think of throwing away some provisions. 1 man drowned yesterday & another to day at the lower ferry. We get ours all acrost in safety. Our boat is composed of 4 log canoes fastened to gether. Here the stream is very rapid & must run at the rate of 12 miles an hour. Oars are fixed & when towed up & the load on, the helmsman steers & rowers pull for the other shore with all dispatch, till they reach a reef or bar, far below on the other side. Men hall it up in the same manner to row it back, by waiding thro' the water above the bar. Here the water may be only ancle deep in one spot & the next a hole over your head. It is amusing to see them go in of a suddent. We then take the wagons to the river bank by hand. We raise tent & I make supper in a jiffy, & boil tea with [thrown] of[f] ox yokes, &c. Plenty of things thrown away, first rate axes, waggons. Tis amusing to read the poetry, the prose, the names, the sayings, the advises given, the mottoes, upon the trees & upon boards posted, from comp. passed. But, the night was beautiful.

After supper I take the dish cloth & dishes out doors to wash, for the bright moon was just riseing directly over Old Nebraska reflecting her silver rays & sparkling upon her rippling bossom. The tall dark trees of Deer Creek waved in the gentle breze on her right, & the indestinct out lines of the Black Hills, releived the star spangled sky. On the reef stood in a row numbers of wagons that had not yet been brot to the banks, casting a dark shade beneath in the water. The Arabs were now ferriying, & a large fire sparkled under the shade of a small groop of cotton wood on the other side. After a hard days work most of our party had taken their blankets & wrapped themselves, & layed down beneath some bushes on a sand bank, & all was still except the occasional curse from the ferrimen or the splashing of an oar. Our tent set beneath a groop of cotton woods, & near one that had lately been fallen, on the edge of the bank,

24. From the island, they hitched up the wagons and forded a narrow, shallow portion of the river to the north shore. Because they were crossing in July, the river was below crest, so such a scenario was possible.

& commanding a fine look down the river. T'was a lovely sight & a scene for the artist, captivating in the extreme, & in deed I felt so, for as I wrung the old dish cloth thro' my hands, I would cast a glance at pale Cynth[i]a as she travelled in the heaven, & a person not very near could distinctly hae [hear] sentences something like, "Clem Brown," "Halk fly high," & the "Boatmens dance," coming from my lips.

[July 7]. We start on about noon, thro' sand hills & gravel, dust blowing. Pass a great many dead & abandoned cattle. Had just passed an ox with blind eye feeding on some beans & were going along the rivers bank, & see an ox over the river feeding. Thought it might have strayed away & be a good one from appearance. [Henry] Ward asked Jno [John] from N. Y. city to go along & he would swim the river & drive him over.[25]

They put out & the current carried them down some 100 yds on a bar. They drove the ox to the shore & swam him acrost. John jumped in & Ward soon after. Ward kept going down stream & didn't gain any. Jno reached the bank, & Henry kept still going down. Ward now began to get frightened & said to [John D.] Thompson & another, help me boys for I cant make the shore. They told him to then swim back. He then made back still going down stream till his head went under. Every body stood on the banks trembling with fearful forbodings. He arose & again went down. They see he was drounding & hollowed, send in a horse. The third time he went down & a cry arose, he is lost. For a few minutes there was a fearful, ancious suspense. Every bodies heart seamed to choke them. At length his head arose from the water. He stood in shallow water, much exhausted. He walked up. He is saved, and a shout arose from the crowd. He did not attempt to come over again. Shannon put on a life preservr, tied his [Ward's] clothes on his sholders & swam over & back, while Ward made for the ferry. He was seized with the cramp in 1 leg. The stag [ox] was found to be good for nothing & the wolves has eaten pieces out of his belly so we left him.

The ferry man said 40 wagons had been sunk in the river while ferrying. Some had been got out & others were lost from sight in the mighty current. 2 more men were drownded to day by riding on horses with "laretts," martingales, saddle, holsters, & equipments all on.[26] It is said no man ever rode a horse over in this current but are always lost. The water running down so swiftly from the mountains carries every thing before it.

Such a dusty windy sandy day I never see. This road for miles ahead is 1 complete desert of dry land. It is so hot that it causes the iron tires to expand, the fellows & spokes to contract, so that what may be considered first rate wheels

25. Henry Ward was in Lorton's mess and related to the Kelloggs.

26. This is a retrospective comment; the two privates in the Mounted Riflemen en route to Oregon Territory drowned on July 4.

fall apart. One [iron] tire run clear of[f] to day & some wheels had to have an extra spoke in between to keep them to gather. We sell the ferry for half price $15 to one of our mess.[27] He kept [his?] poney & intends to ferry a wheek & then overtake us. Tis dark when we haul up under some cotton woods, & camp in a sand heap [east of today's Casper, Wyoming]. Had been a little grass on the bottom but was eaten off & trampled down by the thousands of cattle. Whole groves of trees cut down to brouse cattle on.[28] All the cooking opperations, & dishes, & in fact every hole & corner, nook & crevise, had been penetrated by this piercing wind & dust, & had to all be washed over again before we could [eat]. Plenty of provisions, chests, boxes, bedstead & trunks, broken wagons to make fire of, so we cook bacon, tea, &c., & so have supper. W[h]eather the dust we ate make [may] be considered a desert or not, I wont say. One thing is certain, it came from a desert, stoping up your eyes when you are just aiming for the peach preserves, & geting in between your teeth when you go to grind a piece of delicious bacon, all so fat & greesey. All tired & worn out with the dust & fatigue. Several Kentuckey, Tennesee, & Missisippi comp. camp near us, also 1 from the state of N. Y. Plenty of good waggons, lbs of lead, bags of shot, axes, chains, tobacco, pickled pork, beans, bacon first rate, coats, pants, shoes laying by the way. Dragoons [the deserters] camped up in the mountains. They come down & steal mules & horses.

[Sunday, July] 8th. Start late. Hundreds of dead oxen laying by the rode side. See on tree, "Praise God for our lives & our health." Pass cliffs of brown stone, coal, &c. I take horse, the wind blowing a hurrycane. Thinking to cut off some [distance], I assended a verry high peek.[29] Here the winds houl, whistles & moan, & [as] I emerged above the top, the sever gusts came so suddently that it blew me & my horse back & I had to dismount & lead him down a[s] fast as possible. This wind blowing down between the Black Hills, commences regularly about sunrise, & subsides generly [at] sunset. This is the same the whole year round & which is one cause why the soil is so sterile. Nothing of any h[e]igh[t] could stand. We have to take off our wagon cover, & we with difficulty stem the steady current of air. There is not the least dew so that we just spread down our blankets & breathe free with the mountain air to fan us to sleep, & the bright moon & the

27. They sell to one of the Bartholomew brothers, probably Luzerne, since he is older and appears more independent throughout.
28. Rufus B. Sage described, in the early 1840s, how Indians climbed large cottonwood trees to collect bark for their horses (Sage 1982, 135). Quaking aspen (*Populus tremuloides*), a close relative of cottonwood, is also "good forage for cattle" as is willow (genus *Salix*). "Willows provide one of the principal sources of browse on many of the western mountain ranges...willows are fair forage for cattle" (Forest Service 1937, B111, B141).
29. This was likely the high bluffs north of the North Platte River, east of present Casper, Wyoming.

twinkling stars to light our bed chamber, the great canopy of "heaven." There is scarcely any rain, which is probably owing to there being no evaporation, & [the country] is only water[ed] by passing cloudes.

I see some green spots & ride to them, desend a basen. Green grass & 2 alkali lakes now dried up [Pratt Lakes, six miles east of Casper]. It is white several feet deep, & you could see where the buffalo had trod in it while soft. These alkali lakes causes the death of a great many cattle. The grass any wheres in the vicinity is covered with this saleraetus, & indeed the whole earth is impregnated with it. The dust blowing on your lips makes them sore. Every body has sore lips. See mule laying side the road sick from drinking alkali.

The Rovers leave us to day.[30] 1 wagon up set & some broken. Cross several high Sandy bluffs & at night fall (it being the Sabath) we decended to the Platte bottom & camped on a point. Here the river is filled out with islands, & a great many cattle drove on them. A little below rises a very high hill 200 ft above the water, with projecting [parts]. I hobbled to these cliffs to rest myself after a hard days fatigue. Fired stones in the river. A little below, there was a man found drifted upon a bar. He was burried by a comp.

In the eve'g the moon rises up from amonge the trees on the islands & casts a silver streak across the stream which is very wide here & has a number of channels. The wind had lulled the water to smoothness & appeared to invite us in. We look on the pritty scene. Saw several objects float down, a tea pot for instance. I couldn't wait for my leg to get any well'er, so I stripped, jumped in, swam backwards down the swift current, floundered about a little, washed, tried to swim up current but could'nt.

[July] 9th. Start out ahead of teams a few miles & overdo my leg, so I ride all day. The same wind blowing as usual. Take in water at noon & leave the Platte [near the Mormon ferry, west edge of today's Casper]. Dead oxen with out number. See 1 with brand on his horns & recognized [him] as belonging to the Rovers & was lost in our "stampeed" thus showing that our oxen are on ahead, thus showing how they are rushing things & running the cattle to death. The ox has probably been dead 10 days.

Pass thro' deep ravines & long hills till night. We go 5 miles out of our way to get to the Platte again [at Bessemer Bend], by passing down a wide ravine [Poison Spider Creek]. Here is several boiling springs mineral & otherwise. Here are alkali resavors, poison springs. These are different in quality. Some will take more of it to produce death than others. Even the Platte is impregnated with it, but we drink it. Cattle will drink it but we drive them to the river, & then drive them back to the pasture which is tolerable good.

30. The Lorton mess catches up with the Rovers by July 12, when Lorton speaks of Welch, one of them.

See a large black bear. Here we find the sage chicken, & kill some with clubs. They eat sage, inhabit the sage & are the p[r]ecise collor of the sage, & go a good deal in flush & are hard to desern from the plant. They are larger than the prairie chicken.[31]

[July] 10th. Lay over to recruit our cattle. See bears, panthers, 5 mountain goats & sheep. Killed 2 antelope, 1 Black tail'd deer, flocks of geese. Have singing party. Government train has a horse "stampeed," 40 of which are lost in the mountains. Swim our cattle over the river to keep them from the "alkali."

[July] 11th. Still laid over. Go fishing in Platte & catch a fine lot. Cut grass & make hay to carry along. Kill 2 Black tail bucks. Several [*illegible*] over the river. [Some men] make a small raft & carry guns clothes & amunition & swim themselves [across]. Some like to get drowned. Warm all day, & at night fall the east blackens up & the north wind breathes air only a few degrees above "Zero" & every appearance of snow, & continues so all night. Always a sure sign when you see bears, panthers howl & beasts of prey prowl about the hills. Shoe our Bison ox.

[July] 12th. We leave the Platte for the last time, & take a near cut for the road. We find our selves headed by deep ravines & go around them till noon. We gain the road & camp. While eating dinner an enormous buffalo comes walking leasurely down the hills. Every boddy now prepared themselves for sport. As little noise was made as possible. Footmen commenced going around him & horses galloped around the bluffs, & I guess the old bull must have been near sighted for he did not appear to [see] the camp till he got within 400 yds of us, & then he stood still an instant as if considering what to do, & then he cocked up his bushey tail & commenced lumbering up the hills & down the ravines.

The horsemen had now rounded him & came on to him rather abruptly, so much so that his honor the bullephant dashed on to Proff [Welch], who was mounted on a fine black charger, tearing with his enormous horns the hind quarters of the horse oppen.[32] So suddent had been the interview that he had no chance to fire. Several fired on him but he escaped to a mountain near. Proff thought he had seen the bulephant. Several bears seen to day, but the sportsmen were affraid to fire, for fear of an attack.

The road passes thro' "Rockey Passage" [Rock Avenue]. This is a curious freak in nature, & were it not that the rocks are so large a person could not be convinced it was the hand of nature. The rocks form a complete wall, or

31. Sage chickens, today's greater sage-grouse (*Centrocercus urophasianus*), are still found in the area.

32. The fictional bullephant is mostly bull and a little elephant.

FIGURE 22. Willow Spring, the first good water and forage between the North Platte and Sweetwater Rivers. Photo by LeRoy Johnson.

passage running on both sides of the road tho' the south wall is not so perfect. The north wall runs some 5 hundred feet nearly in a straight line. The top runs from 5 to 50 ft high, & is in some places peeked. The outter surface is smothe & perpendicular, assending & decending hills in its course. In 1 place the wall is double & very perfect, & what appears more curious, there is no stone or rocks any wheres near this passage that does not form the wall, with the exception of pieces that have fallen down, & directly under, the ground is not rockey but rises from the road. On the back it slopes off. While looking at the number of men perched upon the various pinicles, a yong buffalo calf ran up the hill & was shot at but escaped.

Pass some alkali springs & holes [Poison Spring Creek]. See 10 head of oxen laying to gether which had died by drinking water from the poison springs in the vacinity. See three broken down oxen near this place. Find copper oar [ore]. After dark we hall up at Willow Springs where we could hardly find a place to set tent, for the thrown away rubbish & piles of bacon.[33] Feed our cattle hay & turn them over the hill.

[July] 13th.[34] Cattle scattered all over creation & looking for them. Have sage hen for breakfast, large as a turkey. Shoot marmots. 10 o'clock & cattle not half

33. This free-flowing spring is the lowest in the draw that leads to Prospect Hill, today's Ryan Hill, a mile southwest (see Clayton 1983, 66; Haines 1981, 192–93). Mountain willows (*Salix planifolia*) have been extirpated at the spring, but we found a few specimens in a marsh half a mile up the draw.

34. The 3 is written over a 2.

FIGURE 23. Lorton sketch of Independence Rock. He wrote in lower part of sketch: "W.B. LORTON/JULY 13 '49." Courtesy of The Bancroft Library.

found. There are several mineral springs around. Find all but 1 cow. We start on, 3 teams & "caral" on Grease Wood Creek [today's Fish Creek]. Sage here is 6 ft high & wood as thick as your leg. Crackey comes in camp & stays all night.[35]

[July 14.] 13th.[36] Cattle found with difficulty. Plenty of teams near us. Lots of antelope found near spring & killed. At noon we arrive on Sweet Waters [Sweetwater River]. Sweet Water Mountains now appear in the shape of huge piles of rocks. 3 large salaeratus lakes near. Some had entirely evaporated & others soft, & others with water. Some when dry covers acres of ground & in wet season extends 10 miles square. When the sun shines upon the surface it presents the appearance of snow. We next come to Independence Rock.

The rock rises perpendicular on the river side with enormous craggs. Large loose rocks hang ready to fall & crush the passer. Deep seams & fissures run through this enormous mass of stone, while the deep crivaces, chissled up & painted with hundreds of names, & the outer surface covered with 1000s. It is

35. Someone called Crackey is also mentioned by Edward Doty (1872): "Crackey is ded" (also in J. Johnson 2018, 186).

36. The 3 is written over a 4. This is Lorton's second July 13 entry; it is really July 14. Lorton's dates are off by one day and remain so until July 25. He correctly records the date on his sketch of Independence Rock, "Knox co comp/pass July 14th/1849." However, he dates his own inscription "July 13. '49."

indeed a curiosity, made still more so by the stationary directory or Register. Como Co. passed June 29, 1849, David Cairnes Comp.[37] It is about 300 ft high. I climbed up the rugged assent & left my address in the crivaces for future passers. The Rock rises up from the ground, which is leval, & is separate from any of the many rockey peeks & jets of stone. Amonge the thousands of names painted & chissled on this rock, perched upon a high cragg appeard L. S. [L. W.] Hastings 1842, the author. From the top can be seen a large alkali lake [Piaya Lake]. It is the effect (to all appearance) of volcanic eruptions, & the whole scenery around as you follow the river exhibits a volcanic country.[38]

The Sweet Water River heading near the S[outh] Pass runs between 2 distinct chains, both being a part [of, but] diverging from the Rockey Mountains. The north chain is called the S. water mountains [now, Sweetwater Rocks or Granite Hills], & is 1 continued mass of rock thrown promiscuously upon heaps for 5 & 6 hundred feet, many peeked like the crater [cone] of a vol[cano]. Near Ind. rocke we ford the river which is 50 ft broad.

37. Lorton last saw Cairnes in Savannah, Missouri.

38. The country surrounding Independence Rock has a superficial appearance of being volcanic, but it is not.

CHAPTER 6

Independence Rock to Salt Lake City

Background

Beyond Independence Rock, there were three more goals, or points of progress, on the trek to California—South Pass, Fort Bridger, and either Salt Lake City or Fort Hall. The travelers were now following up the Sweetwater River. Even the name sings in the soul; it promises good water and grass all the way to the roof of the continent.

About six miles southwest of Independence Rock is Devils Gate. One of Lorton's best sketches depicts Devils Gate with the angel Gabriel blowing his horn over a burning crown that descends between the rocky walls. The river-cut gorge is 400 feet wide at the top but only 30 feet across at water level. Eons ago the Sweetwater River basin was filled with detritus from the antecedents of today's surrounding mountains. As the river slowly deepened its bed, it encountered a massive granite formation—today's Devils Gate Ridge. The stubborn river was not laterally deflected; instead it cut through this granite barrier and carved Lorton's "demonic majesties gate."

Lorton's comment that the height of the gate is "400 feet on each side" comes from Clayton's Mormon trail guide (1983, 70), and different heights are found in the early literature. However, Craig Bromley, archeologist for the Bureau of Land Management at Lander, Wyoming, supplied these data: "The very highest point on the east side [right bank] of the Gate is 361 feet above the river. This point is about 65 feet back from the edge. The highest point [also] on the east side of the Gate where you can almost look down onto the river is 353 feet above the river. This point is about 15 feet back from the edge" (Bromley, pers. comm., December 9, 2013).

About 25 miles west of Devils Gate, Lorton describes a solitary geological feature that looks like "a house partly broken down, hollow inside" just south of U.S. Highway 287, not far from the river. It is now called Castle Rock, one of several natural features by that name in Wyoming. In the same area, but north of the river, Lorton describes a mountain that attracts his attention that he names "Lortons peek."

After numerous crossings of the Sweetwater and a gradual increase in elevation, the train reaches its next important goal—South Pass (see Bagley 2014). Crossing South Pass was a disappointment to many emigrants. They expected, as did Lorton on July 25, "to see a deep pass between high rocks & only capable of admitting a single wagon," but instead found wearisome rolling hills.

People have been curious about the elevation of South Pass for 175 years. *New* South Pass (where State Route 28 crosses the Continental Divide) is 7,550 feet in elevation. *Old* South Pass (a little over two miles to the southeast) is 7,412 feet as calculated by the United States Geological Survey (Bagley 2014, 24). *Old* South Pass is commemorated with a rock monument a little over one-tenth mile west of the Continental Divide. Early travelers gave various elevations.[1]

Lorton describes a death and burial beside the Big Sandy River he thought mountain fever might have caused, and Captain Haynes suffered from a temporary delirium before reaching South Pass, possibly from the same ailment. While crossing the Rocky Mountians, other emigrants reported symptoms of pain in the head, back, and joints; chills and hot flashes; and general symptoms they lumped as mountain fever (Aldous and Nicholes 1997, 18–23). Altitude sickness, Colorado Tick Fever (not to be confused with Rocky Mountain Spotted Fever), or something in the water are the most likely causes (ibid., 22).

Beyond the summit was Pacific Springs, about three miles southwest of *Old* South Pass and 250 feet lower. The main spring vent is on the bottom of a pond covered with clumps of aquatic vegetation, each clump barely large enough to support a grown person for a few moments. The pond overflows into a small stream only a couple feet wide that flows southwestward seeking the Gulf of California.

About nine miles west-southwest of Pacific Springs, the trail passes a quarter-mile south of Plume Rock, a knob of the Wasatch Formation made from variegated mudstone and sandstone (Franzwa 2007, 195–96). Lorton is one of the few overland diarists who comment on this singular, deeply eroded knob standing out starkly in a flat sea of sagebrush. He compares it to Aladdin's lamp, another example of his whimsical sense of humor. Goldsborough Bruff said, on August 3, 1849, it had "singularly plume-formed projections on top, from the effects of elements" (1944, 1:65, illust. 66 & 398).

A mile and a half west of Lorton's "eastern lamp," he crosses Dry Sandy Creek, and about six miles west of that, he mentions the "junction of Cal. & Oregon

1. Frémont gave 7,490 feet, and Clayton "took a barometrical observation and found the altitude 7,085 feet" (Frémont 1970a, 465, August 13, 1843; Clayton 1983, 72).

roads," also called Parting of the Ways. The left-hand fork heads to Fort Bridger and Salt Lake City; the right-hand fork, commonly called the Greenwood or Sublette Cutoff, went to Fort Hall, in today's Idaho.

Although these names are deeply etched in the literature (Bruff 1944, 1:64; Ware 1972, 26; Kelly and Morgan 1965, 106–7), both "Greenwood Cutoff "and "Sublette Cutoff" are misnomers for this trail. The more accurate name is "Hitchcock Cutoff." In 1844 Caleb Greenwood (ca. 1763–1850) guided the Stephens wagon train (commonly called the Stephens-Murphy-Townsend Party) from Council Bluffs, Iowa, to the Rocky Mountains where his responsibility as guide ended (although he continued as a member of the train).[2] After crossing South Pass, the party camped on Dry Sandy Creek, where "old man [Isaac] Hitchcock was appointed pilot for one day…[because he said] he could take them to Green River by a cut-off that would save a hundred miles' travel" to Fort Hall.[3] After about six miles they came to a point where Hitchcock turned the train directly west across the trackless desert. This *Y* is today's Parting of the Ways. They continued west to Fort Hall from Hitchcock's cutoff, thus avoiding the longer southern swing to Fort Bridger (Stewart 1962, 57–58, 60, 81; Bagley 2010, 223–25).

At the Big Sandy River, Lorton vividly describes the death and burial of J. R. Nelson. Nelson had been hurt and "mortally frightened" in the hill stampede eight days before. A passerby recorded the information Lorton wrote on the headboard and sent it back to the States (see Rasmussen 1994, 96). Lorton was fortunate to have experienced only one burial on the road to Salt Lake City.

The Knox County Company followed the California–Salt Lake City trail southwestward from Green River to its Blacks Fork tributary. Near this stream, a few miles northeast of Fort Bridger, Lorton sat in the shade of what is now called Church Butte (about 12 miles southwest of Granger) to write in his diary.

Lorton provides an excellent description of Fort Bridger and the Indians and traders he meets. He also has quite a conversation with Jim Bridger, who

2. The captain of this party (wagon train) was Elisha Stephens (Kelly and Morgan 1965, 94; Stewart 1953, 32, 41). Contrary to compelling evidence, Stewart (1953, 38) spells Elisha's family name "Stevens."

3. Moses Schallenberger in Foote 1888, 44; in Stewart 1953, 60, 94n10; and in Kelly and Morgan 1965, 106. Schallenberger, a member of the Stephens-Murphy-Townsend Party, was an eyewitness when the party turned off the main trail and created the Parting of the Ways junction. Schallenberger credits the decision for creating this new wagon road to "old man Hitchcock." Apparently, Foote, Stewart, and Kelly and Morgan borrowed this information from a manuscript Schallenberger wrote. Foote (1888, 44) says, "We will follow the…party gathering our facts from Mr. Schallenberger's narrative," and on the following page he says "old man Hitchcock" was their pilot for one day. Stewart contends Foote gleaned about 60 percent of his article from Schallenberger's manuscript.

"was generally considered the ablest hunter, mountaineer and guide of the West" (Chittenden 1986, 1:255). They even discuss the mountain crossings south of South Pass, which again reveals Lorton's wide range of interests. Bridger and Louis Vasquez started building this trading post in 1842 on a beautiful, wide bottom on Blacks Fork. Because of the expansive grassy fields and good water, it became a rendezvous site for Indians and Indian traders as well as a supply stop and place to recruit oxen for the Oregon, California, and Salt Lake travelers.

The next notable landmark after Fort Bridger was Cache Cave. On July 12, 1847, William Clayton and Thomas Bullock were likely the first diarists to record the existence of the cave. Clayton described it as "a cave in the rock about thirty feet long, fifteen feet wide and from four to six feet high." Bullock called it "'Swallows' Cave" because of the numerous swallow nests made of mud attached to the ceiling (Clayton 1973, 291–92; Bullock 1997, 225; see also Kimball 1988, 96–97 and map 7, and Berrett and Anderson 2006, 6:246–54). It is on private land about a mile east-southeast of Interstate 80 exit 187 in Echo Canyon.

After entering Echo Canyon and crossing Weber River, the emigrants faced an arduous climb over the Wasatch Range, where going down was every bit as dangerous as going up. This was the wagon road the Donner Party pioneered in 1846. When nearing Big Mountain Pass, Lorton took time to climb nearby peaks and luxuriate in the astonishing view to the west. His climbing buddy succumbed to a temptation that lurks in the heart of every young man—to roll rocks off a mountain.

Lorton's Journal Continues beyond Independence Rock

[July 14 continued]. After passing thro' rockey passes [Rattlesnake Pass], sandy barren country [for five miles], we camp at "Devils Gate" on the west side.

This is one of dame natures most curious freaks. The river runs dashing & foaming over huge masses of rocks that have been hurled from their native beds. Rocks rise to the hight of 400 feet on each side. The north side is about perpendicular, but the south over hangs its base 25 feet which I ascertained by plumbing it with my eye as I lay on my back, underneath. Near me lay a mountain goat some what fractured, as if it had lately fallen from this awful precipice.[4] It is well known that these goats climb to the highest eminenc[e], & [this one] has probably sliped, in an attempt to scrutinize his demonic majesties gate. The gate reaches 1/4 mile & the river descends 100 feet forming rapids, & three falls

4. Lorton's diary is the only evidence we know that mentions mountain goats living in the Sweetwater River watershed in historic time. Although mountain goats (*Oreamnos americanus*) are native to and still live in the northern Rocky Mountains, they are not currently found in this watershed. Lorton's diary entries on July 4 and 10 make clear he knows the difference between mountain sheep (*Ovis canadensis*) and mountain goats.

FIGURE 24. Lorton sketch. Lorton printed "DEVILS GATE" under the angel. At the bottom is "DEVILS GATE/400 feet high/a passage for the Sw[eetwater]." On the other cliff is "June 16, 1849" and "W.B. Lorto[n]/S. U. B." Courtesy of The Bancroft Library.

FIGURE 25. Devils Gate in 2009, looking northeast. Writes Lorton on July 14: "The river runs dashing & foaming over huge masses of rocks that have been hurled from their native beds. Rocks rise to the hight of 400 feet on each side." Photo by LeRoy Johnson.

over the rock to give terror to the scene. There is an enormous cavern 80 feet deep. In here we found burnt wood, & appearances indicated that the "Crow Indians" had camped there.

Upon firing off a gun the noise is terriffic. It echoes, reechoes, & reverberates along the whole passage, like the laugh of a fiend. There is also a large overhanging table rock on the north which supports the weight above. When you look to the top of this gate to prevent dizzyness you have to clinch the rocks, & thus prevent falling. It is indeed one of Gods noble works, whatever the stain may be upon its name.

Near the top on the south side is [a] large pine, but from below looks like a bush. There is also 3 cedars leaning over the stream, firmly fastened in the crivaces. It is full of wolf dens, the raven inhabits, & owl[s] screech forth their scrill notes. Hideous reptiles lurk around & exhibits their forked prongs to the enthusiast, & lizzards creap around the crumbling fragments. Persons cannot be heard over 10 feet when the water is high. Foaming waters boiling with [will?] pass on till the east pass where the[y] form in to ripples, & finally slumber peacefully along. To pass this we had to wade the river which is not deep except in places, climb over crags, steep places, & run the risk of slipping. In your course, deep seams & fissurs appear in places, & mammoth rocks hang equipoised. Every thing connected with the place is volcanic. In this Gate is the grave of a youth, Richard, died 1847.

The Crow Indians were seen looking from the mountains down upon the camps at night fall & 3 men [were] chased by them. Around here are several mineral & alkali springs. Cold springs by digging down we find ice. Cattle laying dead from alkali. They swell up & burst. The wolves will not eat them.

[Sunday, July 15th, 1849.] 14th [the *4* is written over a *5*]. In the grass of the bottom "Old man" [Edward Kellogg] wakes us up & say—Indians or white men are driving our cattle off to the mountains & [Henry] Ward was on their trail. Wis. [company] camped near us, would not lend us mules or horse[s], so a traveler on horse said he would go & galloped off. We were all up, 6 in all, & armed. Put after them & found them 10 miles off, followed up by about 4 wolves & buffalo rangers. They were driving them up to their dens to kill them at leasure.[5] We soon scattered them & after 20 miles travel reached camp. We hear that last eve'g [July 14] near Ind. Rock & while crossing the ford some loose cattle commenced running which set the whole train in 1 general "stampeed." Waggons were smashed, men knocked down. Canton man broke 2 ribs. Old man [E. Norman] Taylor had his wagon to pass over his boddy, but did not severely injure him. Some [a]head teams unhitched in time to save them selves. I am glad we were absent.

Lay by till near night [still July 15] when we move on 2 miles to better grass. Our comp. goes on 5 miles to day. We entertain 7 of our comp. who had returned

5. The wolves were patiently following the cattle but would soon begin a "rush" and then a "chase" wherein the wolves would wound one of the beasts. The anecdotal notion that wolves would "hamstring" their prey as a mode of attack is not supported by facts (Mech 1970, 200–5, 245).

FIGURE 26. Detail, James Wilkins sketch. "Trail towards South Pass," July 13, 1849. On July 17, Lorton described today's Castle Rock as "a rock perched on a bluff, formed like the walls of a house partly broken down, & hollow inside." WHI Image ID 31294.

from hunting cattle, [& dine] on antelope &c. Have our arms cocked & primed. Keep guard & ready for an attack. Have a grande smoke on my printipus [*principatus*—high point]. Knox comp. lost 2 cattle from alkali tonight. Our cattle some what affected. Pioneer train compel every man to throw away 24 lbs more baggage, first rate clothing, new suits they cut up in ribbins, hundreds of pounds of crushed suggar thrown a[way], spades, kegs of powder blowing up all night. Plenty of waggons left & worn out & broken down cattle by the way. There appears to be a disposition to destroy every thing they leave. Stove[s] are broken, guns are bent, clothes are ripped, & turpintine thrown on sugar. 2 men had caps of fine cloth & the initials of S. M. & T. C., meaning the Saginaw Mereching [Merchandising] & Trading Co. A person wanted to buy them for which they asked cost price, $2. The buyer would give $1.50, but they would not take it, put a stone in each cap & threw it in the river, which the man got out without any trouble, & didn't cost a cent.

[July 16th.] Near daybreak 15th [the 5 is written over a 6] hear great splashing in the water, listen & observe a lot of wolves coming into camp. Fire on them & they disperse. Old giraff ox gone. Wolves probably had a mortgage & now forclosed it. See large salaeratus lake. The edges looks like snow & the in[side] surface like water, but on approaching you can walke over any part. Drove of "mustang" wild horses. Camp on the Sweet Waters, beneath the shade of the mountains, 600 ft high from base. Bets made on time in getting to the to[p]. Done in 20 min. One mass of rocks piled promiscuously upon each other forming pinacles. A person can just be heard from the top, & he looks as small as your hand. Build a large fire on top, of cedars, fire guns off, & such another echoing, clashing & crashing, never broke upon the senses. Bill [Kellogg] finds our cow

FIGURE 27. Lorton's "peek." Today's Lone Mountain, about 10 miles north of the Sweetwater River, is visible from U.S. 287 near Lankin Creek. Writes Lorton on July 17: "Pass some very high mountains & 1 very singular peeke. It is about 10 miles from the rode & about 1200 ft high with hardly a crag. To all appearance smothe & blue rock, so I named it Lortons peek, it haveng no name. It runs up in the shape of a cone." Photo by LeRoy Johnson.

in a train. Ox that we found gives out today & 1 whole team. We throw away 2 Bu [bushels of] Beans.

[July 17th.] I follow the river several miles ahead of the teams, on the 16th [17th], & set up on a large rock writing up my back notes. Lots of goods laying on a camp ground near me, such as shovels, trunk, sea biscuit, bacon, chains, Boxes of soap, yokes, ropes, &c. Pass a rock perched on a bluff, formed like the walls of a house partly broken down, & hollow inside [Castle Rock]. No stone for miles except this. See smoke assending from Crow Indian camp on the S[ou]th mountains.

They had about 100 mustangs grazing, but no Indians could be seen. Pass some very high mountains & 1 very singular peeke. It is about 10 miles from the rode & about 1200 ft high with hardly a crag. To all appearance smothe & blue rock, so I named it Lortons peek, it haveng no name.[6] It runs up in the shape of a cone. We pass thro' mountain passes, cross the river 2 times to day, pass through a mountain pass through which the river mak[e]s its way, & after winding round mountains, camp near mountain & river.

[July 18th.] 17th. Make our way out of the mtn & strike a roleing plain. As we round the rocks a scene [presents itself] varied from that where we had just

6. Lorton's "peek" is today's Lone Mountain, 7,832 feet elevation, about 10 miles northeast of the confluence of Lankin Creek and the Sweetwater River.

passed shut in by rocks & hills. The eternal [snow] caped peeks of the Rockey Mountains [Wind River Range] breaks on our vision in all its grandeur. This is 60 miles off but we could just see their summits 100 miles. Deep gorges are filled with snows & the bright sun throwing his rays at her snow clad hills dazzels the eye. Cross the Sweet Water on our left, go in swimming quite often. In consequence of leaving the Sweet Waters from here for 16 miles, we camped up it [the trail] 2 miles. The other half day where we had good feed, plenty of sage hens. Go guning small bear. Get on his trail & finally over take him. He turned & looked & made of[f]. Fired but took good care not to hit. Lots of antelope. Cooke cruller[s] & doenuts. Lighten our load. Have a good sing in the eve'g.

[July 19th.] 18th. All the morning clouds have hung around the mountains on the south as if storming hard, while the tops protrude above. Pass ice spring 1/4 mile from the rode. Get large cakes of ice.[7] It looks clear, & has a pleasant taste, but there is so much poison mineral around I did not eat much. I go on ahead amonge the sage hills. Almost knock sage hens down with cane.[8] See antelope. See hares [jack rabbits]. They are 2[?] times as large as a rabbit & run like a fawn. See a new reptile of the lizzard species.

While I wrote the above, sitting in the waggon at noon, a "stampeed" occured. That scratch below [a reversed fish-hook pencil mark on the page] was done when they made me start. We halted at dinner time upon a high hill. The snows of the mountains fair to view from its summit. We had all eaten dinner. Some were lying under the waggons assleep. Others set between the wheels, & others in the wagons the same as my self. They say a saddle horse belonging to packers frightened them [the oxen]. The hind teams attached to wagons commenced & as quick as electricity they were all dashing down the steep hill. Capt Talors little boy was run over by waggon & oxen, another had a hand run over, another knocked in the head, another run over the leg, others knocked down, cattle became entangled in chains and wheels, axels broke, wheels [damaged], wheels passed over oxen, & 1 ox was dragged way down the hill under the box with feet up. He had a horn broke off, & otherwise injured. Broken horns lay around, hoofs broken, several rode out the gale in the waggon. Trunks fell out, tubs pans & chains broke. [It was] good for Capt Haynes the cattle broke the chain, he was [still] sick.[9]

7. Ice Spring and Ice Slough (Happy Spring Creek) were often noted by overland diarists. Subterranean water froze in winter and was kept from melting by a couple feet of dense, boggy vegetation. The Oregon-California Trail crossed the slough about 47 crow-miles west of Independence Rock (Franzwa 1982, 139).

8. Lorton is still using a cane to aid his foot injured in the June 9 stampede.

9. By July 19 the Arms–Taylor–Canton–Jayhawker group have caught up with Lorton. Cephas Arms and Lorton both write about the ice spring, the noontime stampede, and the ones following (Arms in Cumming 1985, 59).

A team behind us would have smashed our waggon if [Edward or Luzerne] Bart[holome]w had not frightened them off & thus saved his own life & ours perhaps. They run on every side of the hill. Some [had] on shues & pitched [them] off. They ran some 1 mile, & others to the bottom of the hill. Such dashing pel-mel down such a steep desent is a freightful sight to gaze on when human life is in jeopardy, to say nothing of propperty, & that not more damage is not done & lives sacrificed. I can only account for it, That an all wise Providence looks down on the Knox Co. Comp. with a forbearing eye.

In less than 2 hours after writing the above we had 2 more "stampedes." 1 was caused by a dead ox laying beside the rode. The other was caused by nothing at all. At night while caraling, we could hardly unyoke them & with difficulty & risk of life, they could be held from stampeeding the approaching teams. Enre [Henry Enoe's?] comp. had one at the bottom of the hill where we nooned. Our cattle are all turned out acrost the river but 1 steer just unyoking, impatient for a stampeed, runs away from the teamster carr[y]ing the yoke, & making a terrible noise dashes into the river & is soon in along with the drove, & quick as thought, [they have] sufficient reason for a run, so they all cock up their tails & bound over the valley. At nightfall send guard out, but they all stampeed 2 miles down the river. Drive a few up to camp, but they break [away] as many times as there were minutes, endangering the guards. Try to tie up the few but cant. Get some into the "caral" but it was worth your life to go in. We tie up [those we can] & the rest is gone.

See soap mines to day formed by alkali. Walk 20 miles to day. Sit up on a very high & steap bluff & look down upon the Sweet Water River & gaze upon its various windings. The different camps, the wagons in the distance, the green swarth far below in the bottom, the rivers course thro' the hills & mountains, & the snow clad peaks of Rockey Mountains in the dist. To the north is a roleing plain, with chains of bluffs, level on top, & passes in between. In the night the cattle stampeeded, & several of our comp. who stayed to put new axel on broken waggon & who had come as far as the river [and] "caraled" in the sand, were nearly run over by our cattle as they passed at full speed.[10] Woman got run over by the wagon.

[July 20th. Friday] 19th. Long faces, under lips, grave faces, sorriful countenances, cross men, moody mannered, & discouraged. A great many felt as if a curse had been put upon them. Hundreds of other comp have not seen a stampeed & nothing appears to frighten them, while our comp. is known along the whole rout by the [name of] the stampeed comp. Other comp. are afraid to

10. This was the wagon belonging to Jayhawkers Sidney Edgerton, John Cole, and John Colton (Colton 1849; Arms in Cumming 1985, 60).

come near us & even our own men are afraid to drive an ox. It has become a serious matter. I stand it as well as any & take things easey, willing to leg it thro', which we have to do even now with the wagons. Several have passed us on foot. They take just clothes on their back, a tin pale & by their eatables of teams. One of our comp. started yesterday. Several talk of going Monday. 51 head of cattle found 15 miles north of Sweet[water] & brought in.[11] Men scattered on horse & foot all over the country, ransacking Bluff, ravine, gorge, plains & vallies. Some packers say they seen a number of cattle going as hard as they could go about 20 miles back. At night men still out. Kill several antelope, prairie squirrels, badgers, wolves &c. Do up cooking to day out of first rate waggons to burn. Take the hub of a wheel, set fire to the tar, this making a good stove to fry bacon on. This is the most expensive country I ever heard of.

[July 21st.] 20th. [Robert] Kemble brings in 4 oxen tied together with a rope by the horns. He tried to bring them in last night, but a large bear passing near, his horse commenced snorting & the cattle broke like lightning & ran about 6 miles, & therefore [he] did not get in before [this morning]. [Luzerne?] Bartholomew arrives, says some of our cattle that we lost in our first "stampeed" are 2 days behind & a lot of ours in a Mormon train at Deer Creek ford. He tried to get 1 yoke that he knew, & proceed, but they said he was a d—d deserter from our comp. & wanted to sell them & keep the money. The Badgers stole the boat above him & run him opposition.[12] A man belonging to the Telegraph line [a St. Louis company] tried to steal his horse from him, but a revolver caused him to give up the idea.

One ox lay dead in the "caral" this morn'g. Cattle brought in are skin & bones. Had a fight with E[dward] Bartholomew. He told me I lied, & [I] give it back. He struck me as I lay down. I jumped up & mashed his mug, made the claret fly & tore the shirt right off him, till he thought he wouldn't lick me any longer.

[July 22nd.] 21st. No more cattle found. 28 head yet out. Every man [is] for division [of the company into smaller sections]. 1 ox of Capt [E. Norman] Taylor died. It tumbled into the river, but we got it out & cut it open, & found its kidnies turned black. "Verdic:" died from a deseas called "Stampeed & drinking to[o] much saleratus water." The capt has now but 1 ox left besides a lame one with his leg swelled. He [Taylor] is in poor health, still under the effects of a former

11. Cephas Arms (July 20, in Cumming 1985, 60) said 107 head of cattle were gone with 62 found "and others heard from, twenty miles off."

12. Fifteen days earlier, a Bartholomew (probably Luzerne) bought the Knox County Company ferry for 15 dollars and went into business transporting wagons across the North Platte (Lorton, July 7, 1849). The Badger Company was organized in Kanesville and included the family, who later became Death Valley '49ers (Rasmussen 1994, 1:67).

"stampeed" having had a wagon to pass over him [on July 15th]. He has a wife & 1 little boy. Think of this ye inhabitants of civilization, & fancy yourselves resting upon the sympathy of men, of desperate men, who have lost all & [are] not able to succor their own distresses, men with prospects of starvation, a dreary winter, a mountain[ou]s habitation, & an awful death amid the snows of Sirra Nevada.

Things now look gloomey. Gloom has before spread before us, but have disapeared & bright hopes have been cherishd. We have ben arrested in our progress, we have been delayed beyond forbearance, we have sustained loss after loss, we have been plundered of our property, run over by heavy ladened wagons, trampled beneath the feet of hundreds of infuriated & affreighted animls, swam rappid currents under penalty of drounding, suffered fatigues, privations, thirst & hunger, ran under the tomehalk & scalping knife of the blood thirsty forrest fiend, "caraled" in the sand with no blanket & wild beasts preying & howling a "requiem" around your pillow of sod. Difficulty after difficulty & obsticle after obsticle has presented itself, but from time to time they have been surmounted, & the jovial song has made the "welkin" ring, as they wound their way o'er hill & plain. But now misfortunes to[o] frequently occur, & seam not likely to terminate. Things that before assumed a dark aspect, now begin to look black & serious. Spring came & passed, & summer has passed its medium & we [are] yet east of the Rockey Mountains.

Capt [Asa] Haynes, [afflicted] with sickness, aided by the numerous obstacles has, for a few days back, bordered on lunacy. His countenance looks haggard & his eye wild. He rode down the steep desent at our hill stampeed. The numerous dangers, the delays, the recollections of home, swell the burden on his troubled mind. H[aynes] was crazey & would go down to the spring to get water in his canteen, & drew his knife on those that tried to stop him. He was hurt in the hill "stampeed."[13] I myself am not discouraged & have not been, & whistle off all losses & troubles to the tune of "When I Was a Little Nig."

Have dry thunder showers in the shape of flashing lightnings & dry krashing claps, but out of all we have not a drop of rain till yesterday. Fog has hung low on the bluffs & hills. The heavens looks rainey in the morning. The nights are cold as midwinter but the days are hot. Men [were] sent out to South Pass & the back [road] to hunt for mule & three ponies. I find them in the bluffs. Cattle all brot in but 5. Great rejoicing. I sing Negro melodies & play violin[14] & others play & [a?] flute.

13. Asa Haynes may have suffered from a concussion during a stampede, which may have caused the above symptoms.

14. This is the first clear mention of Lorton playing the violin. There are other mentions of a violin being played, but it had not been certain Lorton was the player.

[July 23rd.] 22d. Comp divides up in 4 parties for travelling. I go on horse back 5 mile. Catch up to train 10 miles from last camp. [They] get catched in a thunder storm with their pants & shirt sleves, & the way forked lightnings play upon the peek & thunder bursting close to your ears is startling, for you are among the clouds. A few cedar trees try to grow, but the lightning burns all the green off & makes them black. We are continually assending the mountains & elevating our selves, with the chain of Rockey Mountains capped with eternal frosts in sight. See bear today. Plenty of dead cattle & lame ones. I forgot to mention that we got our old "giraff," the very identical [ox] that piled his bones on the prairie at devils rock. If it had not been in the oats, Bill [Kellogg] would have took him for the Rocky Mountains.[15]

We, after mounting high mountains & decending hollows, camp on Strawberry Creek, a large tributary to the Sweet Water [about 19 miles east of South Pass].[16] All these streams are fed by spring[s] (mostly ice springs) & melting snows & ice from the mountains. On that creek we find straw berries, yet find banks of snow 3 ft deep, & ice in abundance. There are also ice springs. This is the first of snow & the first I have ate in July. In the snowes I was glad to get off my thin pants, & ten minutes after, wished I had them on, & on assending a high place it was again cold as midwinter. We camped down on the bottom, & I tell you, all the cover we could get was to[o] little. Frost came thick, water froze in the pale 1/4 in. thick. Down in the hollow, the banks of this creek is hills & rockey crags & willows growing along the edge. Grass is tollerable good here. I go down the creek in search of an ice spring & to my astonishment find huge piles of snow & ice with in a few feet of green grass & willows. I get an old sack & bring as much as I can carry into camp. Every one ran after a piece, for it was a novelty. Tw'as now disbelievers believed that the white upon the mountains was snow. They had laughed at the idea of snow laying exposed to the suns rays & not melt away. We now propose making ice cream.

[July 24th.] 23d. Our road is continually on the assent today. We rise upon high elevations & sink into deep ravines. See a popular [poplar] grove on hill side by itself. It is strange for this country. Quaken Aspen Creek [now Rock

15. "Giraff" ox apparently had a hide of contrasting colors, and when standing with a background of uniform color he stood out, but he blended in with mountain terrain behind him.

16. Approaching South Pass they left the Sweetwater River to avoid its narrow, rough canyon. Keeping to the high country on the north, they reached Strawberry Creek. On August 3, Capt. Howard Stansbury, trailing Lorton, recorded that he and his company camped "on the Sweetwater, at a point where the road leaves it to avoid a cañon above, which is impassable for wagons for several miles" (Stansbury 1988, 69).

FIGURE 28. South Pass, looking west. This "Old Oregon Trail 1843–57" monument is near the actual summit of South Pass, whose official elevation is 7,411 feet. Photo by LeRoy Johnson.

Creek], branch of Sweet Water, [and] Willow Creek, runs thro' the mountains. We ford the Sweet Water for the 8th time & pass thro' high mounds.[17] Here on the S[wee]t Water the banks are covered with shining particles, supposed to be gold. The sand is full, but the particles are light & difficult to wash. Camp on a bluff covered with [sage], while our cattle has excelent grass on bottom. Shoot plenty of sage hens, & prairie squirrels. We have another bitter cold night. Cover[s] in demand.

[July 1849] 25th. [Lorton corrects his dates here.] On a/c of the scarceity of feed we cut grass & make hay. After travelling several miles, we pass bet[w]een the twin mounds.[18] We come to the South Pass & dont hardly know it, the assent being so gradual & the ground being so rolling. The ground thro' here is gravel sand & stoney, & 19 miles from 1 mile [camp?] to another. We expected to see a deep pass between high rocks & only capable of admitting a single wagon,

17. Lorton crossed the Sweetwater for the last time. In 1847 this was the Mormon's ninth and last crossing at present Burnt Ranch, about 10 miles east of South Pass (Kimball in Clayton 1983, 73). The "shining particles" were minute flakes of mica eroded from the surrounding mountains. "There were large quantities of yellow mica in the stream [Sweetwater River]...but an application of nitric acid instantly dispelled the pleasing hallucination" (Delano 1966, 100).

18. William Clayton's trail guide called these flat-topped hills "Twin mounds" (1983, 72). They heralded imminent arrival at South Pass, about three miles west.

[but] several roads can be made thro' here. At length we come to the summit of the dividing ridge between the waters of the Atlantic & Pacific ocien. There is 2 ridges upon which there has arisen a doubt as to which is the summit. Altitude of Pass, 7,085 feet above the level of the sea [actually 7,412 feet]. A little on the west of the summit of ridge are the Pacific Springs. You see a little fountain bubbling & running down towards the west in the shape of a stream [Pacific Creek], showing how great streams from little fountains flow, & then notice it feed[s] a larger & both connected feed others of greater magnitude till great rivers are formed. & here is the grave of a young man named Dexter, in loose sand & short [head] board. Here the tall mountains with their deep gorges filled with snow hundreds of feet deep, seem to kiss the clouds. From the springs & creek to the next water is 23 miles with out water, so the comp. decide[s] to await at the creek. We take in some water & travel 6 miles. We there find grass but our supply of water is scanty.

[July] 26th. Start day light without washing, pass a bluff in shape of an eastern lamp or pitcher [today's Plume Rocks]. Cross Dry Sandy, which is watered by 1 spring. The water is brack[ish] & not good for cattle. Next [six miles farther] come to the junction of Cal. & Oregon roads, or Subletts cut off & Mormon rout to Salt Lake. Here we find a grist of papers directed to friends behind, telling them which road they took, as the cut off is to Fort Hall. Here notice says [J. R.] Nelson is not likely to live.

We meet a Mormon woman in a covered wagon, 4 oxen & horse behind with harness on. She said her husband was out hunting antelope.[19] They had 2 rifles & very little load intending to meet Capt [Samuel] Gully's team & lighten their load or pick up things on the road. Provisions were not scarce, & mules & oxen plenty at the Lake, at high prices.

Plenty of Cal. guide boards [dead cattle] as usual & on the new principle you can smell them even on a dark night. Plenty of bear tracks & wolves, antelopes plenty. Shoot a large Rockey mountain [white-tailed prairie] dog [*Cynomys leucurus*]. See plenty of them barking on the edge of their holes. Cross Little Sandy, & after going 25 miles to day we camp on the Big Sandy & have fine feed. I get sore footed & fatigued.

19. The woman was Rachel, 20 years old and the fourth of John D. Lee's several wives. Lee and Rachel were on their way to "the Sweetwater on a Picking up Expedition" (Lee 1955, 1:111; C. Kelly 1984, 11–12). They picked up a kitchen stove for another wife along with hundreds of pounds of discarded merchandise (Brooks 1964, 147–49). Juanita Brooks postulated: "This one trip had netted him more than he could have earned by two years' hard labor.... Surplus tools were always an item of trade; powder and lead worth more than money, clothing of any kind priceless in the fingers of his skilled wives" (ibid., 149). Lee was executed by a firing squad at Mountain Meadows, Utah, on March 23, 1877, for his role in the September 1857 Mountain Meadows Massacre (Bagley 2002, 315–16).

FIGURE 29. Lorton sketch. Depiction of Plume Rocks. Lorton writes: "south/pass/july 26/1849"; "EASTERN LAMP BLUFF"; "WIND RIVER/CHAIN/OR/AM. ALPS." Courtesy of The Bancroft Library.

FIGURE 30. Plume Rocks, now called Bluff Rocks, is about 10 miles southwest of Pacific Springs, north of Wyoming Highway 28. View is north. Photo by LeRoy Johnson.

When we arrived Nelson was lying in his tent upon 2 matresses. Struck with death. His eyes were roled up in his head, his neck streached out, & his breath very short. Every one felt as if no earthly power could now save him. A groop of silent men stood on the out side, some gazing in upon the senseless, dying man. It was thought his lamp would go out with the sun, but was [still] a half hour high when a man came to borrow my spade to dig a grave, for his spirit had took its flight. I then got a flat trunk cover, scraped the paper off, & having no paint I took a brush I carried with me & with tar from the wagon wheel inscribed the following, "J. R. Nelson. Died July 26th 1849 Adams Co. & a Member of the Knox Co Comp." The materials were rough but was the best head board I had seen on the way.[20]

My feet get blistered all over, which causes fatigue, to the extreme, after walking 25 miles. The night is very cold, & the winds sharp.

[July] 27th. We burry Nelson, put on his clothes, wrap him in two blankets, a pillow under his head, & then pall bearers take hold of the blanket on each side followed by the rest of persons present, [and] carry him to his last resting place. The grave was upon the edge of the bluff, the usual depth, while the bottom being hard earth was dug out in shape of a coffin. In here he was deposited. Boards were laid crossways, & upon these were laid willow branches & the earth throw[n] in upon his last remains. The head board placed & the grave rased, in due form.[21] A tall man stood by which was the only person who shed tears & his were principally on a/c of the deceased haveing no coffin. He said he took all his boxes & chests & spliced them to build a coffin for a little girl that died in his comp. Thus we left him with no useless coffin enclosing his head, upon the banks of "Big Sandy."

Tho' it had froze in the night yet the day was close & gave people a pain in the side. Our course lay over very level roads. The air is so light upon these mountains that the mountain fever is prevalent & probably took off Nelson quicker than if it had been otherwise [altitude sickness?]. A person wants lungs like a balloon. Nelson, the last I spoke to him, was sitting by his waggon tongue at the hill "stampeed" [on July 19]. He was hurt on the leg & mortally frightened. Soon after that he became sick.

After a fatiguing days tramp & a [prairie] dog dinner, we camped again on the Big Sandy. During the day a number of men all armed rode up to us & asked if we had seen 4 men pass, one haveing a gray horse. We had seen them pass

20. Nelson's name is not in the membership list drawn up with the Knox County Company constitution. Since Adams County is some distance from Knox County, Nelson may have joined the train at a later date.

21. Emigrants mounded earth or piled stones on a grave to thwart wolves and coyotes from digging up and devouring the deceased.

our camp 7 o'clock in the morning & excited our suspicion. They said they had deserted from [Fort] Larimie, taking with them dragoon horses & arms. On the way they had rob[b]ed & [*blank*] a woman, the wife of an emegrant, & [the soldiers] had pursued them from the fort.[22] Cap[t] Stevens of Larimie was on his way to Cal. & Capt [Thomas Duncan], the comander in the army, with another, had got the help of these others who were on their [way?]. Cap[t] Stevens, formally [formerly] of Larimie, had a number of wagons & was moving his family, bag & baggage. At night when we came up to the river, they had been grazing their horses & taking repose beneath the bushes, for, said they, the deserters had just left as they arrived, & [the officers] were going to travel in the night & take them assleep. We entertained the officers in our "Markee" upon hot buiscuit & good bacon. They wanted to pay, But we told them we did not "keep tavern." They give us the latest news, which was 1 week later from Larimie. Bull Tail, chief of the Sioux nation had died with the cholera & the Indians were flocking around the fort to get cured. Gen [John] Worth died with the same disease in Texas. The Canadians had drove the parliament out of the house & the cholera had subsided in the east. They thanked us & set out for Green River about dusk. The comm't [commandant?] was disguised & said the deserters did not mistrust them on their scent. Night moderately cold.

[July] 28th. We come to Green River about noon. This is a mammoth river for a mountain stream, about 100 ft wide & rappid current. The water looks green. There are some large trees on its banks, but most generally bushes very tall. We meet the officer[s] here. They had their men hand cuffed out in the grove. They found them near midnight fast assleep on the ground, & no guard out. They silently disarmed them of every thing, & the Capt called them up & said it was time to relieve the guard. They were very much freightened & made no resistance. 2 of them cryed.

There is a good ferry boat here made of pine, owned by a Mormon, who has his family on the other side in a tent. He charges $4.00 a wagon & swim your teams. He said he had been to the gold diggings & got as much gold as his mule could carry, & for want of provisions he came away. He said gold had made a fool of a great many at Salt Lake. They had got as much as they wanted & go to work gameing.

We ford the river above here. There are 2 islands. The current is mighty, almost taking the oxen off their feet, & if I had not held fast to a waggon & through [thrown] my clothes in [the wagon], I could not have waided it. It like to have took me down river. The ford is 1/2 mile [above the ferry]. We save $4 dolls. [per wagon] by the operation. 1 [wagon] box slips off with a sick old lady

22. Lorton says later (October 10) the woman was not raped, but the army was trying to "excite the sympathy of emigrants" against the deserters.

in it & children in it. A man was found dead in the woods here, appearently a packer, for there was a saddle near him. Foul play is suspected.

After taking a dinner of hot coffee we travel down the river in a south course over barren sandy & gravelly soil laying thick with quartz of all collors, some resembling stone china. A grave [is] beside the river & a board with this inscription, "Sacred to the memory of a stranger who was found in Green river on the 30th of Apl./49 & intered by a comp. of emigrants." He was appearently a man 25 yrs old, had on his left little finger 2 rings one marked A. C. His grave lay in the sand & cattle had trampled on it, or wolves had tried to dig him up. 12 miles from the ford we camp on Green River again. I am pritty much tuckered out with fatigue, galled feet, & not well. Here there is 1st rate wild oats & flax on the other side, but the current is so mighty we would let no one swim it. Only for this [good feed] we intended to lay up on the morrow, Sunday.

In the grove of trees there is a number of log cabins partly burnt, & chiminies standing.[23] They were either Mormons or trappers that wintered there, for a great quantity of wood had been cut by them. Some Cal. emigrants made boats of their wagon boxes & set sail down Green River.[24] The current runs 8 miles an hour. Green River is a tributary of the Rio Colorado of the west that enters in the Gulf of Cal.

[Sunday, July] 29th. Tho' the night has been freezing & plenty of musquitoes, the sun shone forth with as much power as the hottest day of an eastern August. The atmosphere close in the vallies, & on eminences a breeze. Road level, hilly barren & sandy, & several steep places. Pass 3 curious mounds [Blue Point being the largest and most westerly], & at night camp on Blacks Fork [near mouth of Sevenmile Gulch]. It enters in G[reen] River. The night is extremely cold & [water] freizes thick in the pales, & bad getting up in the morning, but in 1 hour after sun rise the weather is different. Good feed. Wild flax is good for cattle, plenty of wild currants. We find some & make sauce. Drive our cattle acrost to feed, & [*blank*].

23. These cabins, built by Bridger and Fraeb in 1841, were intended to be a trading post (Hafen 1966, 136–37; Gowans and Campbell 1975, 2, 10). Frémont comments on "some old houses" in 1843, and T. H. Jefferson depicted the site in 1846 as "Old Trading Post" on the right bank of the Green River (Map, 1846). Today there is no vestige of the site (Frémont 1970b, 466–67; see also Bryant 1967, 139; Wheat 1959, 94–95, map 624, 95n3; Korns and Morgan 1994; part 3 of pocket Map 1846, Jefferson).

24. Lorton is referring to a group mentioned by James M. Hutchings, who said that 10 men "made a raft and a boat out of a wagon-bed and started down Green River. A man named Quimby was Captain of the party!!!" (Hutchings 1980, 147; Heiskell 1998, 17). The most famous river-runners were seven men from the Charles Dallas train "captained" by William Lewis Manly, but they started their float about four weeks after Lorton crossed the Green River. The Dallas train crossed the North Platte 25 days after Lorton crossed on July 6 (Hutchings in Morgan 1959b, 185).

FIGURE 31. Detail, James Wilkins sketch No. 39. "Cathedral Rock," July 24, 1849. Today's Church Butte, Blacks Fork, Wyoming. Lorton writes on July 30: "Every variety of dome, from a Turkish mosque to a St. Peters dome." WHI Image ID 31698.

30th June [July]. Plenty of fish caught in Blacks Fork, which emties in Green River. I set in the bushes 1 hour after the teams had gone, taking down back notes. Hams Fork 3 miles from here emties in Blacks F. Here is plenty of currants which grow on trees & plenty of scrubbary, wild rye, oats, & flax in abundance & a fine stream of clear water. It is 1 3/4 miles from here [beyond Hams Fork, that] we come to Blacks Fork again. Pull off pants to ford it. The current is so swift that it almost takes me down & the water comes up to my watch pocket & wets every thing. Shoot mountain hare, it looks like a young antelope. The rode pritty level with curious bluffs, looking green like copper. Pass near Blacks 2d ford. [I see] a huge pile or formation of sand stone (brown) with all the carvings of an artist, every variety of dome, from a Turkish mosque to a St. Peters dome [Church Butte]. Large pieces had been hurled from the top & frosts, snows & rains acted upon it. We camp on Blacks Fork. I write this while sitting beneath the shade of these rocks of sand stone & a raven soaring above my head as I write.

[July] 31st. Ford Blacks Fork 4th [third] time & then come to a stream [Smiths Fork] that puts into B'k Fork. Meet the mail from Salt Lake, 2 men on behind to receive letters, postage 25 cts. 4 Indian horses [hitched] to light wagon & going as hard as they can go. Expect to go in 26 days, came from Kainsvill in 30. Babot [Almon W. Babbitt] is the proprietor. [At] noon an Indian dressed in a black coat, fur cap, moccosins & leggings, came dashing up to the wagon on a white horse. He had a skin saddle, buffalo skin "larraetto" & no bit in his mouth, the elk hide bridle or halter passing thro' his mouth. Couldn't swap for his horse.

We came to within 1 mile of Fort Bridger upon a beautiful bottom, green willows following the different streams that run within from 5 to 15 rods of each other. Splendid grass spreads itself on the fine level basins, while the south range of the S. Pass [Uinta Mountains] streaches from east to west, showing to great advantage its piles of snow fil[l]ing the mountain gorges & kissing the hazy sky with their white lips of purity. At first up came an Indian & wanted caps for gun.[25] Then we met an Indian reclining on a pile of bushey haired buffaloes skins, while his squaw lay reclining on her elbow. She was [of] light complection & rather pritty featured, tho' all of small statu[r]e & delicate limbs. She was dress[ed] in a short buckskin frock [and] leggings of the same. At every seam hung a fringe. She had a number of bracelets on her wrist, rings in her ears, a belt around her waist, with bright fixings attached thereto. Upon her back hung some half doz jinggling bells & buttons accompanyed by a large brass ornam[e]nt for which I have no name. Together with those hung a bunch of polished teeth of various wild animals. She was the prittiest squaw I ever see. He had on his head a flashy collored scotch cap, buck[skin] coat, leggings, moccosins &c. He wanted to see what I had in my pocket attached to guard & after looking at it got a little brass toy watch & tied it on to my chain with a piece of grass & then commenced laughing heartily. He was very jocular & full of his fun & all seemed to be in good circumstances & happy.

Every Indian has several horses & some have droves. This bottom is litterally covered with squaws, naked papposes, & Indians on horseback, some riding at full spead, & others lying & lolling on their ponies backs. Here there is some 1/2 dozen lodges formed by long poles 15 ft high crossing at the top to let smoke out. Besides the buffalo hide that form the roof is opened & kept so by long poles. The skins are sewed together with sinues. These are owned by traders. Each man has his squaw & consequently his pappooses. There [Their] wagons stood in a line near them. In one lodge lay an old gray headed trader upon a number of robes. He was as cross a[s] the D—l to his men, & his squaw was cooking. These traders lodges are filled with goods, a great deal bot from Cal[ifornians]. In another lodge was a young, coarse homespun fellow. He has been out 13 years & has not been down to the states in 8 years. Born in Ill. He likes trading, & is acquainted with their language, says there is no regular rule, but they talk just like a lot of homespun fellows would at a country place.

We wade the Blacks Fork close by & then 2 others, & soon come to Fort Bridger. It is situated on level ground, green grass all arou[n]d & form[s] a contrast between the snows on the mountains not far off. The fort is made of logs, or rather the cabins form the fort, & the yard is the middle, a large plank gate way to the entrance. On the north end is the store containing good[s] for traffic. On the east the Indians squaw[s] do the cooking & the other[s] are provision rooms & sleeping apart[ments]. While I was in there, regular Indian hunter came in the yard loaded with game. He had an elk & an antelope on his horse all cleaned.

25. Percussion caps were necessary to fire a percussion-lock rifle. Before venturing west, many of the emigrants had their flint-lock rifles converted to percussion locks.

FIGURE 32. Detail, James Wilkins sketch No. 42. "Fort Bridger," July 25, 1849. Now a Wyoming historic site, a reconstruction of the fort on Blacks Fork is south of Interstate 80 near Lyman, Wyoming. WHI Image ID 31549.

He was dress[ed] in all the splendor that brass & buckskin can do for [one], but having rode on top of the meat for a saddle he had got some bloody.

The roof of the fort & chimnies are made of sod, while on the north is the cattle "caral" made of logs stood end ways. Bridger trades a great deal in cattle & horses & had lots of wagons he had bot up. From here I went to the lodges around the fort, about 50 in number. One Indian beckoned me in. I sat down on his robes. He gave me needle & thread & wanted me to work a button hole on his blue cloth coat, which I did. He then pulled out my watch & made motions to the sun & imitated the sun's rays. I then explained the difference betwen the sec., min. & hour, sun set, sun rise & noon day.

I was in a trappers & traders lodge. He had 3 squaws & supported an aged father of the squaw who was white with age, 4 ft high & lay taking a nap on the robe. The trader had been out here 19 years & wintered on the Big Sandy last winter. [A] hard winter. Snow lay 4 mos. Got out of provision & had to hunt antelope every day [for] food. Dug up the snow 4 ft deep to get grass for his ponies, & if he did not, the ponies would [have died]. Had lots of amunition but hard time of it. Some times they only have snow 2[?] days on these bottoms & when it snows on the mountains it rains below. Every lodge has a doz or 1/2 dozen wolves around & wolf dogs who come & take you by the ear as you sit, [or] finger or close [clothes], but the Indians drive them away.

Indians come to our camp in great numbers with buffalo skins to trade. They vary in their prices. Any thing they take a notion to they will have what ever the price. I see a fine large robe traded for 4 bars of lead, an old sword for 1. The[y] like coats but pants they dont like & laugh at them. A bright vest meets their eye. Ponies they are choice of around the fort, but off in the country you can trade a rifle for a poney if they want one. Flint locks are prefferable, on a/c of getting out of caps. Some of these Indians run large numbers of horses. I see several herds of beautiful horses drove in at night full split. One Indian will drive more [horses] than 3 white men. They dash after the herd full split. At night you see each staked separately around their lodges & a guard on the watch.

At meal times it is imposible to keep them out the tent. They creep in thro' every hole, & even where it is staked down the little "pappooses" stick their heads under.[26] The tent is filled with squaws with their "papoose[s]" lashed on their backs. The chief with his children & half doz. squaws. The old squaw with tottering limbs & wrinkled face. The old man with his daughters, & all asking for corn doggins [dodgers], bacon or any thing we have on the table, with out the least manners, all expecting to get something.

In the eve'g I stroled up to the fort. A number of traders sat around their tents with their squaws talking vengeance on some one. Had a talk with Bridger.[27] [He] said it is very healthy [here], & cant live any wheres else. He used to own Fort Larimie. Sold with every thing around for $7,000 to Am. Fur Comp., & that he could'nt keep his health any wheres else. Said he could make fifty rodes thro' the South Pass. The mountains on the north of the pass are called Wind River Mts., or Am. Alps. [The mountains on] the south are not so abrupt & B says he travels over them all winter.[28] The snows fall in Feb. & some times early in the spring, but last winter snow fell 2 feet in the Fort [Bridger] valley. He has crossed the Sierra Nevada Mts. & says the snows fall generally not before Nov. & we are early enough. Bridger buys up a great ma[n]y things from the emegrants to speculate on. After crossing the several streams I arrived in camp. Indians dogs come in camp in the night.

Aug. 1 [1849]. Pass over a hard hilly road out of Bridger Valley. Some low cedars by the rode. Travel with the Rovers.[29] Pass a large spring very cold.[30] Find [dead] antelope. Pull his teeth out. Take in water at a creek [Muddy Creek, at 13 miles] so as to camp any wheres. Follow up a deep ravine [Soda Hollow] where there is

26. As previously mentioned, although the term *squaw* has become pejorative, *papoose* has not.
27. James Bridger (1804–1881) "was generally considered the ablest hunter, mountaineer and guide of the West" (Chittenden 1986, 255; see also Alter 1962).
28. Capt. Howard Stansbury, U.S. Army Corps of Topographical Engineers, was ordered to explore the Platte River Trail and the Great Salt Lake area. He conferred with Bridger concerning passages over the Continental Divide, and with Bridger as guide, they pioneered and mapped a new wagon road from Fort Laramie to Fort Bridger. Stansbury (1988, 262) concluded, a "route through these hills, [is] not only practicable, but free from any obstructions involving in their removal great or unusual expenditure." Part of the Bridger-Stansbury trace paralleled the Cherokee Trail through southern Wyoming (Whiteley 1999, 94–122).
29. Welch, one of the Rovers, hears that the "Knoxville Co." are 17 miles east of Fort Bridger, indicating separation of the Knox County Company divisions (Welch, 1849b).
30. Cold Springs, a mile southwest of the southern toe of Bridger Butte, is mentioned in Clayton (1983, 77) and Berrett and Anderson (2006, 6:177).

fine grass both in the vale & on the hilltops, & camp on soda spring.[31] Here we get soda water, genuine soda served up with sweet[en]ing in natures fountain. This is rather strong, & stings in your nose. The earth around the spring looks red like iron rust.

Aug. 2d. We go over some of the highest mountains in altitude yet assended. We assend one, altitude 7,315 feet.[32] Go down awful gulfs, pass little trees, berry bushes, over rockey steeps. Take a new rode & go around some mountains & [that?] were formerly traveled, pass around many high projecting curious looking rocks, especially 1 narrow pass, with high precipitous over hanging rocks, a formation of gravel [conglomerate]. Here is a bad abrupt place in the road & we brake an axle. Dash after the boys on poney who are out hunting. Hear a gun go off in a hollow which enables me to find them. Give them the horse to go back with, & I stay up near the road in the mountains. Some Boston gents stops & holds conversation with me & finally their mule train comes up. They pass on, & I lay down in the shade of the bushes, & get in a doze.[33]

Sudently I hear a trampling down the mountain, & a thought startles me[:] I heard Indians. I looked & shure enough a chief & squaw were riding well armed towards me. I felt curious, steped back from the road & looked over the long dist between our teams & myself, & I only armed with [a] knife. However the Indian was small but [a] stout & savage looking customer. I didn't like his looks. Upon discovering me he came out to me & extended his paw, & shook hands. He then took his bow & knocked on my knife & wanted to look at it, but I wasn't such a fool, for that is the way they disarm you, & then he wanted to trade moccasin[s]. I gave him some thread, shook hands with his squaw & they galloped down the hill. At the bottom they met a Missisippi gent & traded a Spanish saddle tree for his coat & shirt which he pulled off to the skin & let them have.

They put rings on the axle & finally our teams came up. We noon at Sulphur Spring. This is strongly impregnated with sulphyr. It is healthy to drink, & the stone over which they run for there is 3 nearly to gether, & another [spring] not a great dist off that tastes very little of it [sulphur]. Shoot mountain eagles. Shoot antelope. Follow down a valley green with verdu[r]e, with a few stragling cedars [junipers] on the mountains & the gorges. Scenery has changed with 2 days. The valleys are green, & verdu[r]e creeps up the mountains top. Camp near a large spring of good water on the south side of the rode. Use sage for fuel & have antelope for supper, which is grand [trail is three to seven miles south of Interstate 80, roughly paralleling it].

31. Soda Spring, also called Copperas, was just under 17 miles west-southwest of Fort Bridger (Bullock 1997, 222; Clayton 1983, 6:76; 1973, 287).

32. Lorton uses the elevation from Clayton's guidebook and journal (1983, 76; 1973, 287). The pass is between Muddy Creek and Aspen Mountain.

33. These men were part of the Boston-Newton Joint Stock Association.

[August] 3d. Pass [at 1 mile] the east foot of the dividing ridge betwen the waters [of the] Colerado & Salt Lake or Great Basin. The assent is steep, narrow & crooked, & decending between mountain[s], very steep also. Altitude of ridge [Aspen Divide], 7,700 feet. We next come to Bear River [having traveled 8.75 miles in all]. This is a rushing stream about 2 feet deep & wide. It is low now, but had lately been high as could be seen from the thousands of prop [?] blocks lying on the west side. 5 or 6 Indian huts are here, but they appear to be poor.[34] They offered me some antelope meat, & we stayed an hour or 2. We crossed [Bear River]. We [surmount a small ridge, then] proceed down a valley with high mountains on either side, some very rockey & projecting [The Needles on Coyote Creek]. Looks like iron & sulphur mixed. Springs gush out all along the mountains, clear cold water. Come to a bad place on Yellow Creek, so we camp with poor water [nine miles from Bear River], but have antelope & apple sause. During the night an arrow is fired at the guard from the mountains. We are now in a deep ravine & a bodey could cut us all off in our present position.

[August] 4th. Continue [over a ridge and] down the ravine till we come to Cache Cave, where there is a fine spring of water. Here we noon. The cave is up about 80 ft from the base of the mountain & is in solid rock, about 25 ft long & broad. In the inside there is a cupalo or dome. This should be inhabited by Indians as a chiminey could be made with ease [see Berrett and Anderson 2006, 246–54]. While eating, the chief I met at the fort & a lot of others, with a great number of packed mules & ponies, came running down the hill & here unpacked their buffaloes [buffalo robes] with which they were loaded, & the chief with his squaw took dinner with us, but we could'nt trade horses. The chief buys up goods the same as the traders & packs them to the fort. Camp on Echo Creek [also called Red Fork of Weber River].[35]

[August] 5th. Travel down deep ravine till we arrive at Red Fork of Weber River crossing the creek a number of times. Camp on [at?] Red Fork because night overtook us. Many curious rocks in the mountains, & plenty of quaken aspen wood on the stream which is prity.[36] Go in bathing.

34. Lorton's mess is now a day behind the Rovers, based on the similarity of Lorton's description of the poor condition of these Indians with Welch's description on August 2.
35. William Clayton (1973, 296) noted on July 16, 1847, Echo Canyon's propensity to repeat sounds: "There is a very singular echo in this ravine.... The report of a rifle resembles a sharp crack of thunder and echows from rock to rock for some time."
36. Red Fork is not a stream of water. It is the name of the junction of Echo Canyon and Weber River. Lorton is following Clayton's (1973, 297) terminology: After coming down Echo Canyon "the camp renewed the journey and one mile farther arrived at the Red fork of the Weber River." At the river Lorton turned right and passed the rock formations now called The Witches, above the right bank.

FIGURE 33. Lorton sketch. Rock formations overlooking the Weber River (Red Fork) between Henefer and Echo, Utah. Lorton labeled heights of 20, 25, and 50 feet. Cut off for closer view is "ROCKS on RED FORK" at the bottom of picture. August 5 or 6, 1849. Courtesy of The Bancroft Library.

FIGURE 34. Witches Rocks near Interstate 80 in Echo Canyon, near the border of Wyoming and Utah. One of several notable formations. Photo by LeRoy Johnson.

[Sunday, August 5] 6th. Get up [at] day light, very cold. Cross the river & camp on a little stream [Main Canyon] that em[p]ties in the fork.[37] The water is mudey & we lay up. Sunday. It is now 40 miles to S[alt] Lake, & we will have to travel over the worst rode of the whole rout. Our road lays over combination of the Wahsatch Mts. We follow up ravines & steep places, deep abrupt holes, rocks in the road, sideling hills, so that some wagons have to be held up by hand & others let down by ropes. We decend to the base of a tall mountain along which runs the Kanyon river [East Canyon Creek], in a northerly course, & probably emties in Bear [Weber] River.[38] Here I went on 5 miles ahead [to Little Dutch Hollow] & see Indians on horses. Follow up gradually assending, fording the creek 13 times in the afternoon. Here there is many short turns, high bushes, with just room enough to pass through, endangering the waggon covers and axle trees in the passage. Here the Mormons had to cut the tall brush & trees for miles. We then take in a westerly direction up a deep ravine continuoualy assending [Little Emigration Canyon], & camp at a spring in the mountain. Stand guard or rather lay guard in the morning watch. Spread buffalo, take a keg for pillow, & sleep with 1 eye open. No Indians come.

[August 7]. Turn cattle out 3 o'clock, moon shining bright & make breakfast. Cattle stray up road making late start. Start up this hill which is 4 miles to top, or summit [2.6 miles from the camp at spring].[39] After arriving at Summit [Big Mountain Pass, 7,420 feet], we climb [northerly] up a very high mountain, follow it about 1/2 mile & then assind a peek overlooking Salt Lake & a great many mountains [Big Mountain, 8,472 feet]. It is a lovely scene. On the S., tall alpine like peeks appear to reach the sky, their deep gorges & summits filled with snow. On the north another ridge intercepts your view, with occasionally a grizzly bear, an antelope or a mountain goat trying to mount the highest peek. Here I tie my red hankerchief to my cane & raise a flag. Tho' in the lower kanyons the air is close & sultry, yet from the ripp[l]ing & flapping of the fabbric, it can be easily decerned from below that a hard breeze is blowing above the mountains.

On arriving where the road reaches its summit we agreed to assend a mountain on our right, appearantly 100 feet. This we reached but instantly saw another, equal in hight which we did not see from the base, but this we would accomplish & so commenced, but the higher we went the greater distance it appeared from the top, & we were forced to rest before we could proceed any

37. At today's small community of Henefer, Utah, they turned southward up Main Canyon Creek.

38. Main Canyon tops out at Hogback Summit, where Lorton descended into Dixie Hollow to the junction with East Canyon Creek (now inundated by East Canyon Reservoir).

39. Little Emigration Canyon, about four and a quarter miles long, is one of the loveliest hikes on the Donner-Reed trail. It averages 330 feet rise per mile. Their camp was at the spring about one and a half miles up the canyon.

farther. At last we reached the top, which was capped with hard rock, which keeps it from washing away. Several burnt pine trees indicated that fire had illumined its peek at some recent period.

We mounted the highest rock & some animal or snake became alarmed at the desecration of it solitary abode amid air. Our teams were now wending their way up the kanyon that streached out towards the east. On either side tall pine trees lifted their green foliage above their huge trunks. The quaken asp[en], tall, straight & slender, covered the various cross kanyons, the major part without leaves & their bodies looking blue which is probably owing to emigrants setting fire to the grass & the trees. Even now I gaze on a burning mountain far above where I stand, to the east. We look down upon the approaching teams, but they remind us of mice rather than cattle, & the wagons of a liliputians vehicle. We look west but find mountains to intersect the objects & view which we desire to see.

We now determine that our labors shall not be in vain, & conclude to make an attempt at another still higher [peak] 1/2 mile to the west. We are some what imbarrassed here in our object by the thick groth of oak brush & berry bushes. Our legs become entangled many times & we had to get out of a bad box [canyon] the same way we entered. At last by going half way down the hill, we got round on tollerable clear ground. We pluck a splendid ragged red flowr & berrys we knew not the name of, & again comm[ence] our assent. This had the appearance of being as high above the others & [as?] the other was from the road. Excelseor. We went with, once in a while, our foot hold giving way & the stones & dirt roling down, but the peek receeded as we assended. We were forced from time to time to stop & rest our legs. At last we reached the summit with a shout of triumph, & set our flag as before related. T'was here a view of splendor broke upon our sences, a scene that I could hardly realize as nature, different from any that I had ever before witnessed, far exceeding my expectations, & satisfying my most sceptical ideas of grandeur, of magnificence.

We gazed forth through a kanyon upon The Great Salt Lake, [which] was one grand object of the scene. The fertile valley streaching out before the eye, the grand ranges of mountains, & winding streams conspired to fill the heart with pleasure. On the south west of my sight a peeked alpine ridge bathing in the moist cloud that lingered over it, its snow capped tops, & on the north another range of singular beauty but nearer, & with now & then a gorge of snow. The range on the south west at a great distance off, say 30 miles [Oquirrh Mountains], presents a dark purple cast, & is striped with snow. From here can be deserned 2 peeks [Twin Peaks?] appearently not 3 feet apart, & yet 2 Mormons say who ascended the foremost, that the other looks some 3 miles off from them. What a variety in scenery can here be decernd. From the lofty snow appareled peek, you look down upon a lovely valley green with virdue [verdure], sloping off gradually from the mountains forming a basin. You look down on a stream called Jordan flowing as peacefully as did the noted ancient river.

Salt Lake appear[s] as to view, its shore lined with snow white salt. Thro' the lake runs ranges of mountains for the distance of 100 miles from where I stand. Every thing is so far off that it assumes an artificial hue, gives every object an unearthly appearance, & a dream sweeps over the sences of the enthusiast, & [he] exclaims in his delirium, "Great are the works of Omnipotence." The great h[e]igh[t]s of the [place where I] stand, which is some 1,500 ft above the basin, & 700 ft above the summit of the mountain road. The road at this place ascends the highest mountain on the whole rout & with one exception the highest elevation above the sea. The dist. that can be seen in this atmosphere is singular, it being so pure [that] 20 miles out east is no more than an equivalent to 120 here. For instance I look down the kanyon gap & desern the number of wagons & cattle near the mouth & would naturally call it 3 miles, but measurment calls it 20 miles.

Satisfied with our view we commenced decending by a south pitch where it was twice as high from the road as where we assended. Down! down! we went, stones roleing from our feet, sometimes faster than we wished. Our legs became so weak be fore we got half way down that we could proceed no farther. I took one road & my companion another. My road lay down a steep declivity, lined with willow & oak bushes & by these only were I prevented, by clinging to them, from pitching below & dashing to pieces on the masses of uncouthly shaped rocks which had fallen in masses in the kanyon below. Many was [the] time during this long decent that we wished we had remained at the base & took for granted that it was a very high mountain. Not only did I run risk of dashing to pieces on the broken fragments but of becoming a frugal meal to some hungry bear.

On arriving at the bottom & following down the ravine, I observed my companion still on the mountain & amuseing himself by hurling huge rocks from the top, roleing down with the rappidity of lightning, & partially assending the opposite mountain before stopping, or breaking in 100 slivers. I was at length joined by my companion at the bottom of the ravine, & 1/2 miles travel brot us to the road, which was welcome to us, & we determined that another high mt we would not assend, for Cal. gold.

At length noon came & we ate bread & milk on the Little Kanyon Creek [now Mountain Dell Creek] under trees. Here we see large pines snaked out for use, remnants of a saw mill & other appearances indicating that the cittizens of Salt Lake get out timber here. A number of comp's were delayed here, on a/c of waggons upsetting. We see a great many wagons capsized, broke down, &c, by the horrible road. Pomeroy's merchant train had 1 wagon turned off a bank into the stream. Pales were broke, coffee spilled, provisions lost, & a barrel of gin [had the] head stove in & lost 40 gall[ons] worth $4 a gall.[40] We lay still a few hours in the afternoon & then yoke up & set out. Mount a very high hill, decend in a kanyon [over the southwest shoulder of Little Mountain Summit into Emigration Canyon], follow a stream & camp in the kanyon 5 miles from the City. The water is not fit to drink on a/c of the cattle crossing above, but we find a spring which comes very acceptable. Here grows plenty of service berries, & a very small grape growing on a low bush 6 ins high. They are called mountain grape.[41]

40. Thaddeus and Ebenezer Pomeroy were hauling trade goods to miners in California. (Concerning the trail over the Wasatch, see Madsen 1983, 26–29).
41. This low Rocky Mountain evergreen is often called creeping Oregon grape (*Mahonia repens*), but true Oregon grape (*Mahonia agrifolium*) is not native to Utah and grows to a height of 10 feet. Although the *Mahonia* genus is not related to the grape family, it is called "grape" because its ripe fruit resembles small, purple grapes, which are sour but laden with vitamin C. Thus, it was used to prevent and cure scurvy.

PART III

The Southern Route

Salt Lake City to Pueblo de Los Angeles

CHAPTER 7

Among the Mormons at Salt Lake City

Background

Lorton's wagon train traversed the Wasatch Range via the difficult road the Donner Party blazed in 1846 (Madsen 1983, 26). On the western flank of the range, the route snakes down Emigration Canyon into the Great Salt Lake Basin, where, on July 24, 1847, a year after the Donner Party, Brigham Young and his entourage also exited the mountains to begin the laborious process of establishing a new Zion for the Church of Jesus Christ of Latter-day Saints in territory outside the United States (Bullock 1997, 237). This nascent settlement grew into today's Salt Lake City and its surrounding megalopolis.

From Winter Quarters (north of today's Omaha, Nebraska), Mormons fled westward—deep into Mexican territory, where they could establish a theocracy in which church and state were inseparable. They established their new Zion between the Wasatch Mountains and Great Salt Lake while the Mexican-American War (1846–1848) raged far to the south. After the war, via the Treaty of Guadalupe Hidalgo, Mexico ceded today's California, Arizona, New Mexico, Nevada, and Utah, and parts of Colorado, Wyoming, and Oklahoma, to the United States for $15 million. Thus, the Mormons had settled yet again in United States territory, where their plans for a theocratic kingdom would soon be threatened once more.

"The Saints who poured into Salt Lake Valley in fall of 1848 boosted the population to nearly 5,000" (Morgan 1947, 217). In August 1849, when Lorton arrived, the Mormon population was somewhat greater than this, with another 1,500 on the way. Most emigrants who left the Oregon-California Trail and detoured to Salt Lake City thought they could replenish their shrunken larders there. Some sold or traded their wagons and oxen for horses and mules to pack through to the goldfields. Others, particularly those with families, laid by to recruit their oxen and mules before venturing north via the Salt Lake Cutoff to the Oregon-California Trail. Still others planned to overwinter in the basin and trek westward in spring of 1850. However, a population swollen with non-Mormons threatened the Mormons' ability to feed their burgeoning church members over the winter; thus, this increase of gold rushers needed to be reduced.

The Mormons also needed an all-season and quicker connection to the eastern states than the long, laborious wagon road across the continent that was closed over the Rocky Mountains during winter. And they needed access to a seaport; thus, a road to the Pacific Ocean was essential to their growth. If they could pioneer and build a wagon road southward to the Old Spanish Trail and turn that trail into a road to Los Angeles, they would have a year-round supply line to the seaports at San Pedro and San Diego.[1]

They knew such a road was possible because some of their brethren had pioneered the route as packers who traveled from Salt Lake City to Los Angeles in winter 1847–1848 (Sutak 2010, 86). In addition, Capt. Jefferson Hunt (and others) made the return trip in spring 1848 with a herd of cattle. In April 1848, Orrin Porter Rockwell piloted "25 Souls in the Company" that included men from the Mormon Battalion, one light wagon belonging to Capt. Daniel C. Davis and his wife and child, and 135 mules and horses from southern California to Salt Lake City (Boyle 1848, 39; Johnson and Johnson 2014).[2] At one point, this wagon had to be either disassembled or belayed in one piece down a 15-foot vertical cliff to descend the steep Old Spanish Trail down Virgin Hill into Halfway Wash (about 16 miles due east of Moapa, Nevada) (Crismon in Bigler and Bagley 2000, 398n18). Lorton refers to this "great hill…almost perpendicular" on November 30, 1849.

How could the needed freight road be built quickly? Fortunately for the Mormon's new Zion, an answer lay close at hand. If they could encourage the gold-seeking emigrants who were recuperating around Salt Lake City to travel the Southern Route, these emigrants would have to build a wagon road to Los Angeles. These strong, young gold seekers were anxious to get to the goldfields and were willing to pay for a guide, and the Southern Route offered a way to circumvent the snowy Sierra Nevada.

Circumstantial evidence points to the Mormon hierarchy devising a plan to convince the emigrants they should travel the Southern Route: (1) Brigham

1. After leaving Salt Lake in September 1849, emigrant J. H. Purdy (1850) wrote: "The Mormons wanted a road made through to the city de los Angelos, which they looked upon as the commercial Metropolis of their state. It is included within the limits" of the proposed state of Deseret. To create a "Mormon Corridor" to the Pacific Ocean, Leonard Arrington (2005, 86) said "the founding of a string of settlements stretching south from Salt Lake City to San Pedro and San Diego, California," was very important, and of course settlements needed roads to tie them together. See also Hunter 1939.

2. Bigler and Bagley (2000, 397, 399) quote Boyle saying there are "35 Souls," and then they quote John J. Riser who says "23 persons." Boyle's handwritten diary clearly says: "25 Souls in the Company."

Young had a vision that emigrants leaving Salt Lake City late in the season would die in the mountains on the Northern Route; (2) tales of death and destruction on the Northern Route were circulated; (3) rumors began that the Mormon crops would not be sufficient to share with emigrants; (4) stories of cannibalism at the Donner Party camp in the Sierra Nevada were retold; (5) a Mormon guide was volunteered to lead a train that would travel the Southern Route (for a price); and (6) the Mormons planned to establish an enclave in southern California, and a road and forts were needed to connect it with Salt Lake City.

Brigham Young preached a "sermon that the Lord had come to him in a vision and told him that no emigrants starting after that time over the northern route to California would arrive there, but would leave their bones to bleach on the plains or in the mountains" (W. White 1927, 207). The emigrants were regaled with exaggerated stories of dangers on the Northern Route. Lorton relates one he was told concerning the heights of stumps at the Donner Party camp. "Stumps of trees are there to be seen 40 ft," Lorton wrote on August 9. This gross exaggeration of snow depth was intended to instill fear of what the gold seekers might encounter in the Sierra Nevada if they took the Northern Route late in the season. Closer to the truth was an account by Dr. Wakeman Bryarly, who recorded on August 21, 1849: "The trees around [the cabin near Donner Lake] were cut off 10 ft. from the ground" (Bryarly in Potter 1945, 113n13, 201; see also McKeeby 1934, 137). On June 22, 1847, Mormon Battalion veterans venturing to Salt Lake City from California visited the Donner Party campsites, and they brought eyewitness accounts of the horrid squalor found in and around the hastily built log cabins. Their doleful firsthand accounts included seeing mutilated corpses that had been pillaged for life-sustaining morsels and a human skull that had been sawn open to get the brains (Jones in Bigler and Bagley 2000, 238).

True stories were circulating about hundreds, if not thousands, of rotting horses, mules, and oxen littering the trail along the Humboldt River and across the Carson Sink. Goldsborough Bruff sketched one such ghastly scene (Bruff 1944, illust. facing 292). William White left Salt Lake City about "the first of September" and took the Salt Lake Cutoff to the California Trail (Northern Route), where he says he was "never out of sight or smell of dead cattle and mules and horses." He also commented that "Brigham Young, their leader and prophet, wanted as many as would, to go by the southern route, and to hire his men as guides and road builders.... Some trains were frightened and went by the southern route, though to their sorrow" (W. White 1927, 207–8).

Brigham Young reported in October: "Several hundred of the emigrants arrived in the Valley too late in the season to continue their journey on the northern route, and many of them contemplated wintering with us. So large an accession of mouths in addition to those of our own emigration, threatened almost a famine for bread." However, the Kanesville, Iowa, *Frontier Guardian* (a Mormon newspaper) proudly announced on August 8, 1849, that "the wheat crop [in Great Salt Lake Valley] has come in bountifully,...[and] there is every prospect of a large surplus of food for man and beast." And Isaac Haight said, "As much as 180 bushels of wheat has been raised from one bushel of seed [sown]" (*Journal History* 1849, October 8; Madsen 1983, 79, 98).

Thus, the gold seekers were inundated with dire information about the northern routes and at the same time urged to move on. There were also reminders of Frémont's fourth expedition—winter 1848–1849—when his men resorted to cannibalism (Nevins 1928, 2:410–11), and newspaper articles amplified the horrors that lay in wait for those trying to cross the Sierra Nevada late in the season. Lorton's journal stirringly sums up the predicament of all the emigrants.

Disagreements over the two routes wrenched apart mess-mates, close companions, and even brothers. Lorton's mess "split up our co-partnership...with much difficulty & dissatisfaction." Five days later he added, "part of our mess with others started for Cal. via north [route]" (August 10 and 15). Lorton, rather than the Kelloggs, seems to have done the work of selling their wagon, oxen, cows, and sundry goods and to have done the dividing.

James Ellery Hale, also a member of the Knox County Company, traveled the Northern Route from Salt Lake City with at least two of the Kelloggs and Luzerne Bartholomew. Later Hale intended to reconnect with "Wm. Petrie, John Evans, Luzerne Bartholomew, Lartes Langford, Wm. Kellogg and his father" with whom he "came through from Salt Lake" (Hale 1850). All the men Hale mentions were members of the Knox County Company.

When Luzerne Bartholomew elected "to rush through" on the Northern Route, he separated from his younger brother, Edward, who opted to take the Southern Route with his Jayhawker buddies. After Luzerne reached Sacramento on November 3, 1849, he was unsuccessful at gold digging and turned to ranching, and during this time he trapped a gigantic grizzly bear that purportedly weighed 1,988 pounds. This would make it the largest grizzly ever recorded. He brought the bear across the Isthmus of Panama in a wheeled cage and exhibited it on the East Coast and in Europe. Luzerne died before the bear did—years later in a New York zoo (Snyder 2003, 166; Runner 1995; L. Bartholomew 1906, 313–18).

Edward Bartholomew stayed with his Jayhawker friends, who took the Southern Route and continued west in southwestern Nevada instead of following the Old Spanish Trail to Los Angeles. He spent Christmas Day 1849 in Death Valley, then stumbled into the Rancho San Francisco (today's Valencia and Newhall, California), on the verge of death, on February 4, 1850. This became the Jayhawkers "day of our relief from starvation, the day of our deliverence, the day we should celebrate," three terrible months after Luzerne had reached Sacramento (Bartholomew in J. Johnson 2018, 176).

One Rover, A. J. Baker, left the others in Salt Lake City and arrived in California in September 1849, but most of the Rovers took the Southern Route (Cumming 1985, xi). James Wasley (1849) and wife took the Northern Route, and their friends, the Ryniersons, took the Southern Route.

The stick and carrot approach worked well for the Mormons as more and more emigrants opted to travel the unbroken Southern Route. Brigham Young gave orders "to Captain Hunt in regard to his mission with the emigrants and to measure the road." They "secured a roadometer which they attached to their wagon to measure distances" (*Journal History* 1849, September 20 and October 2). It was installed on James Brown's wagon that also carried Addison Pratt, Apostle Charles C. Rich, Francis Marion Pomeroy, and Hiram H. Blackwell (Hafen and Hafen 1954b, 224; A. Pratt 1990, 377). In 1847 the Mormons had perfected a wooden roadometer (odometer) that recorded revolutions of a rear wagon wheel to calculate the miles traveled (circumference of the tire in feet and inches times the number of revolutions, divided by 5,280 feet per mile) (Clayton 1973, 136, 143, 152; Wright 1995).

Lorton also witnessed the Pomeroy trial in Salt Lake City. One of the Pomeroy brothers was wrongly accused of participating in the 1838 Haun's Mill Massacre, in which a Missouri mob rampaged through the small Mormon community, killing 15 men and two young boys (Moore 2006, 8, 35, 36, 76). The trial in Salt Lake City exonerated Pomeroy after it was shown that hearsay evidence was used to obtain an indictment (Owens 2004, 276).

In April 1849 the Pomeroy brothers—Thaddeus and Ebenezer—and Gary Peebels "formed a copartnership…for the purpose of loading a [wagon] train with merchandise and supplies for the mines in California. Their outfit cost them 80 thousand dollars. There were forty-three wagons and three carriages, besides five hundred and sixty head of cattle" (Munro-Fraser 1881, 673). While in Salt Lake City, the brothers were allowed to sell some of the merchandise they had intended to haul to the California goldfields (ibid., 674). They also took the Southern Route but started several weeks after Lorton.

While in Salt Lake City Lorton made the effort to study Mormon history. Rather than making snap judgments, he took the time to understand and record it. A large part of chapter 7 is his recounting of that history as it was told to him.

After the breakup of his mess, Lorton was left without wheels. He bought a pony in the city and paid his mess-mates for Dick ox. He found room and board at the fort with the Jonathan Herriman Holmes family. Jonathan had been a private in the Mormon Battalion, Company D (Tyler 2000, 123) and was a shoemaker by trade. Lorton also spent time with the Addison Pratt family, who lived next to the Holmes clan. The Pratts probably provided the closest relationships Lorton had west of Illinois. Addison was 47 years old in 1849. He was also a monogamist, rare among the church hierarchy. He was outgoing, inquisitive, adept at foreign languages, a singer, and a man with an itch to travel. Addison was a man of the sea until he and his wife, Louisa, converted to Mormonism in 1838, after which he soon became an active and successful missionary to the natives of French Polynesia throughout the 1840s and 1850s. His travels often separated him from his family, sometimes for years at a time. Louisa was well educated and taught school from time to time. She was also a trained tailor, another talent that helped her support her family during the many years Addison was away at sea or as a missionary for the LDS Church. For Lorton, the two older Pratt girls (ages 17 and 15) would have been an added attraction to visit the Pratt family (L. Pratt 1998; see also Hafen and Hafen 1954b, 67). We use George Ellsworth's *The Journals of Addison Pratt* rather than the copy in the Hafens' *Journals of Forty-Niners*, which was "marred...by the fact that the editors were supplied [a]...faulty manuscript copy of the original journals" (A. Pratt 1990, xvi).

Lorton opted for the Southern Route, as did many from the Knox County Company, and made his way to Hobble Creek, south of Provo, by traveling with whomever was going that way. Cephas Arms, the Ewings, and the Taylors, who had been in Lorton's division of the Knox County Company, also took the Southern Route.

Lorton writes about the Indians, particularly "Walker the Utah chief & hawk of the mountain." Wakara or Waccara (ca. 1808–1855), the renowned Ute Indian chief white men usually called Walker was sometimes referred to as Napoleon of the Desert Frémont said he was named after Joseph Reddeford Walker. Wakara became notorious because of his daring horse-thief raids into Alta California and his kidnapping of Indian children to sell as slaves (Frémont 1970b, 1:695–96; Hafen and Hafen 1954a, 251). The Mormons attempted to build strong alliances with the local Indians. Even so, they found it necessary to build forts when some of the tribes (or bands) resisted when the Mormons usurped their land.

Lorton's Journal Continues in Salt Lake Valley

[August 1849] 8th day.[3] Comes to our camp 2 fine oxen which I drive down & at the mouth of the kanyon meet the owner who is a Mormon. Here the City first comes to view. After a gentle rise of ground you commence desending [into] the basin.

Here [Salt Lake City] is at present 19 wards, 9 Blocks to a ward, 8 lots to a Block, 1 1/4 acres to a lot. The streets run regularly north & south & east & west.

3. Lorton's name is listed in Emigrant Rosters 1849 (see also Cannon 1999, 146).

FIGURE 35. Engraving by Samuel Manning. "Salt Lake City in 1850." Courtesy National Archives, photo no. 513336.

These wards are cultivated, & the crops irrigated by water running from the Kanyons, in canals. This is equally distributed amonge the inhabitants & each farmer has his day for watering his crops. [For] the land lying on the sideling hill, the water is let in & disperced thro the rows of corn, buckwheat, & vegetables. They have scarcely any rain from Ap[ri]l to Nov[ember], yet I had the pleasure of witnessing 1 shower however. There are no fruit trees in the valley, & I fear they cannot rear them on a/c of the strong winds.

Salt Lake is 32 miles from the city, tho' the mountains which range through it looks to be 5 miles to the eye. There is another range to the left [Oquirrh Mountains] that appears to be only 3 miles, but the actual distance when traveled is 20 miles. When the Mormons first emigrated one thought he would go over & back before breakfast, but he kept on going & going over the level country till the sun struck the meridian, & it was pitch dark before he got home, traveling hard all the time.

This mountain is now on fire, set on fire by Indians (the Utaws). They set the grass on fire to roast crickets & grass hoppers. Then they become an easy prey, & are allready roasted for food.[4] These Indians come down in the valley & steal horses & kill oxen & eat them. This is done by poison which does not affect them for food so that the inhabitants do not know the cause, & makes no persuit. Several were found dead & partly eaten sence I came. When they steal horses the inhabitants pursue them even in their "Wick ee ups" where they either stand or give up the property. Last year the Mormons chased a number into there "wick e ups." They demanded their horses, but they [the Indians] remained obstinate & refused, so they [the Mormons] lit fire as they promised them & killed 4 Indians. Sence that, they have made themselves scarce. [This punitive expedition occurred March 5, 1849 (Bigler 1998, 68).]

4. Some of the fires blamed on Indians were accidently started by emigrant campfires. While camped on the Mojave River, Lorton records on December 31 that "while eating, the grass caught fire & spread rappidly so that we could not extinguish it." In addition to sometimes being set by Indians, fires also originated from lightning strikes.

The river Jordan flows piecefully through the valley to the north.[5] Pine timber is floated down this river from the kanyons. The[y] get fire wood 8 to 12 miles off, maple & pine. Jordan is fringed with high flags & tall reed like vegetation. Wire grass grows in some places upon which cattle do well. There is other kinds resembling eastern grass. This, cattle do well on & is perhaps the most norishing. Cattle will fatten on any of it in 3 mos. fit for beef, even broken down cattle, & cittizens buy up these at from $5. to 20. from emigrants giving fresh cattle in exchange. Many of what they call fresh cattle are only recruited emigrant oxen, which are best if sufficient time is given to recruit.

The settlements extend 50 miles north & south into the Utaw Valley, which is separated from the S. Lake by mountains. They have a farm belonging to the church of several hundred acres, worked by the people. This is to support the poor & neady. They have built a fort at Utaw Valley similar to the former & is increasing rapidly.[6] Utaw [Lake] em[p]ties into the S. Lake by an outlet called Jordan of which we spoke. This connects the 2 lakes.

On the west side of this stream is Hastings cutoff's commencement. It winds through the different mountains to [until?] it oppens on an almost tractless desert, without any feed [or] water for 80 miles & joins St Mary's River.[7] Hastings & his men had difficulty in performing the jorney. Another comp. undertook the rout but went in [to the water] so that nothing but their mules heads & tails [stuck out]. They crawled out with the mail & took the northern rout. Last fall a party of solgers returning from the mines took this cut of[f] & got as far as the point of the mountain on the left. There their horses & mules went in [briny mud] & were lost. The men were also mired, & remained almost starving till they were relieved by persons from the city. The nature of the country is this. It is sandy & barren, a few salt springs, mountains &c. You may travel on over solid earth when of an inst[ant] you are plunged in a gulf. The surface has all the same appearance. This is caused by salaeratus or alkali fermentations.

Tall reed grass grows about the [Salt] Lake valley in abundance to the hight of 14 ft. It makes excelent hay. There is another kind resembling eastern grass. Horses go crazy after eating it, & cattle do not like it. The game is antelope, bear,

5. Fresh water from Utah Lake flows northward via the Jordan River into Great Salt Lake. The water carries minute quantities of dissolved minerals, including table salt, which remain as the water evaporates, resulting in a solution about 10 times saltier than the ocean.

6. The Mormons began constructing Fort Utah (now Provo) in March 1848, and in a year, 150 settlers built their homes within its protective walls. Some Mormon Battalion veterans, including Jefferson Hunt, resided here. The fort was built because Mormon settlers feared reprisals when they began usurping Indian land.

7. Hastings's cutoff was the route the ill-fated Donner Party followed (Tea 2005a and b, parts 1 and 2). Frémont renamed Mary's River for the great German naturalist Alexander von Humboldt (Frémont 1970b, 3:505).

sheep, Black tailed deer, wild geese, ducks, & sage hens. Most of the large animals keep up on the mountains during warm weather.

9th Augt. is spent in discussing & enquiring about the different routs & it was thought by those that have been that rout [Hastings Cutoff] to be impracticable at this late season, but [and?] the hight of abserdity this year on a/c of the great emigration. Part of the Mormon Battallion came through last fall. They started 1st Sept from the mines, encountered some snow storms, but got their oxen through the Sierra Nevada mountains with difficulty. Then there is no difficulty, for you then pass through a lovely summer.

Stumps of trees are there to be seen 40 ft [closer to 10-12 feet tall], having been cut by a party that were forced to winter the year before [Donner Party, winter 1846–1847]. They were cut from the top of the snow showing the great depth you have to encounter. The road is thro' a kanyon most of the 100 miles, & the ravines & kanyons are drifted full hence the eternal snows we find in the mountains.

Nearly all of the Mormon Battalion [now at Salt Lake City] have been to the mines & dug gold. Some got 300 doll[ar]s, others 2[00] & 100 in 1 week. 1 man that has now gone to the states with the mail, found a rich hole by himself, & in 1 1/2 days got 700 dolls.

Towards the middle of the after noon the water that freezes on the mts comes down [and] raises the streams & they have to relinquish their work in the lower diggings. A great many belonging to the Battalion felt so ancious to get home to their families they did not stay long in the mines. Others say they did not realize the benefit. Mr [Addison] Pratt, Mormon missionary from Tahita Island dug some. He paid a blacksmith $40 to set his wagon tire & 2 [men] dug for him while he was doing the work. He came thro' the upper rout [the California Trail]. 3 of their men went on ahead to hunt the road [in the Sierra Nevada] & did not return, & were not found in 2 weeks. They had evidently been butchered by the Digger Indians.[8] They had dug a hole & covered them up with gravel. They were pierced with arrows. Some had the marks of 4 bloody arrows [that] were found near the grave, & the rocks had blood on them. They were killed undoubtedly for their mules, arms, & clothes of which they were stripped. Their comrades burried them in a becoming manner & their graves are marked by

8. The *Oxford English Dictionary* credits the first use of "Digger" to Washington Irving in 1837. Irving reported Bonneville's observation that Indians along Ogden's River "are of that branch of the great Snake tribe called Shoshokoes, or Root Diggers, from their subsisting, in great measure, on the roots of the earth; though they likewise take fish in great quantities, and hunt, in a small way" (Irving 1961, 224). Digger was a name given to many Great Basin and California Indians; it is now considered a pejorative.

trees, with the circumstance thereon. They [the Indians] always ransack every grave, even when they [the emigrants] burry in the road & as the wagons go out, each passing over [the grave]. They are sure to dig them up for the grave clothes [see A. Pratt 1990, 343–45].

The Digger Indians inhabit the Sierra Nevada mts & vicinity & are so called from the fact they live principally on roots. This is their principal food. They seldom hunt & have no horses & are afraid to ride one. The principal root is the "Sago."[9] It resembles an onion & favors the sweet potato in taste. This root is used also by the Snakes of the north, the Utahs on the lake, & the Piutes in the south to a considerable extent & grows profusely west of the Rockey Mountains.

[August] 10th [and 11th]. We conclude to split up our co-partnership. We with much difficulty & dissatisfaction come to terms after a few days consideration. I sell the wagon that cost $180 for $25, divide the provisions, chattles, &c.[10] The cattle left are 1 yoke cows, 1 yoke oxen [Brin & Buck] in good order, [&] 1 Duke ox in fine order. Dick ox got lame before we got in town, & of course depreciated in value. Cows now are worth as much as oxen. I sell Brin & Buck for $69 1/2 & buy Dick for 14 dols. Flour is worth 15 dolls. [per] 100 lbs & has been 50 cts a lbs. before the emigration. Scarcity existed during the winter, but the crops now looks florishing & plentiful. They expect to have some 1000s [of bushels] surplus grain, but do not throw out inducements to emigrants.

[August] 12th. Herd cattle part of the day. Have meeting in the "Bowery" [today's Temple Square]. Trial of Pomeroy takes place, charged with participating with the mob against the Mormons & for detaining their goods in Missouri. He had brot on some 30 tons of goods designed for Cal. but he thought it advisable on a/c of the danger on the north rout to sell out at Salt Lake. His teamsters mutinied against him & he solisited the protection of [Howard] Egan's Mormon comp. for they [the teamsters] threatened him. I[t] was proven that Pomry got in trouble in Mis[souri] for favoring the Mormons. Pomeroy was also chosen by Capt [Jefferson] Hunt of the Mormon batallion as a sutler as far as Santa fee & bore the best wishes of all Mormons that knew him. He was honerably acquited, & allowed to sell his goods. "If Guilty" he would have had to leive the country & sold his goods elswhere.

9. Sago (*Sagittaria latifolie*), Utah's state flower, commonly called wapato, is an aquatic perennial that produces starchy tubers the Indians used for food throughout much of North America. The tubers grow in shallow, muddy margins of bogs, lakes, and streams, but the leaves float on the surface. When cooked, the tubers taste like corn or potatoes, but when eaten raw, they are bitter (Spurgeon 1996, 20, 28).

10. The wagon was a Conestoga, now cut down, called the Ark that Lorton's mess used from Illinois and apparently sold to someone going on the Southern Route. Lorton mentions seeing it December 1 on the trail in Nevada.

They bring up any business matter before the meeting on the sabbath the same as any other day. The farmer is admonished concerning his crops, the mechanic his labors, & the duties of every cittizen is laid down.

[August] 14th. Never was I in [such] a delema before, or ever before struck so forcibly that it was nescesary to do something, & that immediately. I now fancied I see the blues coming rappidly towards me, & the horrors grinning at me with a double row of teeth, & what made it worse, every body was in the same fix. No one knew what to do. To cross the trackless desert [via the Southern Route] was burring [burning? burying?] yourself alive, & to go the Northern rout rushing in to a grave yard & rideing over dead [oxen] bodies.[11] Word comes that the fort hall road is so lined with carrion that new rodes had to be made, & the stench so stifleing as to almost stop the breath, & so thick are they, you can almost step from one to the other. The grass is nearly all ate up & thus alkali.

No food & fatigue causes death in heaps. On a/c of the loss of animals, women & children are seen loaded heavily ploding along, with feet bleeding, women & children crying already for food worn down with fatigue, & fainting by the way. Some halt at the [Salt] Lake, choosing rather to loose [lose] the wealth of the mines than to wade through blood to gain it, or to pass through grave yards to reach it. On, on, they rush. Gold! ahead. Headlong they plunge in ruin, death & dismay. Those that have started may pass, would to God they may. But there a[re] thousands yet to come who have listened so intent to the tingling voise of the Deamon of gold, they are deaf to the voice of warning. They will continue to go as long as there are any left. See Vol. III.

End of Volume II of Lorton's California Journal. Volume III, below, Continues in Salt Lake Valley.

Volume III of the California Journal

Gold! Gold! is the only thing that predominates in the mind of the avericious gold seaker. On they go dodging in between dead cattle amid the crys of half starved children & fainting women, amid the groans of the sick & forsaken, who have been left because of weakness & inability to go any further. This will become so frequent that a careless glance will be the only sy[m]pathy exercized by the more confident gold seaker. They cry for sympathy, for humanity! But the stones will not reiterate the answer given by the cons[i]encious ravisher of the Sierra Nevada mountains. Self preservation crys he. If I delay we will all perish together, is the heartless answer, & gold is almost seen beaming from his

11. By Northern Route, Lorton is referring to the California Trail. To reach it, emigrants trekked north, then swung northwestward on the Salt Lake Cutoff to intercept the California Trail at City of Rocks, Idaho (Bagley 2012, 119, 200).

eyes. Gold! What is the whole contents of [the] west compared to the life of one inocent wife or mother. They now croud to the gorge or kanyon through which they have to pass the mountains, each wedged in behind the other, all eager to cross that barrier. On they croud in countless numbers, climbing the steeps & rocky craggs.

At length the winds from old Pacific's bosom sweep over their heads & whistles through ravine & glenn & the white flakes, the snow white flakes, strew the ground. On it comes in profusion, the skys turn black the leaves tremble in the chilling blast. They whither & are hurled thro' currents of frozen air, & then there comes a frost, a chilling frost. All nature seams inanimate, with the exception of [a] madened storm deamon who now raves in all his fury. Snowey billow, upon billow rolls successively from elevation to the ravines & kanyons below, till all has become one level surface. Now a chilling gloom spreads over animated creation. Cold drops of sweat start from the temples of the emigrant, & dispare deapens upon his countenance. The wife weeps upon the bossom of her husband as she wraps her babe more closely to her heart, but what cares the gold seaker for friendship [or] warning.

The tide still pours in, but they can go no farther, for there is an impassable barrier. Consternation now runs through their ranks. Panic seizes them, provisions have been thrown away to lighten their load, & aid their progress. The "kiotas" [coyotes] have had a frugal meal. On they come, & on they continue to pour in, even when dim death has commenced his ravages. The food is good as long as it lasts, but presently it is all exhausted. Tis then the work commences. The motoe is "Strength is might" & the weak is overcome. Some may manage to make their way through, but what is to become of the helpless women & children. "*Death*" echoes an answer. "Food for the ravinish gold seaker," & these gold canibals now devour the most noble work of *Gods* design. The weak, the helpless & the inocent are sacrificed on the altar of "Hecate."[12] Thus they live in a grave yard till the plains are whitened with human bones & [fill] the kanyons in piles. Would to *God* it were not so, which may be by his strange interposition, but present prospect suggests the above scene to my imagination.

15th Aug. [1849]. Some one had told Brigham Young (at the time Jo[seph] Smith passed through Knoxville) that Capt Ewing said if he had known it, he (Jo) would never have passed out except in a coffin. Today Brigham visited the camp in a carriage with his lady. The subject was broached by Ewing as he had heard that B. [Brigham] had said he had better leave town. B. told him he did not care what people said & bade him go in peace. B. said man after man had passed through this place boasting of having fired our homes & drive us from

12. Hecate, Greek goddess of witchcraft, death, and crossroads was much in evidence in Salt Lake City, a crossroads where the emigrants had a critical decision to make.

our cities, & one made his boast of haveing fired the first shot at our prophit, but we forgive them inasmuch as we have been forgiven.

As the croud collected around his carriage, he related an anecdote, about Dr Franklin & the 41 chap[ter] of Exedos. His opponant was much better skilled in scripture than he was but he determined to out wit him, & quoted from the 41 chap of Exedos, where Abraham entertain[ed] 3 strangers [see Genesis 18:1–11], & he did go to work straight way & prepare food for the strangers, & when they did eat they offered not up thanks to God, & Abram was displeased & said, inasmuch as ye have not offered up thanks to God ye shall not sett under my roof this night, & the lord said unto his servant, Abraham! have I not born[e] up with these men 90 & 9 times & can'st thou not bear up with [them] this once. This was to[o] much for the Dr opponent, & in all his wisdom could not detect him in his 41 chap. The leader [Brigham Young] bad[e] us good day. The driver snapped his whip & off they rode to the "doby" city.[13]

Towards night, part of our mess with others started for Cal. via north [route, with] 6 yoke of oxen, carr[y]ing 1 change & provisions just enough to last & every thing the same as if they packed, intending to rush through.[14] I get boarding place in the fort & take my things to it. Hosts name, Mr Holmes of the battalion. [He was] in the employ of Capt Sutter, & dug in the mines. One man who was in delicate health cooked for 10 & received shares from each, sometimes $15 a piece. They would sometimes wash gold near the tent & in the cool of the day, & under shade of the tent he would crawl out & from the wastings he would collect his powder charger full, which held an oz. every after noon.[15]

The first dinner I ate seamed to me like a feast of fat things. I ate & ate as if I would never stop eating green vegetables. To set up to a table seamed awkward & to lean back in a chair a novelty. The log cabin in which I ate had a homely look, & it seamed altogether as if I had got on board of civilization once more.

13. Many of the initial buildings in Salt Lake City were made with adobe bricks.

14. Luzerne Bartholomew, one of those who elected to "rush through," reached Sacramento via the Lassen Route by November 3, 1849 (Runner 1995). Edward Kellogg and son Bill took at least one yoke of oxen after only a week of recuperation. Edward died in Marysville, California, October 12, 1851 (Hopkins 1903, 584). His son William returned to Elmwood, Illinois, in 1853, where he took up shipping grain and produce. He married Lavinia Bartholomew in 1856, and they had four children (*History of Peoria County* 1880, 744). William Kellogg died July 13, 1910, while living with his daughter, Belle, in Chicago. Henry Ward stayed in California and married Ann Toomy in Marysville in 1857. He "conducted" hotels in several California locations and was a tax assessor in Alpine County at one time. Henry and Ann reared five children. He died in San Jose at age 81 on April 11, 1900 (*Sacramento Bee*, April 11, 1900).

15. A powder charger measured the amount of black powder needed for propelling a bullet from a muzzleloader—a black-powder measuring cup. Presumably this was a troy ounce of gold, not powder. A troy ounce of gold is equal to 1.097 avoirdupois (regular dry) ounces.

I would take up a piece of hot corn, select out three rows for my corn crackers & go to work in my own celebrated stile. Then up come the peas, then the beans, & then the beets. My eyes were very large, as could be seen from the quantity on my plate. By & by they all got done, & I only just began. However, I was not to be backed off, bu[t] kept on till another table full sat up. They were members of the Boston comp. & full of jokes. They finally got done & I by good luck & good management got through as quick as my fellow epecurians. The sun s[e]t to day in all its glory, the high ridges casting its dark shade on the valley, the sun casting its refulgent rays upon the lofty summits of snow. The [area] below lightens up with a blood red glare, & in the west a dark purple mountain [Oquirrh Mountains] reflects the desending rays of the monarch of light & absorbs itself in beauty.

[August] 16th. A haze almost obscures the neighboring mountains from view, & the whirlwinds circle all over the plains more than ever today. These will stand in upright collums appearantly motionless reaching for thousands of feet in the air, a collum of dust. Today heavy clouds lower over the mountains, & heavy showers fall upon these eminences while in the valley scarcely a sprinkle is felt. I have seen heavy showers fall from clouds 1/2 way up the mountain & above all is dry. The mountains attracts the showers, & it is said, by cultivating the soil draws the rain, the same as in Oregon. They have now plenty of rain where at first they had none. Today I witnessed a curious phenonamon of Salt Lake. It is seen frequently before storms. Salt Lake cannot be seen by standing on the level ground near the fort, but on this occation Salt Lake appeared to rise to view. Whether it did or not I cannot say, or whether it was a reflection of [or?] refraction of light.[16] An establishment is about to be erected at the Lake for the manufacture of salt (table salt).

[August] 17th [and 18th]. Today Pres. Young & his counsellors, accompanied by a band of music, took a trip to the lake for the purpose of selecting a place for manufacturing the article. They took buffaloes [robes] for sleeping & provision[s] in plenty. They discovered a new valley [Tooele Valley], nearly equal to their present location. This excurtion is performed in Rockaway wagons & is to the valley what Coney Island is to N Yorkers.

[August] 19th Sabbath. Attend meeting in the Bowery. The Bowery is a shed of pine boards supported by trees with a stand & benches to set on. It is capable

16. Lorton has witnessed a superior mirage caused by refracted light. "When warm air overlies cold air, an atmospheric temperature inversion is said to exist.... Near horizontal light rays passing upward through such a warm layer are refracted downward and we see them above their non-refracted position as a superior mirage.... Superior mirages are even capable of bringing into view objects below the horizon" (Lynch and Livingston 2001, 58).

of holding 1,500 persons. We have a sermon from one or 2 of the bishop[s]. The morning's subject was principally "on tything." They say God requires 1.10th [one-tenth] of a mans property & his interest, to be devoted to the church. During the afternoon the emegrants were adressed in regard to their welfare. They warned them not to go the north rout, for they would go in to a graveyard, they would rush on till gold would be their ruin if they persisted. Their attention was called by Capt Hunt who has been the south rout, [and he will offer some remarks] on the following morning.[17] The brass band does up the choir in elegant strains to say nothing of the spirited tunes at the close of service.

[August] 20th. & in the morning a collection of emigrants gathers around the stand to hear what Capt Hunt late of the battallion has to say in regard to the south rout. At length the capt is seen coming in comp. of Pres. Young, & takes the stand in the bowery. Capt. commenced by saying that he would pilot a comp. thro' to William's Ranchoe,[18] of 100 wagons for 1000 dolls. He then gave a description of the whole rout, the dist. without water, fuel &c. Capt. Hunt afterwards advised the emigrants not to go the northern rout at this late season, & not to start on the southern tour till the 1st [of] Oct. on a/c of the excessive heat on the desert. [He] described the latter part of the journey as almost impassable, & said we might take up the Tularris Valley to San Francisco & the gold regions.[19] Only 1 wagon had ever passed thro here, belonging to capt. [Daniel C.] Davis,[20] & only 1 pack comp. before capt Davis, & they had their throats cut with stone knives. Their bones were burried by capt Davis.[21]

Pres. Young then spoke, & said he wanted to advise emigrants to do the best for themselves, that the people in the valley were very poor & wanted cattle, & if the Capt piloted the comp thro to the ranchoes the capt would buy cattle &

17. Jefferson Hunt had been part of a Mormon pack train that traversed the nascent Southern Route in 1847 and returned in May 1848. Their route from Salt Lake Valley followed a distinct Indian horse trail south to its juncture with the Old Spanish Trail in today's Parowan Valley, Utah. They followed this trail to Los Angeles (Schindler 1966, 176–78; Hafen and Hafen 1954a, 252–53; 1954b, 24–27; Lyman 2004, 1–42).
18. When Hunt was in Alta California in winter 1847–1848, Isaac Williams had verbally agreed to sell his 35,600-acre *Rancho Santa Ana del Chino* to the Mormon Church for $200,000 (Hafen and Hafen 1954b, 175; Beattie and Beattie 1951, 127, 130–34).
19. Tulares Lake is on Frémont's 1848 map, of which many emigrants had a copy. From the lake the gold seekers could follow the Rio San Joaquin north to the goldfields.
20. Orrin Porter Rockwell, once a bodyguard of Joseph Smith and later Brigham Young, guided the Davis family and members of the Mormon Battalion from Los Angeles to Salt Lake City in spring of 1848 (Johnson and Johnson 2014).
21. Burial of "bones" could refer to the desecrated bones of Hernandez and Santiago Giacome, whom Indians murdered at Resting Spring, California, in April 1844 (Frémont 1970, 677, 684). Frémont makes no mention of burying the corpses. There had been pack trains on the trail for years—Frémont, Mexican and Indian traders, or horse stealers. For background on Davis's trek to Salt Lake City, see Bigler and Bagley 2000, 395–400.

bring them back to the valley. Says he [Brigham Young], dont sell your broken down & lean cattle, but turn them out on good pasture & [I give] my word for it, before you go they will be fat enough for beef. I know it would benefit my people, but this is for your own good. Then said he, if other comps. trys to follow your trail with out paying their share, I'll stop them.[22] Woudit you bear me out emigrants. The answer was a unanimous yes. A vote of thanks was then given to the Pres. for his disinterested advice, & the meeting adjourned.

[August] 21st. By the request of pres. Young there was a concert held at [John] Packs tavern. There is a large room 50 by 25 [feet], good floor, rafters plained overhead, & the side walls brown mortar. Every thing looked cleaned.[23] The band belonging to the city played beautiful during the eve'g. About 8 instruments, [William] Clayton Leader, yankee stories. Adam Was a gentleman, & other songs followed. By the particular request of Pres. Brigham Young I was desired to sing on[e] of the latest Ethiopian melodies. I accordingly took the stand, & sang "Dearest May" accompinied by the violin. This brot down thunders of applause. Then came another Irish story, & after that, loud cries for another song from Mr Lorton. I then sung Susanna accompinied by violin & a powerful bass by Mr Kea [John Kay, a Mormon] from G. Brittan. Applause followed.

To the north of the City there is a warm sulphur spring of extensive size. This is dammed up a little & is a fashionable place for bathing. It is just hot [enough] so that you can bear it. It runs out through a subterraneous passage from the base of a high range of mountains having the appearance of sulphur with red spots here & there like Ochre, & if the spring was out east it would make fortunes for more than 1. To the north of this, there is a hot spring sufficiently hot to boil eggs. Hogs have been put in & their hair scalded off. The other day 2 emigrants went up to bathe in the warm spring, but missed their way & came to the hot spring, & prepared to bathe. Before going in, one of the party stuck in his hand & told his companion it was to[o] hot. I dont care exclaimed his companion. I can stand any thing the Mormons can & jumped in, but he had no more than got in when he cried to his companion for assistance. They did not know

22. We find no evidence Brigham Young tried to stop other trains nor attempted to make them pay "their share." Young wanted as many wagon trains as possible to travel the Southern Route because they would improve his needed freight road to California's seaports.

23. John R. Pack (1809–1885), a member of the Council of Fifty (a body of Mormon elders created by Joseph Smith to govern civic matters), moved his family from Winter Quarters to Salt Lake City in 1848, where he built a large home of timbers and adobe. It accommodated the family plus provided a large room for dances or public meetings (Bitton 1982, 104; Jenson 1941, 190; 1971, 714). In 1850, while Pack was proselytizing in France, this room was used for the first month of classes of the newly formed University of Deseret, later University of Utah. Called the Parent School in 1850, it provided classes at high-school level for about 40 students (Bitton 1982, 119–37, 140–42).

there was a [second] hot spring till he asked a Mormon how the devel they stood it, for it like to have made boiled meat of him. It was then explained.

[August] 22d. Have singing at sister Pratts & pritty girls. Indian Walker the Utah chief & hawk of the mountain came in town with his brother on horses. He is a famous horse stealer & the terror of the Spanard & Piede [Indians]. If a Spanard cheats him he will some times levy on a 1000 horses for pay.

The Piedes a[re] a mixture of Indian & Spanard & are in the utmost depth of poverty & misery. They increase to[o] fast for the means of sustaining them, & therefore they kill & sell their young. A child can sometimes be purchased for a plug of tobacco, but most of them are driven in bondage to the Spanish Rancheos.[24] Indian Wa[l]ker [Wakara] deals largely in Piede children & horse-flesh. He agreed with [Isaac] W[illia]ms to purchase a lot of children, & [when] the time came to receive them Wms had left, but bound his successor to fill the contract, but this he refused to do. So he [Wakara] assembled his men & proceeded to the place. Now says he, I want [pay for] the number of children or your scalp. They [the children] were given [to Williams's "successor"]. The guns were loaded in presence of him, & he [Wakara] departed that night. Walker stole 1000 head of horses as a recompense for the Rancheroes dishonesty.

The oxen in the Rancheo are worked by a stick tied to their horns. Walker is a man th[e]y say [is] of good principel when treated kindly & says he wants to live like white people & dont want to live on buffalo meat all the time. He is intilegent & carries the various traditions that have been carried down to his tribe. Mr [*blank*] of [Fort] Utah was discussing [discoursing?] upon the Bible & W[akara] seamed eager to grasp at the subject. He was telling him of the curses that came to Elija in the wilderness, this he had by tradition, then of the destruction of the 1st born of Ejypt. But in this he was interupted by W—, for W wanted to finish it by saying it was so dark that you could feel it with your hands. He also had a tradition of the flood. He the[n] said, why did not the white man tell me of that before. They had never told me any thing but curseing & daming. These Indians have the curses used by the traders, & will some time say "G—d d—d it," if anything displeases them.

To the south of the Piedes there is a nation that has not yet become slaves to the Spanards. They inhabit holes in the ground over which is laid sticks & brush, & everything is kept in as natural order as possible, so that no one can disern their place of abode till they get on to[p] of them, & then their tribe being

24. When the powerful and highly mobile Ute Indians learned the Spaniards and Mexicans in Alta California would "trade horses and white-man goods for children, the Indians found a new field of commerce." Many Indian children were kidnapped, but some Indians "traded their children away [because]... it was the only way they could get horses and guns. [An Indian informant] said they could make more children but they had nothing else to trade for horses and guns" (Hafen and Hafen 1954a, 261, 281).

powerful, they fire through loop holes & some times surround their enemy. They go down into the Spanish rancheos & levy on their horses & drive them off in the mountains. The Spanards pursued them once & got in their homes before they knew it. Then they [Spaniards] were fired on & killed a part while the rest fled in the utmost confusion. Sence that [time] they will not pursue them [the Indians] beyond their own rancheo.

[August] 24th. Ball at Packs tavern. Jas. Brown & my self gets our girls & off [we go].[25] Ba[*unclear*] band present with music. Dance & have songs till 2 o'clock, & then retire to our abodes of inocence.

[*Lorton made no Journal entries August 25 and 26.*]

[August] 27th. Auction at the north gate of the fort. The principal articles for sale were horses, mules, cows, oxen, & three boys. The boys were culprits, arrested for dishonesty. The hopefull youths were arrayed before the audiance who were setting on rail fences, wagons, chicken coops, &c. while others were standing. The platform consisted of the roof of a not very stately house covered with dirt. The first was a small boy, with a light wool hat partly over his eyes. He had a very rogish countenance for a youth & kept grining while the marshal cryed out going, going, & seamed to think it a very curious thing to sell a boy. At first there was no bidding, but finally it arrose to 1 doll & then to 2. He was then struck off to the bidder. He was arrested for stealing from an emigrants pocket while bathing in Jordan, $30, which he divided with the other 2. He had served 1 year before on a similar offense. His benefactors or guardians could not make a Mormon of him or make him come to prayrs, till one night his pious preceptor endevored by the rod to make him come to his prayrs, & got him down on his knees, but [the boy] would not pray, for he said he couldn't. Say anything, said his master, accompanying his command with a blow. "Amen" cryed the boy & up he jumped.

The next was a boy of 14 yrs for passing a $5 counterfeit piece on an old woman that made straw hats. He was cracked of[f] for 6 dols to the city marshall. The other boy looked very sheepish & had one of his arms in a sling. He was sold like the rest for one year.

[August] 28th. Capt Stansburry Comp. sent by U.S. to explore Salt Lake & valley, arrived here to day.[26] Large train on behind with baggage & provisions. They have all their surveying apperatices & mathimatical instruments.

25. James Stephens Brown (1971, 130–44) was six days younger than Lorton. He had been in the Mormon Battalion and was present when Marshall discovered gold. Brigham Young selected Brown to go on a mission with Addison Pratt to the Society Islands (a French protectorate that included Tahiti).

26. Captain Howard Stansbury arrived in Salt Lake City this date; however, the entourage

[August] 29th. Gen. Wilson, app'd [appointed] coll'r [collector] of Costs for the port of San Francisco & head Indian agent for western Cal., arrived with his family under the escort of Col. [R.H.] Morris bound for that place.[27] There is 25 mounted men, & teamsters to every wagon of which they have 20 & more coming, & 8 & 10 mules to the wagon & will start on the north rout for San Francisco. Their mules are very poor & some are now dying for want of breath. I buy a colts revolver from 1 of his men (who got it from a deserter) for $12 1/2.

[August] 31st. Gen. Wilson with his escort starts on the north rout, govt mules in very poor condition. Left several dead on the ground & in marshes. They had about 20 wagons & teamsters & 40 extra mules. These are all of them skin and bone. They do not get good care taken of [them]. If a mule sticks in a marsh they let it go. Consequently they drop down along the road in numbers.

I try to get a berth with Capt [Stansbury] to explore the valley, build boats for the lake &c., & launch out upon the briney wave.

Hist[ory] of the Mormons [According to Lorton].[28]

Jos[eph] Smith the head of the Mormons was born in the town of Sharon Ver[mon]t. He afterwards moved to Manchester N.Y. Ontario Co. About this time there was a religious excitement & amonge the rest. Smith became interested. He went in the woods to pray, & while praying a light came down from heaven & 2 persons full of glory decended down & stood before him.[29] Jos[eph] asked which of the numerous sects were right, & the reply was they are all of the devil, & he found him self lying on the ground facing heaven at the conclusion of the vision. He was then 15 yrs old. He afterwards see[s] another vision, & the angel of the Lord stood before him & told him there were

---

of John Williams Gunnison, Stansbury's second-in-command, arrived on August 24 (Gunnison in Madsen 1989, 135). Stansbury had been scouting a possible new route from Fort Bridger to Salt Lake Valley (Stansbury in Madsen 1989, 147–55).

27. John Wilson was on a secret mission for President Zachary Taylor. His charge was to convince the Mormon leadership and California's military governor to petition Congress for statehood as one gigantic state that would include most of today's Colorado, Nevada, Arizona, and New Mexico, and all of Utah and California. Wilson, Brigham Young, and key church members drafted a memorial that Wilson carried to California, where it was rebuffed (Morgan 1948, 383; Culmer 1947, 329–31). "General" John Wilson is not indexed in Clary and Whitehorne's *Inspectors General* (1987), so it appears "General" Wilson promoted himself to this rank.

28. Lorton's rendition of Mormon history is similar to that published in 1851 in Joseph Smith's *The Pearl of Great Price* (see also Gunnison 1852; Joseph Fielding Smith 1979).

29. In *The Pearl of Great Price*, Joseph Smith (2013, 49) says: "I saw two Personages, whose brightness and glory defy all description, standing above me in the air. One of them spake unto me, calling me by name and said, pointing to the other—*This is My Beloved Son. Hear Him!*" Joseph Smith (1805–1844) said he was 14 years old when this fantastic vision occurred (MacKay and Dirkmaat 2015, 2–3).

plates deposited, which was the book of Mormon & Hist. of the Nephites in a hill convenient to the village in which he lived. Here he found the stone box with the plates [and] Urim and Thumin [stones] as stated by the messenger. He attempted to take up the plates which were of gold, but the messenger forbade him till 4 yrs. should role by. At the end of the term he brought forth the plates to translate, which he did by the Urim & Thumin, & thus he brot forth the book of Mormon.[30] His followers continued to increase.

The plates were found in 1827 & the church established in 1830 in Independence Mo. From there they were driven to Clay Co. [Missouri], & from Clay Co. to Colvell [Caldwell] & other cos. & finally they were driven out of the state by an armed mob. They then crossed the Mississippi to Illinois. Thare they laid out a city in Hancock Co. which they called Nauvoo [on the Mississippi River]. Here they raised a temple of great size, skill & of singular architecture. On the 27th of June 1844 Jos[eph] & Hyrum Smith were murdered in the Cartharge jaol [jail] by a mob [about 22 miles southeast of Nauvoo]. Soon after the death of their leader, they prepared to leave Nauvoo. Jos[eph] Smith see[s] in a vision that they were to depart in[to] the wilderness & locate to a valley. Some of the Mormons went to Mt Pisga[h] Iowa, while others jornied up the Missouri. Brigham Young their president was then their leader & jornied with them.

While they were in the wilderness Tho[ma]s Benton made a speach in the Senate & accused them of being unloyal subjects (it will be recollected that Jos Smith was arrested for treason, he being Gen of the Navoo legeon) & to test the matter he sugested the propriety of testing the matter by making a demand on them for 500 men to join [the] war [with Mexico] which had broke out.[31] It was accordingly done while they were at Council Bluffs. Their leader then picked out the 500. One would say, we have wife & children, another, we have mother & sister to take care of. But he would say, no matter, we will take care of all. Go on, your country calls. There was suffering, crying, parting, fathers, mothers, & children were separated, & the remainder going they knew not whither, forced to leave their houses, their property & cast themselves out on the wilderness.

A number stayed at Winter Qrs on the Mo. [River] & in the spring of 1847 Pioneers were dispatched to hunt up a suitable place for locating.[32] They expected to go to the Pacific.

30. Urim and Thummim are, in common parlance, seer or peep stones. Joseph Smith said God sent a messenger named Moroni to show him where there were "two stones in silver bows (and these stones, fastened to a breastplate, constituted what is called the Urim and Thummim) deposited with the [gold] plates, and the possession and use of these stones was what constituted Seers in ancient or former times, and that God had prepared them for the purpose of translating the book [of Mormon]" (Smith 1878, 49; see also MacKay and Dirkmaat 2015, 62–65, and Van Wagoner and Walker 1982, 49–68).

31. We, and the staff at the U.S. Library of Congress, could not find this speech.

32. Winter Quarters was near the west (right) bank of the Missouri River in today's Florence, part of North Omaha, Nebraska.

In the same year Elk Horn [River] was appointed as the rendezvous & here assembled 506 waggons & 2000 persons, & commenced their jorney thro' the wilderness.[33] Near the south pass they cut in a southwesterly course to fort Bridger & then put over the Wasatch Mountains & thro' the kanyons till they arrived at the Great Basin & valley of the Great Salt Lake.[34] As soon as the leader [Brigham Young, was] at the mouth of the kanyon, & gazed down on the valley, he exclaimed that it was their destined place & the valley of beauty he had seen in the vision.[35] Here they built a Fort the first year, & in 1849 built this city, & emigration is continually flocking in from all parts of the world, & it is destined to be the great stoping place between the States, Oregon & Cal. The emigrant will only provide himself with provisions sufficient to last him to this place, & then recruit. Here is the place to exchange broken down cattle & mules. Besides opening a road to here they have opened a road that joins the Fort Hall road on St Mary's [Humboldt] River.[36] Brigham Young, Pres, Wilard Richards, & Heber C. Kimball, Pres. [are] councelors over all the world, & their 12 apostles [are], Orson Hyde, P[arley] P. Pratte [Pratt], Orson Pratte [Pratt], Jno. Taylor, Geo. A. Smith, Ezra T. Benson, Chas. C. Rich, Erastus Snow, Lorenzo Snow, Franklin Richards, Amisa Lyman, [Wilford] Woodruff. These are apostols over all the world.[37] There are 19 wards in the city & each ward govrned by a Bishop

33. The Mormons who were to gather at the Elkhorn River (about 20 miles west of Winter Quarters) started westward at the end of May 1848 with "2,408 people in 923 wagons" (Bullock 1997, 321). Brigham Young's company of 1847 numbered 143 men, 3 women, and 2 children (Clayton 1995, 295; 1973, 75). Some of those men, in addition to Mormon Battalion members, returned from Great Salt Lake Valley to Winter Quarters in the latter half of 1847 to assist the next wave of Mormons who headed for the valley (Bullock 1997, 267, 319–20).

34. They followed, with minor variations, the wagon road the Donner Party created in 1846. For a brief description of the Donner trail, see Madsen 1983, 26.

35. Brigham Young's revelation of January 14, 1847, now memorialized in the LDS's Doctrine and Covenants, Section 136, provided no destination, only the vague direction they should journey "West" (B. Young 1997, 11–14). But 16 months before, on September 9, 1845, the church's Council of Fifty discussed sending as many as 1,000 families "somewhere near the Great Salt Lake" to escape the persecution they experienced in the States (Grow et al. 2016, 472, 476).

36. Samuel J. Hensley and his packers pioneered the wagon road from Salt Lake City northward to the California Trail in 1848. Hensley's Salt Lake Cutoff joined the trail at City of Rocks in Idaho just north of the Utah boundary, not at Mary's (Humboldt) River as Lorton states (Bagley 2010, 380; 2012, 136). (There is a Marys River that flows into the Humboldt north of Wells, Nevada, but it is not near the emigrant trails.) That same year, Mormon Battalion members returning from California were the first to take wagons over this route to Salt Lake City.

37. After murder and mob violence in the Eastern States "failed to destroy Mormonism… [Mormon leaders] relegated to an undisclosed future date the aspirations of the government of the kingdom to rule the United States and the world" (Hansen 1974, 44).

who superintends all matters whether temporal or spiritual.[38] The streets are laid out at right angles, & the wards wave with ripened grain.

Sept. 2 [1849]. The men sent to explore the valleys south have returned. They did not go to Little Salt [Lake] as anticipated on a/c of Walker the Utah chief who felt afraid of the Indians in that vacinity & he with a small force. While they were sojourning, there came an Indian & hailed the Utah chief & by the Mormon interpriter we get this news. The runner said he had met an Indian who had walked 5 days. He said a party of Americans were driving thro' a lot of cattle, & while on the second drive on the desert they were attackted by a party of Piute Indians. That they fought 3 days till finally the last man was killed & thus the battle ended. The messenger had been out to make a treaty with the Piute tribe. The Piutes say as soon as the Ams see an Indian, they fire on them & then they think they want to fight. In their exploration they discovered a mountain of salt, & a valley suitable for settling in.

While they were there, they see in the bushes a hiddeous specticle. An Indian & squaw, neither of them had any flesh on them but were litterally skin & bones. They said they were 150 summers old. They said they were miserable & were glad the Mormons were come, that they were blind & had no one to provide for them, that they lived from the spring near by. They would poke in their hands & if fish or frogs came in their hands they would catch them. Otherwise they had to chew grass like the ox. They were entirely naked & looked as they sat like withered murder.

Lot of our comp oxen come in [with other wagon trains]. Have trial concerning them in a tent used for selling water mellons in. Verdict in favor of [*blank*].

A man can have as many wives as he chooses as long as he can support them. Brigham Young has 30.[39]

[*Lorton made no Journal entries September 3 through 10 while in Salt Lake City.*]

Sept. 11th. Go over Jordan [River] to look for ox. Meet Indian on horse said he wanted doctor, & that some boddy was sick & crazy. He made motions by pulling his hair, & motions with his hands by leaning his head on them & then as if digging a grave. He made the most pittyful morning noise. On returning at night after a long tramp, it looked red in the west over the lake. I met one Indian on horse back with his squaw, both straddled, one with a bow & the other with a gun. They were in a Spanish gallop & hollowed howdy do as far as I could see

38. This relates to the Mormons' tenet to create a theocracy where there is no separation of church and state (Hansen 1974, 24–44; see also Crow et al. 2016, xxxvi–xxxix, 40, 88, 521).
39. When Lorton wrote this comment, Young had married 44 women. His total marriages were 55 (Jeffery Johnson 1987, 62, 68, 69; see also Hardy 2007, 143).

them. They had a pappoose hanging on the horn of the saddle. By their side ran another Indian painted red around the eyes with vermillion. I give him a pair of pocket combs. As I approached the Indian camp near Jordan bridge (it was just twilight), I heard some of the loudest screaming I ever heard, & as I approached I soon concluded that it was some dance, but afterwards remembering the Indian that I had seen in the morning I concluded he or she was dead & that they were morning over the boddy, which so proved to be, tho I did not dare to disturb them in their revels o'er the dead. Their dogs barked & snarled which were part & all wolf & the "Kiotas" off set in their howlings, & of all the noises no pen can describe. There they were, Old men, women, children & babies, all yelling to one tune, & as they danced about through the bushes, they looked like so many devels.

[*Lorton made no Journal entries September 12 through 20 while in Salt Lake City.*]

[September] 21st. Bot me a nag of [from George G.] Blodget for $55. Went with him after a bridle & in returning home poney ran away from me, up one street & down another & the harder I ran the harder she ran till within a block of the bench land. There I cut acrost fields to head her, thinking she would run home, that is the camp at Big Kanyon, 8 miles. I ran all out of breath till I came to the fence where I hid thinking she would come along, but as she did not, I thought she must have passed. At first I thought I would follow right on, & on 2d thought perposed to stay all night at a house the light of which I see not far off, for I was very tired & out of breath made still more so by carring "Colts revolver." Just then the thought struck me to follow the fence back. I did so & had to cross many deep ravines. These I examined minutely to see if there were any tracks, many of which were difficult & bushey. I arrived at the st[reet] & the first thing that met my eye was Black Bess. She made a desperate push to pass me, but I caught her by the raines, & took her to the fort about 12 o'clock.

[*Lorton made no Journal entries September 22–23. On September 24 he headed south to join others gathering to take the Southern Route.*]

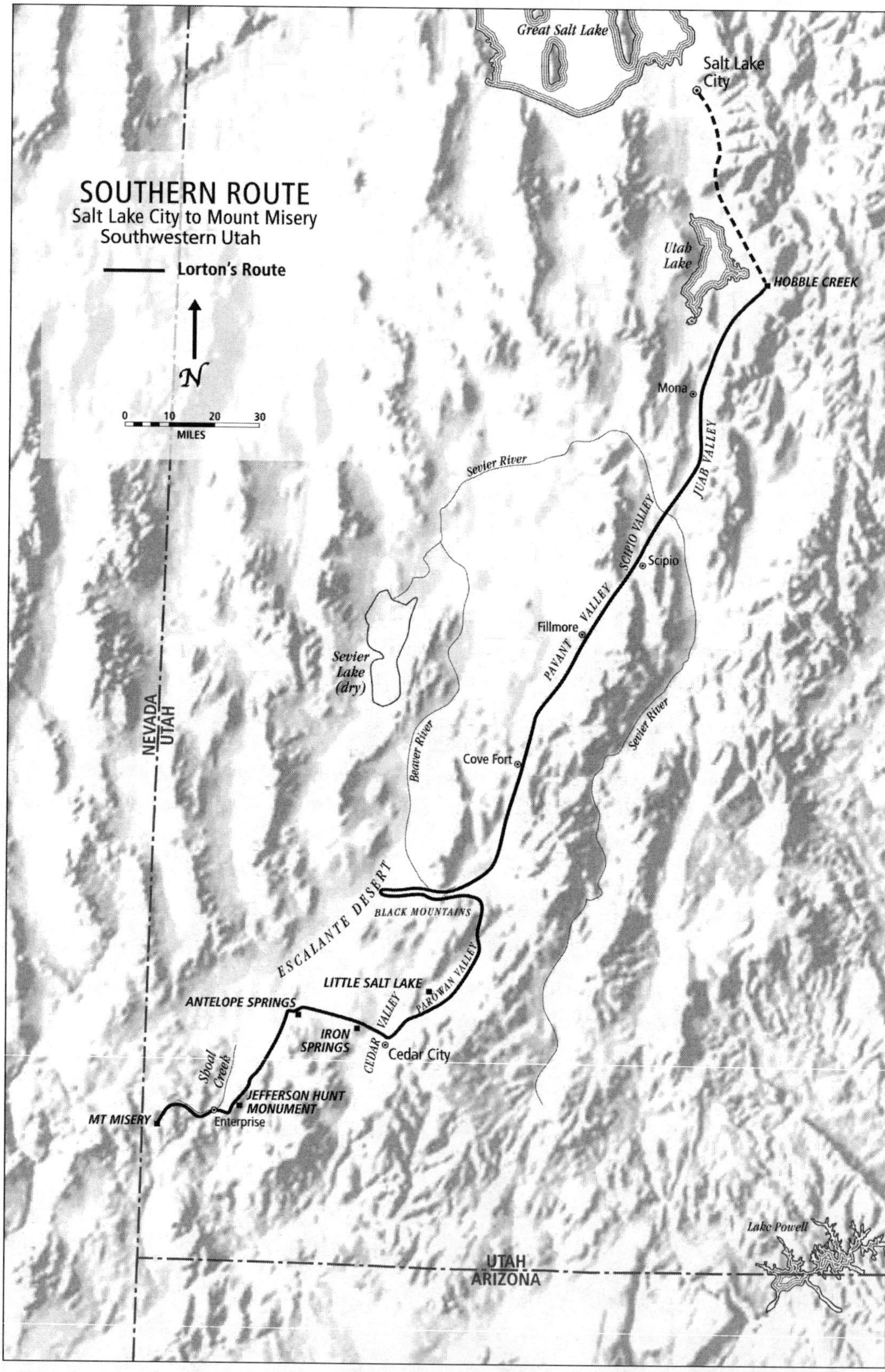

MAP 3. Southern Route: Salt Lake City to Mount Misery, southwestern Utah. Map drawn by Eureka Cartography based on editors' trail analysis.

CHAPTER 8

Salt Lake City to Beaver River, Utah

Background

In late September 1849, an assemblage of hundreds of emigrants with wagons and cattle began to congregate about 60 miles south of Salt Lake City on Hobble Creek at today's Springville, Utah. Their purpose was to proceed to California via the Southern Route to seek either their fortunes in the goldfields or to settle in Alta California. The 400 or more men in the wagon train would provide free labor to break a road to the Pacific Coast.

When Brigham Young (with the help of Jefferson Hunt) convinced hundreds of emigrants to take the Southern Route, he accomplished the task of removing hungry, non-Mormon mouths from the city, thus conserving the fall harvest for the brethren.

A large portion of men in this new train were from the old Knox County Company, the famed "stampede" train, including two fairly cohesive subgroups—the Fayette Rovers and the Jayhawkers. Single men, such as Lorton, needed to band together in new wagon messes. On the Southern Route, Lorton was bounced from one group to another, but he kept his positive outlook and curiosity about what he saw and heard.

When Lorton left Salt Lake City for the rendezvous at Hobble Creek, he and other small groups kept getting lost on the way, but they finally caught up with the Jayhawkers at the Provo River.

The Jayhawkers had taken oaths in the Platte River Valley to help one another. Lewis Manly said they "were not, in general terms, considered a secret order; but they were bound together as firmly as any secret society on earth" (Manly 1949, 25). Many of these men became part of the Jay Hawk or Jayhawker division in the soon-to-be-formed San Joaquin Company with Edward Doty as their division captain. Most of them continued west from Mount Misery in southwestern Utah, through Nevada and Death Valley to the coast via Soledad

Pass in southern California, thus establishing their historical prominence when they became the first Caucasians to blunder through Death Valley.[1]

Lorton's continuing curiosity covered geology, archaeology, and the people around him. For instance, on September 30, at Hobble Creek, Lorton sees five men emerge from Spanish Fork Canyon, and instead of stopping with that observation, he meets and quizzes them about who they are, where they came from, and what they experienced. The leader of this little band was William Lewis Manly, who wrote *Death Valley in '49*, one of the great, true adventure stories of the American West.

Lewis Manly and his Wisconsin trapping partner, Asahel Bennett, planned to travel together to California, but while Manly went north to buy a pony, Bennett started west with his family. Bennett took Manly's "outfit and gun," expecting him to catch up later, but because Manly could not find the Bennett family in the Council Bluffs area, he hired on with Charles M. Dallas to drive one of his ox teams to California. Imagine Manly's surprise when he finds the Bennett family encamped at Hobble Creek. All Manly had when he left Wisconsin was Bennett's "light gun, a small, light tent, a frying pan, a tin cup, one woolen shirt and the clothes on my back" (Manly 1894, 61, 102). Here he is, nearly destitute after crossing the plains and floating 415 miles down the turbulent Green River when, in the middle of nowhere, he serendipitously stumbles upon the wagons carrying his gear and money.[2]

The seven river-floaters were Lewis Manly, Charles and Joseph Hazelrig, Alfred Walton, John Rogers, Richard Field, and M. S. McMahon. They had worked for Dallas's small trade-goods train and quit his employ when they reached the Green River at the Oregon-California Trail crossing in present Wyoming. When they heard Dallas was going to let them go in Salt Lake City, they found and repaired an abandoned ferry boat and decided to float to California. They aborted this venture (after several calamities) when they had a chance encounter with a Ute chief, Wakara, near today's Green River, Utah. Field and McMahon stayed with the Indians a few weeks and ultimately made their way to Salt Lake City. The former five followed Wakara's directions toward Salt Lake City and arrived at Hobble Creek as the San Joaquin Company was assembling (Johnson and Johnson 1987, 51–52; Manly 1894, 74–103; McMahon's story in Manly 1894, 279–319; see also Kane 2008, iv).

1. Their story is graphically told in Jean Johnson's *Grit and Gold: The Death Valley Jayhawkers of 1849* and William Lewis Manly's *Death Valley in '49* (see also Johnson and Johnson 1987).

2. Mileage of 415 is the distance from the Mormon Lombard ferry at the Oregon-California Trail crossing of Green River, southward to the Old Spanish Trail crossing three miles above the town of Green River, Utah (Kane 2008, 3, 94, 203, 208).

The Bennett family had taken the Council Bluffs Road after joining the Badger Company wagon train; several wagons from this company took the Southern Route. Lorton's observations and dates have helped historians figure out where Manly and his friends traveled before they arrived at Hobble Creek.

Lorton's keen observations about soil and rock formations included Mount Nebo, where he comments that just below the peaks "there appears [a] substance resembling sand, upon which there arrose a dispute" (October 6). Welch, listed as a geologist for the Fayette Rovers, climbed Mount Nebo with some other men to satisfy their curiosity. After a trek far more difficult than expected, Welch (October 6), found the mountain to be "limestone with seams of white quartz," but Lorton reported on October 6 the white spots were "sand hardened by the weather, not rock" (Welch in Ressler 1964, 261).

Farther down the trail Lorton comments on unusual sinkholes partially filled with water. Addison Pratt also observed "some of those deep wells, when one of our oxen fell in and would have drownded had we not taken another yoke of cattle and drawn him out" (A. Pratt 1990, 380). Vestiges of sinkholes are still visible five miles southwest of today's Levan, Utah, in Juab Valley, where some have been filled in to level land for farming. Two days later Lorton notes more sinkholes near the northern end of Scipio Valley, and almost 120 years later they are described in the scientific literature: "Numerous sinkholes in the alluvium are aligned along faults…in Scipio [Valley]…particularly in the northern end.… It is believed that the faults penetrate the bedrock underlying the alluvium…and that solution by ground water moving along the fault planes and the fractures…is creating a series of connected caverns in the bedrock. The collapse of some of the caverns…is causing collapse of the overlying valley fill and the consequent appearance of sinkholes at the land surface.… Some of the holes are connected by tunnels" (Bjorklund and Robinson 1968, 18). Lorton correctly surmises that interconnected tunnels drained them. Near today's Cedar City he describes the iron deposits as did Reverend Brier, a Methodist minister in the train and later part of the Death Valley '49ers (Lorton, November 1, 1849; L. Johnson, 2005b, 225–26).

Lorton attempts to discern the differences between the "Ute," "Pyute," and "Piede" bands. Sondra Jones describes how complex it can be to distinguish between them. Jones writes: "The Southern Paiutes were Numic neighbors of the Utes, with whom the Utes frequently interacted, traded, intermarried (usually captives), and preyed upon. Numerous Piaute bands are named in the literature; in general, they were known as Paiutes, Piedes, or Digger Indians.… They were identified as part of an ethnic and linguistic group that included Utes" (Jones 2019, 438). Lorton comments on their dress and customs and attempts to communicate by learning some of their language. He does not fear the Indians, but after his experiences with them, he guards against their penchant for stealing.

Near the Sevier River, Lorton trades the sassy little black pony he bought in Salt Lake City for a white stallion the Indians had stolen in California. Lorton is smitten by this "beautiful Cal. horse, as white as alabaster." He names it Mazeppa after the popular poem that Lord Byron wrote. Mazeppa was the man in the story, not the horse, but Lorton's new stallion likely reminded him of the wild, plunging steed in the 1846 Currier and Ives illustrated edition, which depicts a white horse. Lorton naming his horse Mazeppa was prophetic; Byron's horse also bore its burden into the wilderness and died from the exertion of doing so.

On September 30 at Hobble Creek, after Reverend Granger preached a sermon, the emigrants met to set up committees to form a constitution for this already large wagon train, and to collect the $10 fee from each wagon to pay the Mormon guide, Jefferson Hunt.

Capt. Jefferson Hunt (1803–1879), who had converted to Mormonism in 1835, had been a member of the Nauvoo Legion in Illinois and commissioned as a captain for Company "A" in the Mormon Battalion. Its members were discharged in Los Angeles in July 1847. Hunt's return route to Salt Lake Valley was up El Camino Real to Monterey, thence to Sutter's Fort (Sacramento), east over the Sierra Nevada, and up the Humboldt River. In late 1847, he had traveled by horseback to Los Angeles over a trail that was to become the Southern Route, returning over the same route in May 1848 (Schindler 1966, 176–78; Hafen and Hafen 1954a, 252–53; 1954b, 24–27; Lyman 2004, 1–42). After guiding emigrants along the Southern Route, Hunt helped settle the town of San Bernardino in 1851. He served in the California State Assembly from 1853 to 1857, and founded the town of Huntsville, Utah, the following year (see Sutak 2012).

Lewis Granger, Adonijah Welch, and Thomas M. Marshall were elected to draft a constitution and by-laws. Welch says about 200 folks were in attendance at the meeting to organize the train (but only men were permitted to vote). After this date about 32 wagons joined the train, bringing the ultimate number to 107 wagons.

The San Joaquin Company is often spoken of as the Jefferson Hunt wagon train, but the emigrants formed and administered the train and hired Hunt to guide their wagons through to southern California. On October 3, after about 70 wagons arrived at Peteetneet Creek, 16 miles south of Hobble Creek, the emigrants elected Henry Baxter (captain of the Rovers) as colonel and seven captains to govern the train's seven divisions. Some division names were Hawk Eyes, Wolverines, Bug Smashers, Buckskins, and Jayhawkers (Stephens 1916, 16).

Although the original papers forming the San Joaquin Company are missing, Lewis Manly wrote about its organization 45 years later:

> The train was divided into seven divisions and each division was to elect its own captain. Division No. 1 should lead the march the first day, and

their men should take charge of the stock and deliver them to the wagons in the morning, and then No. 1 should take the rear, with No. 2 in the lead to break the road.... The numbers of animals cleaned out the feed for a mile or two each side of the camp and a general meeting was called for the organization of the whole. Mr. L. Granger got up so he could look over the audience and proceeded to explain the plan and to read a preamble and resolutions which had been prepared as the basis for government. I remember that it begun thus:— "This Organization shall be known and designated as the Sand Walking Company [San Joaquin Company], and shall consist of seven divisions etc."... Capt. J. Hunt was chosen commander and guide, and his orders must be obeyed. All possible trouble that we could imagine might come was provided against in our written agreement, and all promised to live up to it. (Manly 1894, 107–8)

Lorton's Journal Continues as He Leaves Salt Lake City

[September 24th, 1849] 25th. After paying my board bill & singing [cinching] up saddle which was a Spanish tree with marking [?], a "kiote" skin &c. [for a saddle blanket]. I bid good buy to Mr & Mrs Holmes mine hosts. Mr H. asked me if all was right, no hard feelings & Mrs H. said I appeared like one of the family. Mrs Platt [Louisa Pratt] mended an over coat for me & in the pocket put a letter in poetry. Her husband is expected to join me in a few days on his mission to Tahiti isles [together with] Mr Brown, Apostle Charles C. Rich & another, all Mormons.[3] Mr [Joseph] Busby give me a blessing & wished that plenty of gold might be my portion. The sun was setting when I started. I went to the store & got p[ai]r [of] spurs, then went to Blacksmith & Bot "larriet" & took down thro' the church farm. By this time it was dark.

A few miles out I stop[p]ed at a hut & the woman told me there was another house 2 miles farther on. I followed on & met several teams just from the kanyons with wood, & I followed on but on a/c of the multiplicity of roads was somewhat bothered but took those that went to the right till I came to a large mud hole. This I crossed by dismounting & kept on till it lost itself amonge the bushes. Several times I thought I heard noises & see houses, hay cocks &c., but on approaching proved to be trees & bushes. I wandered about knowing not where I went till I though[t] I would go to sleep in the bushes & wait till morn. I got a good place. The wolves were howling around, so I put caps on my pistol. Just then I heard voises & mounted to find the person or persons I heard. I could see thro' the dark an ox team, & 3 [2] persons just came up & said they

3. They left Salt Lake City October 5 and caught up with the San Joaquin Company at today's Nephi, Utah (ibid., 372, 378–80; see also J. Brown 1971, 130–33).

were lost & asked which way the road went.[4] I then came up & found Davis & Clark the persons lost. We 3 went to gether up the road to the kanyons & road to [the] Mills. After traveling a great ways we accidently fell in with Bartholomew & Capt Haynes who had also lost them selves & camped here. They chained up there oxen to the bars & I posted my poney near some bushes to feed on them.[5]

[September 25]. The next morning I put up the kanyon road & then struck down to saw mill & so up to Cotton wood. There is 2 cotton wood creeks. Fremont passed near here in his expedition.[6] I let my horse graze a little at the Cotton[wood] & got drink of butter milk from a woman. After a 15 miles drive I met Old man [C. W.?] Miller,[7] put my poney out on good grass & stayed till next morning on Willow Creek [near present Draper].

[September] 26. Early start with a tall Negro, late steward on Mississippi River [steamboat]. Pass a boiling spring on right of road. Clear pure water, 6 miles & then reach end of G. S. L. [Great Salt Lake] valley. Assend a high dividing ridge [Traverse Mountains] between Utah [Lake in Goshen Valley] & the latter valley.[8] Upon the top is a table land, & the road is steep, sandy & tedious. Upon the top is a beautiful location for a residence looking down on the beautiful lake Utah. It is 60 miles long & 12 wide to all appearances.[9] The [Wasatch] mountains around its edge to the east are high & covered with grass. The rows of trees

4. There was a half-moon plus stars for light.

5. Davis (Urban Davison), Orrin Clark, Edward Bartholomew, and Asa Haynes became Death Valley Jayhawkers. Haynes had been elected captain of the Knox County Company when it first formed. The Knox County Company men who continued west from Mount Misery seeking Walker Pass, became the Death Valley Jayhawkers, and have a star (*) next to their names in the membership list in Appendix A.

6. The northern creek is today's Big Cottonwood Creek in Big Cottonwood Canyon, up which is Brighton Ski Resort. Five miles south is Little Cottonwood Canyon, up which are the Alta and Snowbird ski areas. Several impressive peaks separate the two drainages. Frémont traveled north as far as Utah Lake. Then, "turning our faces once more eastward, . . . we left the Utah lake" when returning to the States during his second expedition to Oregon and California in 1843–1844 (Frémont 1970b, 703).

7. There is a C. W. Miller from Mercer County, Illinois, (northwest of Knox County) on the Knox County Company roster (Appendix A).

8. Wagons (and Lorton) crossed the Traverse Mountains by following the toe of the mountain along the right (east) bank of the Jordan River. The final crossing into Utah Valley required a short, but very steep, up-grade before reaching a gradual descent into the valley (Tea 1999, map 2). Addison Pratt used the same route on October 5 and "found a verry hard hill to ascend which is a divide between Salt Lake and Utah vallies" (A. Pratt 1990, 379).

9. Today the maximum length and width of Utah Lake is 24 by 13 miles, with a depth of 10 to 14 feet. When Lorton viewed the lake, it may have been three to five miles longer.

& the dark lines of scrubbary denote the mountain streams that put into it from the west. We arrived at the Am[erican] fork at noon [north of today's town of American Fork]. Met Boy on horse & another driving cow & calf. 1 team on the fork drying beef on sticks. We then went over some wet ground & at 3 o'clock arived at Provost [Provo] River w[h]ere the Knox Co Comp. are camped. Pritty stream with plenty of trees, water cold as ice. They had built a bower of bushes & brush. Under this I slept on buffalo rob[e]s. Plenty of Indians around.

The fort here is built of logs, the doors inside & 2 gates, 1 at north & other south.[10] An open log shed built of huge logs & a heavy mounted cannon on top brot by Capt Hunt from Cal.[11] Killed a beef out side & sold it at 7 cts [per] lb. Doz[en] Indians standing around waiting for the guts, & offall, which the[y] fight for with as much igerness & [as?] wolves for a carcase. Have a "Fandango" in the fort which lasts till day light. A Mexican sitting out by the door with a steeple crowned hat & Mex. blanket around him. His comp. had left him & he was sick. He could not speek Engl[ish]. Had a trial under the Canon shed between Dallas & the Rovers. I was called on as witness. The cattle were of those that stampeeded on the Platt. The honorable body decided in favor of the Fayette Rovers.

[September 27.] Set out next morning the 27th for Hobble Creek which was 10 miles. Pass 2 creeks, one fringed with trees & the other (Spring Creek) not. As I am crossing Spring Creek, a person tells me Burnett, the man I agreed to go with, had started out. He was to take me thro' for 30 doll to Wm's Ranch.[12] He was formost in getting up The Independent Comp.[13] They first ingaged [Charlie] Mcintosh & he went off with a pack train.

10. The decision to colonize Utah Valley was made March 19, 1849. The Mormon hierarchy selected "thirty men and their families" to move to Utah Valley and erect a stockade in which to build their log houses. This settlement became known as Fort Utah (Sutak 2012, 279–81; see also Ellsworth in A. Pratt 1990, 552n6). Jefferson Hunt and his family were among the first settlers here.

11. After Captain Hunt and fellow Mormon Battalion soldiers were discharged from the U.S. Army at Fort Moore, Los Angeles, on July 16, 1847, they trekked north to Sutter's Fort at today's Sacramento. Here the Mormons purchased two small cannons from John Sutter and brought them to Utah (Ricketts 1996, 169, 203, 330n28).

12. Isaac Williams married into the prominent Antonio Marìa Lugo family and became a Mexican citizen. Williams's ranch—*Rancho Santa Ana del Chino*—was a sprawling 35,600-acre Mexican land grant in the San Bernardino Valley. When Jefferson Hunt was on the ranch in 1847, Williams agreed to sell his grant to the Mormons for $200,000, but he later reneged his offer (Beattie and Beattie 1951, 123–31; see also Bynum 1934, 1–4).

13. Lorton's partnership with the Kelloggs had dissolved, so he intended to join the Independent Pioneer Company (also referred to as the Gruwell-Derr wagon train), the first wagon train that began blazing the Southern Route.

[James] Waters went with another.[14] About 45 wagons we[n]t off.[15] I immediately put after Burnett who was nearly out of sight. Here I spured my horse till my spine & boot was all bloody. I met a doz Indians on horses. One came out to talk with me, the rest went on. I at length over took the wagon but learned that Burnett was on to the creek, that he also had 6 [men] to his wagon. I wheeled my horse & put back to the creek disapointed. I here talked with a man on going with him. Dallas wanted me to go with him.[16] [Charles] McDermet said he wanted me to go with him & he would not charge any thing. Before I decided, Mr [Lewis] Granger the minister said he understood that I wanted to go with some one, that he was pleased with my appearance & would like to have me to bear a share of the burden.[17] He wanted as far as I could understand my horse. I made arrangements to go with McDermit from Kentuckey. He had 2 yoke oxen & 2 horses. My things had not yet come up from [Fort] Utah. [Alexander] Palmer & [Edward] Doty were to bring them up. This was the reason why I did not catch Burnett. To day I was informed by Deacon [Cephas] Armes that the Indians had stolen my bacon (40 lbs) the previous night from of[f] the wagon side & the cloth where in it was wraped flung in a slew near by. This was mellencholly intelegance for me, as it was all the meat I possessed. Bad luck appered to befall me in every form & I swore that if I found the thief I would shoot him & loaded my revolver for this purpose.

[September 30] 30th Sept. was the Sabbath. Mr Granger preached a sermon on profanity &c. The meeting was held under the trees, under which sat a large assemblage of emigrants, & a number of Indians with their rifles & arrows stood a little ways off listening to they knew not what. The ladies sat in the tent. While engaged in the discourse the team with my things arrived.

Not long after I see 5 men with 2 horses packed coming down the big kanyon to the S. east. I went to meet them & learned they were Green River floaters that had left Dallas, made canoes & floated down Green River to [toward?] the Col-

14. James Wesley Waters's pack train arrived at Williams's Chino ranch October 29, 1849, "from the Grate Salt Lake with a party [of] 1.14 [114] men . . . in good helth with loss of abot 30 Muls for wa[n]t of water and grass" (Bynum 1934, 32; Hafen and Hafen 1954b, 47–50).

15. Vincent A. Hoover, a member of the Independent Pioneer Company, is our authority for the number of wagons in this train. On October 17, 1849, he said his group had 23 wagons, and "22 wagons were close at hand," making a train of 45. Addison Pratt (1990, 382) says there were "some 50 waggons."

16. Charles M. Dallas, the owner of a small wagon train, had hired Lewis Manly and John Rogers as bullwhackers at the Missouri River (Manly 1894, 61). Instead of staying in Salt Lake Valley as he had told his men, Dallas was now taking the Southern Route. He moved ahead of the slower San Joaquin Company and joined the Shearer group to create the rear section of the Independent Pioneer Company (Hafen and Hafen 1961, 15:28).

17. Lewis Granger was a Baptist minister who practiced law after he and his family settled in Los Angeles (Granger 1959, 5–7; Manly 1894, 76, 279).

erado.[18] They said they had had a hard time of it & nearly all lost their lives dashing amonge the rocks & down rappids & over falls. They had all lost their fire arms except one, & would have starved to death but for Indian Walker who gave them as much as they could eat, & traded the horses to them for amunition & clothes, put them on a trail & told them it was 8 sleeps to the valley. The Indians were very kind to them. They had hardly any clothing & shoes on them. They said it had been very cold on the mounts, that they had seen mountains of every shape & form. Walker, who is named after the great mountaineer, gave them a map of the country in the sand. He would heap up the sand for mountains, the valleys in between & mark out the roads & rivers with a stick. All these men, but one, got a chance to go to Cal.

Oct. 1st, [1849]. Plenty of Indians around camp, some on horses. Indian boys shoot with great precision at [for?] tobacco. [Chief] Walkers Brother & sister visited us today. His sister has 2 white children, the biggest lashed on a poney & the baby hanging to the horn of the saddle like a small embalmed mummy.[19] Today Capt Hunt come up who is our Mormon guide to the Spanish country. He gets $10 a waggon. We paid him some money to day to take home to his family [at Fort Utah].[20] The constitution & by laws are made & approved.

[October] 2d. Every thing in readiness, we start out from Hobble Creek. Pass a creek 8 miles (Spanish [Fork] Creek) & camp on a creek 8 miles from that [Peteetneet Creek at present Payson].

[October 3.] Here we elect [Henry] Baxter of the Rovers, as Col. of our train of about 80 wagons & more expected. These were divided into 7ths & a capt. to each 7th. See Fremonts brother in law.[21] Fall in with the N.Y. City Col[ony] Guards.[22] Stay up till late singing Negro melodies. Go to bed out doors under

18. In this party were Lewis Manly, John Rogers, Charles and Joseph Hazelrig, and Alfred Walton (Manly 1894, 76).
19. This might sound macabre to some ears, but the baby was safely bundled on a cradleboard, the common baby-carrying device many American Indians used.
20. Jefferson Hunt's price to pilot a train down the Southern Route was an advance payment of $10 from each of the 100 non-Mormon wagons.
21. This was John Randolph Benton, son of Missouri senator Thomas Hart Benton (Johnston 1948, 5).
22. J. Goldsborough Bruff (September 17, 1849) met eight members of the Colony Guard on the Humboldt River after their ordeal on the Hastings Cutoff, and he commented on the others: "The remainder of the Guards, with a considerable number of other emigrants, under the guidance of some Mormons, would pursue a southern route from the [Great Salt] Lake into California, a route, in my humble opinion which will consign many emigrants and their animals to the wolves, and the rest to much suffering" (Bruff 1944, 562n39; see also 176, 290).

our robes & our hats on. In the night we have rain, which comes souse in our faces & pritty cold & in the morning we discover the mountains on the east & north east covered with snow, till half way down there is none.

Clouds still linger about the mountains & snow still falling. How singular it looks to see it snowing on the mount while below there is none whatever. A large cloud 30 miles longe will fairly stick to the mountain by attraction, for half day at a time. Then it will blow off when the wind changes. The mountns are very high, some thousands of ft from the level of the lake with every few miles a kanyon & a stream of pure cold ice water runing from them.[23] On the 3d we lay up all day. Tonight it is very cold. Ice freezes in the buckets very thick.

[October] 4th. Travel 10 miles, then camp. Kill a beef & have fresh meat with apple sause & beef steak.

[October] 5th. Go 8 miles up gradually assending mountains & camp on a small creek with a subteranous passage for a great distance.[24] Utah Valley has a good supply of cool water & fenced in by high mountains. The valley is level, sloping to the beautiful lake by the same name. The soil is beautiful tho' some is saleratus earth.[25] There is abundance of buffalo grass & bunch grass. The latter is dry & tall & is good for cattle to travel on. In fact the valley is supperior to S. Lake Valley tho' both are to[o] cold for me. Utah Lake in my opinion will have boats running on it in time. We can see from our present camp the termination of the lake peeping out from behind a mountain on our righ[t] (west). We form a "Caral," the largest I ever see. The dry timber which is cotton wood & box elder has to take it for large camp fires which are seen blazing all around the "caral." 2 Utahs camp with us to night. For some of the Utah language (see blank page 2 in front).

The following vocabulary and remarks on Ute or Utah bands appear on three unnumbered pages following the front flyleaf but are inserted here in context.

Te cup na nurch [?] — They want to eat
Te cup narrow up — I want to swop [swap?]

23. Utah Lake is about 4,500 feet elevation, and nearby Mount Timpanogos, northeast of the lake, is 11,750 feet, the second-highest mountain in the Wasatch Range.
24. Native Americans called this Punjun Spring (at today's Burriston Ponds) and thought it was bottomless. The spring is a little over a mile and a half south-southwest of Mona, Utah. The Domínguez-Escalante expedition camped here on September 27, 1776, and they named it *Ojo de San Pablo* (Domínguez 1977, 62; see also Farmer 2008, 52, and Welch in Ressler 1964, 260, October 5 and 8).
25. Saleratus—aerated salt—is an alkali. Both sodium bicarbonate and potassium bicarbonate were commonly called saleratus, and both are leavening agents used in baking.

Pequa — Go away! going away
Carrabin (from French) — Gun
Wick e up — Wigwam
Oshe — (Snake) Yes!
Truig [?] u [?] wino — first rate, good
Pungo — poney
Harpa — powder horn
Ohne — arrow
Oware — food
Tah — shirt
Crisha — Leggings
Putso — Moccosins
Agui — Bow
Nowa — Coat
Sarsee — Dog or Wolf
Posin cotain ite — Wild cat skin arrow case
Panshe — Blanket
Timbes — Bullet or Lead
Cootsam — Powder
Noodsup — Precusion camp [cap]
Oo'ah — Yes!
Shoe-shaney — Generally applied to the Snake Indians
Shup — Larrette
Quish e up — Hair hanging behind
Mo'ab [?] — Buffalo Robe
Wi no, (positive degree) — Good (they have no comp[arative] deg[ree])
Tuwig u (superlative degree) — Best
Ta Wag — All gone
Kin-e-kin-nick — A leaf used for Tobacco

There are a great many bands of Utahs in these mountains of which I will only give a few names below —

Walkers band — Ten penny Yutes is pah Yutes
Winter Yutes — of Winter or San Pitch Valley
Touse Yutes — Pyutes farther south & Piedes

Water frezes inch thick to night but we sleep warm. Up early on this morning. Indian hunters come in camp. We hear that a lot of Mormons have arrived from the [California] mines, very rich & that Fremont had bought out [Isaac] William's ranch with the prospect of finding a mine on his grounds, said to have been covered up from the Mexican priests by order of the governor in olden times.[26] Others say it is with the prospect of becoming Gov of Cal.

[October] 6th. Pass up a beautiful valley 4 or 5 miles wide [Juab Valley]. On the east are steep, rugged & lofty mountains [Wasatch Range], the top apparently as sharp as a razor, [as viewed] from below. The mountains on the west [Long Ridge] are not so high. Just below the peaks of the eastern range, there appears [a] substance resembling sand, upon which there arrose a dispute. So Proff. Welch with others assended the range [Mount Nebo] to satisfy them selves, & found it to be sand hardened by the weather, & not rock. The assent was very difficult, & they had to climb 4 or five miles to reach it, instead of one as expected. Coming down was the worst. When they reached the base they found themselves much weakened & it was dark night.[27]

Soon after, the mountains assume a different aspect being more roling & hilley. A large kanyon separates the 2 links in the chane [of mountains].[28] The lat[t]er looks whiter in its general appearance interspersed with sand or red stone peaks.

We find a notice put up at small creek, that [Jim] Waters men had killed 6 of the "Piutes" on the "Sevire [Sevier] River," warning us to looks out for squalls.[29] The Independent Comp'y posted it up & wanted all that wishes to join us [them?] to come along. We camp on a creek [Salt Creek, at present Nephi]. Nothing but brush to burn. This night I determined to watch which way the Indians came from for they are in soon after camping & no one sees from whence they come, but [I] had scarcely had time to look around before 6 Indians were in camp mounted on horses. They had ponies to trade for amunition. Not long after, I see a keg of powder hanging to the saddle which informed me they had

26. This was an unfounded rumor. Frémont provided Thomas O. Larkin, the American consul to Mexico's Alta California, $3,000 to purchase property, but it was not for the Williams ranch. Larkin made "only one purchase for Frémont, *Las Mariposas* [a Mexican land grant] near Yosemite, in early 1847" (Hague and Langum 1990, 181). The grant was 44,387 acres (B. Shumway 1988, 41).
27. The three-quarter moon rose after 9:30 p.m., giving them light for travel after it cleared the mountains (see Welch in Ressler 1964, 261–62, October 6). Six weeks before this, on August 24, 1849, "Wm. W. Phelps ascended to the top of Mount Nebo, south of Utah Valley, to make scientific operations" (Jenson 1899, 37). There are three widely spaced summits in the Mount Nebo massif: (1) Mount Nebo, 11,928 feet, the northernmost peak; (2) the middle peak, 11,824 ft.; and (3) the south peak, 11,877 feet. Welch climbed the south peak.
28. Salt Creek Canyon separates the Wasatch Range (to the north) from the San Pitch Mountains (to the south). Both mountain ranges form part of the eastern border of the Great Basin.
29. Vincent Hoover (September 29, 1849), a member of the Independent Pioneer Company (the wagon train ahead of the San Joaquin Company), recorded these murders in his rewritten journal: "Several of the Utaws came into camp & informed us that the train under the guidance of Mr Waters killed seven Indians. The reason they did not assigne."

made a trade. Very cold night. Ice very thick, & looked as if we were going to have a snow storm but did not.

[October] 7th. Sabbath. Shoot hares & sage hens. Large party start out after "Grizzelies." Do up large baking, with brush [for fuel]. Have a sermon in dutch [German] in the eve'g by the Rev. Crow, missionary to the mines.[30]

[October] 8th. After leaving the creek we see a band of mounted Indians coming down the eastern mountains. I first thought they were some of our comp., but on approaching found them to be Indians. They went to our camp ground to pick up any thing that was left as is there custom. They had their lodges packed on their animals, & were apparently moving for some valley west of the eastern range. Not long after, a fine young looking Indian rode up to [us] in full gallop, & gave their customary salutation of "how'dy do." He had a fine rone [roan] horse. He had a pig tail hanging from behind his head about 4 ft long trimmed with brass rings & [*illegible*], brass plated, attached there to. He called it a "I ushle up" ["Quish e up—hair hanging behind" in Lorton's list of Indian words]. His face had no vermillion on it & his features were more like an Americans than any I had seen. I rode along with him several miles during which time he told me the names of all the things he had on, & the locations of the different valleys.

The soil today is red & produces a grass bearing a seed. All the small streams which do not sink in the ground run near the base of the eastern mountains, following the valley down [and] passes through the hills into the upper or south end of Utah Lake. Camp near some natural wells. Some of these are 40 feet deep & 30 broad, covered with a green skum & surrounded by high grass. The sides are as abrupt as a well. Some times cattle fall in & are halled out by the horns.

This is a pritty camp ground affording abundance of thick matted & short grass, plenty of grease wood 100 yds off, & Cedar on the eastern hills half mile off. While we were getting supper a shower came up & the rain fell copiously. We soon erected our tent & spread our robes for sleep. Mr Platt [Addison Pratt] came up with the rodeometer.[31] He brought me compliments from his wife, daughter & my former hosts. Cattle very troublesome all night & pritty wet.

[October] 9th. Grass covered with frost which made it very cold to the feet & wet. Our road to day is very hilly yet apparently in the same valley. Pass several small lakes, which afford a randezvous for ducks. We strike towards a mountan

30. Welch says Reverend Crow spoke in German, "a portion of the com[pany] being Germans" (in Ressler 1964, 262, October 7). Some of them were from the German California Mining Company, New York (Rasmussen 1994, 34–35).
31. The Pratt mess caught up with the San Joaquin Company at Salt Creek (today's Nephi) so Jefferson Hunt could use their roadometer to "measure the road" (A. Pratt 1990, 380). Pratt was returning to his missionary work in French Polynesia.

FIGURE 36. Mormon wooden roadometer (odometer) similar to the one Captain Hunt used to measure the Southern Route. At Winter Quarters Museum, near Omaha, Nebraska. Photo by LeRoy Johnson.

gap on the west here to avoid a swamp, & then take over the hills.[32] There is very little good grass on todays drive but we pass through some tolerable large cedars for this country. We discover the old trail of the only wagon that ever passed through the country.[33] It was quite visible showing that rains are not frequent even in winter. My poney liked to break her neck in stumbling down hill. The soil appears to be strongly impregnated with saleraetus & looks blue or a light purple.

32. The "swamp" is the area around the numerous springs that produce Chicken Creek. The emigrants traveled southwesterly through the low gap between the West Hills and South Hills.

33. Lorton sees tracks from the Daniel Davis carriage in the Rockwell contingent that left Los Angeles for Salt Lake City in April 1848 (for background see Boyle in Bigler and Bagley 2000, 397; Sutak 2012, 265–69). This is the first wheeled vehicle that traversed the Southern Route from Pueblo de Los Angeles to Salt Lake City. Kelly and Howe purport a second wagon, also in 1848, started on the same route and "was abandoned ... but it had pioneered much of the road that would soon be traveled by hordes of gold seekers, and should therefore be listed with other famous trail-breaking wagons." However, they provide no citation, and we found no corroborating data to support their assertion (Kelly and Howe 1937, 90).

About 2 o'clock we see a lot of Indians running their horses very hard to the eastward, & we afterwards find it is near the banks of Sivier [Sevier] River. The river is about 4 rods wide [66 feet]. Its banks are high, & at this time lays low in its banks, & muddy, probbably occasioned by last nights rain. Where we camp, the bank is 18 ft purpendicular. We make steps down to it while some ties a "larriette" to a pail.[34] Plenty of Indians in camp wanting to "narrowup pungoes for Timbeo" [swap ponies for bullets or lead], bear skins & Buck[skins]. A great many trades are made. I swap my mare off for a beautiful Cal. horse, as white as alabaster. I gave a rifle to boot, 2 Boxes caps, an old shirt &c. The Indian who was a fine looking fellow & no doubt a horse jockey, put his larriette in the mares mouth & of[f] he went full jump. It was afterwards discovered that his horse was swelled in the fore legs & they all cryed they would rather have my old mare, but myself thought it was a good trade yet, & another man said it would get over [it] in a few days. It is a Cal. stallion as can be seen from the brand, & has no doubt been stolen from some ranche, for when a horse is sold they always brand the same on the sholder. I may yet have it take[n] away from me. I had him a little after dark "Larrieted" within 20 ft of where I was washing dishes. A little blaze was burning so I could not see 10 ft. He was going toward the bushes, when he sprang back as if somebody had tried to catch his Larriet. He then became entangled in the "Rietta" & fell down. I am confident there was an Indian in the tall grass that was tr[y]ing to steal him away, so I put him in the "Caral." Presently 3 Indians came from that direction & came up to me saying, "howdy do" & wanted to shake hands. Capt Rone [A. Rowan] & myself proposed watching in turn all night so we loaded our guns, but the Col. appointed a "Caral" [guard] so we went to bed.

[October] 10th. Up very early, orders to fill every thing with water, as we have to make a 20 mile drive without the same, but it is 12 o'clock before all the wagons cross the [Sevier] river.[35] 1 mile below that, we all camp on the other side in good pasture, down in a valley with hills all around us. In the evening the Col., Leut. [Adjutant] & 7 capts assembled in a large "Marque" in court marshal to try a man assuming the name of Davison a deserter from fort Larimie. A charge was made against him as being one [of] the men which committed a rape on an

34. They camped near today's Yuba Dam, which creates Sevier Bridge Reservoir. The river's tortuous course through highly erodible soil in this area contributes to its steep banks.
35. The steep, 18-foot embankment separated their camp from the river the previous night; thus, the oxen were not taken down to drink. Welch explains on October 10 the reason for the long time spent to cross the Sevier River: "The oxen before being yoked ought to have been driven to the water but as this was neglected they were obliged to drink at the ford so that nearly four hours were spent in crossing" (Welch in Ressler 1964, 263).

emigrant, an a/c given by me in the last Vol. [July 27] as recd from the Larimie officer. It was proven that he was not the person, & it was pritty evident that the report was only a bait thrown out to excite the sympathy of emigrants.

[October] 11th. We get all ready to start when word comes that 2 men are not expected to live & we must lay up. We go up to the mounts with 2 yoke [of] oxen, hitch chain to top of the old fir trees & pull up root & branch. Made a cart of the same & fetch large load. Do a large baking, 12 skillets full. In the eve'g have a Negro concert in N. Y. boys tent. Mazappa broke loose in the night & wounded his hind legs with [a] picket pin. Froze hard. Kill an ox & have beef soup.

[October] 12th. Assend a hill & desend in a basin about 8 miles long & 5 Broad [Scipio Valley]. At present there is no water in this basin, any quantity of bunch grass & sage. Road passes near 3 large holes. These have subteraneous passages to let out water in rainy seasons. High mountains range on every side, highest on the east. The mountains have more or less a great quantity of white cedar growing. In the large sage or grease wood harbor myriads of Hair [hare] about the size of a small antelope. As I described in the last Vol., dogs pursue these animals in every direction over the grass but are distanced by the pursued. Load "Mazeppa" with game & follow on to camp. We then follow a ravine on the south W [Scipio Pass] for a great many miles. Some very bad road but no accidents. From the summit [between Canyon Mountains and Pavant Range] we gradually decend [to] a valley of great magnitude [Pavant Valley]. The altitude of this valley is far above that of the "Sivire" [Sevier River].

Night comes on & as there is no moon it is very dark. On we go over a vary good road till we discover signal fires in the distance which we make after passing thro' groves of tall cedar [Cedar Springs, at present Holden]. We find that they [the horsemen in advance] had burnt many cedars & still setting more on fire, and as we behold them in the distance dodging among the firy trees they resemble so many deamons. The last of the train arrives 10 o'clock at night. The whole dist travelled being 23 3/4 miles without stoping & without water. I had not drinked sense daylight & walked & led my horse the whole way. Every body out of humor. It being my guard night I have to go streight off without supper to guard. The boys get it ready & relieve me. It rains some & the wind is very piercing & chilly, & the next morning discover the neighboring mountains cov'd with snow.

[October 13.] Start early next morn'g 13th in a southerly direction. Plenty of feed all [the] way from "Sevire." Cross a creek [Pioneer Creek, seven miles north of Fillmore at] 3 miles. Acres of wild sage & hundreds of sportsmen out mowing down the hair [hare] in great numbers. (Some cedars.) While passing thro' there, a bullet passed by me screaching within a ft of my head. Road winds a little to the east & we keep up [it] 8 miles, on a narrow but deep creek, bed very rockey, plenty of dry wood & grass.[36]

[October] 14th. Sabbath. Lay up all day. Preaching [at] 12 o'clock by Rev'd Granger. Have hare soop again. Heavy snow storm on the eastern mountains all day, weather below chilling. Capt Hunt in a stump speach remarked in regard to the dis[s]atisfaction on a/c of laying up Sundays, said *God* on his throne with 3 hundred angels couldent frame an arrangement that would please every body.

Dr Dry grass [commented] on dry grass, said it was the greatest valley in the world, & that a hundred lbs of dry grass would produce 1 qt molasses. He is going to send some to Europe for anilization.

He is for greater progress, & contended that the cattle would be injured by [not?] so doing. His reasons were that fat would collect on their intestines, & the want of exercise would cause it to chill with the cold of the mountains & produce death. He is taking out 3 or 4 stock horses. He values 1 at 10,000 & the others at 5,000 dolls apiece. He goes off several miles from camp every night to get out of the way of other folks & get the best dry grass. It is expected he will come home one of these mornings minus the crown of his head.

[October 1849] 15th. Morn'g raw & chilley as if going to snow. First part of the road [has] wild sage. Plenty of sage hens flying thro' the air. Some shot while flying. We then pass thro' some of the loveliest grazing grounds the world ever saw [Pavant Valley], being a variety of all kinds of grasses & wild flax. The latter cattle & horses eat with ravinish appetite. Pass a number of small streams together [particularly, Meadow Creek]. At the end of 12 miles we camp on good feed & water, & dry willous 20 ft high [Corn Creek, Kanosh]. 3 wagons & a number of horsemen follow the pack trail [Independent Company's wagon road] to the S.W.[37] Mts on the east look pritty while the sun shines on it while below, green with virdu[r]e.

[October 16th] 15th.[38] Still press onward to the south. About noon we arrive at the Base of a high mountain. This is the end of this [Pavant] valley which is 30 miles long & about 12 Broad. It has 3 streams of water running from the eastern mts [Pavant Range]. The soil is suitable of raising wheat. There is a variety of

36. They camped on Chalk Creek, which now delineates the northeastern edge of today's Fillmore, Pavant Valley. In 1855, Fillmore was the seat of Utah's territorial government.
37. The circuitous route these three wagons used was the same route Frémont traveled in 1844, Hunt used in 1847 and 1848, and the Independent Pioneer Company used just ahead of the San Joaquin Company. For more detail see Sutak 2012, 324–26, map 325).
38. Lorton inadvertently recorded two 15th dates in his journal.

soils such as sand, clay &c. I take the liberty to call it the Wasatch Valley. The pilot [Captain Hunt] assends the gap & requests the train to wait as [at] the base for a signal. They then assend a rough way & wind throu sage, scrub oak & rocks through the mts. then assend a steep way to the summit. The decent is now steep.[39] I dismount & lead Mazeppa down the side of the mt. over sharp stone. The firey steed trembled like a leaf in the chilling wind, afraid to step. While standing above & looking down below, could be seen a large circle of saddles, & men lo[u]nging on the grass. I turn Mazeppa loose & go up to help the wagons down. By locking the wheels they come down tollerable easey in to this deep valley [today's Dog Valley], which is small & called Brown's hole on a/c of a mountaineer wintering there.[40] We cross this & assend again hills & follow ravines, which are stony, cross the divide gradually into a vally & we reach water after dark.[41] Find cedar wood & have supper. Feed not very good. Soil here brown sand.

[October 17th] 16th. Find that Indp[endent] comp. had passed thro' here on our right.[42] Steer south, pass thro' some of the loviliest grass Eye ever beheld, close matted & tall as your waist. Yellow, oster [ochre], brown & green all commingling together fills the heart with pleasing sensations of beauty. The tall rough rugged peeks capped with cedars & scrub oaks. Plenty of cedars on the benches, the grass on the west & the natural boundary makes it a desirable place for forming a settlement, & the only place I have ever selected as magnificent in the extreme [long narrow valley with Cove Fort at the north]. The bottom is capable of producing the greatest crop of wheat in the world. On a/c of its beauty I have named it the "Vale of Ophelia" in honor of my sister. The south part neads no irrogation, the rest probably will. It has 2 streams 4 miles apart [Sulphur and

39. The train waited in White Sage Flat, a small outwash basin about nine miles north of today's Cove Fort. Hunt selected a route that went through a low pass on the west flank of Dog Mountain (0.4 mile east of Interstate 15) and dropped into Dog Valley down a steep, 27 percent slope.

40. There is another Brown's Hole, now Browns Park, over 300 miles northeast, that borders the Green River in the northeast corner of Utah. Louisa Pratt said "Brown's [was] a fictitious name for Porter Rockwell" (L. Pratt 1998, 116). Could this hole have been named for Rockwell or for the color of the soil?

41. They camped along Cove Creek, near the present site of Cove Fort, which was built between April and November 1867 to protect the Mormons from the local Indians. As Mormons expanded their Great Basin empire, they settled on Indian hunting grounds and killed the large game Indians had relied on for centuries to feed their families. When the Indians became destitute, they began slaughtering Mormon cattle, and this, in part, precipitated the Utah Black Hawk War in 1865.

42. Frémont's route, the same used by the Independent Pioneer Company, circled west of Dog Valley from White Sage Flat but returned to Cove Fort Valley (Sutak 2012, 325, map).

Pine Creeks]. The Valley is 12 miles long & 2 wide. The day on which we passed thro' was cool & pleasant.[43]

We assend a high mt. on the south, from the summit of which 2 tall snow capped peaks appear on the east, one looking like a sugar loaf, & the other like an iced ornament on the top of a plumb cake. We decend a ravine & the road varies to the east [Cedar Knoll], & then strikes due south [having re-entered Wildcat Canyon]. Feed good all thro' the mts. Scrub oak in abundance & ugly hill to assend [cross the Hogsback six miles north of today's Beaver]. At length we descend into a valley putting south [dry wash east of the Hogsback]. The pilot & comp. went up in the mts to find water [since] the creeks were dry, thinking they had probabley sank below, but could not find any. From a ridge on the east [Last Chance Bench north of Beaver] could be seen water but it was to[o] abrupt to suit [?] with wagons. So we concluded to follow on, not knowing when we would find water, & the prospects were we would travel all night [with no moonlight].

Nigh[t] came on & about 8 o'clock the fires ahead anounced that water was found [Indian Creek, north Beaver Valley]. On arriving, the banks were found to[o] steep for horses to decend. See the flashing eyes of some wild beast in the bushes while looking for wood. Camp in the wild sage after traveling 25 miles. Fix the crossing.

[October 18th] 17th.[44] Assend a divide ridge [part of Last Chance Bench] & decend in a valley well watered & plenty of various kinds of grass. It has 3 creeks runing west [North Creek, Beaver River, and South Creek]. High ridge on the south [Black Mountains] & the east [Tushar Mountains], high & capped with snow. This [Beaver] valley is as long as wide & I will name it the Valley of 3 creeks. 5 mile from last camp.[45] Plenty of cooking wood. Meet an Indian at first [North] creek. He was almost naked & said he was Utah. This is the first Indian sence we left "Sevier" River.

A young man went back after an ox to day [that] he had left on the road the night before which he found but could not drive him along so he shot him with his pistol. Before he got at the first creek he discovered 2 Indians consealing

43. According to numerous genealogical records, Lorton did not have a sister. He had a brother, Albert, two years his junior, but no record of a sister. However, Cousin Silas (Jr.) had a five-year-old daughter named Ophelia, who may have treated Lorton as a big brother, and he could have reciprocated by calling her his sister. We find no other family member by that name.

44. Both Sheldon Young and Addison Pratt agree the train arrived at Beaver River on October 18 (S. Young 1849a, 1849c, October 18; A. Pratt 1990, 382).

45. They camped two days to refresh their livestock on the lush grass along the Beaver River about a mile east-southeast of today's Adamsville.

themselves in the bushes. They expected he would stop to water his animal, but did not. They however tryed to seize his bridle, but did not succeed. He see them point their arrows at him but was to[o] much frightened to look around to see whether they fired. They then ran & tryed to head him, but the horse was to[o] swift for them, & the man created some excitement in camp, & at night oxen & horses were brot in & a "caral" guard set, & every hour in the night the cry of "all is well" was heard every hour. Have pyramid of men 3 high in eve'g & lofty tumblings. Kill a beef.

CHAPTER 9

Beaver River to Mount Misery, Utah

Background

After the San Joaquin Company crossed the Sevier River and passed today's Scipio and Pavant Valleys, they wanted to avoid, if possible, crossing the Black Mountains via its steep, rocky trail with its 1,300-foot rise in elevation that impeded their path into Parowan Valley (Little Salt Lake valley). Their guide, Jefferson Hunt, knew Porter Rockwell had guided a group with a light wagon around the west end of the Black Mountains the year before (see Boyle 1848, 38–39; Riser in Bigler and Bagley 2000, 399–400; Johnson and Johnson 2014; cf. Heath 1995). George Cannon recalled what Hunt knew about Rockwell's route: "[Hunt] had been told that by keeping down Beaver Creek & then striking across to the left [southward], it would save travel & be a better route. But he knew nothing about it himself only what he had been told" (1999, 22–23, 96). This was the route Hunt wanted to find. He had traveled the Old Spanish Trail both to and from southern California in 1847–1848 with a pack train and was aware of the copious springs plus the Near Muddy Creek (today's Coal Creek) in Cedar Valley west of Parowan Valley.[1]

Hunt and members of the train studied Frémont's 1848 map, drawn by cartographer Charles Preuss. New research (see Appendix B) discusses the reasons this detour into the Escalante Desert to find Rockwell's route was pivotal to the disintegration of the San Joaquin Company.

When Hunt and emigrant scouts did not find the water they expected based on Frémont's map, the large train "began to suffer... [and] a great dissatisfaction prevailed and they tried many of them to blame Capt. Hunt, who was not in the least the instigator of the moove," recalled Addison Pratt (1990, 383). If not the instigator, Hunt was complicit in the move into today's virtually waterless

1. The Old Spanish Trail was primarily a pack-train trail that stretched from Santa Fe to Pueblo de Los Angeles in California.

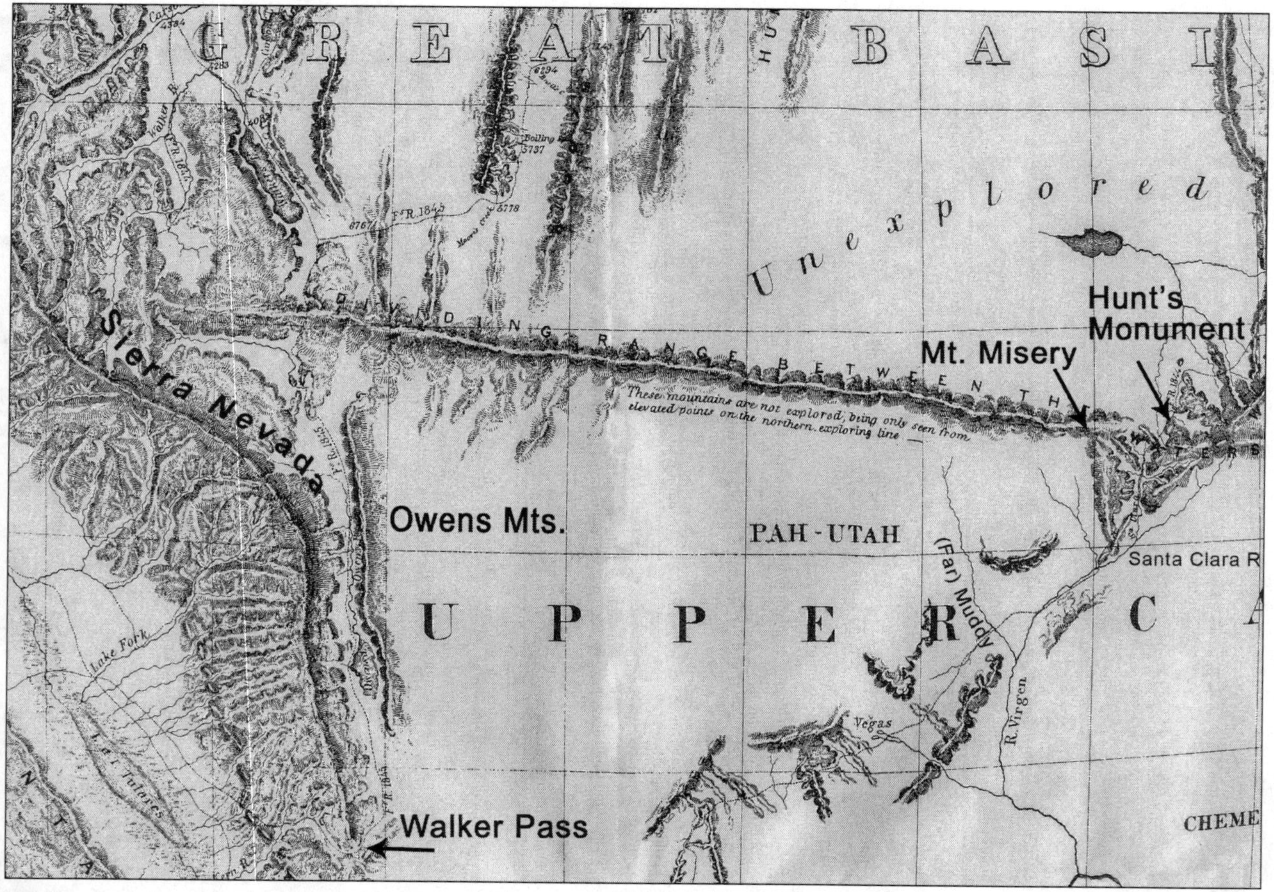

Map 4. Detail, Frémont's 1848 map of Oregon and upper California. The prominent, but nonexistent, east-west mountain range enticed the emigrants to turn west from the Old Spanish Trail. Barney Ward's bogus route crossed the southern toe of Frémont's imagined mountain range in the vicinity of Pine Park Bench and followed its southern side across Nevada toward Walker Pass. Frémont not only warned that the area was "Unexplored," he also labeled it as such: "These mountains are not explored, being only seen from elevated points on the northern exploring line," a warning the emigrants ignored. Included are modern place names and the location of Mount Misery. Courtesy of David Rumsey Historical Map Collection.

Escalante Desert. The detour debacle undermined the emigrants' faith in their guide, and the delay precipitated growing discontent with the slow pace of this unwieldy wagon train. With sublime timing to stir this soup of discontent, a tantalizing idea was injected—the possibility of a shorter, safer route to the goldfields. Nothing could have been more irresistible.

The bearers of this enticing idea were some packers who carried a sketch-map of a route that purportedly cut months of time and 500 miles off the circuitous Southern Route to Pueblo de Los Angeles, thence north to the mines. Captain Orson Kirk (O. K.) Smith and his company of about 20 men caught up with the San Joaquin Company on the Beaver River as it straggled back from the Escalante debacle (Hafen and Hafen 1954b, 33; A. Pratt 1990, 383; Cannon 1999, 23–24).

The sketch-map was drawn by Elijah (Barney) Ward, who claimed he had traveled the route more than once. Apparently his route left the Old Spanish Trail about six miles east of today's Enterprise, Utah, went westward across the present state of Nevada, and over Walker Pass in the southern Sierra Nevada to the San Joaquin Valley, thus saving time and distance to the gold country (Cannon 1999, 19; Welch in Ressler 1964, 267, October 24; Lorton, October 24, 1849; Manly 1894, 327; Stephens 1916, 17).

Barney Ward was a typical mountain man who had traded with the Indians since the early 1820s. He helped build Fort Hall in 1834, and in the mid-1840s had established a trading post in Utah Valley. In March 1849, Ward and Dimick Huntington located a band of Indians on Provo River who were stealing Mormon cattle. After the Indians were defeated, a Mormon colony was sent to Utah Valley to settle and build Fort Utah (later Fort Provo). In August 1849, Ward was on the Bear River in southwest Idaho trying to talk emigrant trains into coming to Salt Lake City rather than going to Fort Hall. He was telling lies about no supplies being available at the fort. When the emigrants reached Pegleg Smith's place 20 miles farther along the trail, they found "that Ward's stories were false and his route 100 miles out of our way" (Stuart 1895, 52; Hafen 1969, 347). Kimball Webster (1917, 72) added that "Pegleg said the Mormon [Ward] was lying." In October 1849 Ward drew his sketch of the Walker Cutoff for O. K. Smith. Sixteen years later, on April 10, 1865, Ward was killed and scalped while hunting cattle at the outbreak of Utah's Black Hawk Indian War (Hafen 1969, 351).

Ward's map was not the only inducement to tempt the emigrants. They had a copy of Frémont's 1848 "Map of Oregon and California," with the trail showing Frémont's route over Walker Pass through the southern part of the Sierra Nevada (although the pass is not labeled). However, "Walker's Pass" *is* labeled on Mitchell's 1846 and 1849 maps, the latter being "of real importance, highly popular, and doubtless published in a large edition" (Wheat 1959, 335 and map 520 facing p. 29; Map, Mitchell 1846a and 1849).[2]

Prominent on Frémont's map was a fictitious mountain range marking what he considered to be the southern boundary of the Great Basin. The range stretched westward from the Wasatch Mountains almost to the Sierra Nevada. However, Frémont also added this cautionary note: "*These mountains are not explored, being only seen from elevated points on the northern exploring line*," a line that was many, many miles to the north (emphasis ours). Barney Ward's shortcut to the goldfields purportedly followed the southern toe of Frémont's mythical east-west mountain range, then crossed the southern Sierra Nevada through Walker Pass to the Tulare and San Joaquin Valleys of California. The pass was an Indian trade route used for centuries and named for the first known white man to traverse it, Joseph Reddeford Walker.

Adonijah Welch wrote on October 26, 1849: "This route the packers who have come up with us intend taking. Capt Smith who is their leader has furnished me with a diagram according to which there is wood water and grass at intervals of twelve or fifteen miles. The [route] runs due west and it cannot be more than 400 miles to the valley of San Joaquim. Mr Ward of Salt Lake City has been through twice and has assured many that it can be traveled with wagons" (Welch in Ressler 1964, 268–69; Welch consistently spelled the company's name *San Joaquim*). Unfortunately, these emigrants were not privy to Pegleg Smith's sage knowledge that Ward was a liar and his "stories were false" (Hafen 1969, 347).

Many, possibly most, of the gold rushers labored under the delusion that each day spent on the trail was one day less they could spend picking up gold nuggets along the Sierra Nevada rivers. Thus, the shortcut was widely discussed—the chance to save time was a temptation too great to resist, and the short-cut plan was eagerly accepted while Frémont's warning was easily ignored.

About this time in their journey several of the emigrants commented on finding unusually fine pottery and tile shards scattered about in the Pavant, Beaver River, and Parowan Valleys. Welch said on October 14 that "they were fragments of clay ware far superior to any possessed by the present Indians. The same men found some fine specimens of variegated tiles." Lorton adds more detail.

These pottery shards were vestiges from the Fremont Indian culture that flourished in this area from about 700 to 1300 AD, named after the Fremont River in south-central Utah. The Fremont beginnings predate the Pueblo people and were distinct from the Anasazi culture. These Indians became farmers

2. A David Rumsey note about the 1846 map says it "was one of Mitchell's most popular and important pocket maps."

(corn, beans, and squash) but still clung to hunting and gathering. They lived in family units, for the most part, although large villages have been excavated near the Fremont Indian State Park and Museum (off Interstate 70 in Clear Creek Canyon) and in Parowan Valley. The Fremont are known for their thin-walled, gray coiled pottery; detailed, trapezoidal-shaped figurines and petroglyphs; and moccasin footwear rather than sandals. They are thought to be ancestors to a wide range of modern western Indian groups (Marwitt 1986, 161–72).

North of Little Salt Lake in Parowan Valley, as the San Joaquin Company begins to dissolve, more calamity visits Lorton: He sees Nig, one of the oxen from his original team, slaughtered for food; the wagon mess he has been forced to join disintegrates; and all his flour has suddenly disappeared. The train council is called upon to litigate the breakup, and Charles McDermott, a mess-mate, leaves to become a packer "without the oxen." For whatever reason, Lorton finds himself "set out on the prairie," but fortunately he is accepted by a Knox County Company man, D. C. Norton.

The final breakup of the company occurred about 50 miles farther along the trail at the southern end of the Escalante Valley (six miles east of today's Enterprise, Utah). The Jefferson Hunt Monument commemorates the location where 100 wagons turned west from the Old Spanish Trail and their guide, Jefferson Hunt. Captain Hunt gave his rationale for continuing down the trail rather than leading the unwieldy train into unknown territory: "You all know I was hired to go by way of Los Angeles, but if you all wish to go and follow Smith I will go also. But if even one wagon decides to go the original route, I shall feel bound to go with that wagon" (Hunt in Manly 1894, 110). He also felt obliged to follow President Brigham Young's order to "measure the road" that was vitally needed to expand the Mormon kingdom in the West. When at least one emigrant wagon decided to follow Hunt, he said, "I cannot recollect the time when I have made so lucky escape from death as I have in getting rid of that company.... Now we will push ahead fast as possible and get out of their way, for they will soon be coming on after us" (Hunt in A. Pratt 1990, 387; see also Sutak 2012, 246–50). We call the remaining seven wagons the Jefferson Hunt wagon train.

Near the monument, Hunt's train detoured around lower Holt Canyon (the route of the Old Spanish pack trail), where it was not passable for wagons. Shearer, in the Independent Pioneer Company just ahead of Hunt, said: "Our road [with the wagons] was over a rising slope to a small stream in the pass of the mountains, leading to" Mountain Meadows, where they camped October 26 (Shearer in Hafen and Hafen 1961, 35). Hunt followed these wagon tracks over the hills east of lower Holt Canyon.

The 100 wagons that turned onto the purported shortcut crossed the southern tip of Escalante Valley and entered Shoal Creek Valley three miles west of today's Enterprise, Utah. It was a gentle grade with plenty of water, abundant firewood, and forage for the hundreds of livestock, just as Barney Ward had promised O. K. Smith. An important guidepost on the route up Shoal Creek (across today's Terry Ranch and into Nephi Draw) is Lorton's detailed description and sketch of "Cave at Cave Canyon." It resembled a fireplace with a hole shaped roughly like a four-foot cavity. Packrats inhabited it for hundreds of years as indicated from the accumulation of amberat in the back. Amberat is fossilized packrat urine that vaguely resembles amber (Grayson 1993, 116–17; Betancourt, Van Devender, and Martin 1990).[3]

The next day they entered Nephi Draw, where "a light snow had just melted rendering the ground so soft that the cattle sunk hoof deep and our progress was consequently slow" (Welch in Ressler 1964, 274, November 5). About a mile southwest, beyond the head of Nephi Draw, they came to an extensive layer of volcanic tuff now called White Rocks. This was essentially the eastern summit of Frémont's mythical east-west range, labeled on his map as "Dividing Range between the waters of the Pacific and the Waters of the Great Basin."

The packers who preceded the wagon train included Captain O. K. Smith's group (which had grown from accretion after he caught up to the San Joaquin Company) and a company of about 20 Mormon packers (and a couple of non-Mormons) who left Salt Lake City October 12, headed for the gold country with James M. Flake as their captain. The Flake party caught up with the Smith packers somewhere before Beaver River, and the two companies then caught up with the San Joaquin Company near today's Minersville, Utah, where O. K. Smith passed around Barney Ward's cutoff map (J. Evans 1936, 181; Cannon 1999, 15; James Brown 1971, 133).

Apostle Charles C. Rich and Francis M. Pomeroy joined the Mormon packers on October 28 in Little Salt Lake valley to investigate the purported cutoff to see if it might be a feasible route for a Mormon freight road to the Pacific Ocean and the southern gold mines. Sutak (2012, 379–80) formulated this hypothesis and we concur.[4] James Flake retained his role as captain, with Apostle Rich as his counselor (Rich in Hafen and Hafen 1954b, 184; Bigler in ibid., 149). The Smith and Flake companies traveled in proximity to one another until they reached Division Spring at the eastern base of the Sheep Range in southern Nevada.

3. Lewis Manly (1894, 274) vividly describes his encounter with amberat in Nevada: "We found balls of a glistening substance looking something like pieces of variegated candy stuck together. The balls were as large as small pumpkins. It was evidently food of some sort, and we found it sweet but sickish.... [We] were a little troubled with nausea afterwards."

4. Charles Colson Rich had been a brigadier general, and later a major general, in the Nauvoo Legion and was appointed to the Quorum of Twelve Apostles in the Mormon Church on February 12, 1849. Francis Pomeroy was not related to the merchants Thaddeus and Ebenezer Pomeroy, who owned a train of freight wagons.

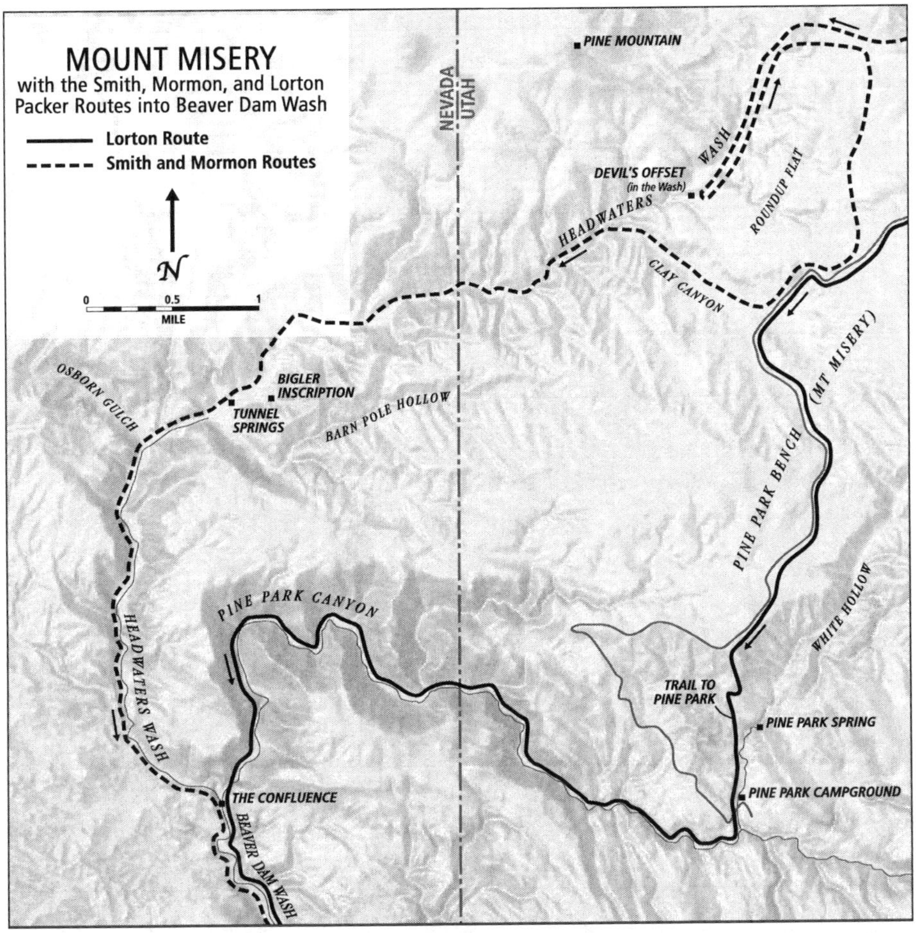

MAP 5. Mount Misery (Pine Park Bench area) in southwestern Utah. The Smith and Mormon packer route down Clay Canyon and Headwaters Wash, and Lorton's route down Pine Park Canyon into Beaver Dam Wash. About 20 additional men became packers who found their way into Beaver Dam Wash to follow the Smith and Mormon groups. Wagons could not follow the packer trails, so about 70 of them returned to the Old Spanish Trail. Twenty-six wagons (about 100 men, women, and children) found a way around the maze of cliffs and canyons and became the Death Valley '49ers. Map drawn by Eureka Cartography based on editors' trail analysis.

From White Rocks (at the head of Nephi Draw) the packers crossed out of the Great Basin and traveled southwesterly searching for the southern toe of Frémont's mythical east-west range. After about four miles, they turned down Headwaters Wash but huge rocks blocked the narrow neck of the wash and stopped their progress. They dubbed this barrier the "Devil's Offset" (Cannon 1999, 38). The packers retreated, circled the toe of today's Roundup Flat on Pine Park Bench, and followed an Indian trail down Clay Canyon to re-enter Headwaters Wash. They camped the night of November 2 at Tunnel Springs. Next day, on the canyon wall across the wash (near the bottom of Barn Pole Hollow),

Henry Bigler, one of Flake's Mormon company, "cut the 3 first letters of my name on a Rock" (Bigler in Hafen and Hafen 1954b, 151; Cannon 1999, 39n13, 102; Kelly 1939). We have visited the inscription five times.[5]

The wagons, unable to follow the packers, spread southward from Roundup Flat for two miles along the rolling hills of waterless Pine Park Bench. Welch said on November 5, "We have found water in a neighboring canon enough for our horses. For cooking purposes we had sufficient in our casks. So the oxen only are unsupplied. Word has come tonight that [there] is a fine stream running in a deep grassy valley or gorge two miles south of us [where White Hollow meets Pine Park, at Pine Park Campground]. We shall probably advance to it tomorrow morning" (Welch in Ressler 1964, 274). Next day, Welch and others may have advanced their wagons along the bench to the brink of White Hollow.

Scouts followed a prominent Indian trail into White Hollow and discovered forage between Pine Park Spring and today's Pine Park Campground. One of the Brier children later recollected, "The only available water flowed at the base of a thousand-foot declivity, and the only man who could get to it was a French voyageur. His risk and labor were easily worth the dollar collected for every bucketful" of water he toted out of the canyon (Brier 1911, 2).

Lorenzo Dow Stephens (1916, 19) recalled that "we came to a bluff, seemingly a thousand feet to the bottom, and straight up and down.... A small stream flowed at the bottom, and by using ropes and buckets we could get enough [water] for camp use, using it sparingly. The oxen had to go without." White Hollow is 540 feet deep (not 2,000 feet as Lorton first thought), and the next day cattle were precariously driven down the Indian trail to water and pasture (Lorton, November 6, 1849).

The splintered San Joaquin Company was now in complete disarray. During the forlorn days spent on cold, snowy, waterless Pine Park Bench, they dubbed it Mount Misery, Deep Diggings, and Poverty Point. Numerous men on foot and horseback scouted for a wagon route westward, some staying out for several days. Based on their reports, Cephas Arms declared the "single [east-west] mountain range as laid down by Col. Fremont" was a "humbug" (Arms in Cumming 1985, 106–7). Right he was. A comprehensive study of Mount Misery is in our article, "Where Is Mount Misery?" (2018).

While at Mount Misery, "Poor Naylor died." Lorton refers to "Nailer" earlier on the trail and seems to have felt some responsibility for his possessions after his death. A "J. Naylor" is listed twice in Rasmussen, as coming from Illinois in company of other men who took the Southern Route, but Lewis Manly says he was from Kentucky (Rasmussen 1994, 38, 55; Manly 1894, 112). Thanks to

5. A local rancher told LeRoy that he "refreshed" the fading inscription by recarving it sometime before 2000. This "refreshing" is obvious by comparing Kelly's 1939 (p. 7) photo that has serifs on the letters to the initials today that do not have serifs (personal observation).

Lorton, the name of this solitary black man now has its rightful place in western history.

In 2016, Tom Sutak arranged for a "cadaver dog" and her trainer, John Grebenkemper, to search for Naylor's grave. We had found an anomaly of small boulders on the hill at the base of Roundup Flat and suspected it was his gravesite. Tom wrote, "Kayle (the dog) DID NOT alert [find smells she was trained to react to] on the rock pile or anywhere else on that ridge.... In John's opinion, it's not likely there is a detectable burial there." So now we assume Naylor's grave was dug in the softer earth of the meadow below the hill.

A few wagons were abandoned at Mount Misery (including that of Mr. Naylor), but about 70 wagon masters gave up the "folly of exploring with ox teams" and retreated to the Old Spanish Trail, reaching it November 13, "having lost ten days travel and provisions" (Arms in Cumming 1985, 108). Here they turned southward to follow the Hunt train to the coastal Spanish Ranchos just as Hunt predicted. Scouts from the remaining wagons finally found a route around the maze of canyons, and almost 100 men, women, and children continued westward toward Walker Pass in the Sierra Nevada with 26 wagons. They became the Death Valley '49ers, who lost everything but the clothes on their backs and the few emaciated oxen they had not yet eaten.

At Mount Misery, Lorton said his "teem gave out" (the wagon he was traveling with), and his life was about to change. He concluded "to pack & make preparations." With those five words, Lorton states his momentous decision to forsake the wagons and follow O. K. Smith and the Mormon packers into *terra incognita* with Mazeppa, his trusty white steed. Other young men made the same decision, such as 11 who were later called the Pinney-Savage party. Lorton planned to travel with some of the Buckskin Division boys from his hometown of New York City who also became packers. In his January letter to the *New York Sun* (see chapter 12), Lorton names them—Charles Burrel, William Sands, William Sherman, J. Hendle, and J. Bucklin.

Lorton's Journal Continues in the Valley of the Beaver River

[October 19, 1849] 18th. Lay up while exprours [explorers] go ahead to explore the road.[6] Stand guard, commences 1 o'clock. Hard time to get up, freezing cold. Grass full of frost, infernal cold to the feet. Almost perishing [I] get wood, make

6. They scout the route the Independent Pioneer Company blazed up California Hollow and over the eastern shoulder of the Black Mountains. Welch relates (October 20): "The canon which was explored yesterday was found to be passable to wagon[s] though rather rough. Its direction from camp [on the Beaver River near today's Adamsville] is a little east of south" (in Ressler 1964: 266). Hunt had twice traversed this route on horseback in 1847–1848.

a fire, collect around it, have all sorts of yarns. Conversation interrupted by the discharge of a gun. Centenal took a wolf for an Indian & fired. Another came near shooting the guard thinking it an Indian. See 2 fires in the eastern mts. First thought they were Indian fires. At length 3 hunters came in. They agreed to make as many fires as they killed bears to [signal how] many horses they wanted [to carry the meat].

[October 20.] Explorers arrive after dark of the 19th [20th].[7]

[October 21st] 20th. Sunday.[8] We make for the south west corner of the 3 creek valley [North, Beaver, and South Creeks]. The train follows Bever Creek, while Mr [Addison] Pratt & myself take up the mountains thro' the sage.[9] Load my pritty Mazeppa with rabits down to the guards making its pritty white coat red with blood. Beaver Creeks follows a kanyon to the west [between the Black and Mineral Mountains]. Very near a wolf [passes]. Fire on it, no shot. Plenty of sage hens. We cross the creek several times. Pass beneath over hanging crags & broken stones crumbling down the hills. At the mouth of the kanyon we over look a valley of great size [Escalante Desert]. I should judge it was 15 miles wide & 40 or 50 long. We fancy Sevire Lake lays to the north west of us. Little Salt Lake [should be possible] to be seen from the top of the mts south of west of our camp.[10] Camp on Beaver Creek [near today's Minersville]. This we suppose em[p]ties in to Sevir Lake or river.[11] Plenty of wood & water, grass scarce.

[October 22] 21. Early start. Pass south [west-southwest] after supplying ourselves with water [from Beaver River]. About 4 o'clock we halt without feed & water.[12] Cattle feed on a weed. Capt Hunt out exploring, not yet returned

7. This is another exploring party. On October 20 James Martin, David Switzer, and Adonijah Welch rode down the Beaver River (west) into today's Minersville Canyon and found a route west along the river that "presents no difficulty for wagons." From an elevation, they "took a view of the valley into which the pass opened [Escalante Desert]. It extended farther than eye could [see] and appeared barren to the last degree." They arrived back at 10 p.m. (Welch in Ressler 1964, 266, October 20).
8. October 21 was a Sunday in 1849; thus, we know Lorton's dates were off by one day.
9. Hunt had never traveled down Beaver River, but he hoped he could find, in reverse, the trace Porter Rockwell pioneered (Johnson and Johnson 2014; Boyle in Bigler and Bagley 2000, 397; Sutak 2012, 265–69).
10. Based on the faulty data on Frémont's map, Lorton assumed Little Salt Lake (in Parowan Valley) might be visible from peaks in the western Black Mountains, but such was not the case. See Appendix B for a discussion of this data.
11. The Beaver River flowed north about 70 crow-miles into the Sevier River, which then flowed into Sevier Lake (now almost dry). Today the Beaver River is diverted for irrigation and no longer flows into the Sevier.
12. They left the Beaver River near today's Minersville and rolled southwestward into the

at dark. This we call Welches cut off as he explored the 1st part [down Beaver River]. There is an old trail passes thro' this valley.[13] We call this Retreat valley in honor of our retreat.

[October 23.] The next morning [some go] back to Beaver Creek for water & feed. Capt Hunt arrived in the night [of October 22]. Our tent was in the "Caral" & all night we were in danger of being crushed by hungry cattle.

[October 23 continued.] Next morn cattle out & scattered all over the valley for 15 miles, & a great many put back for water. All the horses which were not tied had gone. Mine was tied & I mounted & put for water [back to Beaver River]. By the time I got in sight of the stream he wanted to go off on full jump, poor thing. When he got in it he [drank so much he] swelled up like a bladder. Waggons were sent back [from the river] with water casks for the whole comp., 500 gall[on]s. In the eve'g 2 men came 11 miles, 22 there & back, for 2 canteens of water. As the team [with the water casks] had not arrived, women & children were crying for water.

Explorers went out a head to explore the rout on foot. Hunt said he seen fires, supposed to be Indians 25 miles off.[14] 40 wagons at the creek broke [rank on the 23rd], & are going east of [to?] Little Salt [Lake valley]. Guide & explorers not yet a giving up. 40 teams frightened to death.

Packers commanded by [O. K.] Smith & Blogit [George G. Blodget] arrive from Salt Lake. Give a/c of an explosion in the west [Oquirrh] Mts. Bring me letters from Mr Holmes & [Mrs. Addison] Pratt. Find aggate & pottery broken on the creek. Lost my spurs.

[October 24th] 23d. Cattle of all but 40 wagons drove up to camp [on river near present Minersville], not knowing our fate. Good deal talk of going Walkers cut off. Packers were attacked by Indians. 1 shot thro the hand.[15]

Escalante Desert. Addison Pratt (1990, 383) says they "went 12 miles into the dry plains and camped without water." They did not turn south-southwest into the Black Mountains from the Minersville area, the general route of today's Utah State Route 130 (cf. Lyman 2004, 61).

13. Lorton does not see the trail, he only states there *is* one—the Rockwell trace that Hunt was looking for but never found. It appears Lorton wrote several entries at a later date, for there was no talk of abandoning this route on October 22nd. He also intermixes the 23rd and 24th entries based on comments by other diarists.

14. More likely these are campfires of the rear contingent of the Independent Pioneer Company at Antelope Springs (see A. Pratt 1990, 383). This wagon train has variously been called the Gruwell-Derr Wagon Train (Hafen and Hafen 1954b, 51), the Hoover-Derr-Gruewell party, or the same names in different order (Lyman 2004, 6, 36, 77).

15. This paragraph is in retrospect.

The pottery, or pieces of the same found thro this country is artificial as can be seen from the rim & flowers painted on them & impressed figures. Naturalists attribute it to an intelligent race that once inhabeted this region [Fremont culture]. It is reported that the present Indians have [no?] pottery.

I mount the horse, & when a few miles out, I meet members retreating & said they were all coming back [to Beaver River] for it was imposible to proceed [south down the Escalante Desert] on a/c of there being no feed, water or wood. The guide & explorers went out [and back] 40 miles & did not see water. 2 men went on to water. They see the dust made by the other comp's teams & from the direction they made they appeared to be bound for Walkers cut off.[16] When Capt. Hunt arrived at camp this morning he could not speak.[17] The teams not having arrived, I am hospitably entertained by Mr [William H.] Sands & Co this night, & [in the] morn [of October 25th], I saddle up poney & try to catch up team, but have to put back & look for one yoke cattle. Find them & arrive at east mouth of kanyon toward dark [southwest of today's Adamsville].

[October 26th] 24th.[18] Strike [east] over the base of the [Black] mountains which are rockey & covered with wild sage. Here the road is up hill & down dale till we meet the old pack trail ravine we intended to go first off & [this we] took up [California Hollow] several miles & there camp on good bunch feed. Our guard night, 2nd tour. Every sentinal had his own watch fire, as the mountains are densely covered with fir trees [pinyon pine or Utah juniper]. The cattle down in the ravines & the fires on the tops, to prevent the cattle from going back to water. The day had been very cold, but 12 o'clock [midnight] it was moderate. I had a large fire built against a large tree. I spread my blanket, lay on it & smoked my pipe in comfort. If any place ever glowed with brilliancy, it was these hills.

[October 27th] 25th. Rich, one of the 12 [LDS apostles], packed with Pomeroy.[19] We start early to assend the mountains which is the devils own pass, & descending is very steep & tedious. Fir trees very thick & ground very stoney.

16. The Old Spanish Trail heads west from Iron Spring to Antelope Springs; thus, dust along the trail would give the impression some company was on Barney Ward's western cutoff. As far as we know, none of the Independent Pioneer Company had knowledge of the purported shortcut.

17. James Brown noted: "Sometime in the night Captain Hunt came into camp, so near choked from the lack of water that his tongue was swollen till it protruded from his mouth; his eyes were so sunken in his head that he could scarcely be recognized" (1971, 134; see also Cannon 1999, 25). Mormons James S. Brown, Addison Pratt, Francis Marion Pomeroy, Hiram H. Blackwell, and Apostle Charles C. Rich traveled in the same mess in the San Joaquin Company (James Brown 1971, 130).

18. The date October 26 is supported by Welch (in Ressler 1964, 268).

19. Rich and Pomeroy may have decided to pack with the Flake Company on October 27, but they left with them the following day in Parowan Valley (J. Evans 1936, 181; Cannon 1999, 15; James Brown 1971, 135).

See plenty of green stone resembling copper ore. We trace a valley [Little Valley] south east a few miles, & then assend a ridge which enters you into Little S Lake Valley.[20] On the right as you enter is a tall abrupt rockey mountain perpendicular to the base, several thousand feet high. Plain covered with wild sage & bunch grass. After passing a poor spring [Buckhorn Spring] we arrive at a creek with 3 or 4 Branches [Little Creek, Parowan Valley].[21] The largest has a cascade 10 ft high. The feed (wild oats) is very abundant. Dry willows & water cold as usual. The oats is irrogated by it.

[October 28th] 26th. Start next morning & go 8 miles to a creek [Parowan Creek, at present Parowan]. On the way [have] fair sight of the lake which is lined with wild geese & duck. The lake is about 12 [actually 7] miles long & 1 mile wide, water part salt & saleraetus. Here at this creek we found plenty of drift-wood & a species of currant growing on a tree. [Last night] 2 [?] Indians come to the camp. They had neither fire arms or arrows, poorly clad but sociable. One had an infant captive (so I supposed) he wanted to sell for a mule instead. We told him to go & wash its face & we would buy it. He did so, but we did not take the babe. We kept them under guard till day light, & then depart, ("Wino") [Lorton's translation of the Ute word for "good"]. They said they were Walkers Utes but we think they were the "Pyes" [Piedes].

[October 29th] 27th. Go to a creek [Summit Creek] on the upper end [of Little Salt Lake valley], 8 miles, first rate grass. Conclude to lay up.

[October 30th] Soil is irrogated by the stream which spreads. Capt Taylor kill[s] my old Nig ox, hard to [see him] die.[22] Received a steak of the off rump [right rump; farthest off, or away, from the ox driver].

McDermot concludes to pack. I am set out upon the prairie, come near having Blood shed. My 25 lbs of flour is missing. No one knows any thing about it, ("Pyqua") [Ute word for "go away"; see also Arms in Cumming 1985, 94]. Nailer is a nigger & will not reach Cal.[23] Call on the council to have our affairs settled.

20. They crested the Black Mountains at 6,940 feet and dropped 400 feet in about two miles into Little Valley, thence into Dennis Hollow and followed Fremont Wash into Parowan Valley.
21. Little Creek is about two miles northeast of today's Paragonah where the Old Spanish Trail enters Parowan Valley (Crampton and Madsen 1994, maps 68, 69; Friesen and Heath 2015, 54–55). Strangely, no diarists mention the Old Spanish Trail here.
22. Lorton speaks of Nig when crossing Iowa and when he "rode Nig horseback" into Kanesville on May 20. When Norman Taylor was down to one ox on the Sweetwater River, he may have bought Nig from Lorton's mess (Lorton, July 22, 1849).
23. Less than two weeks later (November 9), Lorton records Nailer's death, sees he gets a proper burial, and puts a stop to the pillaging of his possessions. Lorton spells his name "Naylor," which is likely correct.

Mc[Dermet] clared [cleared his gear?] & retreats [to join the packers] with out the oxen.[24] [I] Try to go with [Lewis] Granger. The big load. In the meantime Col. [Henry Baxter] & adjutant [William McCormick] & several capts resign. Knoxvill [Jayhawker division] starts off by day light [on the 30th].

[October 31st] 29th. I get in with [D.C.] Norton. Disention has now commenced. One division [Jayhawkers] goes ahead of the other[s].[25] Great talk of going the Cut off on Walkers Pass. Meeting in the camp. Devil in man. Provisions getting scarce. I have previous to today been on bread allowance 4 days. We hunt hare for meat. Follow up [south in] Little S Lake valley [into today's Cedar Valley] & camp on Little Muddy Creek [Coal Creek, near present Cedar City]. Quite a grove of [cottonwood] timber on it. Have to take to the eastern mountains [foot of Hurricane Cliffs] to cross it.[26]

[November 1st] 30th. Follow up the valley after the storm has somewhat abated which had poured down in torrents during the night. While it was raining in the valley, the snow had fallen on the mountains. I do not know how far the valley extends but suppose it reaches 50 miles farther. As you look south easterly a range of peaked mts [Kanarra, Square, and Cedar Mountains] runs in that direction, white with snow. We now pass thro' a pass in the western mts [between Granite Mountain and The Three Peaks]. Near the gap, tall mts of stone resembling iron ore put up in pyramids & here we find specimens [of] iron, chrystalized, but could not find a general deposit but presume there must be some near.[27] Every thing shows that fire, hot fire has melted the minerals. Pass westward, & camp on a small creek runing thro' this gap [Iron Springs Creek].[28]

24. Charles McDermet became one of the eleven men who headed west over the Sheep Range in southeastern Nevada. Sensational tales of death and cannibalism surround these men, other than Pinney and Savage who made it to the gold camps.
25. Edward Doty was captain of the Jayhawker Division in the San Joaquin Company. Several of the same men had previously been part of the old Knox County Company Jayhawker Division, and 24 of them later became Death Valley Jayhawkers.
26. They were "compelled to proceed far up the stream [Muddy Creek, today's Coal Creek] because it spreads in the valley to form a marsh impossible to cross with wagons" (Welch in Ressler 1964, 271, October 31). Welch and companions rolled ahead and spent this night at Iron Springs, west of today's Cedar City, a day ahead of Lorton.
27. Reverend James Welsh Brier claimed "he found a mountain of solid iron" (L. Johnson 2005b, 255–56). Both north and south of their camp is the Iron Springs mining district, which has "huge ore bodies of hematite and magnetite... [and is] the largest iron producing area in the western United States [in 2007]" (Hacker et al. 2007, 25).
28. Addison Pratt (1990, 385) called today's Iron Springs "Cedar Springs" for the Utah juniper (*Juniperus osteosperma*) growing on the high ground immediately north. The emigrants called them cedars. The nearby iron deposits prompted the name change. The

Commences raining as we camp & get drenched while I cook been soup. Clears after 9 o'clock. We then take guard which lasts till 12, & Cynth[i]a [the moon] shows her face. Mazeppa grazes near my watch fire.

[November 2nd] 31st. Still continue west. As we pass we see the bute [Table Butte] to the south [of where we camped] in retreat valley, or the dry encampment. We now see our folly & see that in 25 or 30 miles [by continuing on] we could have reached water [at Antelope Springs]. Our present valley, on a/c of its size, we will call Wasatch Valley [today's Cedar Valley]. Retreat Valley [is] only separated [from it] by a mountain spur. Retreat may well be the road in future.[29] After 11 mile drive, we camp at a spring [Antelope Springs] found by one of the retreat explorers in a mtn nearly south of the Bute, & can be known by a tall mt [Antelope Peak, 6,557 feet] standing out from the mane [Antelope Range] which we round by [the north]. From he[re] we get an elevated view to the north & west, to look at the ranges of mts one behind the [other], extending purhaps 100 miles north & south, many very high peeks. One in perticular, north west, covered with snow. In the front of the landscape rises in the midst of the valley, a washed mountain, [Table Butte, on which] the sun sets rosey red, the yellow grass at its base being a scene for the artist, unique & imposing.

[November 3rd] November 2d.[30] Up before day, pritty cold & chilling, bake bread. Mazeppa mts [mounts] a bute & as the sun rises he relieves the land scape aided by a wolf. Wolves now begin their yells in every direction & we start round the mt, & make south hugging the western [foot of the] mts over a road that deserves the name of a turnpike made hard by the late rain. Camp on a little spring branch [Pinto Creek at Newcastle, Utah]; but little feed, wood plenty.

Several Indians come in camp & take the entrals of an ox that has just been killed, worked till within a min. before its death. These Indians are evidently Pi Utes. Some had on old pants, evidently traded skins for them to emigrants which have gone before us. Others had robes around their boddies made of hare skins twisted & tied close together with Buck skin strings coming up to the neck like a cloak & down to their middles. On the legs were buckskin leggings & on their heads some had hats & pieces of skins tied on. They are all a gruff, savage looking set, with an eye that is always restless & never remains on any certain

---

springs once yielded enough water to create a small stream but are now dry due to pumping for domestic and agricultural use. In 1978 the largest spring discharged 225 gallons per minute (Bjorklund, Sumsion, and Sandberg 1978, 42).

29. The flat expanse of the Escalante Desert, visible from Antelope Springs, never became a vehicular road to Salt Lake City.

30. For a while Lorton's dates have been two days behind. This day, he catches up one day so his dates are now only one day behind.

FIGURE 37. Jefferson Hunt monument on the Old Spanish Trail in southwestern Utah. Writes Lorton: "SHORT CUT/118 WAGONS TURNED/WEST HERE/1849." The monument was built about 1958 with colorful rocks surrounding the plaques. One hundred (not 118) San Joaquin Company wagon masters forsook the train's guide, Jefferson Hunt, to follow a bogus shortcut toward the California goldfields. Photo by LeRoy Johnson.

object. They move around like a hyena, take very little notice of any person but come up to the fire to warm, with out any apprehenssions. They aproach the nearest to the beast & man united I ever noticed in the savage. As the night was dark & apparently stormy, a guard was appointed over them after they had mad[e] a frugal meal off the ox entrails. I tied Mazeppa to the wagon wheel at my head & went to bed after singing with Coker.[31]

31. Edward C. Coker hailed from New York City and traveled with the Georgia-Mississippi boys (the Bug Smashers) through Death Valley to the goldfields over Walker Pass (J. Johnson 2018, 83–84, 130, 202; Johnson and Johnson 1987, 185n169; Manly 2001, 347n34). They arrived in Aqua Fria, Mariposa County, on January 29, 1850, "after having suffered intensely," and others arrived on February 9, "all in a starving, and some in a perishing condition" (G. Evans 2006, 254, 259).

[Nov. 4th, 1849] 3d.[32] Start southerly & hug the left mountains till we come to a road made by the trains ahead of us. [We are] going on the north rout [toward Walker Pass]. Here [between today's Newcastle and Enterprise, Utah] the 2 roads branch off & as the teams come to the turn off those that chose to go North rout turned right [Barney Ward's cutoff], & those south [turned] left. All but 8 [wagons] turned north [route], & 2 of that number finding no more to follow also turned with the majority.[33] They built a large fire & consulted the matter. The 6 [wagons] contended they were the San Wakin [Joaquin] compy. & had a right to the guide. The guide had now as good as [made] the $1000 & felt free & might as well go back, money quick earned. *[Written at the bottom of the page is this faint notation:]* piles of chrystal piled up by Bugs.[34]

We turned north [westward] also & at last the 6 moved on with 8 men. Hunt said he did not like to risk it with so few but the Mormons said they would go if only 1 went besides their wagon. I bid [Addison] Pratt, [James S.] Brown & the rest farewell & departed. It was a sad parting scene. We going over a rout never explored by the white man, before us all dark & gloom, to enter mountains of great hight subject to dreadful snows & frosts. They going over trackless deserts to follow the Spanish trail never traversed by teams, a gloomy barren soil with out tree or scrub.

The sky was darkening fast & night aproaching as we made [reached?] a dry river [bed]. We enter the kanyons mouth [Shoal Creek], assend the hill & near dark we camp with good feed, water in holes & plenty of dry willows & sage.[35] It now commences snowing & the high peeks around us are soon covered. The drive from water to water is 15 miles [according to Barney Ward].

[Nov. 5th] 4th. Start up the kanyon till we come to a high rock on the right at the top of the mountain & [on] the left a pass. Here it branches to a valley filled with good feed & some wild rye. The day is splendid & every one exclaiming, if it is so all the way how delightful. We will soon reach California. About 4 o'clock we camp at a spring runing out of a kanyon on the left, the water good. As you

32. Pratt (1990, 386) records: "4th. Sunday.... Here the road forks,...the Old Spanish Trail continues south [up Holt Canyon]."
33. Seven wagons, including the wagon Hunt traveled with, continued down the Old Spanish Trail. We call this the Hunt wagon train. Addison Pratt (1990, 386) wrote: "Here the wagons began to file off onto the cutoff, till they left but 7 to go the old trail." Adonijah Welch said, "Company broke up, seven waggons pursuing the old Spanish trail" (Welch 1959, 67, March 1, 1850; Cumming 1985, 120).
34. The separation point is now commemorated by the Jefferson Hunt Monument, six and a half crow-miles east-northeast of today's Enterprise, Utah. The piles were made by ants.
35. They camped near where the small Mormon village of Hebron once stood (six and a half miles west of Enterprise, Utah).

FIGURE 38. Lorton sketch. Fireplace Rock, upper Shoal Creek Valley. He writes: "Wasatch Mts / Nov. 6th 1849"; "Cave at Cave Kanyon"; "saddle found here"; "S.U.B." [or "S.O.B."]. This sketch may have been drawn November 6, but according to his journal, he was at this site two days before, on November 4. Courtesy of The Bancroft Library.

enter the kanyon on the left is a cave resembling an old fashioned fireplace & chimny but no hole to emit smoke. There was a stick laid acrosst & a saddle & bridal thereon.[36] I called this Cave Kanyon.[37] Kill a beef, fry liver, cook beans, organize in the eve'g.

[Nov. 6th] 5th. The road now leads thro' a narrow rockey pass. At 1 mile is water.[38] The grass had been burnt off. Up hill all day. Crooked time up & down, snow laying still on the ground which made it bad going for teams. We pass 2 or 3 dry camps. One in particular, had ravins & wolves picking what had been left. The wolves skulked off. Shot [at] several of these. They gazed at us as if they had never before seen man. We snapped at them but all [guns] mised fire. The cattle nearly exhausted & a great many give out.

After frequent rests we arrive at what we supposed to be the summit, & there for 2 miles strung along up the hill tops appear all the old comp with the exception of the Rovers & they were down about 2,000 feet in an awful gulf which they

36. The artifacts were left by a packer who was a few days ahead.

37. The main water source for Shoal Creek is the overflow from several springs, now impounded by an earth dam on the Terry Ranch in Lorton's "Cave Kanyon."

38. Nephi Draw and Nephi Spring are named after southern Utah pioneer Nephi Johnson.

FIGURE 39. Fireplace Rock on Terry Ranch, upper Shoal Creek Valley, below mouth of Nephi Draw as it appeared in 2006. On November 5, Lorton writes, "A cave resembling an old fashioned fireplace & chimny but no hole to emit smoke." Photo by LeRoy Johnson.

had rushed headlong into & when to[o] late found that they were blockaded in & would have to take wagons to pieces.[39]

39. Nearly a hundred wagons were strung out along the rounded ridge of Pine Park Bench from the headwaters of Clay Canyon south to the brink of White Hollow and Pine Park Canyon. The emigrants named this area Mount Misery about November 5 (Manly 1894, 329; Map 1890, Manly; anonymous letter in *Knoxville (IL) Journal* 1850, April 3; Arms 1850, January 29; Erkson in Manly 1894, 368). The Rovers, part of the Buckskin Division, drove a small number of wagons down the "awful gulf" toward Pine Park Creek, "from which I had seen no possible way of escape," said Cephas Arms (in Cumming 1985, 103–4, 108). This was linear, not vertical feet.

FIGURE 40. Lorton sketch. From Mount Misery looking east beyond White Hollow. Writes Lorton, "Great Gulf or awful Chasm/at attempted pass/1000 ft high." Courtesy of The Bancroft Library.

I decended this gulf or ravine, I suppose 2,000 ft, very steep on one side. [This] side sand & rock, on the other purpendicular with high lofty jets [hoodos] & loose disconnected fragments & mamoth rocks.[40] At last we reach the bottom with ponies & cattle. Here we find a creek where the cattle drink.[41] Several cattle got hurt by falling from the precipices. Some were let down by the bushes easy. There is an outlet for the stream but a wagon cannot go five miles.[42] Packers went down, & [in?] places they had to back out.[43] I arrive up after dark.

[Nov.] 6th. [continued] Arroused up & ordered to prepare for battle as the Indians were attacking the Rovers below. We got our arms ready & soon after learned that Dr Holmes had heard a tremendous firing. As soon as I heard from whence it came, that was all I wanted. He fired at the guard, [who fired] back,

40. This is a fairly accurate description of the descent down the Indian trail into White Hollow, a branch of Pine Park Canyon. However, the depth of the canyon from brink to stream is 540 feet (not 2,000 feet). Lorton's "sand & rock" alludes to the conical and randomly sculpted hoodoos that are characteristic of the volcanic tuff of honeycomb rock common in the surrounding area (Rowley et al. 2008, 4–5).
41. In Lorton's letter of January 20, 1850, he described the canyon more realistically as "an awful chasm several hundred feet in depth" (see chapter 12).
42. Someone scouted down Pine Park Canyon. From today's Forest Service campground to the canyon's confluence with Headwaters Wash is roughly five and a half miles. Below this point the canyon is called Beaver Dam Wash.
43. Sequentially this sentence is out of order: Lorton is referring to the packers who made an abortive attempt to descend Headwaters Wash on November 2 but were thwarted by the Devil's Offset (Cannon 1999, 38, 101).

FIGURE 41. Part of Mount Misery today, looking east from near the trail from Pine Park Bench into White Hollow and Pine Park Campground. Note similarity to Lorton's skyline and crags in foreground. Photo by LeRoy Johnson.

when he went down after water which we reached by letting ourselves down by the rocks. The Rovers had a laugh ov[e]r it. Great time in getting up hill. Greatest hill I ever see.

[Nov.] 6th. [continued] Pioneers still out & some coming in, some from the west & others south. For 20 miles they climbed the highest snowey peeks. They could see a stream to the south & supposed it to be the Santa Clair [Clara] or Rio Virgin.

[Nov.] 7th.[44] No more news till eve'g, [when] explorers come in & report that it is impossible to pass with wagons. Great many discouraged & know not what to do. Some women [take the news] better than the men. Talk of packing oxen. Provisions getting scarce, flour raise to $40 [per] 100 [pounds]. Rovers down in the hole probably have to leave their wagons in there or hall them up with ropes. Capt [William H.] God[d]ard returns & advises all to put for the Spanish trail.[45] Had an arrow to pass by his head while alone. I took [Harry] Wade

44. As Lorton lay in camp on November 7, he took time to write, retrospectively, in his journal.

45. Others at Mount Misery concurred. Mr. Rynierson said he felt "duty bound to seek a safer way than this. I shall hitch up my oxen and return at once to the old trail" (in Manly 1894, 112). The Rovers, "after getting out of the canyon with some difficulty, we began to retraced our steps, and…struck the [Old Spanish] trail, having lost ten days travel and provisions…on the folly of exploring with ox-teams" (Arms in Cumming 1985, 103–4, 108).

FIGURE 42. Hoodoos. These may be the tent-shaped hoodoos Lorton drew in the upper left of his "Great Gulf" sketch (see Figure 40). Photo by LeRoy Johnson.

for an Indian. Our teem gave out. Take away 1 yoke. Conclude to pack & make preparations.

[Nov.] 8th. 1 comp starts out. [I] still make preparations.

[Nov.] 9th. Poor Naylor died. Quarel over his body for his property. I reprove them. Have a trial. I am witness. Sell my trunk for 6 bits. Throw away shirt & give other things away. Burry him on the mountain. Several wagons left & great many splicing.

[Nov.] 10th. All ready & start down the Big hill with the pack on Mazeppa's back & calculated to meet the N. Y. boys 2 miles down [at Pine Park Canyon].

CHAPTER 10

Travails in *Terra Incognita*

Background

There were about 64 packers, including the Smith and Flake companies, who dropped into Beaver Dam Wash supposedly following Ward's purported cutoff map. (The number comes from adding the Smith packers, Mormon packers, some who joined them before Mount Misery, and some who became packers at Mount Misery.) With them were a larger number of horses and mules (until many of them were eaten). These packers became the first known white men to venture deep into the vast desert region west of Beaver Dam Wash, the northeastern wing of the mighty Mojave Desert. Explorers had already skirted this vast territory on its southern and eastern periphery—Jedediah Smith, packers from Santa Fe, and John C. Frémont followed a major portion of the Old Spanish Trail, but none had penetrated the desert into which the gold-rush packers ventured.

After his trek west through Moapa Indian lands, Lorton sketched his first map of this area while at Division Spring at the base of the Sheep Range (Lorton's "horse spring," his last westward camp). This crude map has a couple of details Lorton leaves off a second map he drew later, upon which he added a dashed line depicting his trek from Mount Misery to Division Spring and his return east to Beaver Dam Wash. On the second map he used a three-by-three-mile grid, and with it we can follow his general route of travel (and the movements of the other packers as far as Division Spring). We interpret Lorton's route based on his journal and his two maps, although there are (expected) discrepancies between the journal mileages and the grid map. And we have made numerous trips into *terra incognita* to trace Lorton's route.

When Lorton left Mount Misery on November 10, he traveled down Pine Park Canyon rather than following the Smith and Flake packers' route down Headwaters Wash. He picked up their trail where Pine Park Canyon and Headwaters Wash join to become Beaver Dam Wash.

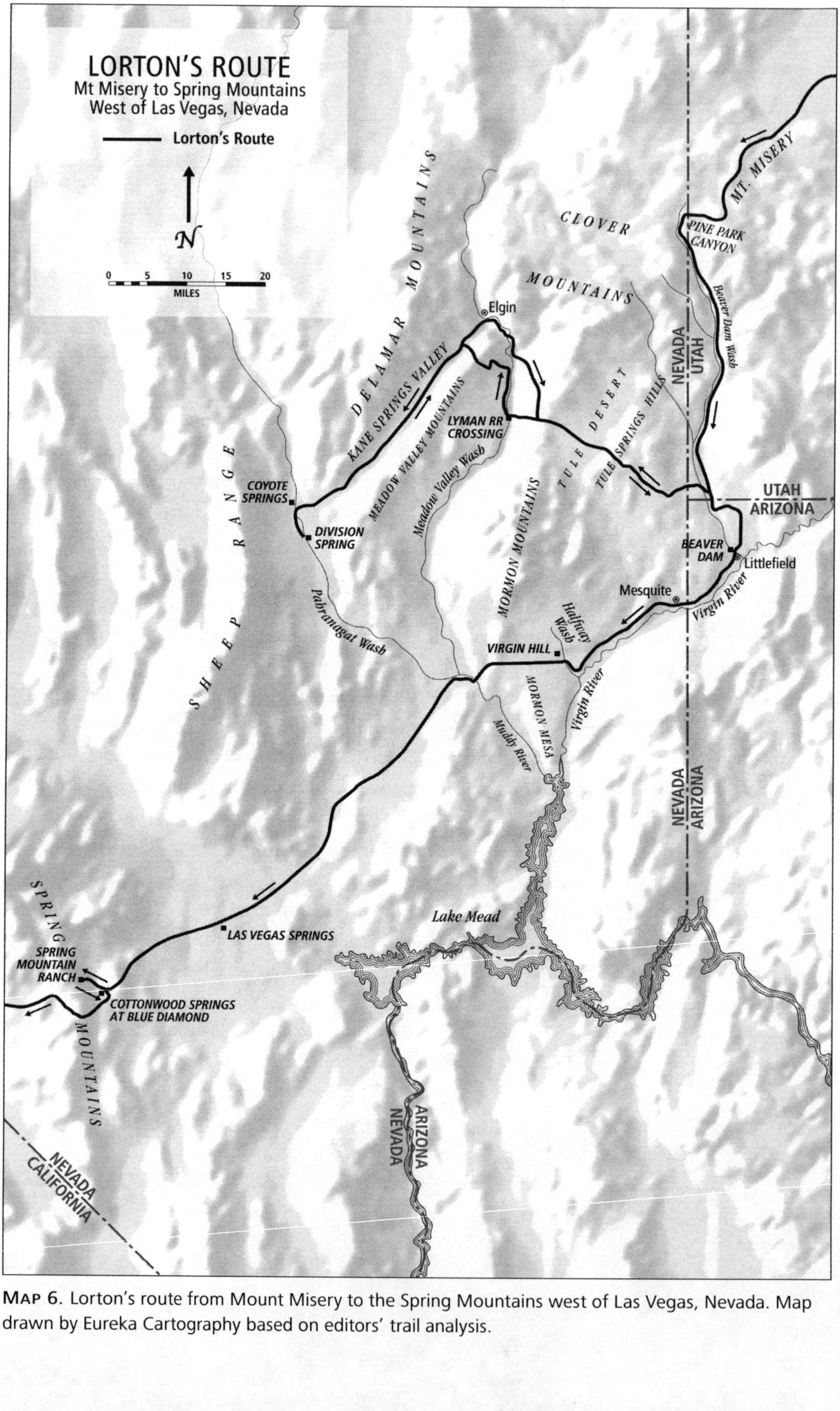

Map 6. Lorton's route from Mount Misery to the Spring Mountains west of Las Vegas, Nevada. Map drawn by Eureka Cartography based on editors' trail analysis.

FIGURE 43. Scene on today's Tule Desert west of Beaver Dam Wash and east of Meadow Valley, Nevada. Photo by LeRoy Johnson.

In a letter written January 20, 1850, Lorton lists the men who came out of the desert with him including the five New York boys he planned to meet "2 miles down" the canyon from Mount Misery.[1] Later in Kane Springs Valley (November 18) he mentions there were "only 3 of us," but others were ahead or behind him.

After a short march down Beaver Dam Wash, Lorton catches up with the New York boys and they camp about a mile south of today's Beaver Dam State Park. Here they are forced to climb out of the wash where the canyon narrows and the water course is littered with big boulders. Lorton draws this detour on his grid map.

About 42 miles down (south) Beaver Dam Wash (Lorton's "Corn Kanyon") the packers find an Indian cornfield where water flowing underground is pinched to the surface. Here they turn northwest up an arroyo to access the tablelands to the west. They are forced southwestward to find a way through the Tule Springs Hills via Steer Flat north of Jumbled Mountain, then northwestward

1. In his January 20, 1850, letter Lorton lists "Dr. Downer, Iowa; two Mr. Sanburns, Ill.; P. Orr, do. [ditto]; Mr. Potter, do.; Gen. G. Blodget, Wis., and servant boy; J. Stoges [Stover], Iowa; Charles Burrel, New York City; Wm. Sands, do.; Wm. Sherman, do.; J. Hendle, do.; Wm. B. Lorton, do.; J. Bucklin, do.; Mr. Springer, Ill.; Mr. [F. B.] Shannon, do." Four of the non–New York men came from the O. K. Smith company.

to cross the Tule Desert. They descend into Meadow Valley Wash just below today's Lyman Crossing on November 15, where the Smith and Flake companies camped without water on November 8.

The Smith and Flake companies continued farther up Meadow Valley Wash to find water than did Lorton's group (north of Leith Siding) because the rains of November 13–14 had not yet left puddle water in the wash that Lorton's packers found. Thus, the Smith and Flake groups had to backtrack to enter a tempting canyon into the northern Meadow Valley Mountains. George Cannon, one of the Mormon packers, said,

> [They] traveled down bed of Creek about a mile & then struck off to the Westward over some low mountains. This day's travel was...an uninterrupted succession of hills very fatiguing for both animals and men we did not seem to make much headway as we had to tack round considerable to avoid heavy hills. After travelling until near night we saw a creek to our right [northwest] down in a Cañon...[we] descend; upon examination we found that it was Providence Creek [in Meadow Valley Wash] & that we had not gained over three miles by our day's travel. (Cannon 1999, 48)

Lorton's group followed the Smith and Flake packers into the Meadow Wash Mountains on November 16.

After the mountain fiasco, Apostle Rich assumed command of the Flake company, citing Flake's failure to listen to Rich's council by doggedly following Smith's tracks through the wilderness (Cannon 1999; Rich in Hafen and Hafen 1954b, 187; Bigler in ibid., 158; Cannon in ibid., 245–46). With the change of leadership, the Flake company becomes the Rich company.

The Smith and Rich packers passed southwest through locally named Riggs Wash into Kane Springs Valley between the Delamar and Meadow Valley Mountains (Averett 1995, xi). After about 40 dry miles they entered Pahranagat Wash (Coyote Spring Valley) at the base of the Sheep Range, where they found a small spring with "lots of tadpoles" on November 14.

Based on information from diaries, we conclude none of the packers camped at Coyote Spring, which has long been assumed to be their Division Spring.[2] Coyote Spring is a little over a mile and a half north-northwest of the junction of Kane Springs and Pahranagat washes. But Bigler says some of Smith's men "found a small spring about *3 miles toward the South*...lots of tadpoles in the spring, it was cleaned out and we had plenty of water" (Bigler in Hafen and Hafen 1954b, 160; emphasis ours). And Cannon says, "Capt. Smith's men found

2. George Perkins thought the packers camped at Coyote Spring, and LeRoy and Ann Hafen accepted his premise (Perkins 1947, 47; Hafen and Hafen 1954b, 160n28).

a small spring in the bottom, *to the Southward*" (Cannon 1999, 52; emphasis ours). This weak spring is extinct now that vast quantities of water are pumped from the aquifer for agriculture, Las Vegas's domestic use, and to keep the local golf course green.

From Kane Springs Wash, dead ahead to the west, stands the Sheep Range with a string of 7,000-foot peaks—a formidable barrier. At its base is Division Spring, as the Rich company called it (Bigler's Tadpole Spring and Lorton's Horse Spring). One of the group, Jacob Stover, uses the name Dead Horse Spring because several horses and mules were slaughtered there to provide meat.

When Lorton arrived, the Smith packers had just returned from an ill-fated trek over the Sheep Range, where they saw an endless desert waste ahead and finally realized Barney Ward's map was a humbug.

At Division Spring the various packer groups reassessed their situation and chose different options based on their divergent purposes. Eleven ardent gold seekers decided to continue west to find Walker Pass. Today, these men are called the Pinney-Savage party, and fortunately Lorton recorded their names (Lorton, November 19, 1849, and letter, January 20, 1850; Cannon 1999, 251). Apostle Rich was convinced that Barney Ward's cutoff was not a feasible wagon route to the coast after Rich climbed to the crest of the Sheep Range (in Hafen and Hafen 1954b, 188). So, the Mormon Packers turned south to intercept Captain Hunt on the Old Spanish Trail. The Smith packers, having probed the desert beyond the Sheep Range, were satisfied they were lost and decided to retrace their steps to Salt Lake City (Bigler in Hafen and Hafen 1954b, 161–62). Lorton and other independent packers decided to return to Beaver Dam Wash and there determine what to do next.

Lorton and his contingent had not yet arrived at Division Spring when the Mormons left on November 16. Their decision was the result of observation, some preplanning, and, as Lorton said, the help of a "revelation" (November 18). Addison Pratt quotes Hunt: "I told Br. Rich, if he found mountains that they could not pass, to be sure and slide back onto this trail [Old Spanish Trail] quick as possible and come on and overtake us" (A. Pratt 1990, 387). Rich's choice was logical, uneventful, and correct. They "parted with Capt Smith's company and took [south] down the creek, found plenty of water and grass after passing a kanion, camped" (Rich in Hafen and Hafen 1954b, 189). The Mormons descended Pahranagat Wash, passed through Double and Arrow Canyons, and camped below a cluster of potable warm springs, the source of the (Far) Muddy River. On the 18th they "continued down creek... [and] came to Capt. Hunt and 7 wagons" on the river at the crossing into California Wash near today's Moapa, Nevada (ibid.).

Why Lorton's group decided to turn back instead of following the Mormon packers is difficult to fathom. Twenty years later, Cannon gave his opinion:

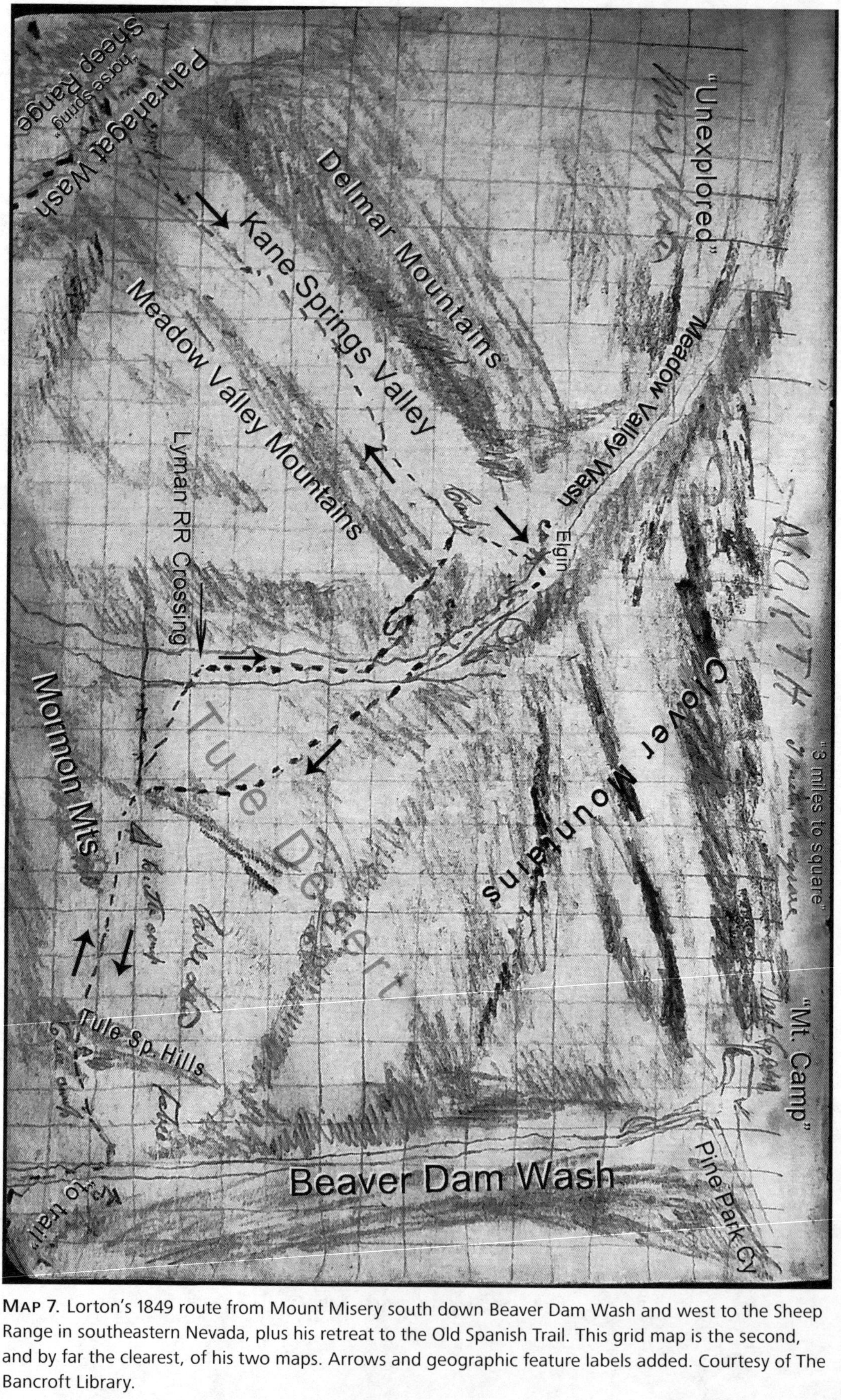

Map 7. Lorton's 1849 route from Mount Misery south down Beaver Dam Wash and west to the Sheep Range in southeastern Nevada, plus his retreat to the Old Spanish Trail. This grid map is the second, and by far the clearest, of his two maps. Arrows and geographic feature labels added. Courtesy of The Bancroft Library.

"They might have followed us, but their pride revolted at this." Lorton's route ended up adding at least 120 miles more than the route the Rich company took.

After turning back, Lorton's group had a dry camp in Kane Springs Wash, where Jacob Stover says they "held council on what we should do. They concluded to follow me, so I was captain to lead them out of the desert and mountains" (Stover in Hafen and Hafen 1954b, 280; see also Cannon in ibid., 251). We refer to this group as the Stover company. After reaching Beaver Dam Wash, the recombined Smith and Stover men had a crucial discussion as to what course to take. The result was Smith and most of his men turned north in the wash, planning to return to Salt Lake City. The Stover company (and four of Smith's packers) turned south, hoping to intercept the Old Spanish Trail.

The Stover company went two and a half miles down Beaver Dam Wash then exited the east (left) bank via Welcome Creek (a dry drainage). Once on higher ground they headed southeastward and soon found the Old Spanish Trail.

Only through the words of another do we get an inkling of the impact this misdirected sojourn had on Lorton. A conversation he had with Addison Pratt reveals the emotional effect of his detour into *terra incognita* (see chapter 12).

As it turns out, Smith's company did not get back to Salt Lake City. They met the Pomeroy wagons December 3 at or near the Near Muddy (today's Coal Creek, Cedar City, Utah). Joseph P. Hamelin noted Smith had 18 men with him and "we gave them all the food we could spare & took in 3 of their number." About 20 miles farther northeast, the rest of Smith's party met the Huffaker-Egan wagons in Parowan Valley, where Ransom G. Moody successfully negotiated with his fellow travelers to have Smith and his men join their train. Thus, they were brought through to California (Hamelin in Hafen and Hafen 1961, 85; Thurber in ibid., 117–18; Moody in ibid., 109, 113).

Lorton's Journal Continues as He Leaves Mount Misery

[November 1849] 10th. All ready & start down the Big hill with the pack on Mazeppa's back & calculated to meet the N. Y. boys 2 miles down [in Pine Park Canyon]. When we arrived at the spot we did not find them, but the trail showed that some persons had went on, so we followed on the deep dark ravine up steep assents & precipitous gulfs, decended thro' thick cedars and rockey passes. We hollowed at every valley but the rocks reiterated back what we said in hollow tones.

We see paper [saying] come on boys. Finally dark came & as we came to a fine little spring, & some grass, we make a fire amonge the rocks & after taking a lunch [?] we laid our bed up on a hill under the trees & examining our revolvers we made them our bed fellows fearing Bear or Pi Ute.[3] We were awake every 30 min. during the night to see if our animals [were all right] & rivaly [reveille] to every rustling & sound the night bird or wolf made. Miles [*blank*].

[November] 11th. Up by day[break] & start. Pass over a very rough & stoney road till we come to a high mountain where we had to make [a] road & almost let our mules down. By the time we got down in the valley & crossed a fine stream [Beaver Dam Wash] we entered an opening of tall trees when a loud shout made the welkin ring. We were not long in seeing that they were our boys. They were just [about] to start & we all went on together. We cross the creek about 150 times today. In fact we almost wade the stream down. Assend 1 hill that is almost perpendicular [because the stream bed is littered with big boulders]. See several Wic e ups deserted. See many[?] Indians track, plenty of grape vines, but grapes all gone. Indians live on them. At last we "carall" without any grass.

[November] 12th. Ready to pack by day light & go on for grass. Find a little [at] 9 o'clock & stop till 12. See a very large Cactus of 2 species. Sell [?] [*several words illegible*] $5.00. See several wic e ups lately inhabited. See where the Indians ate horse, picked bones. Come to several Indian farms where they had raised small corn. One in particular [had] a fine soil & trenches dug to irrogate, & furrows in between. Our course is now somewhat widened by narrow valleys. We camt 3 o'clock. Plenty of birds, quale & partrage. 15 miles [or] 20 miles. 12th [continued]. Road still down kanyon (south). See many wic e ups, large cactus, & footprints. Hard & rough days drives. 15 miles drive.[4]

[November] 13th. Pass thro' a succession of narrow valleys. Curious phenonama in relation to the creek which drys up near night & runs again at midnight.[5] Keep strict guard, & put out fires & double our watch. Leave the creek where it sinks & continue our course down. Comes on a hard rain. At length, we come to a gentle stream with green fringed edges of grass. Near it a corn patch of this

3. They made a short march down Beaver Dam Wash and camped about a mile south of today's Beaver Dam State Park near the Utah-Nevada state line.
4. Here Lorton is repeating the above 15 miles. The first "15 [or] 20 ms" are interlined. It appears he later put this interlined mileage in as a total for that date.
5. In 1769 Don Pedro Fages observed this same phenomenon while descending the Santa Clara River, west of today's Castaic Junction, in Santa Clarity Valley, California. His party came to "the bank of a stream which, although it has a moderate flow during the night and early morning, soon dries up from the heat of the sun—a peculiarity observed in some other streams from this point on" (Fages 1937, vii, 17). This phenomenon is linked to the normal diurnal evapotranspiration cycle. When the sun sets, vegetation shuts down its photosynthesis and respiration mechanisms that, figuratively, suck the water out of the soil. As the process abates, groundwater is available to move into a drainage.

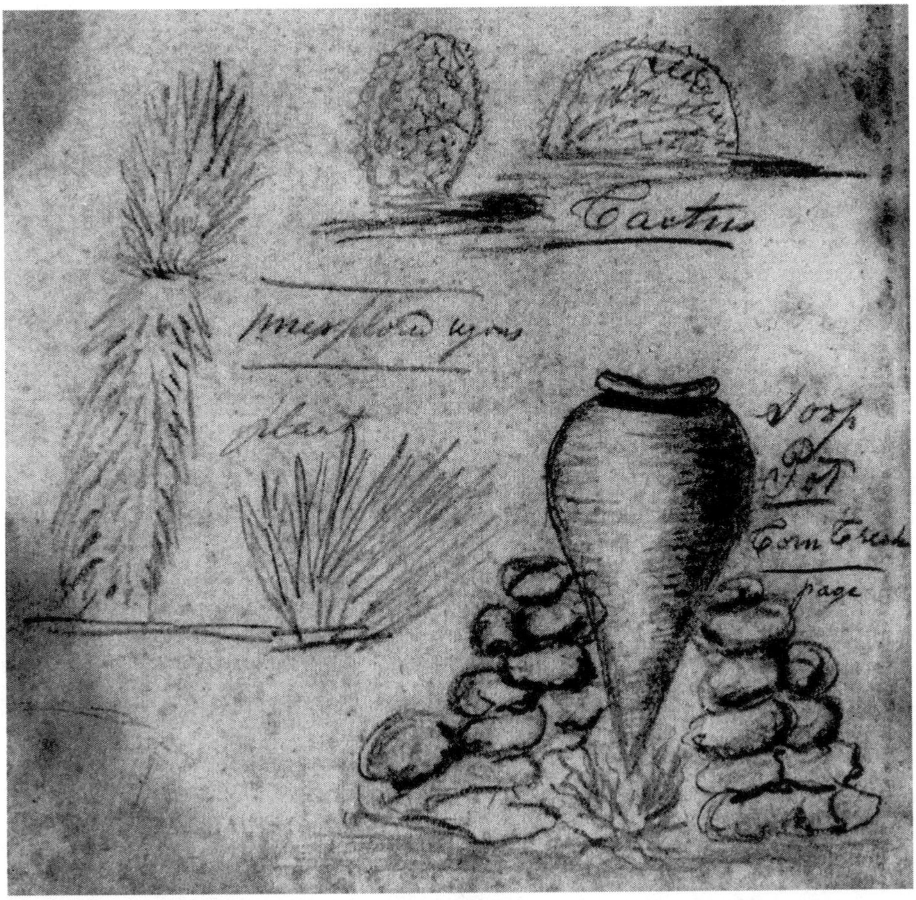

FIGURE 44. Lorton sketch. Desert plants and Indian soup pot. Lorton's labels are: "Cactus," "unexplored regions," "plant," and "Soop Pot/Corn Creek/page." Courtesy of The Bancroft Library.

years groath where the Indians had irrogated it. Their furrows are about 3 ft wide & the corn grows in abundance, for the surface [is] cultivated. They had 2 large thatched houses but partly destroyed. We turned our animals out in the stalks to feed while we sat under trees to rest. We come acrost 1 or 2 other fields, but smaller.

We turn to [the] West out of the kanyon [Beaver Dam Wash] & assend a table land. Here all is gloom. High mountains all around in dist & relievs the solitary appearance[?]. The storm is also approaching & clouds hang low on the mountains. A little scrub, & here & there a sort of palm plant.[6] Whole dist down kanyon, 45 miles.[7] We camp in a cave in the rocks, build a fire, drenched

6. The Joshua tree's (*Yucca brevifolia*) natural range begins in this area. Lorton sketched one inside the cover of Volume III.

7. We conclude Lorton's 45 miles "dist down kanyon" began where White Hollow joins Pine Park Canyon.

FIGURE 45. Lorton sketch. Joshua tree on tableland west of Beaver Dam Wash. Writes Lorton: "grow/very/high"; "on Table land/unexplored regions." Courtesy of The Bancroft Library.

to the skin with rain.[8] We get on the wrong tract. The storm comes on & rain decends heavily. We spread oil clothes & set pans to catch water. Terrible night for the natives. Guns, pistols hanging up in cave, [creating a] robbers scene. We spread buffalo [robes] & cover up head & ears tho' the rain drips on our bed of stones. Hard night for the guard.

[November 14th] 13th. Travel (20 miles) over a trackless desert without water.[9] We get a little from holes in rocks. Wolf dung [in the water] is no object now.[10] Have rain throughout the day. Our jorney still over the table lands. At length we camp on a bluff.[11] Good bunch grass & seed grass which the Indians cut.[12] Storm

8. We determine this camp was about a mile north of the Utah-Arizona east-west state line in a rugged arroyo between Beaver Dam Wash and the Terry Benches.

9. They crossed the Tule Springs Hills via Steer Flat and descended into the Tule Desert.

10. Desert mammals, particularly packrats, defecate in small basins of ephemeral water to mark them. I (LeRoy) have reluctantly had to drink water from polluted rock puddles on several solo research treks.

11. "Butte camp" on Lorton's grid map (see Map 7) might be the bluff above Sams Camp Wash.

12. This perennial bunchgrass, Indian ricegrass (*Achnatherum hymenoides*), is found throughout the Great Basin. "Nutritious seed of Indian ricegrass was one of the staple foods of American Indians" (Ogle 2006, 1). Lewis Manly observed the same thing farther north about the same time: "Among the sage grew also a bunch grass a foot high, which had seeds like broom-corn seeds. The Indians had gathered the grass and made it in piles of one hundred pounds or so, and used it for food as I found by examining their camps"

FIGURE 46. Joshua tree on Tule Desert, Nevada, Lorton's tableland. Photo by LeRoy Johnson.

lowers. Scoop up muddy rain water & make tea. Sleep out on the plain.[13] Rains hard & wets thro' every thing.

[November 15th, 1849] 14th. 18 miles [today]. Start out again without water & the weather looking clear. We now feared the consequences. Got a few sucks [of water with pipe stems] from holes in rocks & we continue on over bleek gravelly rolling ground till we come to a dry river [Meadow Valley Wash]. Here we see Smiths Camp. No water.[14] Packsaddle &c. [abandoned]. We follow up

(1894, 115). "When the seeds were nearly ripe, grass bunches were gathered into a pile, threshed by beating with sticks to loosen the seeds, then winnowed in basket trays to concentrate the seeds" (Rhode 2002, 174).

13. Lorton camped overnight near the western edge of Tule Desert, about 20 miles northwest from his "cave in the rocks" camp.

14. There was no surface water where the packers entered Meadow Valley Wash at Lyman Crossing. The Smith and Flake parties were here November 8.

north his trail in search of water, every boddy almost famished & animals had none in 3 days. We are very much fatigued. At last near night a mud puddle done by the late rain is discovered. We quickly fill our canteens & pails & then let in the cattle who drink it to the earth.[15] All is joy & all say God sent it, for at a dry season we must have perished. We go up further & there find puddles in plenty, either from rain or [where the] creek choked up her water. Little feed. We here camp [Meadow Valley Wash south of today's Leith Siding].[16]

[November 16th] 15th. [Today went] 10 miles. Start up the mts on the left [west]. Up ravines & down ravines, at one time travelling south, then east & very little west. Very rough & craggy rocks to assend & go down.[17] Coming down a steep decent we find water in rocks dripping down from the late rains. We water & go on moderately till we come to a valley running a little south of west [Kane Springs Valley].[18] We see an old sway back mare that had been left & pack it. See Smiths trail where he turned back. We camp without water [northeastern end of Kane Springs Valley]. Plenty of dry ravines.

[November 17th] 16th. [Today went] 10 miles. Still down the valley at good speed. Found a little rain water in puddles, we fill our canteens. Thinking to find more we let in the horses & soon brot it to a crisis. Go on all day. I go to the north mt [Delamar Mountains] & look [for water] in the ravines but near night I see the men at a dist. camping & Waitin all without water.[19] At first we thot to let our animals bate & then go on but did not till day light [second dry camp in Kane Springs Wash].

[November 18th] 17th. [Today went] 28 miles. 8th day [since leaving the wagons]. We follow down after a sleep with fanciful brooks, rivers, puddles of

15. "Cattle" were the horses and mules. It is doubtful any oxen or cows were with them.
16. Lorton's contingent found puddle water from the November 13–14 storms. The Smith and Flake packers, having traveled here before the rains, found no puddle water; thus, they camped farther up the canyon where the upside-down stream is pinched to the surface. The Mormon packers christened this place "Providence Cañon" and "Providence Creek" (Cannon 1999, 45; Bigler in Hafen and Hafen 1954b, 157). They retraced their steps the next morning and turned west into the Meadow Valley Mountains.
17. Lorton and company entered the northern Meadow Valley Mountains in the vicinity of Leith, following tracks of the O. K. Smith and Flake companies, who exited the Meadow Valley Wash on November 11.
18. Lorton's bunch did not follow the Smith and Flake packers out of the mountains but headed westward and exited into Kane Springs Valley, whose name implies water but there is none. Kane Springs are in the Delmar Mountains north of, and well above, the valley. Lorton looked for but did not find them.
19. We interpret his 10-mile trek to include the miles covered searching ravines for water.

water. Dream of a puddle down the rim which I find. [Dream of] drinks taken years agoe. We find some [water] in puddles but not more than we wanted for ourselves. Our horses went almost crazy & run every way in search of drink. All this was agonizing. 1 horse [we] left, others about to give out. At the west, running north & south, is a very high chain [the Sheep Range]. To avoid this we strike over the bluffs north of west, & in our course we see foot prints & pack mule prints.[20] On our left [south] we see smoke & dry canes, then 2 fires. There was only 3 of us. We got our guns in order & said we would risk Indians if we could find water. As we approach we see animals & then guns fire. We approach & find it Smiths train, in a delirum.[21] They had been 11 days [from Mount Misery], with the exception of 2 which had been spent in going on in search of water, & failed.[22] They had lost 1/2 their animals. The foot packers lost all but 2 [out of 5]. They had killed 2 animals & some of the meat jerked [was] hanging up in a tree. They had lived on this several days & half starved at that. They were all discouraged. [*Written at bottom of page:*] Smith relates the soop flight [fight?] in corn kanyon [Beaver Dam Wash].

Some one [Apostle Rich] had found water up a steep mt [Cherry Spring? in the Sheep Range], but to[o] steep for animals. He said he see a lake to the south 40 or 50 miles.[23] The Mormons took down south [in Pahranagat Wash]. Gen. Rich, Pomeroy, [and companions, determined] to make a life & death attempt to head [intersect?] the wagon train, a leap in the dark. Gen. Rich said he had a revelation that if they went west they would all perish.

We know not where we are. We are in unexplored Regeons, south of the range seen by Freemont from a peek.[24] All discouraged. Smith goes in for [returning to] S[alt] Lake. They had found a little Indian spring [in Pahranagat Wash]. This they dug down several ft & let it run full. My Mazeppa drank itself about crazy, & run around & would not eat, however after repeated attempts he got a little satisfied.

Gen Blodget gave out altho' mounted, & said he could go no farther & laid down [waiting for his Negro servant to bring him water], 22 hours without

20. They veered northwest toward a lower part of the Sheep Range to cross it.
21. This was the tadpole spring the Mormons called Division Spring, in Pahranagat Wash, about five miles south of today's Coyote Spring (see background material in this chapter; also Bigler in Hafen and Hafen 1954b, 160).
22. Smith's aborted trek over the Sheep Range and retreat to Division Spring consumed two days.
23. Rich may have found Cherry Springs on the eastern flank of the Sheep Range and seen a skim of water on the large Three Lakes Valley playa about 35 miles away (Rich in Hafen and Hafen 1954b, 188).
24. Frémont's map (1848) warns, "These mountains are not explored, being only seen from elevated points on the northern exploring line." Lorton astutely and concisely assesses the shaky basis on which the emigrants turned west from the Old Spanish Trail.

water, his tongue cracked.[25] Another left a gun on the way, fearing he could never reach camp. He offered $30. to any person who would get it. They found a cave with water in it.[26]

To day we kill Utah, a poney 3 year old, & an old, gave out white horse.[27] Shot them & jerked their meat. We fryed some & made soup, very good. We know not what to do. It was now life & death to all. Horse meat had already come in play & I longed for fat little Nero of S. Olmsted, Jr.[28] There had been several Indians seen, & Smith tryed to catch them but they are as wild as deer. 1 man chased into camp by them.

[November 19th] 18th. A party of 10 have concluded to go still westward. Chas. McDermet, Jno. Adams, Savage, Willey Webster, Pinney, 2 Wares, Baker, Semore, Allen.[29] They all had their mule meat on their backs, no blankets. Plenty of ammunition. They left us to day [at] 12 o'clock for the top of the high mountain [Sheep Range], where there is a spring. Horses cannot get up.[30] This is a daring adventure, & hardships & triales & troubles will thicken around them. Some said they would go to Calif or to Hell.[31] Tears droped when they left. Ore [P. Orr] & Potter went with Smith to Salt Lake.[32] They cryed when they left, & by & by

25. George Blodgett was "a lawyer from Milwakee who has left as report says a wife and children at home and is traveling with a prostitute" (Welch in Ressler 1964, 267, October 24).

26. This appears to be a reference to four men traveling with the Smith-Flake packers, who failed to reach the watered camp at "Providence Cañon" (Meadow Valley Wash) November 10. The next morning 12 men backtracked with canteens and "a spade…hoping that, if murdered, we might, at least, find their bodies, and give them as decent a burial as we could" (Cannon in Hafen and Hafen 1954b, 244). After "about four miles from Camp; we were glad to see them…they had found water in a cave," somewhere along Meadow Valley Wash (Cannon 1999, 47).

27. Jacob Stover says, "We camped for the night at Dead Horse Springs [a.k.a. Division Spring], as we called it. In the morning we killed our first horse to eat here, an old gray one of mine" (in Hafen and Hafen 1954b, 279).

28. Silas Olmstead Jr. (Lorton's cousin near Monmouth, Illinois) apparently had a fat little pony named Nero. Now Division Spring takes on additional names; Lorton's map labels it "horse spring."

29. Historians call this group the Pinney-Savage party (Wheat 1939, 114). Lorton adds a "Mr. Moore" in his letter of January 20, 1850 (see chapter 12), totaling eleven men.

30. Apostle Rich brought information about a spring back to camp before the Mormon packers left Division Spring to intersect with Captain Hunt on the Old Spanish Trail. We do not know where the Pinney-Savage party crossed the Sheep Range; however the canyon that contains Cherry Spring ends at a pass (6,750 feet) in this high part of the range, and over the summit is Cabin Spring. An Indian trail likely followed this route.

31. Messrs. Pinney and Savage made it through to the goldfields, but the fate of the other nine men is not known although fantastic conjectures, such as cannibalism and skeletons found in a circle, have been rampant ever since they left the other packers.

32. Orr and Potter changed their minds later and became part of Lorton's company that

we left on the back tract determined to make no more cut offs. We ration on 1/2 allowance.

[November 20th] 19th. Start back all gloomey, the only thing that ever discouraged me & even now I am not [totally discouraged], tho' disheartened. Feel very weak, with 25 lbs about me on a/c of scant allowance. 18 mile drive [from Division Spring] & camp [in upper Kane Springs Valley] with out water. Mazeppa threw his pack & himself.

[November 21st] 20th. Go still back in a N.E. course & tired & fatigued. Strike Creek [Meadow Valley Wash] at base of mountains 25 miles. Left 2 animals & picked up 1 of Smiths. All tired.[33]

[November 22nd] 21st. Lay still all day. Rains hard but clears up. We build tents, [have] horse soop.

[November 23d] 22d. Take down the kanyon, late start. Awful chasm [narrows of Meadow Valley Wash].[34] Gen Blodget goes back after his animals & finds that Indians had taken them [along] with every trap[ping] we had left on the ground. Several saddles, straps, papers & all, but see none. We had no guard last night. Have to wade the creek where it rises amonge the cane brakes. Meet Capt Smith, [coming back] after his lost mule. See 4 carcases they had killed for food which they jerked. He said he had plenty of provisions, such as it was. They had no salt or pepper & "Diareah" had seized on them. I take hide to make moccosens for my poney, which is foot tender. We camp 1 mile from K[anyon] mouth, no feed but water [south of the junction with Cottonwood Canyon].

[November 24th] 23d. Follow down K[anyon] a few mile & take S. E. over a labyrinth of hills & so strike the former trail.[35] Find Lawrenc [Lawrence Hudson].[36] Others came 5 miles by [a] cut off. At dark we camp at the Butte we

---

went down Beaver Dam Wash to the Old Spanish Trail, according to Lorton's letter of January 20, 1850, (see chapter 12).

33. Smith's company was on ahead. Lorton's group, now led by Jacob Stover, camped a mile or two southeast of today's Elgin, Nevada, in Meadow Valley Wash.

34. Years later a tunnel was bored through these narrows for the railroad.

35. They exit the wash near today's Leith Siding and head southeastward toward Lorton's "Butte camp." See Lorton's grid map. Hafen and Hafen (1954b, 280) quotes Stover as saying he "left all trails, made one of my own southwest." The correct direction was southeast, not southwest.

36. This cryptic statement is interlined. Lawrence Hudson was a member of the Smith company who could not keep up. Jacob Stover rescued Hudson and brought him into camp (Stover in Hafen and Hafen 1954b, 281).

camped at before [on November 14]. Good grass but dry camp. Determine on starting 3 o'clock next morning.

[November 25th] 24th. Awakened at 2 by a pistol. Billy [Sands] fired at mule & shot the side of his head off, still standing. Buch kills him & goes in to his meat. We all breakfast & are about to get ready when Lawrance, who had been left by his crowd, we gave him [a] horse to ride, was now taken sick & we determined to bate till day light. Up at day break & off after supplying ourselves with mule meat. We make a big drive & arrive at 2 in camp at Corn Creek [Beaver Dam Wash], beating the boys that started at 3 in A. M. [by] 2 hours. Here we meet Smith, & deliver up Lawranc[e] to his comrades. Make been soop with mule meat. Our feet worn out by sharp stones. "Caral" under a big tree, near my fancy fire place.[37]

[November 26th] 25th. Our stock all in the Indians cornfield. Give letter to Capt Smith to carry to S. Lake. Send out 2 explorers to find a pass to Spanish trail. Smiths [company] depart today up the kanyon [north in Beaver Dam Wash]. I tell Smith it is the best way for him to take the Spanish trail to go back to S. Lake. He thinks the trail is 40 miles. I offer to wager my hat it is not 10 [miles] in a direct course. I feel confident in striking it. All ready, we start down the kanyon. A dispute as to the best course, over the table land or down [the wash]. Follow down 2 miles & then strike S. West [actually southeast] over a myriad of hills & roleing ravines. Come to a gap but cannot on a/c of rocks put south. Cut up the Cactus, or as we call it cabbage & eat it. Pritty good.

About 3 o'clock, those ahead "hurrah" for the Spanish trail which they had struck. 12 cheers for the trail by all the comp. Before reaching it I thought it curious on finding a mules hoof. It might be a 100 yrs old. 2 men dreamed that we struck the trail just where we did. Happy Jubile the best luck we had had in a long while. Every man felt better. After dark, after followin[g] down a gradual decent, we strike the Rio Virgin, & where Corn Creek [Beaver Dam Wash] puts in.

River a few miles above runs thro an enormous chasm in the mountains.[38] Great many trees on its bottom. Feed poor. Marked on tree, 7th div. passed on 17th, another [message] 2 days later. Tracks indicated that wagons had passed since the late rain [on November 22] 4 or 5 days [ago]. Mule & horse meat in demand.

37. This is where Lorton and friends stopped two weeks before.

38. The Narrows is a gorge where the Virgin River and Interstate 15 cut through the Beaver Dam Mountains. Since Lorton did not see it, he likely based his comment on Frémont's description of May 10, 1844: "A gap of two thousand feet deep in the mountain ... where no man or beast could follow it" (Frémont 1970b, 691).

CHAPTER 11

Old Spanish Trail into Southern California

Background

Once on the Old Spanish Trail, Lorton's contingent continued southward and camped southeast of today's community of Beaver Dam, Arizona. From here the wagon road traversed the northwest (right) bank of the Virgin River on elevated tableland, thus avoiding the dense vegetation and quicksand in the shallows along the river. Addison Pratt said the road "crossed the dry bed of the stream [Beaver Dam Wash] above the springs and went down the river on the desert which is high and dry, covered with hard gravel as if set in cement." The route paralleled old U.S. Route 91, not far from Interstate 15. Pratt continued, "[We] traveled some 5 miles and descended a steep slope into the river bottoms," following the Old Spanish Trail down the Virgin River with as many as 17 crossings in 32 miles to today's Halfway Wash—about 16 crow-miles southwest of today's Mesquite, Nevada (A. Pratt 1990, 390; for more on the trail, see Steiner 1999, 104, and Crampton and Madsen 1994, 81).

At Halfway Wash the road turned northwest up the dry wash 2.4 miles to the base of the notorious Virgin Hill that a handful of diarists, such as William Lorton (November 30), Addison Pratt (1990, 392), and Harold Egan (in Hafen and Hafen 1954b, 313), have described. Here the travelers stopped and gazed at the daunting task looming above them.

A nearly vertical final pitch of 10 to 15 feet topped the steep hill at the brink of Mormon Mesa. The steep and narrow ancient Indian footpath became the Old Spanish Trail. With difficulty, animals, walking single file, could traverse the final short section, but wagons could not cross the steep side hill lest they topple over.

In 1848 the first wagon known to traverse the Old Spanish Trail from Los Angeles into southern Utah was lowered over this precipice in one piece or disassembled. When the Davis party, mostly Mormon Battalion veterans, reached the eastern brink of the mesa, the men "had to lower the wagon down in sections with ropes" (Crismon 1905). We interpret this to mean they lowered the whole wagon, rather than parts, down the steep sections of the hill.

The only feasible way for emigrant wagons to ascend the top part of Virgin Hill was to first unhitch and unyoke the oxen and drive them single file up to the mesa. Here they were again yoked and a rope or chain secured the oxen to a single wagon. The upper, nearly vertical pitch of the hill required from 12 yoke of oxen (A. Pratt 1990, 392) to 18 yoke (V. Hoover 1849, November 4) or 20 yoke (Cheesman 1850, 293) to pull a wagon up and over the brink of the mesa. One wagon, reportedly weighing 1,400 pounds, required 30 yoke of oxen to do the job (V. Hoover 1849, November 4)! Today, a wide notch at the brink of the mesa attests to where oxen had to drag the wagons up and over it.

From the top of Virgin Hill, teamsters and packers traveled west across Mormon Mesa about nine miles to where the trail crossed what is now Interstate 15, about a mile northeast of Airway Beacon Hill. Near the hill, along a steep downgrade, boulders show faint scars where the metal tires scraped desert varnish off the rocks (cf. Steiner 1999, 116). The Old Spanish Trail entered Weiser Wash (less than two miles east of today's Glendale, Nevada) and descended the wash southward to the (Far) Muddy River, where the animals found potable water and ample forage. The steep pitch into the Muddy was later realigned to the southeast with a more moderate grade.

On November 30 Lorton and his fellow packers caught up with the company at the Muddy, a joyful occasion. For a man who had been on starvation rations for weeks, a good meal was high on Lorton's list of desires.

The Muddy River emanates from a cluster of five warm springs (90°F) collectively called Muddy Springs (Orsak 2004, 7). About 10 miles below the springs, the "blood warm" water merges with cool water from Meadow Valley Wash (near Glendale), and the resulting water vapor condenses into Lorton's "steam." Addison Pratt "found some fish in the creek much resembling a well-known fish in the rivers of New England, called carp." He added they were easy to catch, and his largest fish weighed almost a pound, but he also noted "lumps on some of their sides. I cut them open and found them sacks, containing a sort of wireworm" (A. Pratt 1990, 393).

After the emigrants left the Muddy River at what was called the California Crossing, they entered their first *jornada del muerto*, a waterless 55-mile trek to the *vaga* (meadow), where several large springs watered a fertile valley. Las Vegas Creek once flowed from the springs at today's Las Vegas Springs Preserve, a mile west of the junction of Interstates 95 and 15, in the heart of the city. The springs ceased flowing in 1963 due to excessive pumping of the aquifer. The site is on the National Register of Historic Places (USDI 1978).

In this area Lorton saw both screwbean mesquite (*Prosopis pubescens*) and honey mesquite (*Prosopis glandulosa*), which provided the native population with considerable nourishment. "Mesquite [seed] pods...are high in protein and sugars and represent a potentially important...food for humans" (Ramawat 2010, 399). The Indians ground or pounded the seedpods to make them digestible before mixing with water for gruel or flatbread.

At Las Vegas, Lorton left the wagons to accompany several men who were sent ahead to the Spanish Ranchos for supplies to send back to the wagons (Arms in Cumming 1985, 111). His decision to pack lasted as long as Mazeppa was able to stand.

The packers headed for Cottonwood Valley along the northern toe of the small Bird Spring Range at the eastern foot of the much larger Spring Mountains, where Charleston Peak looms to 11,918 feet. Lorton mentions a "spring branch" that once emanated from Cottonwood Spring at today's Blue Diamond, Nevada. Henry Bigler stopped here November 23 and commented that "camping was poor as most all the grass had been eaten off by emigrants animals ahead of us" (Bigler in Hafen and Hafen 1954b, 166). Two weeks behind Bigler, Lorton noted on December 8 that there was "no feed," so they pushed on another three miles to recruit.

The weary emigrants then had to cross the Spring Mountains, where a thick blanket of snow covered the ground. They turned south to the pass (5,500 feet elevation) where Highway 161 now crosses, and were fortunate to camp near single-leaf pinyon pine (*Pinus monophylla*), which burn with a hot flame, being heavily impregnated with pitch.

Once out of the Spring Mountains, the trail continued westerly to Stump Spring, two miles east of today's Nevada-California border and about five miles south of today's Pahrump, Nevada.

Stump Spring is somewhat misnamed. It was a shallow well. In Frémont's "Table of latitudes and longitudes" on May 1, 1844, he listed it as "Deep Spring hole on a river [bed] which loses itself in the sands" (Frémont 1970b, 1:782). In 1848 Orville C. Pratt (in Hafen and Hafen 1954a, 356) called it *Escarbado* (to dig), and in 1853 Gwinn Harris Heap (in Hafen and Hafen 1957, 242) called it *Aqua Escarbada* and said he "expected to have to dig for water; but the ground had been so deeply excavated, that a running spring had been reached." The historic flow of Stump Spring was only half a gallon a minute (D. Thompson 1921, 266). We have visited it several times over the past 40 years and have never observed standing water or wet ground now that large quantities of water are pumped from the Pahrump Valley aquifer.

Mazeppa is dying. Lorton is now on foot without his faithful steed, who has carried him and his gear across mountains and through deserts with sore hoofs and scant rations until he can no longer stand. Without his horse, Lorton cannot keep up with the packers and must find someone with a wagon to take him in.

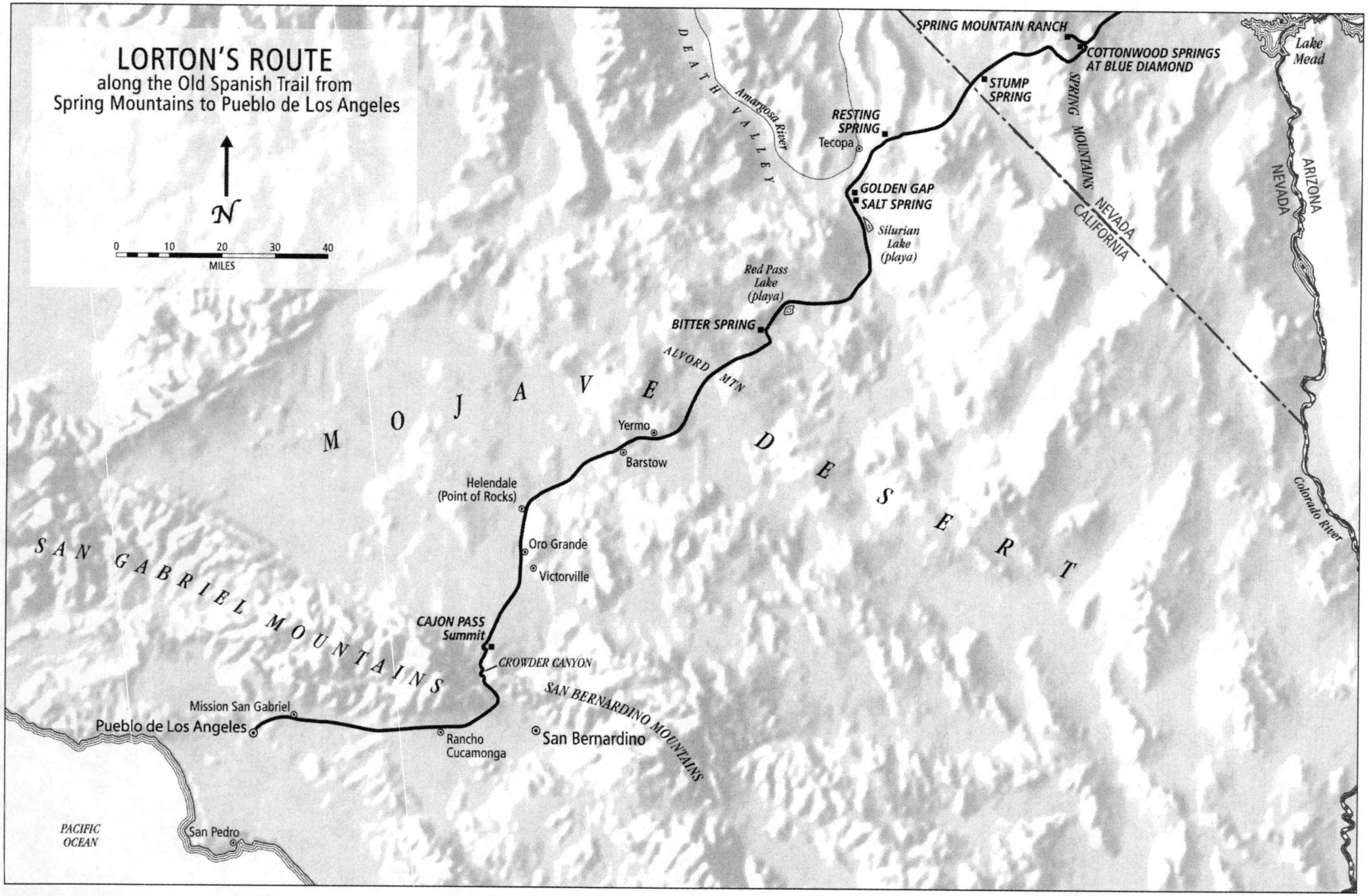

Map 8. Lorton's route along the Old Spanish Trail from Spring Mountains, Nevada (west of Las Vegas), to Los Angeles. Map drawn by Eureka Cartography based on editors' trail analysis.

West from Stump Spring, the distance to water is about 24 miles to Resting Spring (four miles east of today's Tecopa, California). The country is desert with two rocky passes: a spur ridge (2,980 feet), which separates Pahrump Valley and California Valley, and Emigrant Pass (2,920 feet) that crosses the Nopah Range.

Emigrant Pass is the quintessential spot to see the differences between a pack trail and the wagon road. Less than a tenth of a mile north of the paved road at the summit of the pass is the original two-track wagon road; in another tenth of a mile is the narrow packer trail with a concrete obelisk standing next to it designating this the Old Spanish Trail. About six miles after crossing Emigrant Pass, Lorton reached Resting Spring, where "waters well up from sandstone and are clear and wholesome." In 1915 the water was 80°F with a flow of 260 gallons per minute (Mendenhall 1909, 40; Waring 1915, 319). Both these experts refer to springs (plural) although the official title is Resting Spring.

Frémont changed the name of Archilette Spring (today's Resting Spring) to Hernandez Spring in 1844 in recognition of Pablo Hernandez, a young boy whose parents were killed by Indians while camped there. They were part of a six-person party driving horses from southern California to New Mexico. After the attack, Pablo Hernandez and Andreas Fuetes, the only survivors, managed to drive about 20 remaining horses southward down the Old Spanish Trail to Bitter Spring only to have other Indians steal them. Hernandez and Fuetes intercepted Frémont's party on the Mojave River, where Frémont took them in. At Bitter Spring Kit Carson and Alex Godey tracked the stolen horses Hernandez and Fuetes had been driving southward and killed two of the Indians (probably not the ones who committed the murders at today's Resting Spring). Various old maps use one and sometimes both names to label springs in the area. For instance, Frémont (Map 1845) uses *Hernandes Spr.* and *Archilette.* Mitchell's map (1846a) uses *Hernandez*; Tanner (Map 1849) uses *Hernandez Spr.* and *Archilette*; Trask's map (1853) uses *Archilette* and *Resting Sps.*; and Wheeler's map (1876) has *Resting Sps.* (see also Frémont 1970b, 1:676–77).

A fresh look at Frémont's journal plus analysis of several early diaries allows an updated interpretation of the route the packers used between Resting Spring and Amargosa Canyon (Johnson and Sutak 2017). Now we know the Old Spanish pack trail went southwest from Resting Spring to today's China Ranch date farm tucked, in the hidden oasis at Willow Spring (old China Ranch Spring), where its creek flows into the Amargosa River. Southward from Resting Spring the pack trail crossed some mud hills, ascended the alluvium incline to the crest of the hills (China Ranch Pass), then followed down the deep gully into China Ranch Wash. This gully contained a dry fall that was bypassed on the left side to allow pack animals to traverse it, but it was impassable for wagons.

Captain Frémont, a man of science trained in survey work, has been misinterpreted for years. On April 29, 1844, his pack train traveled northward after

FIGURE 47. Old Spanish packer trail over mud hills about a mile southwest of Resting Spring, heading south for Willow Spring (China Ranch), California. Photo by LeRoy Johnson.

camping at Willow Spring (China Ranch), and he wrote, "after crossing an intervening ridge [China Ranch Pass], we descended into a sandy plain…[to] the *Archilette*" (today's Resting Spring). Had Frémont followed up the Amargosa River to Tecopa, thence to Resting Spring, his entire trek would have been over a gradually *ascending* grade and would not have needed to cross "an intervening ridge" (Johnson and Sutak 2017).

On December 20, Lorton traveled from north to south, the opposite direction Frémont traveled. Lorton's trail "*assends* a table[land]" from Resting Spring (1,760 feet). Had the wagons rolled to Tecopa (1,320 feet) to enter the Amargosa Canyon they would *descend* 440 feet. The trail of packed earth across the mud hills southwest of Resting Spring is still visible where the Old Spanish Trail headed southward.

Upon leaving Resting Spring, the wagon masters skirted southwest around the soft mud hills, then ascended the plain about three miles, where they left the Old Spanish Trail and turned west down an "awful pitch" into upper Cowboy Canyon (so named by area residents). The complacent floor of the lower canyon debouches into the Amargosa Canyon about three miles above the confluence of Willow Spring Creek and the Amargosa River.

Addison Pratt, who was with the Jefferson Hunt wagon train 20 days ahead of Lorton, commented on November 30 about getting into the canyon that fed into the Amargosa gorge: "We had to descend into it on a sharp and crooked ridge which was a divide between two ravines, that discharged water into it in wet weather. The lower end [of the ridge] was steep and it was with much difficulty we descended without upsetting our wagons" (A. Pratt 1990, 398). Several other diaries also support these descriptions (Crosby 1858, 704–5; V. Hoover 1849, November 27; Peck 2009, 129–30; Mowry 1965, 340). Lorton's next camp was either near the mouth of Cowboy Canyon or one-third mile north up the Amargosa River Canyon at a good spring.[1]

Just below the confluence of Cowboy Canyon Wash and Amargosa Canyon spreads a 65-acre meadow, where Dan Modine grazed his cattle and hogs in the 1930s; thus, the local name—Modine Meadow. The meadow is now covered with a dense stand of native mesquite and exotic tamarisk (a.k.a. salt cedar, *Tamarix* spp.).

The emigrant wagons continued down the Amargosa River through the Sperry Hills and emerged at today's Dumont Dunes Off-Highway Vehicle Area. From here the wagons cut southwest across the plain to the west side of the Salt Spring Hills. Salt Creek originates from Salt Springs, located between the southern and northern Salt Spring Hills. In years of high precipitation, the creek flows for three miles into the Amargosa River, but in normal years both Salt Creek and the river are dry in this area. When the Amargosa River reaches the Dumont Dunes area, it sinks below the surface to become an underground river. It surfaces again after turning northward around the toe of the Black Mountains (Amargosa Range) to terminate in Death Valley.

Approaching Salt Springs from the north, the wagons again detoured from the Old Spanish Trail, which ascended a pass between the north Salt Spring Hills and the Little Dumont Dunes to the weak, freshwater Amargosa Spring nestled near the top of the hills. The wagons stayed on the plain where the road circled between the north and south Salt Spring Hills (same as today's Highway 127), and their camp was near Salt Springs or the pools that run from them. Frémont first described the packers' trail and Amargosa Spring on April 28, 1844, when his entourage camped at or near Salt Springs.

The Mormons, three weeks ahead of Lorton, discovered a gold-laced quartz vein just above Salt Springs on December 1, 1849. Several men were enticed to return a couple months later to prospect (A. Pratt 1990, 399; Welch in Cumming 1985, 132–36). Adonijah Welch went with these men as their geologist.

1. Locals call this spring Frémont Spring, although Frémont never visited it. It is refreshing to drink and consistently flows "neutral" water at pH 7. The Amargosa River, above the confluence with the spring branch, was pH 8, the alkalinity of sea water (measured personally with litmus paper).

South of Salt Springs the trail crossed Silurian Lake, a large playa eight miles southeast of Salt Springs. These desert playas are composed of very fine clay that turns into quagmires when wet. Based on Lorton's description, at least the margins of the lake were dry. Fortunately, there was almost a full moon, which gave ample light for his nighttime travel.

Lorton's Christmas camp was about five miles southwest of Red Pass overlooking Red Pass Lake, normally a dry playa, but at Christmastime that year, it had a skim of water on it.

Jefferson Hunt's train camped here December 2, 1849, 23 days before Lorton arrived. "This is a dry bed of a lake some two miles acrost. It is composed of dry clay on a water level, and in winter it is covered with water," wrote Addison Pratt. They found "some muddy water standing in holes, and some dry bunch grass" (A. Pratt 1990, 399). Here Hunt's train remained until January 4 and then advanced to Bitter Spring.

When Lorton camped within sight of the lake, recent rainstorms had inundated the playa, and inch-long, lobster-like "insects" had hatched in the shallow water. An observant Lorton examined the beavertail fairy shrimp (*Thamnocephalus platyurus*), a primitive freshwater crustacean that lives in ephemeral playa lakes during the short time they contain water.

The northern portion of Red Pass Lake is now fenced to mark the southern boundary of Fort Irwin, a restricted-entry U.S. Army training facility. On this playa J. Fish (1850), traveling with or near Lorton, noted rocks that moved, leaving a telltale track through the mud. There are currently no rocks on this playa, but we found one pebble with a two-inch trail, indicating wind had moved it. The famous moving rocks in northern Death Valley National Park gave rise to naming that playa the Racetrack (J. Johnson 2006, 1).

When Frémont visited Bitter Spring on April 25, 1844, he referred to it as *Agua de Tomaso* and said, "Its water was a pool; but near by was a spring, which Indians or other travelers had dug out. Its water was cool—a great refreshment to us under a burning sun." Walter Mendenhall pointed out that the "water contains too much sodium sulfate to be wholesome, but it can be used." Addison Pratt commented: "As this water was bad and no grass here, we left it about sunset.... It began to rain a little...and soon after it began to snow." Pratt left the spring via "a gradual ascent," indicating they went northward around the Whale (a large basalt outcrop), gaining elevation, thence southwestward toward the crest of Alvord Mountain (Frémont 1970b, 1:679; Mendenhall, 1909, 61; A. Pratt 1990, 399; "the Whale" is a local name not yet sanctioned by the U.S.G.S.).

Lorton's traveling companions also decided not to camp at Bitter Spring. To continue their arduous trek, they first headed south-southeast (losing 120 feet elevation) before swinging around the southern end of the Whale. From this camp the jaded oxen had a sustained uphill grind of almost 10 miles to the pass over Alvord Mountain. The Hafens use the name Impassable Pass for the brutal traverse over the mountain (Hafen and Hafen 1954a, 144; see also Steiner 1999, 185–86). This night Lorton and company had a full moon, and after the initial steep descent, the road went down a fairly complacent wash with no possibility of going astray. Thus, they kept rolling until they exited Spanish Canyon and camped high on the *bajada* overlooking the Mojave River.

They reached the river near today's Yermo where the river rises to the surface to form ponds or short sections of flowing water. Here emigrants expected to find provisions to resupply their depleted foodstuffs. Men had been sent ahead to arrange for these supplies from as far back as Las Vegas (Granger 1959).

The Gruwell brothers had already met their families (part of the Independent Pioneer Company) on the river, and the Hunt wagon train got supplies December 11 from a man named Davis who was camped at the upper crossing of the Mojave River, but no relief party had penetrated the desert as far as today's Yermo (A. Pratt 1990, 403).

On December 31, Lorton followed the men who were hiking ahead to meet the relief mule train from the coastal ranchos. He came across Captain Avis, Mr. Shaw, and another man near today's Barstow, and together they followed the trail south to Point of Rocks near Helendale (Fish 1850; for details of the route, see Steiner 1999, maps 191, 197, 200, 201).

They met some "yankees" they thought might be charlatans, so Lorton and Shaw continued southward to catch up with the Spaniards, who may, or may not, have turned back with the expected supplies. The two men continued southward all night and part of the next day before they "relinquished our design" and turned back to meet the wagons. Not surprisingly, Lorton's mileages for these two days are difficult to reconcile. Part of his hiking was at night, he was on meager caloric intake, and he was hiking through sand and over rocky ground for 19 hours. Some miscalculation can be expected.

According to J. Fish, the suppliers were "under the command of J. H. Davis," an acquaintance of Fish's from the States. Davis's name was mentioned as someone who supplied food to Hunt's train and Stover's packers, who were now well ahead of Lorton (A. Pratt, 1990, 403; Stover in Hafen and Hafen 1954b, 284). Stover mentions Davis had a wagon, but Lorton and Fish speak of a mule train. It seems Davis created a temporary depot at today's Hodge among some cottonwoods, and mule trains from the ranchos supplied his depot (for location, see Steiner 1999, 200, Map 36).

Lorton remained with the wagons until January 7 because the river rose from a heavy storm, and no one could cross at Lane's Crossing, a mile south of today's Oro Grande (see Steiner 1999, 203–6). Aaron Lane was a gold rush '49er who returned to the desert for his health in 1858 and became a trader at the last crossing of the Mojave River. He remained here for many years. On January 8,

1850, the water dropped 18 inches, and Lorton again became a packer with 30 pounds on his own back.

Stover comments on an earlier flash flood at the Mojave River, where he "saw the water coming three or four feet high abreast, carrying with it sticks, brush and logs, and on top six inches of foam" (Hafen and Hafen 1954b, 284). He climbed out of the wash just in time. This flood was one of several that occurred in the weeks before Lorton camped at Lane's Crossing about four miles northwest of today's Victorville.

The winter of 1849–1850 was very wet and cold, which brought good fortune in the form of puddle water along the route but misfortune in the form of flash floods, snow, and frozen feet. Pomeroy's train had snow in the Mountain Meadow area in Utah; remnants of the San Joaquin Company had snow over the Spring Mountains west of Las Vegas; Pratt had six inches of ice along the Mojave River and snow on Cajon Pass; the Death Valley party had lifesaving snow in the Fortymile Canyon area in Nevada 80 miles north of Salt Springs; snow closed Walker Pass after 22 men got through, but halted westward progress for the remaining Death Valley '49ers; and the Death Valley party crossed snow on Soledad Pass in the San Gabriel Mountains in February and March 1850.

After crossing the Mojave River at Lane's Crossing, the Old Spanish Trail traversed a southerly course to the summit of Cajon Pass, which separates the San Gabriel Mountains on the west from the San Bernardino Mountains on the east. Lorton's zenith was about 4,200 feet. At Cajon summit, the wagon and mule trails inexorably funneled into the upper reach of Crowder Canyon.

Lorton's Journal Continues Down the Old Spanish Trail

[November 27th, 1849] 26th. Late start. Road takes [up] on the table[land] & then on the bottom, crossing [Virgin] river several times. See some old camps. Great overhalling, lots of wagons burned, yokes thrown away, cow bells, clothing of every description, first rate trunks, boxes, shoes, moccosins, lbs of pepper, salt pills in piles, chests of tools, axes, picks, & every thing [the] mind could think of. We take such things as we want. Also find an ox, drive him on to camp & soon have him skined. While performing the opperation, we find a Cow, pritty good [condition]. We kill her to[o] & then devide, have more than we want. Have excellent beef soup, eat the meat half raw, & almost [become] sick.

[November 28th] 27th. Follow down the pritty river with its precipitous banks. On the south, [Virgin] mountains covered with snow. Cross river several times, on Mazeppas back. He crosses the river ahead of me after going over a long road without crossing, & I have to wade up to my middle. I drop my revolver in the dashing element, stop instantly & feel for it with my foot & recover it. The moon which is nearly full rises as we make camp. Fire guns for those behind. Grass impregnated with saleraetus & opperates on animals as will be seen hereafter. Up till 12 making soop. Woke up for 4th guard [at] 1 1/2 o'clock.

[November 29th] 28th. Our animals are full but feel rather bad. We however streak it to catch up with the boys who are ahead, I having discharged all my shots the eve. befor for signal. I feel like going the 50 mile drive to day. Ground pliable to the feet & moccosins feel well. Pass more old camp grounds [with] lots of boxes thrown away, medicine, libraries, clothes &c.[2] See 2 Piutes acrost the river. They hollowed for us to come over & we to them. They made a great noise. We camp with out feed after a 20 mile drive, & where the road leaves the river [at Halfway Wash].

[November 30th] 29th. Leave the Rio Virgin & strike up a chasm to the west [northwest up Halfway Wash]. Heavy sand, & up hill. For 8 m. see 1 doz ox carcases & Indian bare foot tracks.[3] Finally we come to the great [Virgin] hill so mutch talked of, almost perpendicular.[4] Here they halled up oxen & wagons with ropes. The road leads S. west over a hard road [across Mormon Mesa] till we come to heavy sand & a little bunch grass where we bait. Finally at 20 miles we see deep chasms leading to [a] lower valley on the south, & continuing on we arrive at the top of the high eminence from which the roads drops down in the large valley [Moapa Valley]. From this hill we see the Far Muddy & sever[al] smokes assending amonge the hills.[5] We follow over 5 miles before reaching our place of destination. Sand very deep. Horse drops his pack twice. Terrible time in crossing a slew. Old Red throws me off in the sand, stubbing tows [toes].[6] Left 3 horses to day at the bottom of h[igh] hill, against [because of?] stones & hard ground.

2. Lorton failed to record mileages for November 27 and 28.

3. Lorton's eight miles is a retrospection of the total miles traveled that day. From the Virgin River to the base of Virgin Hill via Halfway Wash is 2.4 miles.

4. In two places the ancient Indian and Old Spanish Trail is still visible, but most of this original trail has been obliterated by the wagon road. One of the editors of this volume (LeRoy) has hiked the trail and road several times. The road is just over 0.6 miles (per GPS measurements, averaged up and down measurements) with a vertical rise of about 350 feet. The last 15 to 20 feet of the original wagon road are almost vertical. The steeper sections of the current road are at a 17% grade (measured with a Suunto clinometer).

5. The adjective "Far" differentiates this river from the "Near" Muddy (today's Coal Creek), which flows through Cedar City into Cedar Valley, Utah.

6. Lorton seems to be packing Mazeppa and riding another horse. He correctly refers to the horse's hoofs as toes.

Finally, I hear some one say, here is a white horse & hollow, who are you? By golly, that is Lorton & that is his horse, & Jo [John Ewing?] & one of the R[overs?] welcome me to their camp. I ask them for Old Man Norton saying may be I might get a supper there. Oh! you need not fear, says they, the supper is prepared for you. They see to our packs, carry our goods & wait on us like guests. We cross [the Muddy River], & of all the suppers this was the richest—rising bread, boiled fat beef, sugar & hot coffee & buiscuit, every boddy shaking hands, how do you like horse meat &c. all in one breath. There was 17 of the gladest hearts in existence. We knew how to apreciate good things. The word was, eat, boys, as much as you want. I am invited in a good tent with good bed clothes & I have a fine nights rest. The boys stay up 1/2 the night relating & recapitulating our adventure.[7]

[Dec. 1st, 1849] 30th. Our horses on good grass. Norton lost both oxen. Partner [Robert C. Price?] had his 2 left & his wagon made into a buggy. Invited down to Div[ision] No. 2 & there meet our friends with joy.[8] They treat us to liquor & buiscuit with sugar. They divide their flour with N.Y. boys. They have an Indian who [they] have caught or coaxed to go with them as guide. He says he knows where there is water on the desert. He says any person that goes the way we went will die. He is inteligent & was stolen by the Piutes from the Piuedes whe[n] a boy, & now is the only time he has had the chanse to escape. Several Indians have been seen, one was shot to the knees while running. A white rag will cause them to approach you. This caught Indian trembled like a leaf. 500 was seen off on the plains. 2 were seen on the hights & hollowed [as] Cal[ifornians] pass.

The dutch [German] Doc. that stole the peaches &c. was left on the Rio [Virgin] alone with his wagon. They attacked his cattle during the night & run one arrow 2 ft in him. Another they carried off down the river. He made a fortification of his wagon & trunks. They would not approach the tent for fear.[9] The

7. D.C. Norton was an original member of the Knox County Company, Illinois (Appendix A; Rasmussen 1994, 65). Lorton says there were 17 men but names only 16, including himself, in his letter of January 20, 1850 (see chapter 12). Cephas Arms said "they were sixteen in number, twelve of them formerly of the San Walkin company, and four of Smith's pack company" (in Cumming 1985, 110).

8. Cephas Arms corroborates this joyful reunion. "Saturday, Dec. 1st, just at night, the cry was raised, 'the packers are coming.'...They proved to be part of those who packed from the canyon [Mount Misery], whence we turned back to the [Old Spanish] trail" (Arms in Cumming 1985, 109–10).

9. In a trial near Little Salt Lake (Parowan Valley) this German, convicted of stealing bread and peaches, "was sentenced to travel twenty rods [110 yards] behind the comp and never to encamp nearer than that distance to the corrall under pain of receiving twenty lashes upon the bare back" (Welch, in Ressler 1964, 270, October 28). Thus, he was denied protection and was easy prey for Indians.

boys went in pursuit & drove them from their cave. Got the ox. Took their skins, baskets, arrows poisoned & bore them off as trophyes to camp. Stones placed up [at the cave mouth] with place to look out.

Grass good at F[ar] Muddy. Creek bridged by the comp. [using] Noahs Ark.[10] Prepare grass for ox teams, & lug water [for the 55-mile *jornada del mureto* to Las Vegas Springs]. One of Capt Arms men shot a Piute while running. He fell to his knees & then run a little ways.

[Dec. 2nd, Sunday] 1st. The ground above the Muddy is very springy, water running thro' the grass at intermediate places. This water is cool at first [stream from Meadow Valley Wash], but when kept in a canteen becomes bitter. The other water in the creek [Muddy River] is blood warm & a steam constantly arises therefrom.[11] The river is winding, about 3 yds wide & deep, & produces fish. It is mirey & horses & cattle are constantly getting into it & cannot extricate themselves. We hall them out with ropes. Capt [Thomas M.] Marshals poney found in creek almost dead. Been in 3 days. Hall him out & shoot him. Billy Sands Bisin fell in while attempting to cross the bridge made of my old wagon (Noahs Ark). Nearly exhausted, they leave him. The water does not agree with animals first rate.

All being in readiness we start 11 o'clock on our jorney at the rate of 2 miles an hour. Follow the creek 1 mile [westward] & then strike S. west up a gradual assent [in California Wash] for 12 miles, where we camp for supper, & start on [at] 7 o'clock, the moon rising not long after.[12] The road is good but the journey is tedious. The horse & foot [men] going on ahead build fires & wait till the train comes up. About 3 o'clock [a.m.] they halt on a/c of a notice found, stating that the Indian guide had found water 1 1/2 miles from the road to the right. The oxen & animals are taken over, but no water is found [but] good grass. Back they all come, disapointed & angry at having been fooled.

[Dec. 3rd.] We lay still this morn'g, & find water in holes about 3 miles in that direction [the notice indicated above], almost enough to satisfy them. Start at 12, camp at 6.

10. Another hint the Kellogg-Lorton mess had used (and sold) a Conestoga wagon. Figuratively, Lorton's *Ark* was scuttled at the California Crossing of the Muddy River. The bed would not have been wide enough for a wagon to use as a bridge; thus, they probably took the bed off the undercarriage, removed the side rails, and added them to the bed to make a bridge.
11. The trail crosses the "cool" water from Meadow Valley Wash, which flows into the Muddy River two-tenths of a mile southwest of today's Glendale, Nevada. The trail then crosses the Muddy River about two miles farther on and enters California Wash.
12. They had ample moonlight for safe nighttime travel just three nights after a full moon.

December [4th] 3d. Start at 12 [midnight], & arrive at the [Las Vegas] spring 9 in A.M. after a tedious, wearysome, sickening jorney of 55 miles [from Muddy River over] barren desert. Fires were built every 2 miles where we could warm. Cloudy during the night. Mountains on each side all the way. Befor reaching the spring [in Las Vegas], we passed over 4 or 6 miles of "Acacia" wood.[13] The land is level & the spring lays upon a bench. Good grass spreads over it & several good springs of water, scarcely no wood in good dist. Ducks & geese constantly fly over here, even to disturbing of ones sleep in the night. They fly very low in foggy weather. We have rain soon after camping. We allowance ourselves now very small. Go to bed with out supper. Rainy all night. Comfort of a tent, all dry.

December [5th] 4th. Make a bite, cant find horse, give him up for gone. After wards find him. Ground very soft. Kill a beef ox that had given out in the rain. Have been [bean?] soup. Start for next springs 3 miles on, road half knee deep in mud. Camp on good grass & good water. It is called Cash Spring.[14] Think of staying with train.

[Dec. 6th] 5th. Drying beef all around camp. 4 or 5 cattle killed, all poor. Piute has taken his flight after jerking his meat. Packers fitting out. Great many footing & carrying packs of 20 & 30 lbs. 2 or 3 springs near here of warm water. Spoke of by Frémont.[15] Take supper with Norton. Been very sick today with too much fresh meat.

[Dec. 7th] 6th. All camp preparing for packing. Get my horse shod all round. Conclude to pack. Take the things for 2, furnish[ed] 10 lbs for 1.[16] Start 1 o'clock, road very stoney. Cross several dry creeks, mountains all around covered with snow, wind blowing from the north cold & keen. We enter the mountain gap, & at 15 miles find water in a hole of sufficient quantity to water a whole train. We camp here, 6 P.M. Elect Mr. [Robert C.] Price capt. & estab'h guard.[17] No one sleeps during the night on a/c of the extreme cold. Take turns sitting up by fire.

13. This so-called acacia was a mesquite along the stream from the Las Vegas Springs.
14. What an ironic name for a spring in the middle of today's Las Vegas, where money is king. In all probability, Lorton should have spelled it Cache Spring, where many men left all but the barest essentials and became packers.
15. This is at today's Las Vegas Springs Preserve. On May 3, 1844, Frémont relates: "Two narrow streams of clear water, four or five feet deep, gush suddenly, with a quick current, from two singularly large springs.... The taste of the water is good, but rather too warm to be agreeable; the temperature being 71° in one, and 73° in the other" (1970b, 685–86; see also Crampton and Madsen 1994, 90–92).
16. This sentence is unclear. We think it means that because Lorton had a horse, he could take his own things plus those of someone on foot, and that he took food for one person furnished by those who had wagons.
17. Packers camped in the main wash about five miles east of today's Blue Diamond, Nevada.

[Dec. 8th] Breakfast before daylight, & start [at] daylight. Road takes up north [northwest] for ways thro' a rockey pass, snow becomes 2 in. on the level, hard walking. 5 miles to spring branch [flow from Cottonwood Spring at Blue Diamond], no feed. [At] 3 miles little rivulet to the left & puddles.[18] Feed good but cov'd with snow. Mts cov'd with snow & alpinish. Pull off our packs & take a lunch. Looks like aproaching xmas in earnest. See wild cat tracks in snow & mt sheep horn. Find poles sticking up by road side telling of a gun cached 5 paces north of road.[19] 1 mule & 1 dead ox. From the guides we could not discover with positive certainty how far it was to the next watering place, so we let our animals pick what they could of grass & weeds which was partly covered with snow. About 1 o'clock we repacked & soon turned about south & commenced assending a mountain kanyon [upper Cottonwood Valley and into Mountain Springs Pass].

This we continued to assend, the snows growing deeper, & as the sun fast sank in the west it grew colder. At the dist of 7 or 8 miles [from Mountain Springs Stream] we judged from appearances of the kanyon (for the snow was now over 14 in. deep) that the road struck thro' this narrow defile of rocks & finally after assending 200 ft up a steep hill we again decended on our former level, & continued to push up the mountain [toward Mountain Springs Summit]. On a/c of the lame ancle I could not keep up & my horse was driven by Ken. He soon now show[ed] signs of fatigue & turned out [of] the road to rest. The boys & foot packers had made a fire of cedars & were warming themselves, for fear their feet were frozen. We could look over the mountain & see the valley we had left which I call, "Vegas Valley." Every thing looked red & as the sun set, the eastern sky turned green & dismal. It appeared to us like an approaching snow storm. We continue up passing perpendicular rocks, & finally camp in a gully filled with pine or cedar trees. Many of the boys [feet?] were frozen, as was seen by the fire. We dig away the snow, make a large fire & cook a kettle of soup which did not get done till 12. Mazeppa has given out & [there is] no feed. Cold & chilley. Spread down horse blanket & wrap up in robe by the fire. Sleep warm as the fire burns all night.

[Dec. 9th] 7th Dec. As the sun tinges the mountain peeks we again resume our jorney up the mt. & reach the summit 2 miles. Our decent is now rappid. Road turns south [actually west] & then south west into the gully. Snows lessen but

---

Price and Lorton were both in the Knox County Company along with Ewing and Taylor, who went with Price to have food sent back to the wagons (Arms in Cumming 1985, 111).

18. This is at today's Spring Mountain Ranch, three miles northwest of Blue Diamond. Hunt's train also had to move up to these springs because all the forage at Blue Diamond had been eaten (A. Pratt 1990, 396).

19. Roadside messages were placed along the trails west for people behind. They told of directions taken, conditions ahead, and caches of food and other valuables.

does not disapear. We reach the plain, which after a 20 mile drive from camp we come to the bed of a creek & beside some tall willows find a spring [Stump Spring].[20] Find plenty of wagons on the ground which we burn to cook with. Every thing laying a round from a chisels to a rifle. Post office on tree, stating that Dallas [and] 7th division, were at the next spring [Resting Spring] & Capt Hunt ahead. [Find also an] a/c of "cut off" packers arriving [and] stating that Capt Smith train were in a starving condition.[21] With difficulty I got Mazeppa in camp & I fear [he] will go no farther having been 72 hours with out feed. Lay up next day to recruit. Left 3 or 4 animals behind.

[Dec. 10th] 8th Dec. Near night Dr Ormsby arrives stating that a portion of the train was close here. He stated that all the oxen were yet standing, that they had been going all night. Several teams had been left & part of a division were yet in the mounts. Several were frozen in the feet & disabled. A great many wagons [were] left & whole teams unable to proceed. The destruction of property great. The rest arrive 12 at night. Fatigued I tell you.

[Dec. 11th] 9th. I cannot proceed with our packer[s] as Mazeppa can go no farther & my lame ancle will not admit of a push. I stay with the train. The boys go on, all in a sad state of mind. Oxen "versus" horses & mules. Feed due south 2 miles. At night my horse falls down & cannot be drove. Give him up. On a/c of scarsity of water animals have to be rationed the same as at horse springs [Division Spring]. Watering all night.[22] I sleep with Capt Avis.

[Dec. 12th] 10th. Mend my breeches & cut grass to carry along. Also water, by orders of Holton who I got in with. We have pritty good living. Kill a poor steer & cut it up. Cook up a lot [of meat] for the next 30 miles. Great difficulty in getting water for both teams. The Buckskins start out to night. The water here is sulphyey [sulfury]. My Mazeppa would not get up. Suffice it to say he starved to death. I shot him & cut out a steak, for every boddy said white horses eat best. This spring I named Mazeppa Spring & Valley in memory of the death of him [Stump Spring and Pahrump Valley, Nevada]. Leave my Spanish saddle & knapsack on the ground. A great many articles of value left: 2 vol of ShakeSpear worth $10, first rate saddles & several wagons.

20. West of Spring Mountains, the trail crossed Lovell Wash alluvial fan to Stump Spring, Nevada, two miles shy of today's Nevada-California state line.
21. Lorton would have been relieved to hear the Mormon packers had escaped *terra incognita* and were ahead of him. The news they provided about Smith was not new since Lorton had seen the Smith train more recently than had the Mormon packers.
22. Emigrants had to periodically scoop water out of the shallow well in order to get enough for both humans and livestock. This tedious process continued all night.

[Dec. 13th] 11th. We start about 11, & find a little grass 8 miles & there camp for the night. Comes up a great tarnado which lasts all night accompained by hard rain. The clouds disperse & the wind goes down with the riseing sun.

[December 14th] 12th. Our course now laid thro' a mountain pass, which we took to be a mountain & feared the snow. Decend a hill over a rough road, at the bottom of which the road is good.[23] Noon & take a bate. Cross a valley [California Valley] of some extinct [eruption] surrounded by volcanic turnups, & mts coming to a tremendous high hill over which the road led up a steep [mountain], we supposed. Give the cattle hay & water, & assended by resting many times. After dark, on reaching the top [of Emigrant Pass, Nopah Range, 6,920 feet elevation], the road decends abrupt, then gradually down ravines & bad road, till about 10 [P.M.] we come to ground that looked springy, & at 11 we camp on a spring called Hernandez Spring [Resting Spring], so called in memory of the murder of the Spanard & his mother [who] were murdered while in advance of the Santa Fe carravan.[24] 2 men escaped to tell the tale. They were ahead to recruit their animals. There are many skul[ls] & other human bones laying strewed around these grounds. I suppose some of these to be Hernandez, & other murdered victims. No doubt this is the sight of many dark murders. Mule, horse, & ox bones are abundant. Wolves are plenty, & lay dead near us & a brazing [brazen] puppy was looking off of a bluff near us.

[Dec. 15th, 1849] This morning the 13th. The ground here is alkali earth. The grass is white with the mineral & the cattle get full. Plenty of "Acasha" [mesquite] which I draw to camp with cattle for baking & boiling meat.[25] The spring here is blood warm, very strong. Some cattle get mired here. This valley is small filled with dreary looking ash heaps or bluffs. Rough volcanic matter compose the rugged peaks by which it is surrounded. During the night we are awakened by the doleful moanings of a woman which we soon learn has lost her baby. O! crys she, My baby is dead. My dear baby.

[Dec. 16th] 14th. Make a box & inter the dead child of Mrs Mose [Mrs. S. Mowe] upon a hilloc. The mother feared the wolves or Indians would dig it up. She took it hard.[26]

23. This hill is in the nameless range that separates Pahrump and California Valleys.
24. The boy, Pablo Hernandez, survived the massacre, but his mother and father did not (Frémont 1970b, 683; Carson 1966, 83–85).
25. He fastened a chain or rope around the trunk of a dead tree, and a yoke of oxen pulled it out of the ground.
26. J. Fish had teamed up with the Mowe family at the Muddy River. Since Lorton describes helping with the burial of their child here at Resting Spring, he surely knew Jeremiah Fish.

FIGURE 48. Cliffs in Amargosa Canyon. Writes Lorton on December 20: "High erect sand bluffs on each side." Photo by LeRoy Johnson.

[Dec.] 17th [correct date]. The Buckskins start for [the] next spring. Dallas left 200 lbs flour & one bu of beans to sell to us at 50 cts a bu for flower & beans, to be paid for in Cal. The Buckskins take all, so as to average 9 lbs each in their train & then send word to us that they have 40 lbs for us.[27]

[Dec. 18th] Call a meeting, devide the breadstuff all around & declare ourselves independant. Lay here shoeing oxen, baking Bread, fixing meat, & preparing for the desert. Some mince pies made in camp.

[Dec. 19th] Hav[e] a rain & finally start for the next camp 5 miles on.[28]

[Dec.] 20th. The road assends a table[land] at 3 miles & then thro' rough rugged bluffs, along a narrow ridge, steep pitches, & awful pitch into the valley of the spring.[29] See pritty table land on the west before we desend. Here is a strong alkali creek [Amargosa River] with numerous cascades, & bad places for cattle

27. This indicates there were now about 18 members in the Buckskin Division, including the Rovers.
28. Lorton's expectation of getting to the camp "5 miles on" is a prospective statement. They camped two miles southwest of Resting Spring on the spring branch where there was water, wood, and forage before ascending the tableland the following day.
29. They ascend south to China Ranch Pass and turn westward down Cowboy Canyon (Johnson and Sutak 2017).

to get in. High erect sand bluffs on each side & a good spring tho' warm.[30] Wic e up on hill. The sand is here piled up perpendicular in shapes, cones, & in shape of collums, domes, perspective edifices with turrets, cupalos, & fantastic shapes. With the exception of the stream bed the country presents the apearence of a mountain desert, the mountains far off capped with volcanic ash. This stream is said to be a continuation of Hernandez Spring creek.[31] There are many bones scattered around of animals, & I see the horns of a mountain sheep. Some cut hay here [Modine Meadow] for the desert. We Burn up an Indian wic "e "up" [*sic*] that set on a hill just above camp.

[Dec.] 21st. After breakfast I go down the creek to cut hay for the desert, get nearly stalled in alkali mud.[32] The bottom [of Amargosa Canyon] for 8 miles down there is more or less grass & mostly sweet hansome grass & canes. At this point there is a spring.[33] The sides of the kanyon has the same abrupt perpendicular appearance all the way as described above, & the creek, enlarged by the fresh aditions of rain water, goes dashing down over short rapids & pritty cascades. The ground is ireogated by it & you have to wade thro a great deal of water. The water verry cold at this season. We travel on till about 8 o'clock.

While going over a sandy road at where the kanyon widens out into a valley [at today's Dumont Dunes] one describe[s] camp fires ahead, & are soon after "Caraled" & have warm supper. I caral in the sand.

[Dec.] 22d. Come to the [Salt] creek & take in water which is very salt. The road east of south hard pulling thro' sand. Have to ease the cattle every few min's. Thermomoter at 70°. We conclude to stop till the heat of the day has passed. To the west, snowey mts [Owlsheads and Panamints]. On the south, high mts [Avawatz] & the east mts of rocks looking like iron [Kingston, Clark, and

30. The spring is one-third mile up the left bank of the Amargosa River from the mouth of Cowboy Canyon wash. The locals called it "Frémont Spring" before recent research established Frémont did not go to this spring (ibid.). Frémont and his entourage turned up Willow Creek and camped at today's China Ranch. He did not proceed farther north in Amargosa Canyon to "Frémont Spring."

31. Had the wagon road continued down this spring branch from Resting Spring to Tecopa, as tradition has held, Lorton would have known whether or not the creek flowed into the river.

32. A mile south of Fremont Spring is Modine Meadow then covered with desert saltgrass (*Distichlis stricta*). The saltgrass genus "in general have little value for forage, but in the interior basins...[saltgrass] is grazed when better grasses are not available" (Hitchcock 1950, 175, 177).

33. This sentence is out of sequence. They got fresh water at the spring the local folks call Frémont Spring, 0.3 mile north (upriver) from where Cowboy Canyon reaches the Amargosa River. Modine Meadow is one mile south of the spring.

Ivanpah Mountains]. We, however after striking easterly up a kanyon find the water or spring [one of the Salt Springs] with tolerable good grass & cane. We go down [and around with wagons] but the pack trail cuts off 2 miles & passes thro' a gap.[34] There is the bitter spring laid down in [trail] guides called Bitter Spring. We find holes of excelent rain water, which we lay in for the desert. Here we find salt mixed with, I think, "magnitia."[35]

[Dec.] 23d. Lay still till 2 o'clock [p.m.]. Springs up a sea breeze. While I write, news comes that the Indians are driving off our cattle & all the camp are rushing with their arms in pursuit & proves to be a false alarm. We emty out the stream water [from Salt Creek] & take in rain water. Our [cara]van leaves camp slowly [at] 4 o'clock after pulling out an ox which had fallen in a hole. Road some sandy till supper time 6 1/2 [p.m.]. Not moving over 2 miles an hour. The moon at our 2d set out appeared in the center of high heaven, smiling amonge the twinkling orbs, upon the night. The Thermom. stood 60° & it was a beautiful eve. At last we struck a plain of great magnitude hard as a ten pin alley & as level.[36] The oxen tripped off to a more lively gate & we made good time stopping once in a while to unyoke some steer that had fallen in the yoke, or turn out [of] the road for one which had lain down & would not get up. Whips are cracked & dogs set on but barely do they succeed when once they [the oxen] lay down from fatigue. About 1 doz head were left this night. This is a barren desert scene all level with hard, light, cold sand or gravel & shining black rocks, hard on cattles feet. The road side whitened with animal bones & dead oxen partly eaten by wolves. Pass a waggon box setting on end, & wheel gear near by. We make a stop & rest [at] 12 o'clock [midnight] & at 2 camp, feed & go to bed till day light.

[Dec.] 24th. Start out without breakfast & stop 9 o'clock, [where we stayed] till night. Go down to a well & puddles of water on our left, but it proved in-

34. This low pass in the Salt Spring Hills is now called Golden Gap, where, on December 1, 1849, members of the Hunt train found gold. "On looking I saw that he [Rowan] had discovered some in a stratum of quartz, about 4 inches wide running through a ledge of granite. It was a collection of small particles, the largest about the size of a pea" (A. Pratt 1990, 399).

35. Amargosa does mean "bitter," but Lorton has confused Amargosa Spring (three-quarters of a mile north-northeast of Salt Springs in the hills) with "Bitter Spring" in the emigrant guide books (Frémont's Aqua de Tomaso) roughly 38 miles south over another dreaded *jornada del muerto*. Lorton may be referring to milk of magnesia (magnesium hydroxide suspended in water), which gives a milky appearance. It is used as an antacid and a laxative.

36. Silurian Lake, usually dry, is eight miles southeast of Salt Springs. The moon was approaching full, which gave ample light for safe travel.

FIGURE 49. Red Pass Lake, usually a dry playa, shown here with water on it. Stones "travel across in a straight line...each one leaving its mark, some like a trail of a large muscle in its element. This is strange but positively true." Jeremiah Fish, December 25 or 26. Photo by LeRoy Johnson.

sufficient for the train. Start [at] sun down.[37] After a while the road commences assending up a hard gradual road for ten miles to the summit, the road passing thro' a kanyon [Red Pass]. We camp near the summit & let our cattle browse on weeds, & then wish each a happy Christmas. 12 oxen give out.[38]

[Dec.] 25th. Road m[oun]ts the summit & then road assumes [the character of] a high mountain desert, barren & destitute. About 6 miles travel brings us to some bunch grass, & water in puddles. It is now xmas. We take breakfast [at] 11 o'clock. All [in] camp leg weary. There is allso a lake of water looking green around the borders [Red Pass Lake]. We are now again on 1/4 rations & part of that carrion, the latter being nearly exhausted. We drive up a sickly looking scheleton of a steer, knock him down with an axe, cut his tongue out, heart, but his liver was partly rotten which we throw away. Took some meat of the rump

37. The sun set at 4:45 p.m., and the moon was 71 percent full until 2:19 a.m.; thus, they had ample light for nighttime travel.
38. They camped about a mile east of Red Pass (elevation 1,560 feet) where it cuts through the southern tip of the Avawatz Mountains (See Steiner 1999, 180–82, map 29).

FIGURE 50. Wagon swale on south side of Alvord Mountain, twelve miles north of the Mojave River near Yermo, California. Photo by LeRoy Johnson.

& left his carcase. This, cooked, served xmas dinner. I must say eating this went against the grain, & I hope to God it will be the last carrion we will have to eat.

Great doubts are entertained about finding any other water previous to crossing this other desert, thinking that it may be covered up by the Lake, & that this is the veritable "Ague De Thomasa." All the water is thick with mud & full of white insects 1 in. long & when viewed thro' a glass of 200s magnitude somewhat resembles a lobster [fairy shrimp].[39] We find a puddle which is less muddy.

[Dec.] 26th. Lay up all day. Cook beens, & cut grass for cattle, & carry it on our backs 2 miles.

[Dec.] 27th. About 8 o'clock we strike S. W. Take in water at the lake [Red Pass Lake] & pass thro a gap in the mountains [around the northwest spur of Soda Mountains], & then commence a rappid desent for 8 miles when we arrive at "Ague De Thomasa" [Bitter Spring], spoken of by Freemont, & sup [have supper]. Here we find a regular post office without any master. News! [Notices] contained Be careful of your teams for this is a bad sandy mt to assend, when the packers left, grass at 2, 6, & 8 miles.

Dallas left 3 wagons loaded, tent &c. for which he intended to return for. The gen. [gentlemen] lay in there till morning.

39. The "glass" was likely a 20-power hand lens.

Our road is heavy sand & down hill. We turn a rockey point & strike west down hill. The road now commences assending the great mountain [Alvord Mountain], with several stoppages during the night & constant tumbling out [of?] fallen oxen. At 12 miles we camp till morn'g.

[Dec.] 28th. Start again [at] day light & go to noon [and] camp, & 2 o'clock go on thro' thik sand till night when we reach the summit [of Alvord Mountain], & the Mohoughly Rio [Mojave River] appears in sight with its fringed shores.[40] On reaching the summit, we then desend a steep & from that [point] in 10 miles the road gradually decends. We camp 8 o'clock.

[Dec.] 29th. Go on before breakfast 5 miles & find grass & water puddles for cattle. Start [at] 2, & when about 2 miles meet Irish Charley, one of the first packers from this camp, returned. This news was hailed with joy & all ran with eager haste to hear what he had to say. [He said,] After suffering from swelled feet & many giving out altogether they reached the Catholic mission, this side of Wms. Ranche & were taken good care of.[41] Charley being a Catholic went to the priest. Told him the suffering condition of his and other trains, & the priest prepared *instanter* to send out relief which took 8 days. 11 packed mules loaded with flour, beans, Coffee, sugar, salt, & Spanish liquor, are now waiting 16 miles from where we first strike the [Mojave] river.[42] He tried to get the Spanyards to accompny him out on the desert but such is their dread & terror for a "hornatha" [*jornada*], they would not venture a mile. The Buckskins met him [yesterday] & bought some provisions & made up a purse of $15. Our road is a level plain & traveling 12 miles from our last camp, rise [we climb?] 2 or 3 hills & a 1/2 mile on the bottom brings us to the Mohoughly Rio [Mojave River near Yermo].

40. Sunset occurred about 4:45 p.m. and the moon had risen about 4:20 p.m. with 99 percent illumination. From the summit of the pass over Alvord Mountain (3,120 feet), you can see the Mojave River, 20 miles away, through a "V" in one of the westward ridges. To see the river, Lorton must have used a monocular—then commonly called a "glass."

41. What Lorton says makes sense if Charley arrived at Rancho Cucamonga, once part of Mission San Gabriel, which was located closer to Cajon Pass than Williams Ranch. At Rancho Cucamonga the men would have been taken care of. Charley may have then continued 30 miles farther west to Mission San Gabriel to speak with the priest.

42. Lorton and the other emigrants misunderstood Charley. Charley was not referring to where "we" (Lorton and wagons) would "first strike the river" at today's Yermo. He was referring to where he (Charley) first struck the river on his return from the rancho (or mission) to the wagons (at Lane's Crossing). Thus, the Spaniards were 16 miles south of Lane's Crossing of the Mojave River (near the foot of the mountains), not 16 miles from Yermo. Lorton would have no reason to hike 60 or more miles along the trail toward the mountains looking for the suppliers, as he does on December 31 and January 1, if they were only 16 miles from where Lorton struck the Mojave at Yermo.

[Dec.] 30th. Lay over all day to recruit our cattle & ourselves. We expected to see the Spanyards come with provisions, but as they did not come, fears were entertained that they had gone back. The river here flows in a south easterly course & is devided in 9 divernt [different] branches forming islands that suport good grass & rushes. Acasia [mesquite] is plenty & the dead trees afford good fuel. Cotton wood fringes the borders, & small ducks are plenty. On the south side runs a spur of mountains [Newberry Mountains]. The water is clear & is melted snow.

[Dec.] 31st. No provisions yet. I eat my last lb of flour & know not where I am to get the next mouth full from. Every body that had [any] are now nearly exhausted of provisions & therefore cannot give or lend, & then the plea of women & children comes in. They are all getting frightened & think they are now in a bad row of stump[s]. I feel perfectly reconsiled in [this] regard having ate a full breakfast.

The captain [Avis] & 2 men started out this morning in chase of the Spanyards on foot. I start 1 hour after & walk at the rate of between 4 & 5 miles an h[our] for 12 miles till I here come to where the road crosses the river [at Barstow] & mount a high rockey bluff [B Hill] & am scanning every object with in ten miles, when a "hollow" from below causes me to look down & there sat the trio eating there dinners previous to crossing. We continued our course up the river for 20 miles when we come to a large rockey mound on our right [Point of Rocks a mile north of Helendale].[43] Plenty of beautiful grass all the way. We notice fresh tracks of 2 oxen. One of our men mounts a bluff to look out & soon discovers the Spanyards coming. We fire off our guns as a salute as they appear thro' a grove of trees, but find on their approach, & that they salute us in our mother tongue, & are yankees. They said the Spanyards had sold out to the buckskins & Dallas & being affraid of Indians went back. He bore a letter to Capt Avis stating flour [was] worth $12 a "fanego" (140 lbs), beef very cheap & also said no dependence could be placed in the bearer.[44] We therefore took him for a sharper, thinking he had been to[o] quick for the "Spanolos" & probably pass[ed] them in the night. We therefor conversed together & Mr Shaw & myself agreed to go on in pursuit & bring them back. In the mean time they [Capt. Avis] would buy sparingly of the speculators, & we would meet them & take them [the speculators] back [to the wagons] if the Spanyards could not be found.

43. Lorton's trek up the river was along the east (right) bank where he followed the Old Spanish Trail on elevated ground (see Steiner 1999, maps, 32, 35, 36, and 37). This was considerably easier than slogging over the sandy river bed where the river flowed underground.

44. *Fanega* is a loosely defined Mexican measurement for grain that varied between one and a half to two and a half bushels. A bushel of unground wheat weighs 60 pounds.

We accordingly walked on till dark & camped till the moon should rise.[45] We made a fire in the grass, roasted a rabit, & the capt gave us a large pan cake & Shaw had meat in a bag. While eating, the grass caught fire & spread rappidly so that we could not extinguish it. Spread on among trees making the timber crack & brush snap. The fire soon encircled us & we were forced to place ourselves in the space it had burnt. At length Cyntho arose amonge heavy dark clouds & we soon crossed 2 branches of the river. The water is very cold. After walking 1 mile we cross 7 divisions of the stream [Lane's Crossing?] & then strike out on the 16 mile desert.[46] This is heavy sand & nothing but weeds out. The road then strikes the river, & by following up 2 or 3 miles find good camp for grass.

Jan. 1, 1850 [before dawn]. 10 miles further & intermediate places are camps. A few miles on we go then I swear I wount go any further till morning haveing strained every nerve for the last 19 hours & traveled 55 miles in that time.[47] For a little while we slept very well but a chill soon strikes you.

As the day cracked we set out for several miles over a hard road & level. On & on we went expecting to see [the Spaniards] at every turn of the river or road. At last mounting a small hill we describe a blue smoke curling up amonge the trees 5 miles ahead. We now are shure of the camp & push on with renewed vigor. It seamed a great ways. At last we reached it & to our chagrin & discomfriture it was a burning stump. At a place thro' some bushes I thought I see a temporary "wic eup" & 2 Indians reclining under it. We examined our pistols & approached but were mistaken. No one appeared. All was forsaken & we had to make the best by presing on 5 miles further when we relinquished our disign [to find the Spaniards with supplies] & put back, for we h[a]d ate up all our provisions.

A[f]ter making a cup of tea, all we had for a New years breakfast, we took a sleep for an hour. This very day, with out a mouthful to eat of any kind, while I think of the many happy N years I have spent, & this very A.M., & all the folks, eating more than they want of the fattest [foods], how different. It is painful & I feel low spirited, but we must up & off for we are now 50 or 60 miles from camp [near Yermo]. Near sun down near our mornings knap ground the Good Lord sends us for our N years supper a big fat hare & 2 fine quail which we soon broil

45. On December 31, 1849, the sun set about 4:45 p.m., and the almost-full moon rose at 7:35 p.m. along the Mojave River.

46. Again, Lorton describes a braided river. He is probably at what became known as Lane's Crossing a mile south of Oro Grande.

47. This day's trek of 55 miles was an extraordinary feat of endurance considering their malnourished condition. Assuming Lorton walked "55m," we judge he and Mr. Shaw turned around roughly in the vicinity where Highway 395 crosses Oro Grande Wash, west of Hesperia, California.

by our noble camp fire beneath a large tree on the banks of the river. We keep up a good fire all night & rest our weary bones on some grass which we collect for a bed. Keep up the fire with big logs during the night, tho' the wind is chilly.

Jan. 2. A deer comes near us & crosses the river attracted by our fire. Go on [back] 10 miles & breakfast on the remainder of the hare, & 2 miles further, which we made by 3. We come on the Ranche mens camp, & the train soon after roles up & we all "caral." The packers had already been bought out, on condition that we would pay them on our selling our property at the Ranches. I therefore supply my self with 12 lbs of flour (Spanish bran in it), 1 lbs sugar [$]5/, one pound coffee [$]4/, salt one quart [$]2. I also get 10 lbs of tollerable beef (not carrion) & oh! what a supper I have of slabjacks &c.

Jan. 3. Packers & mule wagons [from Howard Egan's company] overtakes us, say there is Pomeroy's & a family train yet behind us.[48] When they last seen Pomeroy he was on the big mount laboring thro' 3 ft snow.[49] His cattle were giving out & his teamsters about to leave him. He started with only 40 days provision. Amonge the packers were some of the Horse Spring boys. Smith overtook Pomeroy & got provisions & put for the [Salt] Lake.[50] They ate 8 more animals after leaving us, making 18 in all.

[Jan. 7th]. I keep with the [wagon] train till the "7th Jan." when we arrive at the last crossing of the Mo-hah-ve, but the water is so high we cannot cross.[51]

[Jan.] 8th. [The river] fell 18 in. I get out of breadstuff, have hard work to get any more.

[Jan.] 9th. I with a young man from Rochester, wades the rio, which on a/c of swifter current nearly carries us down. I have a load of 30 lbs. [About] 12 miles overtake mule packers & go with them. One man from Arcansas named Park [traveled] with his slave. Our road is one gradual assent toward the mountains

48. The "family train" were wagons of Simpson David Huffaker and Howard Egan that merged November 24 near Konosh, Utah, 158 miles south of Salt Lake City (Hafen and Hafen 1961, 103).
49. A two-day snowstorm temporarily halted the Pomeroy train at Mountain Meadows December 6, 1849 (Hamelin in Hafen and Hafen 1961, 86; see also Walter Van Dyke 45 years later in Hafen and Hafen 1954b, 302).
50. The Smith packers did not get to Salt Lake City. Near Cedar Valley, they were taken in by the Huffaker-Egan train and taken into southern California.
51. Torrential rainstorms in the Cajon Pass area sent voluminous flows of water that kept the wagon train camped on the right bank of the Mojave River at what later became known as Lane's Crossing, a mile south of today's Oro Grande.

for 11 miles then takes up a deep ravine, mounts a hill & finally we commence decending [Cajon Pass through Crowder Canyon] in the dark.[52] Down! down! down an almost intermedable cahsm, over fearful steeps as if plunging in an ahful abys & high lofty peeks mingling with the stars. At last after several hours work we come to a pass that desends gradually. This is Calhoons [Cajon] Pass. We follow till we come to a spring & there camp under an oak.[53] Build large fire. Plenty of good wood. I sleep with slave.

52. After crossing the river, they traveled southwest 18 miles up Oro Grande Wash to near the summit of Cajon Pass (see Swisher 1995, 171–72; Robinson 2005, 173, 474n32). A 12 percent moon did little to illuminate Lorton's difficult passage.
53. Lorton traveled about 21 miles this day. He camped at the unnamed spring on the right bank in upper Crowder Canyon, which drains part of the southern flank of Cajon Pass.

CHAPTER 12

California!

Background

Having crossed the summit of Cajon Pass, Lorton and his companions were finally out of the horrid clutches of the great southwestern desert that brought near death from want of water and lack of food to both men and beasts that survived this far.

They descended a rough defile called Crowder Canyon (some authors use the early name Coyote Canyon) (Beattie and Beattie 1951, index; Robinson 2005, 173). When the Jefferson Hunt wagon train tried to descend this canyon on December 17 and 18, 1849, they were forced to camp two days at a nameless spring above the narrows because a torrent of water was gushing through the canyon. The day after the storm they passed through with great difficulty, as Addison Pratt (1990, 407) related: "[Some wagons had] to be lifted and pried to get them up and down [the boulders]. After all was through this roughest place we found between Salt Lake and California, our wagons went down a few miles and camped." James and Sarah Waite and their five children were in the Hunt train when they descended the canyon. Sidney, eleven years old at the time, wrote (or dictated) an account when he was about age 81, wherein he recalled his family had to "take the wagon apart and pack a wheel at a time down over the boulders and slide the axle trees and heavier portions on sycamore poles down over the precipices and boulders" (in Hafen and Hafen 1954b, 129; Sidney's age comes from Newmark and Newmark 1929, 90, dwelling 387). Three weeks later, Jeremiah Fish (1850) said it was "the roughest canyon that we had ever passed through. It was very narrow and crooked, … and in the bottom rocks of all sizes, from that of a stack of hay to that of a bushel measure, and in any other country would be considered impassable." It may have been the roughest place in terms of being boulder-strewn, but the near-vertical hoist up Virgin Hill was a strong contender for the most strenuous short section of the route.

Before leaving Salt Lake City, Jefferson Hunt described "the latter part of the journey as almost impassable" in his orientation discussions with the emigrants (Lorton, August 20, 1849). When he traversed this area with pack animals in 1848, either the canyon looked passable for wagons or the pack trail detoured around this section of the canyon and he never saw it.

A probable scenario for this rough section is this: A gully washer scoured the canyon two days before the Hunt train descended it on December 19, 1849. Thousands of cubic yards of sand and gravel would have been sluiced from between the boulders, thus lowering the floor of the canyon and exposing still more boulders. We have personally seen the drastic results of such gully washers in the desert.

Adding credence to this hypothesis is Charles Rich's comment on December 8. Ten days ahead of Pratt and Hunt, Apostle Rich and his Mormon packers encountered a wagonload of supplies at the spring above Lorton's "tremendeious rockey place." Isaac Williams provided it (Rich in Hafen and Hafen 1954b, 192, 192n73). By analyzing Rich's dates and mileages, we conclude the supply wagon ascended the canyon before the torrential gully washer sluiced it out. The Pacific Crest Trail now traverses Crowder Canyon on the right bank and follows the hand-built wagon and auto road.

At last Lorton crossed the final barrier into the lush coastal plains of southern California, where he celebrated the vivid greenery while, on January 10, the Jayhawkers, his fellow travelers from the San Joaquin and Knox County Companies, were still struggling deep in the heart of the desert some 110 miles due north. The Jayhawkers, Brier family, and other assorted men still had 24 more days of near starvation and constant thirst as they grappled with the clutches of the unforgiving desert. The Bennett and Arcan families were waiting in Death Valley to be rescued, and a handful of other Death Valley '49ers—Nusbaumer, Hadapp, Schlögel, the Wades, the Earharts, and a couple of others—were struggling south from Death Valley.

Finally, Lorton stumbled onto Rancho Cucamonga, a disjunct livestock-grazing rancho that had been part of Mission San Gabriel. When the missions were secularized after 1834, most of their grazing lands were granted to Mexican citizens, which included a few naturalized foreigners.

The large adobe house at Rancho Cucamonga was built on top of Red Hill, where it faced south with a gate at the north and wings on each side. The roof was sealed with tar from natural bituminous springs (M. Hoover et al. 2002, 41, 327–28; E. Black 1996, 199; Beattie and Beattie 1951, 143.) On March 1, 1850, Welch mentions examining tar springs on Isaac Williams's Rancho Chino. Maria Merced Tapia and her husband, Leon Victor Prudhomme, owned the Rancho Cucamonga when the '49ers passed through (B. Shumway 1988, 68). It was possibly the first commercial winery in Alta California, other than the missions whose padres had perfected the art of viticulture and wine making in the region (Beattie and Beattie 1951, 138–69; E. Black 1996, xvii, xviii, 187–207). Alfred Robinson noted that the padres "make yearly from four to six hundred barrels of wine and two hundred of brandy, the sale of which produces an income of more than twelve thousand dollars" (in Engelhardt 1927, 157).

A black man named Jackson was the majordomo of the rancho (Pearson in Hafen and Hafen 1961, 15:51). When Peter Derr arrived in December, he reported that "they found a Negro who...knew how to treat...[these starving men by] giving them but a little [food] at a time, thus saving their lives" (Derr in Hafen and Hafen 1954b, 53). When Jacob Stover arrived, the overseer was pressing his open-fermented wine grapes with three naked Indians stomping them, and the emigrants began drinking the wine as it flowed out of the hide container. Drinking freely, "they began to tumble over and the wine came up as fast as it went down" (Stover in ibid., 286). Alexander Erkson told the editor of Lewis Manly's book (1894, 371) "that wine [at Cucamonga Rancho] wrecked us all. All had a little touch of scurvy, and it seemed to be just what we craved. I bought a big tumbler of it for two bits and carried it to my wife. She tasted it at first rather gingerly, then took a little larger sup of it, and then put it to her lips and never stopped drinking till the last drop was gone. I looked a little bit surprised and she looked at me and innocently asked— 'Why! Haven't you had any?' I was afraid she would be the next one to be dead drunk, but it never affected her in that way at all."

While Lorton proceeded to Rancho Cucamonga, Mr. Park and his slave, with whom he crossed Cajon Pass, went to Rancho Jurupa, 17 miles southeast of Rancho Cucamonga. Years before, Isaac Slover and his wife had settled in *Agua Mansa* on the northern edge of Rancho Jurupa (now part of Colton in San Bernardino County). They built their home near the southern base of a limestone outcrop now named Slover Mountain, which became an important source of limestone for cement (Belarde in Brown and Boyd 1922, 2:680; Hafen and Hafen 1954a, 224–25; National Park Service 2001, 10, 13, 52).

Many of the emigrants went directly to Williams's Rancho Chino, about 10 miles southwest of Rancho Cucamonga. Rancho Santa Ana del Chino also had been part of Mission San Gabriel. In 1841 Governor Alvarado granted five leagues (22,234 acres) of land to Antonio Maria Lugo (B. Shumway 1988, 69; Bynum 1934). Lugo's daughter married a 40-year-old Los Angeles merchant named Isaac Williams, and Antonio turned over management of the ranch to his son-in-law. Williams was later granted additional acreage. He was generous with his home, his crops, and his animals to help the beleaguered emigrants, although Lorton provides another slant to Williams's generosity.

Lorton says he met a man named Gruwell, who was employed as an overseer at one of the ranches. This implies one of the Gruwell brothers had already found a job. When in Salt Lake City, the Gruwell families planned to travel in

FIGURE 51. Indian plowing mission field using oxen with head yokes, as Lorton described. From Engelhardt 1927, 40.

the Independent Pioneer Company, which the Hafens called the Gruwell-Derr wagon train. This is the train that started down the Southern Route five days before the San Joaquin Company.[1] Just as the Independent Pioneer Company was ready to start its trek to California from Fort Provo, Jacob Gruwell, a Methodist minister, and Robert, one of his brothers, learned they were on a Mormon hit list for alleged hostilities toward the Mormons back in the States. To prevent their demise, the two men quickly separated from their families and headed to California on horseback via the Hastings and Lassen routes and pledged they would meet their families in Pueblo de los Angeles or somewhere on the Old Spanish Trail (V. Hoover 1849, December 16). Asa Gruwell, the third brother, stayed with the families. After arriving in the Los Angeles Basin, the Northern Route brothers headed out from the Spanish ranchos to meet their families, now destitute, on the Mojave River and bring them over Cajon Pass (Hayes in Hafen and Hafen 1961, 15:29–30, 29n5).

At the ranchos, Lorton saw oxen "worked by the horns." The Indians used head yokes lashed tight with rawhide straps directly behind the horns. Both

1. While the San Joaquin Company lingered for other wagons to arrive and finally departed on October 2, the Independent Pioneer Company moved quickly ahead on September 27, putting several days between the two companies. The Gruwell and Derr contingent moved ahead of the Shearer and Dallas wagons October 14, creating an "advance party" of the Pioneer Company (Hafen and Hafen 1961, 15:28). Jacob, Robert, and Asa Gruwell (also spelled Gruwel or Gruel) and their families "all spent the first winter in Los Angeles" after their arduous trek from Salt Lake (Gruwell in Foote 1888, 566–67).

head and neck yokes can weigh as much as 60 or 70 pounds, and their heftiness was "more of a problem for the person lifting the yoke up onto necks of the oxen than it is for the oxen" (Kramer 2000, 5). The head yoke is still popular in parts of the world and is celebrated with ox-pull contests in places such as Nova Scotia (Kramer 2000, 1; Conroy 2007, 111–14; Watts 1999, 23; James 1992; for illustrations of head yokes, see Engelhardt 1927, 40, 66; James 1992).

Lorton left Rancho Cucamonga for Williams's ranch on January 12, where he had a long talk with Apostle Rich and Addison Pratt. That same day Pratt left, packing for San Francisco, where he caught the brig *Frederick* to Tahiti (A. Pratt 1990, 414, 432). After spending several days at Williams's ranch, Lorton joined a fellow New York packer and another man and headed for Pueblo de los Angeles via Mission San Gabriel.

Mission San Gabriel Arcángel, the fourth mission established in Alta California, was founded September 8, 1771, at a site five miles southwest of its present location. A flood forced the padres to relocate on higher ground in 1775, where the mission is still active (Yenne 2004, 48–55; M. Hoover et al. 2002, 151–52). Before secularization in 1834, the mission had 16,500 cattle, 8,500 sheep, 1,200 horses, 40 goats, 60 pigs, and 42 mules (Engelhardt 1927, 279). Father Blas Ordaz was the Franciscan priest in charge of Mission San Gabriel when Lorton passed by. Known as a free spirit, Ordaz "had an unsavory reputation among his brethren as being a priest of notoriously loose morals" (Osio 1996, 270n9).

Father Ordaz had justifiable reasons to dislike the invading Americans. Some of the emigrants considered the dilapidated mission buildings, orchards, vineyards, and livestock spoils of the Mexican-American War. In 1847, when Ordaz had responsibilities at Mission San Fernando, Col. John C. Frémont and 400 troops "occupied the convento, where they committed acts of thievery and left behind visible scars of their presence." Frémont also allowed his troops to help themselves to the mission's sheep and cattle (Pauley and Pauley 2005, 171).

From the mission, Lorton made his way to Pueblo de Los Angeles, where his journal abruptly ends mid-sentence. Obviously, he planned to continue writing, but all subsequent booklets are apparently lost. However, we do have the letter Lorton wrote from Los Angeles on January 20 to the *Sun* in New York City.[2]

2. We use the *Sun* copy. The article was also reprinted in the *New-York Daily Tribune* on May 17, 1850, and in the Cleveland *Plain Dealer* on May 11, 1850, with the erroneous date of January 30, 1850, and other misprints. LeRoy and Ann Hafen used the *Plain Dealer* transcription in their *General Analytical Index...Supplement*, 15:71–75. We strongly suspect there were additional journals because Lorton's obituary said he was working on a history that "would have contained the personal experiences of the writer on his trip across the plains and *his stay in the mining region*" (*New-York Daily Tribune* 1892, March 26, emphasis ours).

We have no firsthand information about Lorton's northward passage to the mines. Considering the state of his finances, Lorton most likely traveled by land, perhaps up the coast via *El Camino Real* or via the inland road through the Rancho San Francisco to the southern mines. By the end of April, he was in the northern mines on the Feather River, northwest of today's Oroville. The only further record we have of his California experiences in his own hand is a sketch of a camp scene captioned "Sierra Nevada mountains. Feather River April 30th 1850." But eight days after Lorton sketched this scene, we pick up his trail and briefly track him until mid-September 1850, through several references in Dr. Charles R. Parke's very fine overland and California diary.

Dr. Parke was the physician in the same train as David Cairnes, Lorton's cousin from northwestern Illinois. The Como Company crossed the Missouri River at Old Fort Kearny, then took the Oregon and California Trail to Fort Laramie.

Charles Ross Parke was born June 25, 1823, in Parkesburg, Pennsylvania, grew up on a farm, worked in his father's mill, and attended local schools before he went to Science Hill, a boarding school. In 1843 he studied medicine in the office of Dr. Wilmer Worthington, a well-respected physician, then attended medical classes for three years at the University of Pennsylvania in Philadelphia, where he graduated in 1847. He soon moved to Como, Illinois, and in April 1849 became physician for the Como Pioneer Company bound for California's gold country (Davis in Parke 1989, xxviii–xxix).

This company traveled the northern trails to California after crossing South Pass, and was one of the first to take the new Hudspeth Cutoff to the vicinity of City of Rocks, just north of where the Salt Lake Cutoff intersected the established California Trail. They crossed Donner Pass August 31 and reached Sacramento September 15, 1849. The following day, as Dr. Parke records, "Capt. Sampson, David Cairnes, John McWhirter and myself started north for Feather River." By the 19th they were prospecting the river, and the following day they "made a claim 5 miles above Bidwell's Bar and half a mile above Oregon Bar" (about 12 miles east-northeast of today's Oroville) (Parke 1989, xxvii, 48, 84, 87).[3]

They helped start the Union Bar Company, organized "to turn the channel of the river this coming winter. And in the Spring when the Oregon Bar is

3. Bidwell's Bar, on the Middle Fork of the Feather River, is now inundated by Lake Oroville (reservoir). Goddard's 1857 map shows an Oregon Bar on the South Fork, about five miles cross country from Union Bar on the Middle Fork (see also Gudde 1975, 8, map 3, 33–34). Or Parke's Oregon Bar may have been a short-lived bar at or near Union Bar on the Middle Fork. He lists members of the Union Bar Company immediately after speaking of Oregon Bar, and his reference about going up "the river to Evans Bar after beef" places their camp at or near Union Bar (Parke 1989, 92; Map, Goddard 1857; Map, Trask 1853).

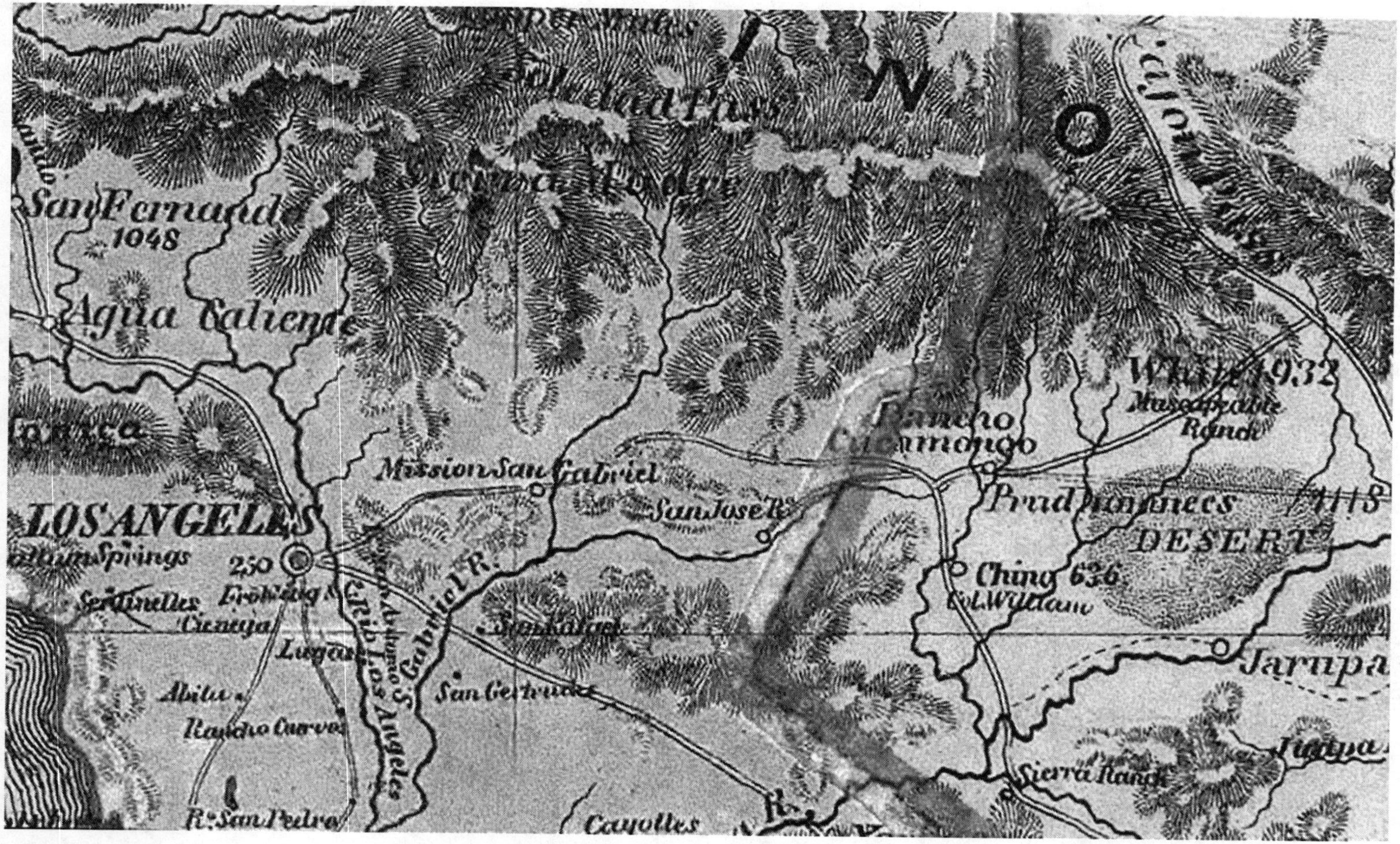

MAP 9. Detail, Goddard's 1857 map with the southern California ranchos Lorton mentions. Courtesy of David Rumsey Historical Map Collection.

worked out, we will take out the dam so as to drain the lower part of our bar." A few months later, in spring 1850, William B. Lorton arrived at Union Bar on the Middle Fork of the Feather River, now under Lake Oroville (Parke 1989, 87, 93–99; Map, Goddard 1857; Map, Trask 1853).

Lorton's Journal Continues on Cajon Pass

[January 1850] 10th. Up & off by day light. Follow the [Cajon] pass [southward] thro its windings, the water ishuing from every rock & hill & widening the stream. As we proceed, at length we come to a tremendeous rockey place of 1/2 mile with cascades apparently imposible for wagon to pass. The country has already taken a change. Every thing is green & instead of the barren black mountains & black sandy deserts we see the whole—one lofty scene of green to the mtn top. The oak has put forth leafs the winter pine & the cedar. About noon the road strikes south [southwest], & opens broad [into Cajon Canyon] & the stream covers the whole width. Here we see 3 handsome deer but could not shoot them. We follow down thro' this Sierra Navada [canyon], till we come to 2 roads, 1 south [southwest], [the] other east [southeast near the junction of Interstates 15 and 215]. Here we camp on good grass amid a lovely scene & springs every 20 rod[s] from last spring, 15 miles [traveled today]. At the foot of this mountain is several persons camped. They cut poles & herd there cattle for Coco Mungo [Rancho Cucamonga].

[January] 11th. Parks puts for Slogers [Slover's] ranche [today's West Colton between Ranchos Jurupa and San Bernardino] & we for Coco Mungoes. On east road we come to campers. They hav[e] 2 saddles of ven[i]son hanging in the tree & skins streached on the ground. We cross many streams & one powerful torrent which we could hardly wade [Lytle Creek?]. We now strike out in a valley of great beauty [Cucamonga Valley], high mountains covered with snow all round while below is perpetual spring, one vast expanse of green swarth studded with here & there a pritty tree. Green benches or seats on the mtn sides look lovely. This is mid winter in Cal. As we jorney along, the meadow larks mounts the sky with its song & the beautiful dove which appear in thousands fly around you like tame pigeons & eat the sun flower seeds, flax, clover, oats that have fallen on the ground. After a 15 mile walk we see hundreds of cattle & horses roming over the plains. 2 Spanyards [Mexicans] & an Indian all on wild horses come dashing down the road, with their brod panama hats & Mex. blankets swinging in the wind, their large spurs jingling. They appeared not to notice us, but jabed in the flanks of their animals [with] these tremendous irons when the animal stops. We soon see they are breaking horses, & soon arrive at their caral near a running stream shaded by large trees [Cucamonga Creek].

Every thing was green & a splendid hurd of fine horses run from us so fat they could hardly toddle. We come to the house which is built of dobies with a portico in front. A molatto man lying in bed [Jackson, the overseer] invited us in, saying, "Come in stranger." He gives us a glass of wine. I go in the kitchen & get another glass of wine.[4] We tell him we have no money. He gives us 6 lbs of beef, which we roast on coals. He brings us hot corn bread & buttermilk. An old Mex. soon after sends us a large plate of potatoes & greens. We get prickly pears from the Mex. woman as large as an egg.[5] In the eve'g they cook up a fine pan of meat & homony.

[January] 12th. Get a fine breakfast of liver, beef steak, hot cakes & butter, coffee, homony, &c & for the whole not 1 cent charge. The overseer is an emigrant just from the mines. He was said to have participated in a[n] [anti] Mormon mob & was obliged to make his escape on the north rout, to escape their vengence. His name is Gruell [Jacob or Robert Gruwell].

They [José and Manuela Valdez] have [a] fine vineyard here & a small farm. Here I see oxen first worked by the horns. Indians do the work.[6] Before day light this morning we are awakened by a most horrible noise. The old Spanyard with his wife would sing once a long time & then all the little ones join in. I was not long finding out that this was their morning pray[er]s.[7]

We start for Wms. [Williams's Rancho Chino] which we see [to the south-southwest] from the hill 11 miles dist. Our road lays over a fine laun, which is covered with sun flow[er]s at certain seasons, & flocks of dove & other birds live on the seeds that fall to the ground. The whole plain [Cucamonga Valley], every nook, every hill & valley, as far as the eye can reach is spotted with cattle & horses. As you approach the sway backed creaters, they lift their high horns, cock their tails high in air, & run, bow & kick.

By climing several fences made of clay sheded with brush to protect them from washing, & jumping ditches, I arrive in the vineyard & peach orchard. Williams has 2 "carals" or forts, built of dobies & porticoes in front. Here I

4. These starving men craved the vitamins and minerals found in fruit juice of most any kind.

5. These are the fruits, *tunas*, of prickly pear cactus (*Opuntia ficus-indica*). This New World species is cultivated worldwide for its nutritious fruit laden with vitamin C (Griffith 2004). It grows to a height of 16 feet, and when planted in rows, makes a cheap and formidable barrier to livestock. Progenitors of these plantings are still seen on the grounds of some California missions.

6. These were skilled laborers and craftsmen who had learned their trades from the mission padres.

7. They were not Spaniards; they were Mexicans (possibly of Spanish descent) who were soon to become U.S. citizens. José Maria (37) and Manuela (33) Valdez and their six children lived on Rancho Cucamonga. The entire family was born in Alta California (Newmark and Newmark 1929, 34; E. Black 1996, 204–5).

meet Gen[eral] Rich & Mr Pratt. The Gen. informed me that from the cut off he struck the Rio Muddy in 15 miles, followed it down & [on Nov. 18] found Cap. Hunt camped thereon.[8]

I stay at Wms Ranch, [January] 13th, 14th, & 15th [1850] with only 50 cts which was lent me. I leave Davis my vest & neckerchief & buffalo [robe] in pledge to satisfy Erkon [Alexander C. Erkson] & Davis [the food purveyor in the desert]. [Isaac] Williams said he used to keep the pavillion at Cooney Island, that he came to Cal. in 1827. He said he would present a bill to the U.S. of [$]40,000 for services rendered emigrants. In my opinion he is a niggerdly upstart. He has a cane, the head of which weighs one lb gold.[9] To day I start with McKey & [William] Sherman [packer from New York]. We strike west over beautiful green hills covered with clover 6 in[ches] high in which the cattle almost roll. Thousand[s] of head appear running & jumping from every hill. As you proceed over sideling hills & moist valleys a bubble gushes from every hill ravine & the sweet smell of clover comes in the nostles.

We rest awhile & gather prickly pears which eat well. We constantly pass ranches after a while which are prittily located & have their Indians plowing their fields. Near sun down we stop near a ranch on the brook, but could get no "Carne" [beef]. I go to another fine old ranche & the old Don, dressed in blue broad cloth gives me plenty of jerked Carne for 1 "onereal."[10] By this time the boys had a fire made & had baked cakes. We then toasted the meat on the coals & had a good supper. By that tim[e] dark came & we traveled on 2 or 3 miles. The moon went down & it was dark. By & by we heard dog barking to the left & knew a ranch must be there. We first crossed a brook over a fallen tree but 50 dogs apparently bounded out on our yelling. A light appeard at the door born by a small Spa[n]yard apparently frightened. We told [him] we wanted to "B[*illegible*]" "sleep" & we walked in. Not long after they brot in a large plate of "tarteers" [tortillas], hot coffee & sugar. We had quite a chat & we compared words in Spanish. He was from Santa Fee. There were several women & children. He spread his "sarapa" over us when we went to bed. Next morning they gave us breakfast, tartiers, meat & samp [coarsely ground corn] & no charge. I gave him a few notions & sold breast pin for 11 "onreals."

8. After traveling down Pahranagat Wash about 22 miles from Division Spring, the Mormon packers struck the Muddy River. The next day they "continued down creek 15 miles where we came to Capt. Hunt and 7 waggons" (Rich in Hafen and Hafen 1954b, 189). The distance from Muddy Spring to California Crossing, following the river, is closer to 10 miles.

9. We assume this was a troy pound (twelve troy ounces), a value of roughly $20,750 using the April 2020 price for gold. It was worth $192 using the gold rush standard of $16 per troy ounce.

10. Possibly a Spanish 8 Reales. These coins were often cleaved into eight pie-shaped parts—pieces of eight or eight bits. Most likely Lorton bought the meat for one bit.

FIGURE 52. Lorton sketch. Lorton writes, "San Gabreal Mission/Jan 17th 1850." Courtesy of The Bancroft Library.

[January] 16th. Went to Rolands, a fine large ranche 15 miles from Wm's [Rancho].[11] Got a drahn of "Bieno," & 9 miles of level land brings you to the gardens of the Mission of San "Gabrael." These are fenced in by cacti or prickly pears & trees. These are partly broken down. The church is a long white building [with] plaster over bricks, 8 pilasters on the [side], 100 ft long, & a vestry in which hang the chim[e]s. The interior looks like some old prison with the exception of the west end which is decorated off in the usual Catholic stiles & 2 effegee figures on each side. There is a massive "doby" "caral" [courtyard] formed by a large rows of rooms, & heavy portion in front & rear supported by heavy collums of brick. Part of this caral has tumbled or been pulled down, & the rest dirty & fast decaying. This belongs to U.S.[12] The emigrants have taken possession of nearly all the rooms, & they build fires any wheres, under the porches or in the rooms.

The Alkalda [Alcalde] lives in this building & so does the priest.[13] The N.Y.

11. Rancho La Puente (the bridge) was a Mexican land grant 15 miles west of Rancho Chino and the largest rancho granted from the San Gabriel Mission lands. It was owned jointly by John Rowland and William Workman (B. Shumway 1988, 139; Hoover et al. 2002, 167).

12. Ownership of the missions and their adjoining property was nebulous at the time. Presidents James Buchanan and Abraham Lincoln formally returned the mission churches and some of their lands to the Catholic Church (Yenne 2004, 20; N. Harlow 1982, 290–92).

13. An *alcalde*, under Mexican rule, was an appointed administrator who held judicial authority in a village. "The Americans, after the occupation of California in 1846, revived the alcalde system. Wherever a group of Americans collected, they proceeded to elect an American alcalde" (California State Senate 1963, 303). Their duties were spelled out in a "Memorial" to the U.S. Congress dated October 12, 1849 (Browne 1850, xxxiii).

boys are invited to sing for his wife. She plays a trick with eggs & aloger [?] water. The Maegarette [Magistrate?] is taken with a fit of histerick. There is also a young priest [Father Blas Ordaz] who dresses in a dark frock.[14] He is a smart fellow & has great authority over the Spanyards. When he walks out they all doff their sombreyoes. They say he was the ring leader in the last war against U.S. He is a great polititition, & hates the Am[ericans] & asks the Spanyards why they dont kill every one of us. Some emigrants take his rooms away. A great part of the mission is in ruins. The whole is built appearently in a substantial manner with cloisters, arches, halls, dungeons. There is a fine Oranges and Olive orchard contiguous to the buildings. The Spanish women are very fond of the yankeys & strange to say the Spanyards are not gelous. There is N.W. of the Mission a chain of high mts [San Gabriel Mountains] & plenty of groves of timber at their bottoms. Emigrants build fires any wheres about the mission & do as they d—d please.

From the Mission to Angelos is 8 miles, 20 miles to San Pedro.[15] De Los Angelos is, tho' not a large town, one of long standing & is by interpretation The City of the Angels, fallen ones of course.[16] The city is approached on the east by crossing a creek [Los Angeles River], passing up roads with high "doby" walls on either side, or fences made by trees growing & in bloom. These enclose vineyards, orchard, & gardins of great beauty, & here you see trees hanging with delicious oranges. Many an old Don holds forth here in private, in his low built habitah frequently with balistrade on top. Indians do their pruning &c. The City lays at the bottom of a high hill, has 2 principal st[reets] running N & south. Several buildings are now going up. Several Am. merchants have stores and make money. The principal Am. house is the Am. Exchange by Mathes. Kearney [Gen. Stephen Watts Kearny] mounted his ordinance on the top of the high hill, & the Span[iards] prepared for defense. Plenty of copper shot from...

Lorton's journal ends here.

Lorton's journal ends mid-sentence, about January 20, 1850. How we yearn for more of his insightful descriptions. We include Lorton's letter, written January 20, after an excerpt written by Addison Pratt about a conversation with Lorton, then we pursue Lorton into the goldfields of California via Charles Parke's diary, another fine diary in The Huntington Library.

14. Father Blas Ordaz (1792–1850), a Franciscan, was in charge of Mission San Gabriel from 1847 to his death November 11, 1850 (Engelhardt 1927, 302–4, 306).
15. San Pedro was the seaport for the Los Angeles area.
16. Pueblo de Los Angeles was founded in September 1781 as El Pueblo de Nuestra Señora de los Angeles de Porciuncula (Engelhardt 1927, 47–51, 341–46). Little wonder the name was shortened.

The excerpt from Pratt's diary was written about January 12, when both he and Lorton were at Williams's Rancho Chino. Pratt was there from December 22 until January 13, before starting north to San Francisco. It gives us insight to Lorton's emotional travails not found in his own journal. In his letters and journal, Lorton does not moan or express self-pity for the trials and dangers he endures as a packer from Mount Misery into unknown territory. Only in the following conversation does he give a hint of the emotional ordeals he faced daily.

Lorton was an independent young man in the first place or he would not have ventured alone from New York City to western Illinois in the fall of 1848, and then to California. Yes, it was a lark, an adventure, and maybe a way to get away from home, but in doing so, Lorton forsook the normal support groups we find in society. He did not travel with family nor with close friends. He did not belong to a coalesced group, such as the Jayhawkers or the Rovers. His first messmates, the Kelloggs, were a family group, but Lorton was not related to them nor was he a longtime family friend. Although wagon trains formed companies to provide a social structure, that support system broke down during times of disagreement or stress.

Lorton was not a loner by nature. He wrote his cousin David Cairnes to come down to go sleighing in Illinois, he asked David to travel with him when they met in St. Joseph, Missouri, and he mined with David in California. But he does not mention yearning for home nor does he yearn for family or girlfriends in his journal. The closest persons west of the Mississippi who represented family to Lorton were members of the Addison Pratt family. Mrs. Pratt mended his coat and put some poetry in his pocket to read on his travels, and he was often in the Pratts' home in Salt Lake City. At that time, he expected to travel with the Mormon mess that included Pratt, Rich, Pomeroy, and Brown. Then Lorton decided (we do not know why) to go with the Independent Pioneer Company, but that arrangement fell through. He rarely mentions the names of the men he travels with, but the messes are inconsistent all along the Southern Route. From his journal we get the impression Lorton was a welcome traveling companion—he stands guard when expected to, collects hay for the team he is traveling with, does his share of the cooking, entertains with his singing, and assists when someone dies.

Studies of those who died in the Donner Party found that single men were the first to succumb. A major reason given was they had no family support group to help them emotionally as well as physically (Grayson 1990, 233–34, 241). Addison Pratt extends some emotional comfort to Lorton, but that is all he provides.

In hindsight, Lorton's trek to California was an unlucky one. He missed going with the "lightning" Findley train in Illinois by only a couple of days and traveled instead in the calamity-prone "stampede" Knox County train to Salt Lake City. Then he hoped to travel with the smaller Independent Pioneer Company down the Southern Route, but he got stuck in the large, slow, and eventually disintegrating San Joaquin Company. When it disbanded in southern Utah, he joined the packers who got lost in eastern Nevada and had to return (by various routes) to the Old Spanish Trail. A presumed self-portrait (figure 53) that Lorton sketched in the goldfields conveys "the vicissitudes, trials, incidents, and dangers" he suffered—a man no more than skin and bones topped by a bountiful head of hair (Lorton 1849b).

Excerpt from Addison Pratt's Diary, Early January 1850

As we were about ready to leave Williams'es, there was a young man came up that I had become acquainted with at Salt Lake, by the name of Lorton. He is from New York, and is a painter by trade. As he boarded at Br[other Jonathan] Holmes's while there he was frequently in at my house, and the subject of salvation was frequently brought up, but he thought but little about it, as he was of a volatile turn of mind. But when I met him last, he was quite serious, and said to me, "We got to be quite religious, while we were in the mountains." "Ah!!" said I, "why so?" He answered, "When we thought we all had got to starve to death, we used to pray, and ask the Lord to help us out," and said he, "I believe I know how the Mormons get revelations, and we believed Gen. Rich was led out by revelation," and ask if it was not so? Said I, "If I should tell you, perhaps you would not believe." Said he [Lorton]:

> When we got out of water and some of our men were insane for the want of it, we prayed to the Lord to shew us water, and two of us dreamed the same dream, that there was water in a certain canion about a mile and a quarter off, both told our dream in the morning, and both went and found it, and our dreams shewed the place so plain to us, that it seemed to us both that we had been there before. And another of our company dreamed he saw an Indian, stand on the top of a mountain, and cried to us aloud, and said 'thus far ye can come and no farther, and now if you do not turn back you all will starve.' We came to such a mountain [Sheep Range, Nevada] as the man saw in his dream, but there was no Indian, and there was no pass by it for us, and we took for granted that it was salvation for us to turn back, but to press forward would be starvation. We had eaten nearly all of our horses, and some of our company had drank their blood for want of water.
>
> With one voice we all turned back and in two or three days struck your waggon trail. [Lorton's group traveled six days, November 20–26, before reaching the Old Spanish Trail.] None can describe the joy the sight of it gave us. We had now been for two or three days without anything to eat, and the cry among us was, look out for worn out cattle that have been left by the waggons that have gone ahead, and we ranged along

> the road like so many hungry wolves, and soon to our satisfaction, we saw an ox that had been left, and so poor he could not stand alone. We cut his throat and soon had him onto a sagebrush fire, and before it was het through by it, we began to eat, and I never tasted anything in my life that was so sweet. We soon devoured it and went ahead to look for another, and so continued on till we came to the Far Muddy. Here we found some of Dallas's company [at the California Crossing of the Far Muddy, about three miles southwest of Moapa, Nevada]. Some boddy had gone ahead with a horse and told them that we were a comeing, and they prepared supper for us. We sat down and I ate the best supper I ever ate in my life. There was another waggon company [the Buckskins] a mile ahead of this, and they sent word that they had supper prepared for us. We went there and ate just as hearty again, and it tasted just as good, but all did not seem to abate my craving appetite, and I could not account for it.

This is a part of the tale of wo[e] he told me and I pitied him, for he was a verry friendly young man. He had lost all but what he stood in on the road, and he needed help, and [I could not assist him] as I was dependant on Br. Rich, and he had helped men in just such circumstances, till our company had increased to some sixty or seventy men, and his means were all exhausted. Our waggons had already gone ahead, and we were on the point of starting when I bade him good by. (A. Pratt 1999, 410–11, 557n39)

Lorton's Letter from Pueblo de Los Angeles

Fortunately, on May 8, 1850, the *New York Sun* published the letter Lorton wrote after his journal inexplicably stops. Lorton's journal probably did not end but continued in another notebook not available to us. The following letter fittingly concludes his westward travails across the continent.

CORRESPONDENCE OF THE NEW YORK SUN
OVERLAND EMIGRATION — TERRIBLE SUFFERINGS
OF THE EMIGRANTS — THRILLING DETAILS

De Los Angelos, Jan. 20, 1850.
About the time I wrote the last letter several mountaineers offered themselves as guides to conduct trains through to California,[17] by way of the Spanish trail, and

17. His previous letter was "dated, Utah Lagoon, October 1st, 1849. — Eds [of the *Sun*]." We do not have a copy of this letter, nor does it seem to have been printed. It is not the letter he gave to "Capt Smith to carry to S. Lake" on November 26. We don't know where that letter is, either.

a wagon train of 150 wagons started on the 2nd of October, by way of this route.[18] This was the first attempt ever made by wagons on this trail.[19] The difficulties we had to encounter were quite apparent from the guide's representation. There would be probably 1000 miles more travel than on the north route—long and tedious deserts to pass, which ox teams had never before encountered.

Everything went on pleasantly as far as Little Salt Lake when a hearsay delusion seized the camp [in the Escalante Desert before they reached the valley of Little Salt Lake]. Mr. A. heard Mr. B. say that he had heard from a mountaineer by the name of [Barney] Ward, who distinctly told him of a pass that took into the mountains near the Great Basin, that by taking this course a safe and expeditious route could be had to California and the mines, and water every 15 miles, and thereby avoid the dreadful deserts of the Spanish trail. Great speeches were made by the learned, the Rio men put their heads together, and wondered why it had never been thought of before. Fremont's map was perused by the knowing, and sure enough he had seen a high range stretching east and west, but did not explore it, and then they consulted the matter thus: Now, say they, wherever there is a chain of high mountains there must be snow, and wherever there is snow there must be streams emitting therefrom; so we will not go the out of the way [route], the Spanish trail, but the short and expeditious route to the mines, and future generations will navigate this great winter route to California, and Fremont will be thrown into the shade. To this all but six wagons consented, and turned to the right [a seventh wagon belonged to Jefferson Hunt's mess].

Passing up fine kanyons, here we found good grass, plenty of water, and prospects brightened as we proceeded [up Shoal Creek]. At length the rim of the Great Basin was reached, and we came to an awful chasm several hundred feet in depth [while at Mount Misery]. Things were now brought to a crisis, for we could go no farther in that direction [with the wagons]. Here we lay over a week trying to find a pass, but to no purpose; pioneers were sent out to observe, and explorers ascended every snowy peak, but all returned unsuccessful. Such was the nature of the mania, they would not give it up. Some thought they had struck into the mountains too soon, others not soon enough. A large number of wagons [about 26] started north of the Basin rim, which is the last we have heard

18. The San Joaquin Company accumulated 107 wagons. The Independent Pioneer Company (with 23 wagons in the Gruwell-Durr section and 22 in the Shearer-Dallas section) moved out in advance of the San Joaquin Company (Hoover 1849, October 17; Hafen and Hafen 1961, 15, 28).

19. It is probable the Slover-Pope wagon train followed the Old Spanish Trail from Taos, New Mexico, to the Los Angeles basin in 1837 (Leroux in Hafen and Hafen 1957, 32). We know for certain there was one wagon (or carriage) in the Rockwell-Davis Company that rolled from Los Angeles to Salt Lake City in 1848 (Robinson 2005, 176–77; Bigler and Bagley 2000, 396–99).

of them. A heavy snow fell soon after [on November 14], which would prevent their retracing, should they so desire. They had provisions for 80 days only.[20]

Capt. [O. K.] Smith passed us [the San Joaquin train] and struck south of the rim with pack animals. A party of 13 packed from the wagons, some days in the rear of Capt. Smith, while the remaining wagons went back to the Spanish trail. Our route lay among fearful rocks and steeps from which our animals fell and were dashed to pieces. We penetrated about 200 miles into this vast region,[21] and travelled five days without any water for ourselves or animals, except what we could get from the rains, and suck up through pipe stems from the crevices of the rocks.

The sufferings of some were intense, a water fever seized the senses, they could not eat for want of water, every rustle of the wind was a bubbling brook to the imagination, and all the delicious drinks that the subject had taken for years arose before him to torture. Sleep was out of the question at such times. Some went nearly crazy.

At the end of the 4th day we camped, having found a puddle of mud and water, which enabled us to repose. The next morning a bold push was made for water, as in a very few hours our faithful animals would all be dead. A blue smoke arose among the hills to our right.[22] Here we expected to find Indians, and if Indians, water. Two out of the number being several miles ahead, made desperate by hardships, rushed for the spot. Instead of Indians, appeared Capt. Smith's men, who had been in the mountains [and deserts after leaving Mount Misery] 11 days. They were out of provisions, and had already killed 2 horses, and the meat then hung jerking in a bush. Here we found a small Indian spring, holding about 2 quarts of water, and not very strong at that. This had to water 100 animals and 30 men.[23] This was strongly impregnated with salts and salaeratus. Here we learned that Capt. Smith had suffered extremely in crossing the "Hornather" [*jornada*]. Some had cut their horses throats and drank their blood. General Blodget then lay down in the valley waiting for his Negro servant to bring him water. The tongues of others swelled to an enormous size, and cracked in their heads. Gen. Rich of the Nauvoo Legion, had a revelation,

20. From Mount Misery, some of these emigrants (now called the Death Valley '49ers) got to settlements after 57 days, some after 82 days, and some after 113 days. Lorton wrote his letter before they came out of the desert.

21. From Mount Misery they traveled about 130 trail miles to Division Spring; their total mileage from Mount Misery to the Old Spanish Trail was close to 218 miles.

22. Lorton has his directions reversed here. His journal, Nov. 18, says, "On our left we see smoke." Lorton is traveling southwest in Kane Springs Valley near its junction with Pahranagat Wash, Nevada.

23. The number of men is fairly accurate if one excludes the Mormon packers who had already left Division Spring and also excludes the 11 Pinney-Savage group who are about to leave.

to the effect that all that continued onward [westerly] would perish. He, with his Mormon followers, struck South, towards the Spanish trail, and arrived safe in the settlements. Eleven men, with not a pound of bread stuff, packed horse meat on their backs, determined to pass the mountains [that] animals would not go over, and continued on, and the last we saw of them they were going up the blue mountains [Sheep Range].

Their names are as follows: Chas. McDermot, Kentucky; Mr. Savage, Illinois; Jno. Adams, G. Wiley Webster, T. Ware, J. Ware, Mr. Baker, editor, Utica, N.Y.; Mr. Semore, Mr. Allen, Mr. Moore [and Mr. Pinney from Ohio].[24]

The next day Capt. Smith went back to Salt Lake with his men, while our party of sixteen struck the Spanish trail on the Rio Virgin.[25] Here we found cattle which had been left, these we shot and packed on the animals we had left. In this attempt to penetrate the unexplored regions, we lost, altogether, about 60 mules and horses, and ate 6 horses and 4 mules.

The names of those that arrived safe in by way of this trail, are as follows: — Dr. Downer, Iowa; two Mr. Sanburns, Ill.; P. Orr, do. [ditto]; Mr. Potter, do.; Gen. G. Blodget, Wis., and servant boy; J. Stoges [Stover], Iowa; Charles Burrel, New York City; Wm. Sands, do.; Wm. Sherman, do.; J. Hendle, do.; Wm. B. Lorton, do.; J. Bucklin, do.; Mr. Springer, Ill.; Mr. [F. B.] Shannon, do.

No pen can describe the sufferings and fatigue endured by those coming the Spanish trail. Thousands of oxen and horses laid their bones upon the deserts. Hundreds of men, women, and children have had nothing to eat for one and two months but the carcasses of the oxen giving out from starvation and fatigue. We encountered mountains of snow, and a great many people frozen badly. Great has been the destruction of property, and all have suffered more or less, from travelling over a country blasted by nature.

With this brief report of the route, I leave you.

Truly yours,
W. B. Lorton

Lorton in the Goldfields

We take up Charles Parke's diary at Union Bar on the Middle Fork of the Feather River in Butte County to follow Lorton, indirectly, in the goldfields for the first few months. We use the transcription in *Dreams to Dust*, edited by James E. Davis, since it is more accessible to readers than the original in The Huntington Library. Davis uses conventional spelling, capitalization, and punctuation.

24. These 11 men are now called the Pinney-Savage party. Lorton listed 10 names in his journal, which include Pinney and Savage, but he did not list the eleventh person enumerated above—Mr. Moore. Stover said Pinney was from Ohio (in Hafen and Hafen 1954b, 280).

25. Although Smith intended to retreat to Salt Lake City, he and his men continued to California when the Pomeroy and Huffaker-Egan wagons agreed to take them.

FIGURE 53. Lorton sketch. Lorton writes, "Sierra Nevada mountains/Feather River/April 30th 1850." Courtesy of The Bancroft Library.

Charles R. Parke's Diary Begins Below

[Wed.] May 8 [1850], Dave Carns [Cairnes] accidentally met his cousin [William B. Lorton] today. He left Illinois last year in the Holt [Knox] County train. Arrived in Salt Lake last summer, where they spent six weeks, sold their oxen, and bought mules and horses, and with a *guide* took the South Trail for California with one hundred horses. Thermometer to day Stand 90° in the shade....

May 15, Mr. Lorton (Carns' cousin) entertained us to day with many anecdotes about the Mormons....

June 8, Had Some fine vocal music last night from Mr. Lorton, reminding me of home. River falling slowly.

June 18, Great excitement prevails along the river regarding the discovery of a Certain "gold lake" on the headwaters of North Yuba river.[26] Every pan of dirt is

26. Gold Lake was a phantom lake. "The name commemorates what seems to have been the first large-scale hoax perpetrated after the discovery of gold" (Gudde 1974, 122; Bagley 2012, 295–96). Lewis Manly, who continued westward from Mount Misery and ended up naming Death Valley, was taken in by the hoax: "The point we were seeking to reach was a new discovery called Gold Lake on Feather River...the lake was believed to have at least a ship load of gold in it." Fortunately, he learned of the hoax before traveling all the way to the Feather River (Manly 1894, 396–97).

FIGURE 54. Washing gold in California. Hand-tinted lithograph, 1853. From Brownell 1853, 608.

said to yield from $32.00 to $200.00. Six of our Company have packed the mules and gone in search of the hidden treasure....

June 26, Men returned from their Search after "gold lake." The lake could not be found but "Nelson Creek" was found and three claims made.[27] On the bank opposite upper claim, [they] took out in an hour or two over one hundred dollars in very coarse gold—nuggets.

June 27, Some of our Company preparing to leave for Nelson's Creek tomorrow, which will leave but 11 at this bar.

July 1, Thermometer 115°.

July 4, Worked on Bensley Bar today, raising dam. Some of the boys on opposite side went up to the Fairfield Bar to attend a celebration. Did not find an extra dinner as in the States.

We turned the water in our new race yesterday and will commence our dam tomorrow. Weather still warm—100°. I worked with a long drill nearly all day

27. Nelson Creek drains into the Middle Fork of the Feather River. The diggings were highly profitable: "Four men took out sixty-one ounces in one day.... [But] the riches were soon exhausted" (Gudde 1975, 236–37; Map, Goddard 1857).

yesterday, with the view of blasting a large granite rock in our new race. Two of us alternate with drill. While one drills, the other slides off the rock into the water, cools off, and comes up on the opposite side and takes the drill.

July 7, Sunday. Yesterday and the day before, we worked on our dam, making good headway against the current....

July 27, Was down at Bidwell's Bar yesterday. Saw many long faces on account of the failure of so many "bars..."

August 13, As yet very little gold taken out of the river bed....

August 20, Prospects for working out our river bed claim this year poor. Have concluded to sell out and try city life.

August 25, Capt. Sampson, Carnes, and myself wound up our connection with Union Bar Company today and make our first step toward *home.*

September 6, Left Feather River in August in Company with Capt. Sampson and Wm. B. Lorton and came to this city [Sacramento], where I have been loafing until a few days ago, when I went in partnership with Dr. Greenman of Illinois, practicing medicine and merchandizing in a small way. Selling pies and other necessaries of life. Must do something to live....[28]

On September 15, letters from home enticed Captain Sampson to return east, and Dr. Parke decided to go with him. The doctor sailed for Nicaragua in a schooner on September 20, 1850. On several occasions Parke mentions New Yorkers going home at the same time, but he supplies no names.

According to Lorton's obituary in the *New York Times* on March 26, 1892, Lorton remained in California until he returned to New York City in 1853 or 1854 "with a handsome fortune." But we are left with a feeling of incompleteness, a lack of closure, by not having his final notebooks and by the loss of the book manuscript he was preparing for publication at the end of his life. Nevertheless, Lorton's description of his journey across the country has been enthralling.

28. The 1850 California census in Sacramento records a "Wm B Lorden," age 22, from New York; occupation, house painter. Our Lorton turned 22 on June 29, 1850.

CHAPTER 13

Afterword

There were few, a very few, born writers of journals,
like William B. Lorton, who set down for us history of the most direct
and transparent kind, accounts of their experiences so personally
detailed yet so piercingly general that none who read them can ever forget.

—Dale Morgan

William Birdsall Lorton returned to New York after about four years in the Golden State. About 1853 he may have taken a ship from San Francisco to Panama, where he would have crossed the isthmus, then taken another ship to New York City.

Lorton was listed in the New York City Directories for 1854 as a manufacturer and wholesaler of clocks at numbers 3 and 15 Dutch Street (Palmer 1950, 234). A couple years later he had a thriving clock business at 1 Cortlandt Street (one door from Broadway). This was a prime commercial location in today's World Trade Center district, two blocks east of the National September 11 Memorial. This business was successful for almost 20 years (Davis 2017, 493).

He was granted a patent, number 641, for a design of a cast-iron, cathedral-design, mantel clock front on April 25, 1854, and another patent, number 700, dated May 1, 1855, for an ornate cast-iron clock front. The latter patent included a drawing and a three-page description of the shape, crest, cornice, various scrolls, and other embellishments used in the design (Davis 1917, 494; Report, Commissioner of Patents 1855, 102; Frazer 1855, 384). He was awarded additional design patents in following years. Lorton's mantel clocks stand about 23 inches tall, and the ornate 1855 design is deep enough on the sides to allow the clock to be self-supporting. Many are elaborately painted. His table clocks are about 11 inches tall with faces equally detailed in decoration, some painted, some not. After 165 years his clocks are still desirable collectibles.

Lorton's obituary in the *New-York Daily Tribune* said that as "a young man he was engaged in the clock business," but there is no mention of this trade in his

FIGURE 55. William B. Lorton's cathedral-design, iron-front mantle clock. He received patents for several of his iron-front designs. Courtesy of Burchard Galleries, St. Petersburg, Florida.

California Journals—only his ability as a house painter. He gives no hint where he learned metal casting and the art of designing metal-front clocks.

In 1857 Lorton's name was proposed, and he was unanimously elected, to become a private in the 7th Regiment, Company A of the New York State Militia. Called the "Silk Stocking" regiment early on, it became a Union Army infantry regiment during the Civil War, when it was known as the "Blue-Bloods" because many of the men were part of New York City's social elite. Lorton's dues were one dollar per month (Lorton Certificate 1857; Guide to Records of 7th Regiment). In 1862, however, Lorton's name was dropped from the rolls, apparently for not paying his dues.

That same year Lorton, at age 34, married Mary W. Briggs, age 27, on July 16 (New York City Marriage Notices, 1835–1880). Their first child, Edith, was born August 17, 1863, and their first son was born April 8, 1865, named William Briggs

FIGURE 56. Two of Lorton's ornately painted iron-front mantel clocks from his 1855 patent design. Used with permission. This image was originally published in L. Davis, "Two William B. Lorton 'Iron Front' Clocks Made to His May 1, 1855, Patent Design." Nov/Dec 2017, *Watch & Clock Bulletin*, a journal of the National Association of Watch & Clock Collectors, Inc.

in honor of Mary's father, William D. Briggs, a jeweler in the city. Baby William, "aged 6 months and 6 days," died of "congestion of the brain" on October 14, 1865, according to the *New York Times*, October 17, 1865. The Lortons lived at 318 Lexington Avenue in Manhattan's Upper East Side at that time, just a couple blocks from Central Park.[1]

Ten days later, on October 24, 1865, Lorton signed the papers to purchase a beautiful house and grounds on seven acres just south of the village of Hastings-Upon-Hudson for $25,000—"only five minute walk from the [commuter train] depot" (Lorton [1874], 1). He put $10,000 down and had a mortgage for the remainder (Lorton 1865, 209). Based on an online inflation calculator, were Lorton to buy the property today it would cost about $4.27 million, and the down payment would be $1.7 million, presumably in cash. Had Lorton made a bigger pile in California than we realized? Did his clock business become extremely

1. Most genealogy references record William Briggs Lorton's birth year as 1855 and dying October 4, 1865. This places the birth before the Lortons' marriage in 1862 and belies the *Times'* comment "infant son of William B. and Mary W. Lorton, aged 6 months and 6 days."

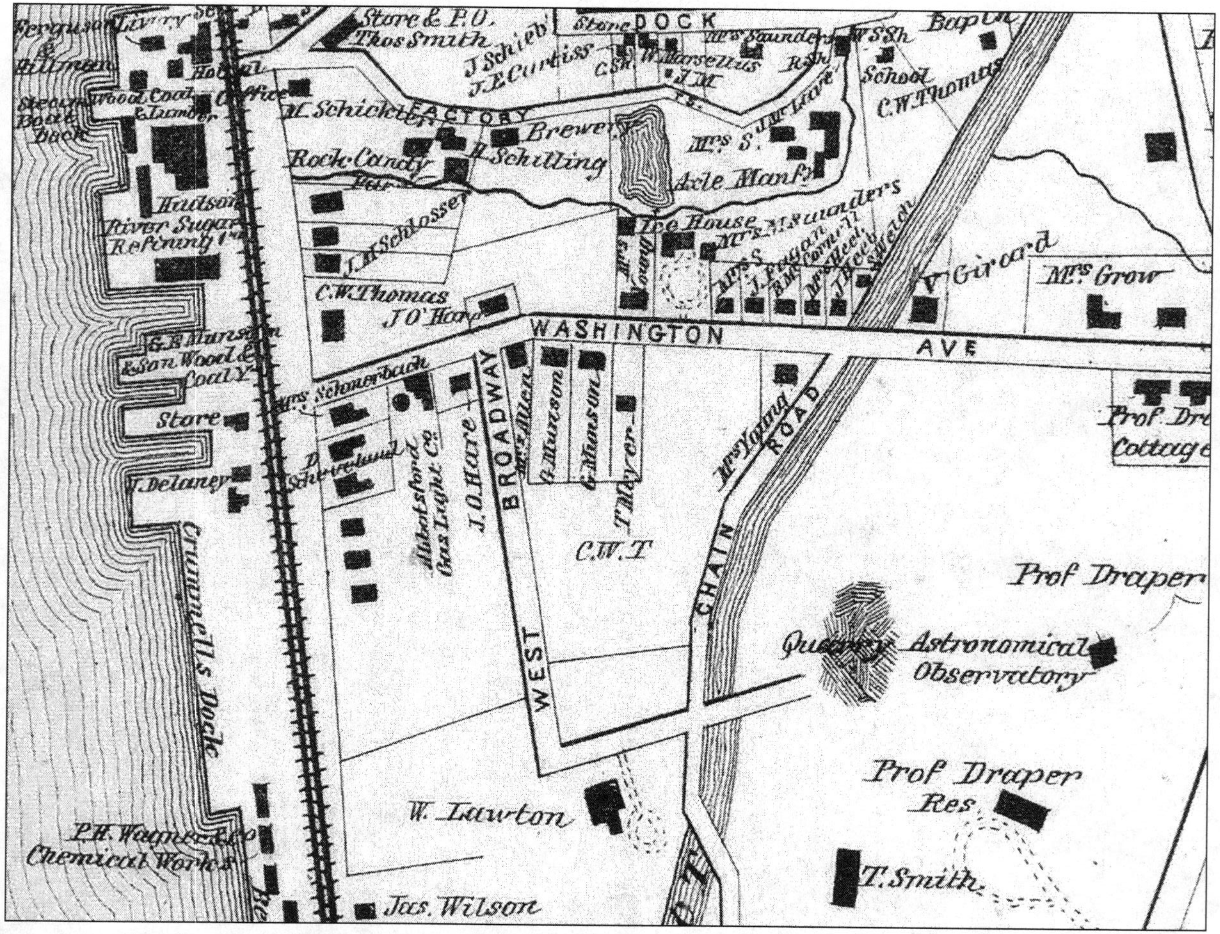

Map 10. Detail, Beer's 1868 map of Hastings-Upon-Hudson showing Lorton's seven acres (mislabeled as "W. Lawton"). West Broadway is now Warburton Avenue. Hudson River on left. Courtesy of David Rumsey Historical Map Collection.

lucrative? Did Mary Briggs Lorton bring money into the family or have access to family money? We don't know.

Lorton's detailed, handwritten description of the property in 1874 said it comprised about seven acres that extended down to the Hudson River. The house had a 165-foot veranda and was built of solid blocks of white marble with a tower in one corner. The carriage house with a stable was also built of white marble. There had been a quarry of white dolomite marble on the original 50-acre property, and quarrying was the leading industry in the area for many years.

The house was built for year-round living, with modern improvements such as bathrooms, hot and cold water, water closets, speaking tubes, bells, and more. "The dwelling is large and commodious & is elegantly painted, grained, & decorated throughout.... [T]he dining room, halls etc. are elaborately paneled in oak, walnut and satin [finished] woods." The parlor and hall are "grand and stately in the extreme" and "all the hinges on this floor are plated silver." There was a "fruit room & milk room and sufficient closet & pantry room to accommodate any family.... The Land is beautifully laid out in Lawn, Flower garden, Vinyard, Vegetable garden—The Grounds are terraced and are of singular and rare beauty." The woods had three or four hundred trees. The stable and a "little cottage, which is a gem of its own kind" were also built of marble from the quarry (Lorton [1874], 1–3).

In the early 1830s, George Harvey (1801–1878), a famous English landscape painter, bought 50 acres just south of Hastings village and built a stone cottage of white marble from the quarry on his property in 1834. Later owners built a second, larger home of the same style, embellishing it with a square, white marble tower and a ballroom on the second floor. This large house ultimately became the Lortons' home.

By the 20th century, other homes and commercial establishments crowded the old house. In the 1940s, the owner described the kitchen as being 19-by-23 feet. A marble driveway led to the ballroom that "had beautiful plaster scrollwork. A winding staircase led to the small tower room, which had two by two-foot windows" (Hastings Historical Society July 2019, pers. comm.). The square tower, also built of white marble, caused the mansion to be called "The Castle" during the 1900s.

Had the Lortons planned to move to Hastings-Upon-Hudson as a wonderful place to rear their children in a serene and comfortable setting? It did become a beautiful place for Mary to rest and recover after the death of their first son.

A second son, Claude A., was born in Hastings-Upon-Hudson on May 25, 1868. Claude unfortunately died April 18, 1871, shortly before his third birthday. He was buried next to his older brother in Green-wood Cemetery, Brooklyn,

FIGURE 57. Detail. The Castle that had been on today's Warburton Avenue in Hastings-Upon-Hudson was constructed of white marble quarried on the original property. 1924 photo. It was probably the Lorton family home from late 1865 until 1874. The view west includes what had been the front of the house in the 1800s, based on the Beers 1868 map, and became the back of the house in the 1900s. The Hudson River cliffs are in the distance. The house was demolished in 1963. Photograph courtesy of the Hastings Historical Society, Westchester County, NY.

a Revolutionary War site.[2] The Lortons' final child, Bella Louise, was born the following year, July 25, 1872, also in Hastings.

Trow's New York City Directory for 1867–1869 lists Lorton's work address still at 1 Courtlandt and his home address as Hastings. But there is no listing for Lorton's clock business in 1872, and it did not survive the big financial crash of 1873. In 1874, after the crash, Lorton put his "elegant property" in Hastings on the market. To part with such a lovely home must have been very difficult after losing his business. Two of his children were born and one died there. The Hine, Cole & Gray Real Estate and Auctioneering Company offered Lorton $16,000 for this beautiful property in early 1874.

In 1963 The Castle was considered structurally unsound and demolished. The site today includes a vest-pocket park between 408 and 414 Warburton Ave-

2. Mary W. Lorton (née Briggs), was buried next to her sons in lot 5066, section 80, Green-Wood Cemetery in Brooklyn on November 10, 1917 (www.green-wood.com/burial_search/). This appears to be the Briggs family plot.

nue (earlier called West Broadway). The 1868 and 1872 Beers maps show the location of the property and the house, but Beers labeled the owner "W. Lawton."

The New York City Directory lists Lorton as a painter, probably a house painter, in 1882. Seven years later he is listed as having a sewing machine business in the 200 block of East Houston Street, about a 10-minute walk from his home at 43 St. Marks Place in the East Village, Manhattan. During this time he started work on a book about his travels to California and his stay in the goldfields based on his journals (see below). What a book that would have been! With Lorton's gift for writing, and his honed sketching skills for illustrations, he would have presented a vivid account.

William B. Lorton died March 24, 1892, at age 63. Taped inside the front cover of his first California Journal is his obituary, clipped from the *New-York Daily Tribune*. It provides brief information on his later life and intended use for his California Journal. His obituary in the *New York Times* provides the following information in addition to that in the *Tribune*: it says Lorton died from asthma, he returned from California with a handsome fortune, he started in the clock business at 1 Cortlandt Street, and he was in business for nearly 20 years before unfortunate business ventures caused reverses. The *New-York Daily Tribune* obituary, published March 26, 1892, said:

> William B. Lorton died suddenly from heart disease on Thursday night [March 24] at 11 o'clock at No. 43 St. Mark's Place. He was born in Peakskill in 1828. His birthplace joined that of Chauncey M. Depew.[3] When a baby he was brought to New-York and was educated in the city schools here. When a young man he was engaged in the clock business. In 1849 Mr. Lorton went West and remained in the gold fields for several years. He returned to this city in 1854 and at the time of his death was engaged in the sewing machine business at No. 276 East Houston St. The grandfather of the dead man was a property holder under the Trinity Church grants and owned the property where Clinton Market now stands and also that occupied by the piers the Pacific Mail steamers used.
>
> During the last years of his life Mr. Lorton had been engaged in preparing his "history of '49." The work was not completed, although he had hoped soon to publish it. The work would have contained the personal experiences of the writer on his trip across the plains and his stay in the mining region.
>
> Mr. Lorton was an old member of the 7th Regiment and in 1862 he went out with the militia to suppress the draft riots. He leaves a widow and two children.

3. Chauncey Mitchell Depew was president of the New York Central Railroad System and a U.S. senator from New York, 1899–1911.

APPENDIX A

Constitution, By-Laws, and Roster: Knox County Company, Illinois

An article published May 30, 1849, in the *Kanesville (IA) Frontier Guardian* includes the constitution, by-laws, and membership roster of the Knox County Company, Illinois. The constitution and by-laws were written May 12 while still in northwestern Missouri, heading north to Kanesville, Iowa. The first membership roster was signed May 16 (Lorton, May 16, 1849). At that time, most of the men were from Knox and surrounding counties in western Illinois, hence the name of the company. The membership roster published by the *Frontier Guardian* includes additional groups that joined at Kanesville, which doubled the original membership. Women and children were not listed.[1]

Names with a star (*) indicate men who turned west at Mount Misery (west of today's Enterprise, Utah) and entered Frémont's "unexplored" country—the deserts of Nevada and California. They crossed Death Valley and were later called the Death Valley Jayhawkers. Twenty-four of them are listed in the Knox County Company roster.[2]

Constitution and By-Laws of the Knox County Company, Illinois[3]

For a more perfect organization of the above named Company, we mutually bind ourselves to observe in the strictest manner the following Constitution and By-Laws:

ART. 1. The officers of this company shall consist of one Captain, one Lieutenant, four Sergeants and one Clerk. To hold their offices until the arrival of the company at its destination, to be elected by ballot, by a vote of a majority of the company.

ART. 2. It shall be the duty of the Captain to take the command of the company and direct its movements — determine the number of men to be detailed on

1. "Constitution and By Laws" (*Kanesville [IA] Frontier Guardian*, May 30, 1849).
2. Thirty-six was the number most often used, but this number varied from year to year.
3. Carl I. Wheat was the first to find this news item in the *Frontier Guardian*, and he published it with a short introduction (Wheat 1940, 103–8; see also Arms in Cumming 1985, 137–42; Rasmussen 1994, 64–65). We use the *Guardian* copy.

guard — direct as to the time of turning out — herding and yoking cattle, and see that all the provisions of the constitution are strictly complied with.

ART. 3. It shall be the duty of the Lieutenant to perform the duties of the Captain, in case of his absence or inability.

ART. 4. It shall be the duty of the 1st Sergeant to keep an alphabetical roll — call the same each morning, and detail the guard and sergeant of the guard for the following night.

ART. 5. It shall be the duty of the clerk to prepare a roll of the company for the First Sergeant and record the proceedings of the company.

ART. 6. A committee of three shall be elected whose duty it shall be to inspect all the teams, waggons and outfits of the company before leaving the Missouri river, and none shall be permitted to start with the company unless found sufficient in these respects. It shall also be their duty to report to the captain any abuse or mismanagement of teams while on the route.

ART. 7. No one shall be considered a member of this company until his name is signed to this Constitution and code of By-Laws.

ART. 8. Other persons may become members of this company by a vote of a majority of the same, and signing the Constitution and By-Laws.

ART. 9. This Constitution and By-Laws may be altered or others substituted in their place by a vote of two-thirds of the company.

By-Laws

ART. 1. No fire-arms shall be discharged within forty rods of camp, except under the directions of the sergeant of the guard.

ART. 2. No loaded guns with caps on shall be permitted in camp except by the directions of the Captain, and never in wagons while traveling.

[*ART. 3. None printed.*]

ART. 4. No spirituous liquors shall be used in the company except as a medicine.

ART. 5. The Captain may call a meeting of the company at any time — and it shall be his duty to do so upon the request of five members of the company.

ART. 6. A horse shall be furnished for the use of the guide by the company — to be ultimately disposed of for the benefit of the company.

ART. 7 For the first wilful violation of any of the provisions of the above Constitution and By-Laws by any member of the company, he shall perform extra duty in the discretion of the Captain. For repetition of the same offence — for refusal to obey orders or Intoxication, any person may be expelled from the company by a vote of majority of the same.

ART. 8. Any person selling or giving spirituous liquors to an Indian shall be expelled from the company.

Names[4]

J. L[eander] Woolsey, Knox [County], Ill.*
Nath. Hurlbut, do [ditto]
J. Grooscup [John Groscup], do*
Ubin [Urban] P. Davison, do*
Oren [Orrin] Clark, do *
H[arrison] B. Frans, do*
C[harles] B. Mecum, do*
J[ohn] B. Colton, do*
M[arshall] P. Edgerton, do*
N. D. [John?] Morse, do*
J[ames] E[llery] Hale, do
A[lonzo] C. Clay, do*
John Cole, do*
J. W[ilson] Semple, do
Alex[ander] Ewing, do
R[obert] C. Price, do
E. N[orman] Taylor, do[5]
L. D. Montgomery, do
Cephas Arms, do
John H. [C.?] Ewing, do
Edw. McGowan, do
Asa Haynes, do*
J[ohn] W. Plummer, do*
George Allen, do*
Thos. McGrew do*
John L. West, do*
Edward Doty, do*
Bruen Byram, do*
W[illiam] B. Rude, do*
Aaron Larkin, do*
Alex. Palmer, do*
Thos. [Thomas] Shannon, do*
Robert Kimble, do
H[enry] J. Ward, Warren [Co.], Ill.[6]
Jno. D. Thompson, do
J. Mackey, do
F[rederick] S[axton] Kellogg, Peoria [Co.], Ill.[7]
L[uzerne] Bartholomew, do[8]
[Edward] F. Bartholomew, do*[9]
Edw. Kellogg, do
Wm. Kellogg, do
Wm. B. Lorton, N.Y. City
S[idney] P. Edgerton, Galesburgh [Ill.]*

4. The starred (*) names are men who went west from Mount Misery in southwest Utah and crossed Death Valley. All of these men reached the California coast and are referred to as the Death Valley Jayhawkers of '49.
5. With Mr. Taylor were his wife and young son.
6. Henry Ward had been married to Edward Kellogg's daughter, Esther Jane, in 1845. She died in 1847. Henry was in Lorton's mess along with Edward Kellogg; Edward's grown son, William; and Edward's cousin, Frederick S. Kellogg.
7. Frederick Saxton Kellogg (1810–1885) was 39 when he went to California. He married Martha Rice Bartholomew in 1838, another Kellogg-Bartholomew marriage.
8. Luzerne (1812–1865) and Edward (1828–1891) Bartholomew were brothers. Death Valley literature is cluttered with faulty information professing the two Bartholomews were father and son or possibly father and two sons (De Laney, 1908, 101; Ellenbecker 1938, 88, 99; Rasmussen 1994, 65). The family genealogical record mentions the brothers went to California in 1849 but makes no mention of the father doing so (Bartholomew 1885, 211–12, 319–20, 321–22).
9. Upon return from California, Edward Bartholomew married Edward Kellogg's youngest daughter, Cordelia. (Edward Kellogg was Lorton's mess-mate to Salt Lake City.) And just to keep it in the family, Noyes Ellsworth Bartholomew, Edward's older brother (named for his father), married Cordelia's twin, Cornelia Kellogg.

D. C. Norton, Knox [Co.], Ill.[10]
J. R. Parker, Fulton [Co.], Ill.
Jacob Grimm, do
J. B. Anderson, do
S. Wise, do
Theodore Ingersol, do
John Chatterton, do
John Lawrence, do
F. B. Shannon, do
H. D. Walker, do
R. Cunningham, do
Orville Jones, do
James Dunn, do
Wm. Whaley, do
J. B. V. Wallace, do
John Short, do
Otho Berkshire, do
R. Baldwin, Erie Co., Pa.
H. Surmeier, Adams [Co.], Ill.
J. B. Surmeier, do
John Lake, do
F. Muer, do
John A. Roth, do
Fred Ketzler, do
John Spees, do
J. D. Campbell, Washington County, Iowa
D. L. Fidler, do
Peter Buck, do
J. H. Cooper, do
Alex Sandilan, do
Geo. W. Buck, do
J. Hasbrook, Rock Island, [Ill.]
S. Shelhammer, do
John Herald, do
Wm. Petre [Petrie?], do
C. W. Miller, Mercer [Co.], Ill.
John Evans, do
L[artes]. F. Langford, do
Thos. Gordon, do
James Merrifield, do
James H. Ellis,
Joseph Ellis,
A. Barton,
Henry Baxter, Capt., Fa[y]ette Rovers of Jonesville, Mich.
G. W. Halsted, Lieut. [of the Rovers] do
H[irman] W. Platt, Sec'y. [of the Rovers] do[11]
J[ohn]. S. Lewis, Treas. [of the Rovers] do
C[alvin] R. Ralph, do
Adonijah S. Welch, do
[Gustavus] C. Cooley, do
A. J. Baker, do
Ira Latham, do
A[mbrose] M. Dibble, do
Andrew Hartman, do
J. F. Underdonk, M.D., do
P. P. Acker, Kalamazoo, Michigan
G. A. Gale, do
C. L. Cobb, do
Henry Gregory, do
Robert Taylor, Knox [Co.], Ill.
Ira Wells, (surgeon of the company,) Rock Island Co., Ill.[12]
Luke Wells, do
Alex Wells, do

10. The names below this point appear to be those who joined the Knox County train at Kanesville.

11. First names with brackets [ ] come from Rasmussen 1994, 58. The Rovers had been in Kanesville for at least a week before they joined the Knox County Company on May 22, 1849.

12. Ira Wells and his cousins Luke and Alex left the wagon train May 28, after crossing the Elkhorn River a few miles west of the Missouri River. Lorton mentions Wells more than once in his journal.

At a meeting of the Company on the 12th of May, — this Constitution and code of By-Law were adopted and the following persons elected under it, as provided by the Constitution, viz: Asa Haynes, Captain — Cephas Arms, Lieutenant — Thomas Shannon, First Sergeant — Edward Doty, E. N. Taylor and Charles B. Mecum, second, third and fourth sergeants — H. C. Price, Clerk. Committee of Inspection — J. L. West, F. S. Kellogg, and J. R. Parker.

APPENDIX B

The San Joaquin Company's Disastrous Detour into the Escalante Desert

On October 18, 1849, the San Joaquin Company, guided by Capt. Jefferson Hunt, arrived at the Beaver River in central Utah, where Addison Pratt wrote: "A range of mountains [the Black Mountains] separates us from Little Salt Lake [valley], and as we came onto this creek, we saw some of those wagons that had gone ahead of us, high up the mountains. To avoid this mountain, some pioneers were sent out [west] to search a pass through a canion on this creek into a valley below [Escalante Desert]" (Pratt 1990, 383).

The wagons Pratt saw were the last segment of the Independent Pioneer Company, which was ahead of San Joaquin Company. Hunt had been over this route to southern California and back. In November 1847 he left Salt Lake City with 18 other packers, including Orrin Porter Rockwell. While in the Los Angeles area the men purchased 200 milk cows, some horses and mules, wheat and vegetable seeds, and fruit tree cuttings, then returned to Salt Lake City (without Rockwell) "about the 23 of May," 1848 (Sutak 2012, 241, 261; Riser in Bigler and Bagley 2000, 395).

From Los Angeles, Rockwell agreed to guide a party of Mormon Battalion veterans to Salt Lake City via the route the packers had blazed a few months before. In the party were between "23 persons" and "25 soles" that included the Davis family. The veterans drove a herd of "135 mules and horses" with them (Boyle in Bigler and Bagley 2000, 397, 399). Captain Davis; his wife, Susan, and their son, Daniel Jr., rode in a light wagon or buggy. This is the first-known wagon to roll northeastward over the Old Spanish Trail, thence northward to Salt Lake City on what became known as the Southern Route.

In the vicinity of today's Cedar City, Utah, Rockwell's party approached the formidable barrier of the Black Mountains north of today's Cedar Valley. To avoid the grueling Indian/pack trail over the mountain, they sought an alternate route. Captain Davis, as a U.S. Army captain, may have seen or procured a copy of Frémont's 1845 map of his 1844 expedition. On it is labeled "St Joseph's Spr.," near today's Enoch, and "[Little] Salt Lake," in today's Parowan Valley. Beaver River is drawn north of the unlabeled Black Mountains. Based on Frémont's 1845 map, if the party went northwest from St. Joseph's Spring[s] they could intersect Beaver River and avoid taking a wagon over the Black Mountains.

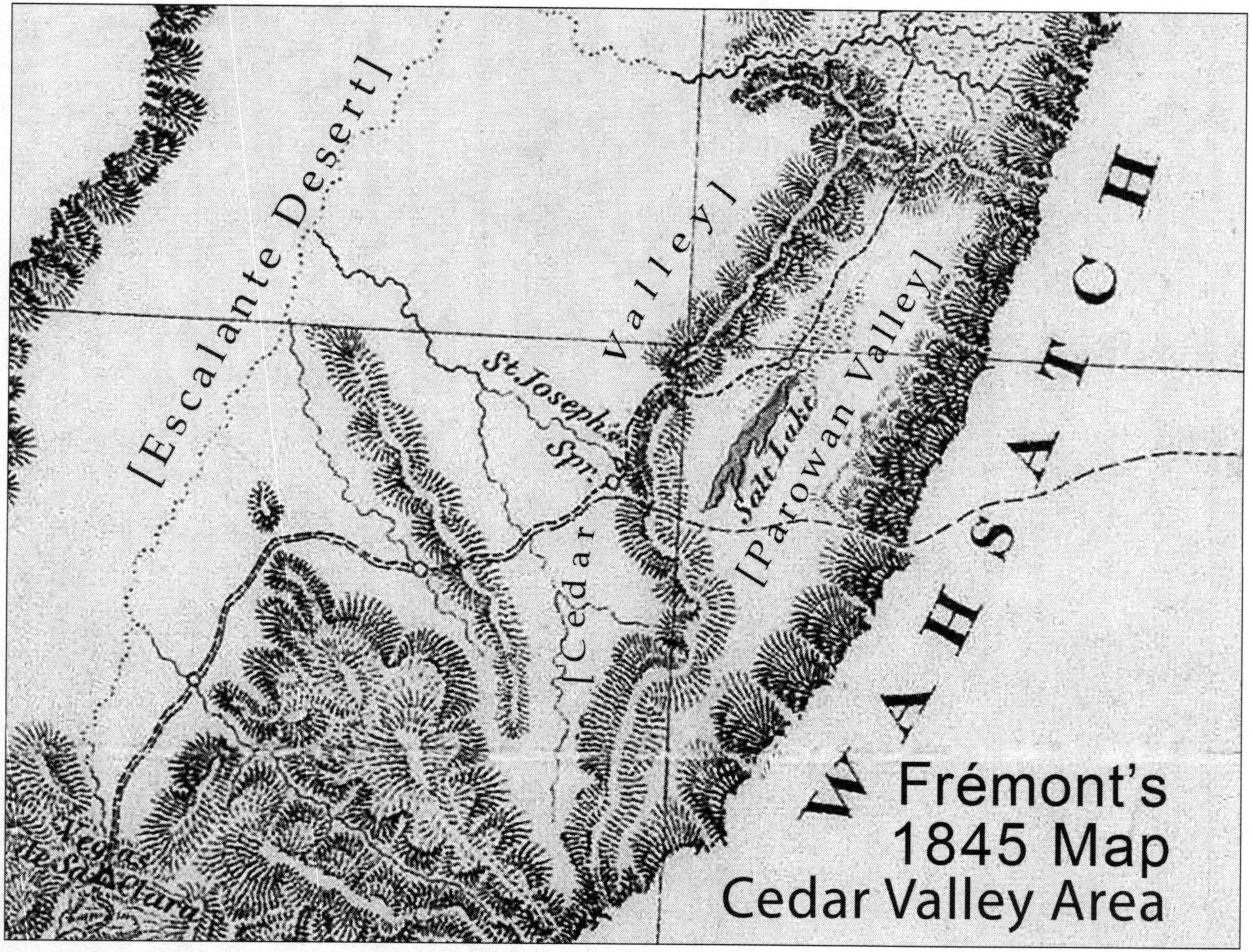

MAP 11. Detail, Cedar Valley, Utah, area of Frémont's 1845 "Map of an Exploring Expedition to the Rocky Mountains in the Year 1842, Oregon & North California in the Years 1843-44. By Brevet Capt. J. C. Frémont of the Corps of Topographical Engineers." Courtesy of David Rumsey Historical Map Collection.

This scenario is supported by a cryptic description of their route in the Mormon Church's *Journal History* (June 5, 1848): "[Rockwell's trail] followed the old Spanish Trail from Williams' Ranch (San Bernardino), through Cajon Pass, across the Mohave Desert to Las Vegas, *up the Muddy Valley and across the Escalante Desert to Beaver Creek*... [thence] to Great Salt Lake City" (emphasis ours).[1]

The "Muddy" or "Near Muddy" Creek of yore is today's Cole Creek, which once debouched into Cedar Valley to create a large quagmire. The Old Spanish Trail passed over this marshy area, but a wagon could not do so. Rockwell had to lead his party either south or north around this part of the valley to access the copious springs just north of today's Enoch.

North of the springs about six miles is Rush Lake, now dry, at the foot of the Black Mountains. Again based on Frémont's 1845 map, to gain the Beaver River the party would have traveled north in Cedar Valley to Rush Lake and followed the complacent Mud Spring Canyon northwest about 12 miles to Mud Spring at a dip in the rim of Cedar Valley. From here they could look west into the Escalante Desert.

A statement by John J. Riser, a member of the party, confuses the issue, however. In 1887, at age 63, he wrote or dictated his autobiography and said of the trip: "Passing up the Utah Basin from the Santa Clara River, and through little Salt Lakevalley.... We arrived in Salt Lake City... on the 5th of June 1848" (Riser in Bigler and Bagley 2000, 397–98). Had the party gone to Little Salt Lake they would have been forced to cross the Black Mountains, placing them many miles from the Escalante Desert. This route is in direct contradiction to the Mormon Church's *Journal History*. We contend Riser affixed the well-known name of "Little Salt Lake" onto the unknown and unnamed Rush Lake in Cedar Valley to describe the general location of this part of his long journey.

From Mud Spring there was likely a well-beaten Indian trail onto Mud Spring Bench, which parallels the 5,200-foot contour around the west end of the Black Mountains toward present-day Minersville, where they struck the Beaver River. They then traveled eastward to Rockwell's 1847 trail from Salt Lake City.

Jefferson Hunt had heard about Rockwell's route with a wagon, and he wanted to retrace it around the Black Mountains to eliminate the grueling steep and rocky grade over them—a major accomplishment in fulfilling Brigham Young's dream to establish an all-weather commerce and migration road to seaports at San Diego and San Pedro.

1. The *Journal History* does not say this was Porter Rockwell's route but by inference both we and Steven Heath conclude it is. The journal gives no information whence this information came. For an in-depth analysis of this route, see Johnson and Johnson 2014; cf. Heath 1995.

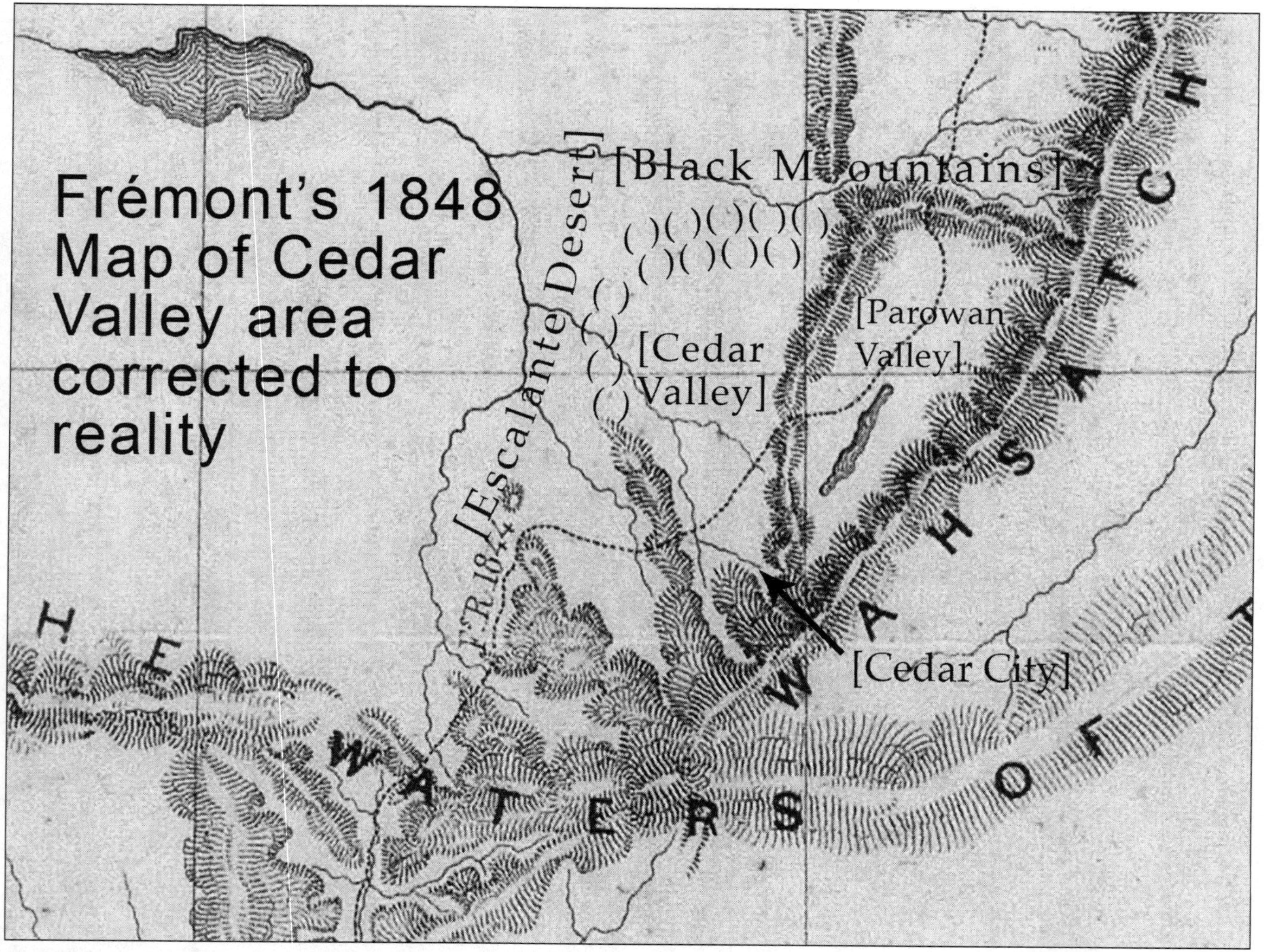

Map 12. Detail, Cedar Valley area of Frémont's 1848 map. Parentheses represent topography missing from Frémont's map—the western Black Mountains, and Mud Spring and Bald Hills, which connect with the hills of The Three Peaks to enclose Cedar Valley. Lake in upper left is mythical. "FR 1844" is Frémont's 1844 route along the Old Spanish Trail. Red Hills separate Parowan and Cedar Valleys. Courtesy of David Rumsey Historical Map Collection.

While the San Joaquin Company baited their livestock along the Beaver River, in late October 1849, scouts checked out the rough road the Independent Pioneer Company had broken over the Black Mountains into Parowan Valley (Little Salt Lake valley) where it connected with the Old Spanish Trail. Welch (in Ressler, 266, October 20) recorded: "The cañon which was explored yesterday was found to be possible to wagon[s] though rather rough." At the council meeting the same day, Captain Hunt said by going over the mountain they would "be obliged to camp one night without water." Hearing "these facts led the Council to decide that another gorge lying west of south west leading out of the Beaver Creek Valley" might be a possible route around instead of over the mountain (ibid.).

Adonijah Welch, James Martin, and David Switzer volunteered to ride down the river to see if wagons could make it through the gorge just east of today's community of Minersville. From an elevation they "took a view of the valley [Escalante Desert] into which the pass opened." Welch added, they found the route presented "no difficulty for wagons" as far as they could see (Ibid.).

Next day, October 21, Hunt told the council that once they got to the west end of the mountains, they "could strike the Spanish trail by taking down [south] the valley beyond and that *plenty of water would be found on the road* from the fact that Little Muddy River runs across its further extremity" (Welch in Ressler 1964, 266–67, October 21, emphasis ours). Hunt was describing the copious springs along the eastern edge of Cedar Valley and today's Coal Creek, which runs through today's Cedar City. Based on information from the scouts and what Hunt told them about water, plus what they could clearly see on Frémont's 1848 map, the wagons rolled west down Beaver River, camped near today's Minersville, and on October 21 rolled southwest into the Escalante Desert.

While men were out scouting routes on October 19 and 20, Hunt and the other men did the logical thing: they studied Frémont's 1848 map based on his exploratory route of 1844. Whereas Rockwell's group may have used the far less detailed 1845 map, copies of the 1848 map had been printed before January 28, 1849, with plenty of time for gold seekers to purchase them (Benton 1970, 16). This is the map the emigrants used. However, Hunt and the emigrants did not realize Frémont's 1848 map not only included direct observations of the country he traveled, but also was fraught with erroneous assumptions about the country his expedition could not see. Carl I. Wheat noted:

> [The 1848 map was] the single case in which Frémont and [his cartographer Charles] Preuss failed to follow their standard course of showing cartographically only the geography actually seen by them.... On their 1848 Map...Preuss shows two east-west, wholly non-existent mountain ranges.... It was the southerly of these two spurious ranges of mountains

that led the gold seekers who discovered Death Valley late in 1849 to adopt their tragic "cut-off to the diggings" (Wheat 1956, 14)[2]

Use of Frémont's 1848 map also led to the dreadful suffering endured by the Smith packers and the emigrant packers who followed them and to the probable deaths of nine of those packers now called the Pinney-Savage group.

Two incorrect assumptions depicted on Frémont's 1848 map deceived Hunt and the emigrants and drew them into the disastrous Escalante Desert debacle. One was the great distance (18 miles) the Black Mountains extend westward beyond its juncture with the Mineral Mountains (at the Minersville Canyon). The other misleading aspect was not depicting the hills that enclose Cedar Valley on the west. The Mud Spring Hills join the Bald Hills that overlap The Three Peaks Hills to create the western border for Cedar Valley, which separates it from the Escalante Desert. This division is not depicted on either of Frémont's maps.

According to Hunt's assertion about finding water, seemingly verified by Frémont's map, all the emigrants needed to do to find plentiful water was to follow the Beaver River west through the gorge just east of today's Minersville, turn southwest, keeping the Black Mountains on their left, and they would come into Cedar Valley.

On October 22 Hunt and Henry Baxter scouted ahead for water in what they thought was Cedar Valley but in reality was the almost waterless Escalante Desert. Not finding any water, Hunt sent Baxter back with word to make camp (Welch's "Dry Diggins") while Hunt continued to search southward far into the night. Addison Pratt (1990, 383), who traveled with a wagon that had a roadometer, said they "went 12 miles into the dry plains and camped without water."

Welch explained the terrain and summarized the crux of the Escalante Desert debacle when he wrote: "There was a small valley [Cedar Valley] between that of the L. S. L. [Little Salt Lake, Parowan Valley] and the Valley of Errors [Escalante Desert]. This fact explained the mistake made by our guide who had intended to enter the valley [Cedar Valley] contiguous to that of L S L" (in Ressler 1964, 269, October 27). Lorton also reflected on the Escalante debacle as he looked north into the desert from Antelope Springs. "We see the bute [Table Butte] to the south [of where we camped] in retreat valley, or the dry encampment. We now see our folly & see that in 25 or 30 miles [by continuing on south]

2. Frémont's 1845 map shows his exploratory route, but it is lacking the cartographic blunders depicted on his 1848 map. A note on the David Rumsey Historical Map Collection information panel says about the 1845 map: "Fremont and Preuss mapped only what they saw along their routes, leaving large areas blank." This 1845 map does, however, annotate "St. Joseph's Spr." near today's Enoch in the southeast part of Cedar Valley. The 1848 map does not show any of the several large springs in this area. The lack of using "St. Joseph's Spr." in emigrant diaries attests to the emigrants using Frémont's 1848 map, not his 1845 map.

we could have reached water [at Antelope Springs]. Our present valley, on a/c of its size, we will call Wasatch Valley [today's Cedar Valley]. Retreat Valley [Escalante Desert] only separated [from it] by a mountain spur" (November 2).

Back in the Escalante Desert, several events occurred on October 23 while Hunt and scouts were again looking for water: (1) a couple wagons were sent from Dry Diggins to Beaver River to bring back water; (2) many of the cattle were driven back to Beaver River from Dry Diggins for water and some forage (near today's Minersville); (3) all of Captain Thomas M. Marshall's division went back to the river; (4) the Mormon packers, whose leader was James Flake, arrived and set up camp on the river; (5) the O. K. Smith packers also camped on the river (they carried with them the Barney Ward cutoff map); and (6) Lorton took Mazeppa back to the river for water and forage.

Also on the 23rd, Hunt left Dry Diggins with Peter P. Acker, James D. Martin, G. Wiley Webster, and David Switzer on another scouting trip, but again they did not find water. Welch said they decided "one man should return to camp with Capt Hunt while the others should go forward with the two horses." They were far enough south on this scouting trip that Hunt recognized, from his pack trips in 1847–1848, the distinctive Table Butte farther to the south, with Antelope Springs six miles beyond it on the Old Spanish Trail. Hunt and Acker turned north and "walked nearly all night & entered the corrall [at Dry Diggins] by 9 this morning in a state of extreme exhaustion" on October 24 (Welch in Ressler 1964, 268).

Later on the 24th, all the wagons and stock at Dry Diggins returned to the Beaver River, vacating the Escalante Desert—Lorton's "Retreat Valley" and Welch's "Valley of Errors."

Why didn't the scouting parties find some vestige of Rockwell's route? We surmise the Rockwell group stayed high on the slopes of Mud Spring Bench that curve around the mountain below the rough mountain canyons and above the soft soil of the Escalante Desert floor.

In 1776 the Domínguez-Escalante expedition came up the Beaver River from the Sevier, entered the Escalante Desert near Milford, and successfully exited eastward between the Black Mountains and Mud Spring Hills through Mud Spring Canyon to water and forage in Cedar Valley (Domínguez 1977, 74n300; Auerbach 1941, 120). This route is tucked between the overlapping Mud Spring Hills and Black Mountains. It was the route Rockwell used in reverse—the route Hunt and the explorers did not find.

The San Joaquin Company's digression into the Escalante Desert was the catalyst that precipitated the disintegration of the company. It cast unwarranted doubt on Hunt's leadership, wasted time, and allowed the packers carrying the tantalizing Barney Ward short-cut map to catch up to the train at a time when the emigrants were particularly vulnerable to such an alluring idea.

References

Note: Maps from the online David Rumsey Historical Map Collection are designated DRHMC.

Maps

Map. 1814. Allen, Paul, Nicholas Biddle, William Clark, and Meriwether Lewis. *Map of Lewis and Clark's Track, across the Western Portion of North America.* Philadelphia: Bradford and Inskeep. DRHMC.

———. 1836. U.S. Topographic Bureau. *Map Showing the Lands Assigned to Emigrant Indians West of Arkansas & Missouri.* [Documents concerning Col. Henry Dodge's expedition to the Rocky Mountains.] Serial no. 289. Washington, DC: U.S. Government Printing Office.

———. 1845. Frémont, J. C. *Map of an Exploring Expedition to the Rocky Mountains in the Year 1842, Oregon & North California in the Years 1843–45.* Washington, DC: Blair and Rives. DRHMC.

———. 1845. Tanner, Henry S. *Iowa.* Philadelphia: Carey and Hart. DRHMC.

———. 1846. Frémont, John Charles. *Topographical Map of the Road from Missouri to Oregon.* Map 4, Section 2 in "Map Portfolio" of *The Expeditions of John Charles Frémont,* edited by Donald Jackson and Mary Lee Spence. Urbana: Univ. of Illinois Press, 1970.

———. 1846. Jefferson, T. H. *Map of the Emigrant Road from Independence Mo. to St. Francisco, CA.* Part III. [Map in pocket of Korns and Morgan.]

———. 1846a. Mitchell, Samuel Augustus. *A New Map of Texas, Oregon, and California with the Regions Adjoining.* Pocket Map. Philadelphia: S. August Mitchell. DRHMC.

———. 1846b. Mitchell, Samuel Augustus. *Iowa.* Philadelphia: S. A. Mitchell. DRHMC.

———. 1848. Frémont, John Charles. *Map of Oregon and Upper California: From the Surveys of John Charles Frémont and Other Authorities. Drawn by Charles Preuss under the Order of the Senate of the United States, Washington City 1848.* Map 5 in "Map Portfolio" of *The Expeditions of John Charles Frémont,* edited by Donald Jackson and Mary Lee Spence. Urbana: Univ. of Illinois Press, 1970. DRHMC.

———. 1849. Jefferson, T. H. *Map of the Emigrant Road from Independence Mo. to St. Francisco, California by T. H. Jefferson. Part 3.* Library of Congress website. JPEG2000 (for best resolution).

———. 1849. Mitchell, Samuel Augustus. *A New Map of Texas, Oregon, and California with the Regions Adjoining.* Includes insert of *Map of the Gold and Quicksilver District of California.* Pocket Map. Philadelphia: Thomas Cowperthwait & Co. DRHMC.

———. 1849. Tanner, Henry S. *Map of California New Mexico Texas &c.* Philadelphia: H. S. Tanner. DRHMC.

———. 1851. Henn, Williams & Co. *Township Map of the State of Iowa.* Burlington, IA: Henn, Williams & Co., J. F. Abrahams. DRHMC.

———. 1853. Mitchell, Samuel Augustus. *A New Map of the State of Illinois.* Philadelphia: Thomas, Cowperthwait & Co. DRHMC.

——. 1853. Trask, John B. *Map of the State of California*. San Francisco: Britton & Rey. DRHMC.

——. 1856. Chapman, Silas. *Sectional Map of the State of Iowa*. Milwaukee, WI: Silas Chapman Publisher. DRHMC.

——. 1857. Goddard, George H. *Britton and Rey's Map of the State of California*. San Francisco: Britton & Rey. DRHMC. Also in Shumate 1969.

——. 1868. Beers, F.W. *Hastings upon Hudson, Dobbs' Ferry, Irvington*. New York: J.B. Beers, Ellis, and Soule. DRHMC.

——. 1872. Beers, J.B. *Hastings upon Hudson. Dobbs' Ferry. Irvington, New York*. New York: J.B. Beers & Co. DRHMC.

——. 1876. Union Atlas Co. *Map of Henderson County and Oquawka*. Chicago: Warren & Beers. DRHMC.

——. 1876. Wheeler, G.M. *Parts of Eastern & Southeastern Nevada & Southwestern Utah*. Washington: U.S. [GPO]. DRHMC.

——. 1890. Manly, William Lewis. *Showing the Trail the Emigrants Travailed from Salt Lake to San Bernardino in 1849*. Route from Salt Lake City to Rancho San Francisco, Santa Clarita Valley, CA. HM 50895, Palmer Collection, The Huntington Library, San Marino, CA. (Manly sent map to T.S. Palmer in 1894.)

Other Sources

Aldous, Jay A., and Paul S. Nicholes. 1997. "What Is Mountain Fever?" *Overland Journal* 15, no. 1 (Spring): 18–23.

Alter, J. Cecil. 1962. *Jim Bridger*. Norman: Univ. of Oklahoma Press.

Arms, Cephas. See also John Cumming.

Arms, Cephas. 1850. Letter, January 29, 1850. In *Knoxville (IL) Journal*. Published April 24, 1850.

Arrington, Leonard J. 2005. *Great Basin Kingdom: An Economic History of the Latter-day Saints' 1830–1900, New Edition*. Urbana: Univ. of Illinois Press. First published 1958.

Auerbach, Herbert S. 1941. "Father Escalante's Itinerary." *Utah Historical Quarterly* 9, nos. 3–4 (July, October): 109–28.

Averett, Walter R. 1995. *Through the Rainbow Canyon*. Grand Junction, CO: Privately printed.

Babbitt, Charles H. 1916. *Early Days at Council Bluffs*. Washington, DC: Press of Byron S. Adams.

Bagley, Will. 2002. *Blood of the Prophets: Brigham Young and the Massacre at Mountain Meadow*. Norman: Univ. of Oklahoma Press.

——. 2010. *So Rugged and Mountainous: Blazing the Trails to Oregon and California 1812–1848*. Norman: Univ. of Oklahoma Press.

——. 2012. *With Golden Visions Bright Before Them: Trails to the Mining West 1849–1852*. Norman: Univ. of Oklahoma Press.

——. 2014. *South Pass: Gateway to a Continent*. Norman: Univ. of Oklahoma Press.

Bancroft, Hubert Howe, ed. 1888. *The Works of Hubert Howe Bancroft*. Vol. 23. *History of California*. Vol. 6, 1848–1859. San Francisco: The History Company.

Bancroftiana. 1960. Newsletter of the Friends of The Bancroft Library, no. 24 (November): 6.

Bartholomew, [Edward A.], Jr. 1885. *Record of the Bartholomew Family: Historical, Genealogical and Biographical*. Compiled by George Wells. Austin, TX: Published by the compiler.

Bartholomew, Lura H. 1906. "Capturing a Grizzly." *Western Field: Sportsman's Magazine of the West* 8, nos. 4–5 (May–June): 313–18. San Francisco: The Western Field Co.

Beattie, George William, and Helen Pruitt Beattie. 1951. *Heritage of the Valley, San Bernardino's First Century*. Oakland, CA: Biobooks.

Bennett, Richard E. 1987. *Mormons at the Missouri 1846–1852: "And Should We Die."* Norman: Univ. of Oklahoma Press.

———. 1992. "Council Bluffs (Kanesville), Iowa." In *Encyclopedia of Mormonism: The History, Scriptures, Doctrine, and Procedure of The Church of Jesus Christ of Latter-day Saints*. Vol. 1, edited by Daniel H. Ludlow, 325–26. New York: Macmillan Publishing Co.

———. 1997. *We'll Find the Place: The Mormon Exodus 1846–1848*. Salt Lake City, UT: Deseret Book Co.

Benton, Thomas Hart. 1970. To unknown correspondent, January 28, 1849. In *Map Portfolio, The Expeditions of John Charles Frémont*, by Donald Jackson, 16. Urbana: Univ. of Illinois Press.

Berrett, LaMar C., and A. Gary Anderson. 2006. *Sacred Places: Wyoming and Utah, A Comprehensive Guide to Early LDS Historical Sites*. Vol. 6. *Sacred Places*. General Editor LaMar C. Berrett. Salt Lake City, UT: Deseret Book Co.

Betancourt, Julio L., Thomas R. Van Devender, and Paul S. Martin, eds. 1990. *Packrat Middens: The Last 40,000 Years of Biotic Change*. Tucson: Univ. of Arizona Press.

Bidlack, Russell F. 1960. *Letters Home: The Story of Ann Arbor's Forty-Niners*. Ann Arbor, MI: Ann Arbor Publishers.

Bieber, Ralph P., ed. 1937. *Southern Trails to California in 1849*. Vol. 5 of *The Southwest Historical Series*. Glendale, CA: Arthur H. Clark Company.

Bigler, David L. 1998. *Forgotten Kingdom: The Mormon Theocracy in the American West, 1847–1896*. Logan: Utah State Univ. Press.

Bigler, David L., and Will Bagley, eds. 2000. *Army of Israel: Mormon Battalion Narratives*. Vol. 4 of *Kingdom in the West: The Mormons and the American Frontier*. Spokane, WA: Arthur H. Clark Co.

Bitton, Davis. 1982. *The Redoubtable John Pack: Pioneer, Proselyter, Patriarch*. N.p: The John Pack Family Association.

Bjorklund, L. J., and G. B. Robinson Jr. 1968. *Ground-water Resources of the Sevier River Basin between Yuba Dam and Leamington Canyon, Utah*. USGS Water-Supply Paper No. 1848. Washington, DC: U.S. Government Printing Office.

Bjorklund, L. J., C. T. Sumsion, and G. W. Sandberg. 1978. *Ground-Water Resources of the Parowan-Cedar City Drainage Basin, Iron County, Utah*. Technical Publication No. 60. USGS and the Utah Department of Natural Resources, Division of Water Rights.

Black, Esther Boulton. 1996. *Rancho Cucamonga and Doña Merced*. Redlands, CA: San Bernardino County Association.

Black, Susan Easton, and William G. Hartley, eds. 1997. *The Iowa Mormon Trail: Legacy of Faith and Courage*. Orem, UT: Helix Publishing.

Blaine, Martha Royce. 1996. "Pawnee." In *Encyclopedia of North American Indians*, edited by Frederick E. Hoxie, 472–74. Boston, MA: Houghton Mifflin Company.

Blair, Roger P. 1997. "'The Doctor Gets Some Practice': Cholera and Medicine on the Overland Trails." *Journal of the West* 36, no. 1 (January): 54–60.

Bonsal, Stephen. 1912. *Edward Fitzgerald Beale: A Pioneer in the Path of Empire, 1822–1903*. New York: G. P. Putnam's Sons.

Boyd, Robert E. 1975. "Another Look at the 'Fever and Ague' of Western Oregon." *Enthnohistory* 22, no. 2 (February): 135–54.

———. 1999. *The Coming of the Spirit of Pestilence: Introduced Infectious Diseases and Population Decline among Northwest Coast Indians, 1774–1874*. Vancouver: Univ. of British Columbia Press.

Boyle, Henry Green. 1848. "Diaries." MSS 156, Box 3, Folder 1, April 12, 1848, to June 5, 1848. L. Tom Perry Special Collections. Harold B. Lee Library, Brigham Young Univ., Provo, UT.

Brewerton, George Douglas. 1930. *Overland with Kit Carson: A Narrative of the Old Spanish Trail in '48*. Edited by Stallo Vinton. New York: Coward-McCann.

Brier, J[ohn] W[ells]. 1911. "The Argonauts of Death Valley." *Grizzly Bear* 9 (June): 1–4; "A Lonely Trail." *Grizzly Bear* 9 (October): 1–2.

Brody, Fawn M. 1960. *No Man Knows My History: The Life of Joseph Smith the Mormon Prophet*. New York: Alfred A. Knopf.

Brooks, Juanita. 1964. *John Doyle Lee: Zealot, Pioneer Builder, Scapegoat*. Vol. 9 of *Western Frontiersman Series*. Glendale, CA: Arthur H. Clark Co.

———. 1964. *On the Mormon Frontier: The Diary of Hosea Stout*. 2 vols. Salt Lake City: Utah State Historical Society.

Brown, James S. 1971. *Life of a Pioneer: Being the Autobiography of James S. Brown*. New York: AMS Press. First published 1900.

Brown, John, Jr., and James Boyd. 1922. *History of San Bernardino and Riverside Counties*. Vol. 2. Chicago, IL: Lewis Publishing Co.

Brown, Randy. 1987. "Childs' Cutoff." *Overland Journal* 5, no. 2 (Spring): 17–21.

———. 2010. "Letters: The Readers Respond." *Overland Journal* 28, no. 2 (Summer): 95–96.

———. 2004. *Historic Inscriptions on Western Emigrant Trails*. Independence, MO: Oregon-Trails Association.

Browne, J. Ross. 1850. *Report of the Debates in the Convention of California, on the Formation of the State Constitution, in September and October 1849*. Washington, DC: John T. Townes.

Brownell, Henry Howard. 1853. *The Discoverers, Pioneers and Settlers of North and South America from the Earliest Period (982) to the Present Time*. Boston: H. Wentworth.

Bruff, J. Goldsborough. 1944. *Gold Rush: The Journals, Drawings, and Other Papers of J. Goldsborough Bruff, Captain, Washington City and California Mining Association, April 2, 1849–July 20, 1851*. 2 vols. Edited by Georgia Willis Read and Ruth Gaines. New York: Columbia Univ. Press.

Bryant, Edwin. 1967. *What I Saw in California*. Minneapolis, MN: Ross & Haines.

Buck, Rinker. 2015. *The Oregon Trail: A New American Journey*. New York City: Simon & Schuster.

Bullock, Thomas. 1997. *The Pioneer Camp of the Saints: The 1846 and 1847 Mormon Trail Journals of Thomas Bullock*. Edited by Will Bagley. Spokane, WA: Arthur H. Clark Co.

Bynum, Lindley, ed. 1934. "The Record Book of the Rancho Santa Ana Del Chino." *Historical Society of Southern California, Annual Publication* 16: 1–55.

California State Senate. 1963. *Constitution of the State of California: The Constitution of the United States and Related Documents*. Sacramento: State of California.

Cannon, George Q. 1999. *The Journals of George Q. Cannon*. Vol. 1. *To California in '49*. Edited by Michael N. Landon. Salt Lake City, UT: Deseret Book Co.

Capace, Nancy. 1999. *Encyclopedia of Nebraska*. St. Clair Shores, MI: Somerset Publishers.

Carson, Kit. 1966. *Kit Carson's Autobiography*. Edited by Milo Milton Quaife. Lincoln: Univ. of Nebraska Press.

Carter, Harvey Lewis, ed. 1968. *'Dear Old Kit': The Historical Christopher Carson, with a New Edition of the Carson Memoirs*. Norman: Univ. of Oklahoma Press.

Catron, John. 1849. "The State of Missouri, Complainant v. The State of Iowa, Respondent. / The State of Iowa, Complainant v. The State of Missouri, Respondent.—*Cross Bill*." 48 U.S. (7 How.) 660 (1849). In Benjamin C. Howard. 1849. *Reports of Cases Argued and Adjudged in The Supreme Court of the United States. January Term, 1849*. Vol. 7. Boston: Charles C. Little and James Brown.

Cavanaugh, James Michael. 1868. [Testimony on the floor of Congress.] *Congressional Globe for the Second Session Fortieth Congress, Part III. Congressional Globe: Containing the Debates and Proceedings of the Second Session Fortieth Congress; To Be Entered with an Appendix, Comprising the Laws Passed at that Session*. City of Washington [DC]: Office of the Congressional Globe.

Cheesman, David W. 1850. "By Ox Team from Salt Lake to Los Angeles, 1850: A Memoir by David Cheesman." Edited by Mary E. Foy. *Historical Society of Southern California, Annual Publications* 14 (1930): 271–337.

Child, Andrew. 1946. *Overland Route to California*. Los Angeles: N. A. Kovach.

Chittenden, Hiram Martin. 1986. *The American Fur Trade of the Far West*. Vol. 1. Notes by James P. Ronda. Lincoln: Univ. of Nebraska Press.

Chittenden, Hiram Martin, and Alfred Talbot Richardson. 1905. *Life, Letters and Travels of Father Pierre-Jean De Smet, S.J. 1801–1873*. Vol. 1. New York: Francis P. Harper.

Clary, David A., and Joseph W.A. Whitehorne. 1987. *The Inspectors General of the United States Army 1777–1903*. Washington, DC: Office of the Inspector General and Center of Military History.

Clayton, William. 1973. *William Clayton's Journal: A Daily Record of the Journey of the Original Company of "Mormon" Pioneers from Nauvoo, Illinois, to the Valley of the Great Salt Lake*. Edited by Lawrence Clayton. New York: Arno Press, New York Times Company.

———. 1983. *The Latter-day Saints' Emigrants' Guide: Being a Table of Distances, Showing All the Springs, Creeks, Rivers, Hills, Mountains, Camping Places, and All Other Notable Places, from Council Bluffs, to the Valley of the Great Salt Lake*. Edited by Stanley B. Kimball. Gerald, MO: Patrice Press.

———. 1995. *An Intimate Chronicle: The Journals of William Clayton*. Edited by George D. Smith. Salt Lake City, UT: Signature Books.

Coates, Lawrence G. 1984. "Cultural Conflict: Mormons and Indians in Nebraska." *Brigham Young Univ. Studies* 24 (3): 275–300.

Colton, John. 1849. Letter. "Camp on the Banks of the Sweet Water, July 17–24, 1849." In *Galesburg (IL) Gazetteer* about September 27, 1849, reprinted as "Camp on the Banks of the Sweet Water" in the *Oquawka (IL) Spectator*, October 3, 1849, and as "From on Route to California," *Monmouth (IL) Atlas*, October 5, 1849. It is also found as a typescript in Guide to the Dale Lowell Morgan Papers, microfilm pages 362–67, The Bancroft Library, Berkeley, CA; in *Overland Journal* 37, no. 1 (Spring): 6–15; and portions are in Jean Johnson, *Grit and Gold*, 42–45.

———. 1895. "The Jayhawkers/A Terrible March." *Kansas City Journal*, February 5, 1895. Scrapbook 2, Jayhawkers of '49 Collection. The Huntington Library, San Marino, CA.

Conroy, Drew. 2007. *Oxen: A Teamster's Guide*. North Adams, MA: Storey Publishing.

Crampton, G. Gregory, and Steven K. Madsen. 1994. *In Search of the Spanish Trail, Santa Fe to Los Angeles, 1829–1848*. Layton, UT: Gibbs Smith.

Crisman, Kevin J., and Arthur B. Cohn. 1998. *When Horses Walked on Water: Horse-Powered Ferries in Nineteenth-Century America*. Washington, DC: Smithsonian Institution Press.

Crismon, George. 1905. "'Mormon' Pathfinders Guests of Senator Clark: Crismon's Experiences." *Deseret Evening News*, Great Salt Lake City (UT), October 7, 1905.

Crosby, Caroline Barnes. 1858. "Diary." In Jonathan Crosby Papers, Mss. B89, Box 3, Folder 18, Utah State Historical Society, Salt Lake City, UT.

Culmer, Frederic A. 1947. "'General' John Wilson: Signer of the Desert Petition Including Letters from the Leonard Collection." *California Historical Society Quarterly* 26, no. 4 (December): 321–48.

Cumming, John, ed. and comp. 1985. *The Long Road to California: The Journal of Cephas Arms, Supplemented with Letters by Traveling Companions on the Overland Trail in 1849*. Mount Pleasant, MI: The Private Press of John Cumming.

Davis, Lee. 2017. "Two William B. Lorton 'Iron Front' Clocks Made to His May 1, 1855, Patent Design." *NAWCC Watch & Clock Bulletin* 59, no. 6 (November–December): 493–96.

Delano, A. 1966. *Life on the Plains and among the Diggings*. Ann Arbor, MI: Univ. Microfilms. First published 1854.

Dixon, William Hepworth. 1868. *Spiritual Wives*. Vol. 1. London: Hurst and Blackett.

Dobbs, David. 2013. "Restless Genes." *National Geographic* 223, no. 1 (January): 44–57.

Domínguez, Francisco. 1977. *Domínguez-Escalante Journal: Their Expedition through Colorado, Utah, Arizona, and New Mexico in 1776*. Translated by Fray Angelico. Edited by Ted J. Warner. Provo, UT: Brigham Young Univ. Press.

Doty, Edward. 1872. To Friend J.B. Colton. San Jose, CA, January 21, 1872. JA378, Jayhawkers of '49 Collection. The Huntington Library, San Marino, CA.

Easton, Hosea. 1837. *A Treatise on the Intellectual Character, and Civil and Political Condition of the Colored People of the U. States; and the Prejudice Exercised Towards Them: With a Sermon on the Duty of the Church to Them*. Boston: Isaac Knapp.

Ebstein, R.P., and R.H. Belmaker. 1997. "Saga of an Adventure Gene: Novelty Seeking, Substance Abuse and the Dopamine D4 Receptor (D4DR) Exon III Repeat Polymorphism." *Molecular Psychiatry* 2 (5): 381–84.

Ellenbecker, John G. 1938. *The Jayhawkers of Death Valley*. Marysville, KS: Privately printed. See also 1993 edition that includes a supplement.

Ellison, Robert Spurrier. 1930. *Independence Rock: The Great Record of the Desert*. Casper, WY: Natrona County Historical Society.

Emigrant Rosters. 1849. LDS Archives, Salt Lake City, MS 15494, "List of the names of the Knox County Company, Illinois" [ca. August 10, 1849. Lorton's name is on this expanded list of the wagon train's members first made on August 8, 1849.]

Engelhardt, Zephyrin. 1927. *San Gabriel Mission and the Beginning of Los Angeles*. San Gabriel, CA: Mission San Gabriel.

Erkson, Alexander Combs. n.d. "Mr. Erkson's Statement." In Manly, *Death Valley in '49*, 367–76. Written before 1893 about his 1849 experiences.

Evans, George W. B. 2006. *Mexican Gold Trail: The Journal of a Forty-Niner*. Edited by Glenn S. Dumke. San Marino, CA: The Huntington Library Press.

Evans, John Henry. 1936. *Charles Coulson Rich: Pioneer Builder of the West*. New York, Macmillan Company.

Everett, Derek R. 2008. "To Shed Our Blood for Our Beloved Territory: The Iowa-Missouri Borderland." *Annals of Iowa*. Third Series 67, no. 4 (Fall): 269–97.

Fages, Don Pedro. 1937. *A Historical, Political, and Natural Description of California by Pedro Fages, Soldier of Spain*. Translated and edited by Herbert I. Priestly. Berkeley: Univ. of California Press. First published in Spanish in 1770.

Farmer, Jared. 2008. *On Zion's Mount: Mormons, Indians, and the American Landscape*. Cambridge, MA: Harvard Univ. Press.

Favour, Alpheus H. 1962. *Old Bill Williams: Mountain Man.* Norman: Univ. of Oklahoma Press.

Federal Writers' Project. 1986. *The WPA Guide to 1930s Iowa.* Iowa City: Univ. of Iowa Press.

Findley, William. 1849. Letter from "Gold Diggings, 40 Miles East of Johnson's." August 16, 1849. Published in *Oquawka (IL) Spectator*, October 31, 1849.

Fish, J[eremiah]. 1850. Letter, "Doleful Desert Which Had Threatened Us with Annihilation." March 1, 1850. Published in *Iowa Democratic Enquirer* (Muscatine, IA), June 1, 1850.

Foote, H. S. 1888. *Pen Pictures from the Garden of the World; or, Santa Clara County, California.* Chicago, IL: Lewis Publishing Company.

Forest Service. 1937. *Range Plant Handbook.* Supervised by W. A. Dayton. U.S. Department of Agriculture. Washington, DC: U.S. Government Printing Office.

Franzwa, Gregory M. 1982. *Maps of the Oregon Trail.* 2nd ed. Gerald, MO: Patrice Press.

———. 1999. *Maps of the California Trail.* Tucson, AZ: Patrice Press.

———. 2007. *The Mormon Trail Revisited.* Tooele, UT: Patrice Press.

Frazer, John F, ed. 1855. *Journal of the Franklin Institute, of the State of Pennsylvania, for the Promotion of the Mechanic Arts.* 3rd series, 29:384. Philadelphia: Franklin Institute.

Frémont, John Charles. 1970a. "Report of the First Expedition, 1843." In *The Expeditions of John Charles Frémont.* Vol. 1, *Travels from 1838 to 1844*, edited by Donald Jackson and Mary Lee Spence, 168–285. Urbana, IL: Univ. of Illinois Press. [A map portfolio is also included as part of the four-volume set.]

———. 1970b. "A Report of the Exploring Expedition to Oregon and North California in the Years 1843–44." In *The Expeditions of John Charles Frémont.* Vol. 1, *Travels from 1838 to 1844*, edited by Donald Jackson and Mary Lee Spence, 426–806. Urbana, IL: Univ. of Illinois Press.

———. 1984. *Travels from 1848 to 1854.* Vol. 3 of *The Expeditions of John Charles Frémont*, edited by Mary Lee Spence. Urbana, IL: Univ. of Illinois Press.

Friesen, Ruth, and Steven Heath. 2015. *Driving the Old Spanish Trail through Utah and Arizona.* Albuquerque, NM: Old Spanish Trail Association.

Frontier Guardian [Kanesville, IA]. 1849. "Constitution and By-Laws of the Knox County Company, Illinois," May 30, 1849.

Fullerton Archeological Site [25-NC-07]. 1974. Nebraska National Register Sites in Nance County, Nov. 1, 1974. Nebraska State Historical Society, Lincoln.

Garr, Arnold K., Donald Q. Cannon, and Richard O. Cowan. 2000. *Encyclopedia of Latter-day Saint History.* Salt Lake City, UT: Deseret Book Company.

Gay, Theressa. 1967. *James W. Marshall: The Discoverer of California Gold, A Biography.* Georgetown, CA: Talisman Press.

Gentry, Leland H. 1981. "The Mormon Way Stations: Garden Grove and Mt. Pisgah." *BYU Studies Quarterly* 21, no. 4 (Fall): 445–61.

Gordon, James W., ed. 1911. *Historical Encyclopedia of Illinois and History of Henderson County.* Vol. 2. Chicago, IL: Munsell Publishing Co.

Gowans, Fred R., and Eugene E. Campbell. 1975. *Fort Bridger: Island in the Wilderness.* Provo, UT: Brigham Young Univ. Press.

Granger, Lewis. 1959. *Letters of Lewis Granger: Reports of the Journey from Salt Lake to Los Angeles in 1849, and of Conditions in Southern California in the Early Fifties.* Edited by LeRoy R. Hafen. Los Angeles: Glen Dawson.

Grayson, Donald K. 1990. "Donner Party Deaths: A Demographic Assessment." *Journal of Anthropological Research* 46, no. 3 (August): 223–42.

———. 1993. *The Desert's Past: A Natural Prehistory of the Great Basin.* Washington, DC: Smithsonian Institution Press.

Griffith, M. Patrick. 2004. "The Origin of an Important Cactus Crop, *Opuntia fiscus-indica* (Cactaceae): New Molecular Evidence." *American Journal of Botany* 91 (11): 1915–21.

Grow, Matthew J., Ronald K. Esplin, Mark Ashurst-McGee, Gerrit J. Dirkmaat, and Jeffrey D. Mahas, eds. 2016. *The Joseph Smith Papers: Administrative Records, Council of Fifty, Minutes March 1844–January 1846.* Salt Lake City: Church Historian's Press.

Gudde, Edwin G. 1974. *California Place Names: The Origin and Etymology of Current Geographical Names.* Berkeley: Univ. of California Press.

———, ed. 1975. *California Gold Camps: A Geographical and Historical Dictionary of Camps, Towns, and Localities Where Gold Was Found and Mined; Wayside Stations and Trading Centers.* Berkeley: Univ. of California Press.

Guide to the Records of the 7th Regiment, 1767–1983 (bulk 1830–1947). 7th Regiment Records. New York City: New-York Historical Society Museum and Library, New York State Militia.

Gunnison, John Williams. 1852. *The Mormons, or Latter-day Saints: A History of Their Rise and Progress, Peculiar Doctrines, Present Conditions, and Prospects, Derived from Personal Observations, During a Residence Among Them.* Philadelphia, PA: Lippincott, Grambo & Co.

Hacker, David B., Michael S. Petronis, Daniel K. Holm, and John W. Geissman. 2007. "Shallow Level Emplacement Mechanisms of the Miocene Iron Axis Laccolith Group, Southwestern Utah." In *Field Guide to Geologic Excursions in Southern Utah*, edited by W. R. Lund and D. B. Simon. Geological Society of America, Rocky Mountain Section 2007 Annual Meeting. N.p.: Utah Geological Association Publication 35.

Hafen, LeRoy R., ed. 1966. *The Mountain Men and the Fur Trade of the Far West.* Vol. 3. Glendale, CA: Arthur H. Clark Co.

———, ed. 1969. *The Mountain Men and the Fur Trade of the Far West.* Vol. 7. Glendale, CA: Arthur H. Clark Co.

Hafen, LeRoy R., and Ann W. Hafen, eds. 1954a. *Old Spanish Trail: Santa Fé to Los Angeles.* Vol. 1 of *The Far West and the Rockies Historical Series, 1820–1875.* Glendale, CA: Arthur H. Clark Co.

———, eds. 1954b. *Journals of Forty-Niners.* Vol. 2 of *The Far West and the Rockies Historical Series, 1820–1875.* Glendale, CA: Arthur H. Clark Co.

———, eds. 1957. *Central Route to the Pacific by Gwinn Harris Heap.* Vol. 7 of *The Far West and the Rockies Historical Series, 1820–1875.* Glendale, CA: Arthur H. Clark Co.

———, eds. 1960. *Frémont's Fourth Expedition: A Documentary Account of the Disaster of 1848–1849.* Vol. 11 of *The Far West and the Rockies Historical Series, 1820–1875.* Glendale, CA: Arthur H. Clark Co.

———, eds. 1961. *General Analytical Index to the Fifteen Volume Series and Supplement to the Journals of Forty-Niners, Salt Lake to Los Angeles.* Vol. 15 of *The Far West and the Rockies Historical Series, 1820–1875.* Glendale, CA: Arthur H. Clark Co.

Hafen, LeRoy R., and Francis Marion Young. 1984. *Fort Laramie and the Pageant of the West, 1834–1890.* Lincoln: Univ. of Nebraska Press.

Hague, Harlan, and David J. Langum. 1990. *Thomas O. Larkin: A Life of Patriotism and Profit in Old California.* Norman: Univ. of Oklahoma Press.

Haines, Aubrey L. 1981. *Historic Sites along the Oregon Trail.* Gerald, MO: Patrice Press.

Hale, J[ames] Ellery. 1850. To "My Dear Parents, [written from] Bodega, California, January 8, 1850." Reprinted in *Knoxville Journal*, April 10, 1850.

Hansen, Klaus J. 1974. *Quest for Empire: The Political Kingdom of God and the Council of Fifty in Mormon History.* East Lansing: Michigan State Univ. Press.

Hardy, B. Carmon, ed. 2007. *Doing the Works of Abraham, Mormon Polygamy, Its Origin, Practice, and Demise.* Vol. 9 of *Kingdom in the West: The Mormons and the American Frontier.* Norman, OK: Arthur H. Clark Co.

Harlow, Neal. 1982. *California Conquered: War and Peace on the Pacific 1846–1850.* Berkeley: Univ. of California Press.

Harlow, William M., and Ellwood S. Harrar. 1968. *Textbook of Dendrology: Covering the Important Forest Trees of the United States and Canada.* 5th ed. New York: McGraw-Hill.

Hartley, William G. 2002. "Pushing on to Zion: Kanesville, Iowa, 1846–1853." *Ensign* 32, no. 8 (August): 14–23.

Hartley, William G., and A. Gary Anderson. 2006. *Sacred Places: Iowa and Nebraska, A Comprehensive Guide to Early LDS Historical Sites.* Vol. 5 of *Sacred Places.* General Editor LaMar C. Berrett. Salt Lake City, UT: Deseret Book Company.

Hastings Historical Society. 2019. Pers. Comm. Natalie Barry, President, 407 Broadway, Hastings-on-Hudson NY 10706.

Hastings, Lansford W. 1994. *The Emigrants' Guide to Oregon and California.* Bedford, MA: Applewood Books. First published 1845.

Hatch, Jane M., comp. and ed. 1978. *The American Book of Days.* 3rd. ed. New York: H. W. Wilson Company.

Heath, Steven H. 1995. "Jefferson Hunt, Bad Judgement, the 49ers and the Mormon Battalion." *Pioneer* (Summer): 6–7.

Heiskell, Hugh Brown. 1998. *A Forty-Niner from Tennessee: The Diary of Hugh Brown Heiskell.* Edited by Edward M. Steel. Knoxville: Univ. of Tennessee Press.

Hileman, Levida. 2001. *In Tar and Paint and Stone: The Inscriptions at Independence Rock and Devil's Gate.* Glendo, WY: High Plains Press.

Hine, Cole & Gray Real Estate Brokers and Auctioneers, New York City. 1874. Letter to William B. Lorton. February 23, 1874. Editors files.

History of Andrew and DeKalb Counties, Missouri, from the Earliest Time to the Present. 1888. St. Louis, MO: Goodspeed Publishing.

History of Davis County, Iowa, Containing a History of the County, Its Cities, Towns, Etc. 1882. Des Moines, IA: State Historical Company.

History of Henry County, Iowa: A History of the County, Its Cities, Towns, &c. 1879. Chicago, IL: Western Historical Company.

History of Johnson County, Iowa, Containing a History of the County and Its Townships, Cities and Villages from 1836 to 1882. 1883. Iowa City, IA: N.p.

History of Peoria County, Illinois. 1880. Chicago: Johnson and Company.

Hitchcock, A. S. 1950. *Manual of the Grasses of the United States.* 2nd ed. Revised by Agnes Chase. USDA Misc. Pub. No. 200. Washington, DC: U.S. Government Printing Office.

Honigsbaum, Mark. 2002. *The Fever Trail: In Search of the Cure for Malaria.* New York: Farrar, Straus, and Giroux.

Hoover, Mildred Brooke, Hero Eugene Rensch, Ethel Grace Rensch, and William N. Abeloe. 2002. *Historic Spots in California.* 5th ed. Revised by Douglas E. Kyle. Stanford, CA: Stanford Univ. Press.

Hoover, Vincent A. 1849. "Vincent A. Hoover Diaries." Original diary, Vol. 2, July 19–November 23, 1849. HM27628. The Huntington Library, San Marino, CA.

Hopkins, Timothy. 1903. *The Kelloggs in the Old World and the New.* I. San Francisco: Sunset Press and Photo Engraving Co.

Hornaday, William T. 1889. "The Extermination of the American Bison." *Annual Report of the Board of Regents of the Smithsonian Institution, Showing the Operations, Expenditures, and Condition of the Institution for the Year Ending June 30, 1887*. Part II, 367–548. Washington, DC: U.S. Government Printing Office.

Hunt, Charles B. 1974. *Natural Regions of the United States and Canada*. San Francisco: W. H. Freeman and Company.

Hunter, Milton R. 1939. "The Mormon Corridor." *Pacific Historical Review* 8, no. 2 (June): 179–200.

Hutchings, James M. 1980. *Seeking the Elephant, 1849: James Mason Hutchings' Journal of His Overland Trek to California*. Edited by Shirley Sargent. Glendale, CA: Arthur H. Clark Co.

Hyde, George E. 1974. *The Pawnee Indians*. Denver, CO: Univ. of Denver Press, 1951. Reprint, Norman: Univ. of Oklahoma Press.

Illinois, Cook County Deaths, 1878–1994. Chicago: Cook County Courthouse, record number 18278, FHL microfilm 1,239,857.

Irving, Washington. 1961. *The Adventures of Captain Bonneville, U.S.A., in the Rocky Mountains and the Far West*. Edited by Edgeley W. Todd. Norman: Univ. of Oklahoma Press.

Jackson, Donald. 1970. *Map Portfolio, The Expeditions of John Charles Frémont*. Urbana: Univ. of Illinois Press.

Jackson, W. Turrentine. 1949. "The Army Engineers as Road Builders in Territorial Iowa." *Iowa Journal of History* 47, no. 1 (January): 15–33.

James, Terry. 1992. *In Praise of Oxen*. Halifax, Nova Scotia: Nimbus Publishing Limited.

Jensen, Richard E. 1994. "The Pawnee Mission, 1834–1846." *Nebraska History* 75, no. 4: 301–10.

Jenson, Andrew, comp. 1886. *Supplement to the "Historical Record." Church Chronology; or, A Record of Important Events*. Salt Lake City, UT: Deseret News Publishing Co.

———. 1899. *Church Chronology: A Record of Important Events*. Salt Lake City, UT: Deseret News Publishing Co.

———. 1941. *Encyclopedic History of the Church of Jesus Christ of Latter-day Saints*. Salt Lake City: Deseret News Publishing Co.

———. 1971. *Latter-day Saint Biographical Encyclopedia*. Vol 4. Salt Lake City: Western Epics. First published 1936.

Johnson, Jean. 2006. *Strolling Stones: The Mystery of Death Valley's Racetrack*. Death Valley, CA: Death Valley '49ers.

———. 2018. *Grit and Gold: The Death Valley Jayhawkers of 1849*. Reno: Univ. of Nevada Press.

Johnson, Jean, and LeRoy Johnson. 2017. "Adonijah Strong Welch, 1849er." *Overland Journal* 35, no. 1 (Spring): 22–30.

Johnson, Jeffery Ogden. 1987. "Determining and Defining 'Wife': The Brigham Young Households." *Dialogue: A Journal of Mormon Thought* 20, no. 3 (Fall): 57–70.

Johnson, LeRoy. 2005a. "Hard Bread." In *Nuggets & Snippets of Death Valley History, Proceedings, Seventh Death Valley Conference on History and Prehistory, February 3–6, 2005*, edited by Jean Johnson, 269–70. Bishop, CA: Community Printing and Publishing.

———. 2005b. "Reverend Brier's Mountain of Iron." In *Nuggets & Snippets of Death Valley History, Proceedings, Seventh Death Valley Conference on History and Prehistory, February 3–6, 2005*, edited by Jean Johnson, 255–56. Bishop, CA: Community Printing and Publishing.

———. 2010. "Letters, The Readers Respond." *Overland Journal* 28, no. 1 (Spring): 46–47.

Johnson, LeRoy, and Jean Johnson, eds. 1987. *Escape from Death Valley as Told by William Lewis Manly*. Reno: Univ. of Nevada Press.

———. 2014. "Porter Rockwell's Route Home." *Spanish Traces* 20, no. 3 (Winter): 27–31.

———. 2018. "Where Is Mount Misery?" In *Proceedings, Tenth Death Valley Conference on History and Prehistory, November 5–8, 2015*, 10–43. Death Valley, CA: Death Valley Natural History Association.

Johnson, LeRoy, and Tom Sutak. 2017. "Unscrambling the Old Spanish Trail and the Southern Route: Salt Spring to Resting Spring, California." *Overland Journal* 34, no. 4 (Winter): 134–65.

Johnston, Wm. G. 1948. *Overland to California by Wm. G. Johnston: A Member of the Wagon Train First to Enter California in the Memorable Year of 1849*. Oakland, CA: Biobooks.

Jones, Sondra G. 2019. *Being and Becoming Ute: The Story of an American Indian People*. Salt Lake City: Univ. of Utah Press.

Journal History of the Church of Jesus Christ of Latter-day Saints. 1830–1973. Compiled by Andrew Jenson. A day-by-day multivolume scrapbook of church history housed in the LDS Church History Library, Salt Lake City, UT.

Kane, Michael David. 2008. "William Lewis Manly." PhD diss., Department of Parks, Recreation, and Tourism, Univ. of Utah, Salt Lake City.

Kelly, Charles. 1939. "On Manly's Trail to Death Valley." *Desert Magazine* 2, no. 4 (February): 6–8, 41, 43.

———, ed. 1984. *Journals of John D. Lee: 1846–47 and 1859*. Salt Lake City: Univ. of Utah Press.

Kelly, Charles, and Maurice L. Howe. 1937. *Miles Goodyear: First Citizen of Utah*. Salt Lake City, UT: Privately printed for the authors by Western Printing Company.

Kelly, Charles, and Dale L. Morgan. 1965. *Old Greenwood: The Story of Caleb Greenwood: Trapper, Pathfinder, and Early Pioneer*. Rev. ed. Georgetown, CA: Talisman Press.

Kimball, Stanley B. 1988. *Historic Sites and Markers along the Mormon and Other Great Western Trails*. Urbana: Univ. of Illinois Press.

Knoxville (IL) Journal. 1850. "Emigration of 1849." April 3, 1850.

Korns, J. Roderic, and Dale E. Morgan, eds. 1994. *West from Fort Bridger: The Pioneering of Immigrant Trails across Utah, 1846–1850*. Revised and updated by Will Bagley and Harold Schindler. Logan: Utah State Univ. Press.

Kramer, David. 2000. "Building an Ox Yoke." *Tillers International Tech Guide*. Scotts, MI: Tillers International.

Kraus, Carroll J. 1969. "A Study in Border Confrontation: The Iowa-Missouri Boundary Dispute." *Annals of Iowa* 40, no. 2 (Fall): 81–107.

Larkin, Thomas O. 1848. "Mr. Larkin to Mr. Buchanan." In *Messages from the President of the United States to the Two Houses of Congress*. 13th Cong., 2nd sess. House Ex. Doc. No. 1: 53–56. June 28, 1848. Washington, DC: Printed by Wendell and Van Benthuysen.

———. 1960. *The Larkin Papers*. Vol. 7, 1847–1848. Edited by George P. Hammond. Berkeley: Univ. of California Press.

Laveille, E. 1915. *The Life of Father De Smet, S. J. (1801–1873)*. Translated by Marian Lindsay. New York: P. J. Kennedy & Sons.

Lavender, David. 1983. *Fort Laramie and the Changing Frontier*. National Park Service Handbook 118. Washington, DC: U.S. Government Printing Office.

Lee, John D. 1955. *A Mormon Chronicle: The Diaries of John D. Lee—1848–1876*. Vol. 1. Edited by Robert Glass Cleland and Juanita Brooks. San Marino, CA: The Huntington Library.

Lord, Israel Shipman Pelton. 1999. *A Doctor's Gold Rush Journal to California*. Edited by Necia Dixon Liles. Lincoln: Univ. of Nebraska Press.

Lorton, William B. 1849–1850. *The Diaries* [Journals] *of William B. Lorton*. C–F 190 vols. 1–8. The Bancroft Library, Univ. of California, Berkeley.

———. 1849a. To *New York Sun*. "From the California Adventurers." St. Joseph, Missouri, May 9, 1849. Published June 8, 1849.

———. 1849b. To *New York Sun*. "From the Overland Emigrants." Fort Laramie, June 30, 1849. Published September 7, 1849.

———. 1850. To *New York Sun*. "Correspondence of the New York Sun: Overland Emigration—Terrible Sufferings of the Emigrants—Thrilling Details." De Los Angelos, January 20, 1850. Published May 8, 1850. [Reprinted as "Wanderings and Sufferings of a Party in the Great Basin." *New-York Daily Tribune*, May 17, 1850.]

———. Certificate. 1857. New York State Militia, 7th Regiment, 3rd Brigade, and First Division, Company A.

———. Indenture. 1865. "James A. Ferguson and Wife to William B. Lorton." Elmsford, NY: Westchester County Clerk's Office, County Archives. Records are online PDF files. October 24, 1865.

———. [1874]. "Valuable Country Seat for Sale at Hastings." Handwritten, 3 pages. Authors' collection.

———. 1957. *Over the Salt Lake Trail in the Fall of '49*. Introduction by John B. Goodman III. Los Angeles, CA: Privately printed.

Lyman, Edward Leo. 2004. *The Overland Journey from Utah to California: Wagon Travel from the City of Saints to the City of Angels*. Reno: Univ. of Nevada Press.

Lynch, David K., and William Livingston. 2001. *Color and Light in Nature*. 2nd ed. Cambridge, UK: Cambridge Univ. Press.

MacKay, Michael Hubbard, and Gerrit J. Dirkmaat. 2015. *From Darkness unto Light: Joseph Smith's Translation and Publication of the Book of Mormon*. Provo, UT: Religious Study Center.

Madsen, Brigham D. 1983. *Gold Rush Sojourners in Great Salt Lake City: 1849 and 1850*. Salt Lake City: Univ. of Utah Press.

———, ed. 1989. *Exploring the Great Salt Lake: The Stansbury Expedition of 1849–50*. Salt Lake City: Univ. of Utah Press.

Manahan, Stanley E. 2000. *Environmental Chemistry*. 7th ed. Boca Raton, FL: Lewis Publishers.

Manly, William Lewis. 1894. *Death Valley in '49*. San Jose, CA: The Pacific Tree and Vine Co.

———. 2001. *Death Valley in '49*. Edited by LeRoy and Jean Johnson. Berkeley, CA: Heyday Books. [Santa Clara University and Heyday Books published this edition as part of the University's California Legacy series.]

———. 1949. *The Jayhawkers' Oath and Other Sketches*. Edited by Arthur Woodward. Los Angeles, CA: Warren F. Lewis, Publisher.

Marwitt, John. 1986. "Fremont Cultures." In *Great Basin*. Vol. 2 of *Handbook of North American Indians*, 161–72. Warren L. L'Azevedo, volume editor. Washington, DC: Smithsonian Institution.

Mason, R. B. 1848. "Head-Quarters, 10th Military Department, Monterey, California, August 17, 1848." In *Message from the President of the United States to the Two Houses of Congress at the Commencement of the Second Session of the Thirtieth Congress*. 30th Cong., 2nd Sess., Ex. Doc. No. 1, No. 37: 56–64. Washington, DC: Wendell and Van Benthuysen.

Mattes, Merrill J. 1969. *The Great Platte River Road*. Vol. 25. *Nebraska State Historical Society Publications*. [Lincoln]: Nebraska State Historical Society.

———. 1988. *Platte River Road Narratives*. Urbana: Univ. of Illinois Press.

McChristian, Douglas C. 2008. *Fort Laramie: Military Bastion of the High Plains*. Vol. 26 of *Frontier Military Series*. Norman, OK: Arthur H. Clark Co.

McGilligan, Patrick. 1999. *Clint: The Life and Legend*. New York: St. Martin's Press.

McKeeby, Lemuel Clarke. 1934. "The Memoirs of Lemuel Clarke McKeeby." *California Historical Society Quarterly* 3, no. 2 (July): 126–70.

McKinstry, Byron N. 1975. *The California Gold Rush Overland Diary of Byron N. McKinstry 1850–1852*. Edited by Bruce L. McKinstry. Glendale, CA: Arthur H. Clark Company.

Mech, L. David. 1970. *The Wolf: The Ecology and Behavior of an Endangered Species*. Garden City, NY: Natural History Press.

Mecum, Charles B. 1878. To A. C. Clay, Dear Brother Jayhawkers. Rippey, IA, January 26, 1878. JA716, Jayhawkers of '49 Collection. The Huntington Library, San Marino, CA.

Meldahl, Keith Heyer. 2007. *Hard Road West: History & Geology along the Gold Rush Trail*. Chicago: Univ. of Chicago Press.

Mendenhall, Walter C. 1909. *Some Desert Watering Places in Southeastern California and Southwestern Nevada*. Water-Supply Paper 224, USGS. Washington, DC: U.S. Government Printing Office.

Milikien, Herbert C. 1996. "'Dead of the Bloody Flux': Cholera Stalks the Emigrant Trail." *Overland Journal* 14, no. 3 (Autumn): 4–11.

Moore, Beth Shumway. 2006. *Bones in the Well: The Haun's Mill Massacre, 1838, A Documentary History*. Norman, OK: Arthur H. Clark Company.

Morgan, Dale L. 1947. *The Great Salt Lake*. New York: Bobbs-Merrill Company.

———. 1948. "The Administration of Indian Affairs in Utah, 1851–1858." *Pacific Historical Review* 17, no. 4 (November): 383–409.

———. 1959a. "The Ferries of the Forty-Niners." *Annals of Wyoming* 31, no. 1 (April): 4–31.

———. 1959b. "The Ferries of the Forty-Niners." *Annals of Wyoming* 31, no. 2 (October): 145–90.

———, ed. 1959c. *The Overland Diary of James A. Pritchard from Kentucky to California in 1849...With an Introduction, Bibliography, and Chart of Travels by All Known Diarists West across South Pass in 1849*. Denver, CO: Fred A. Rosenstock and Old West Publishing Company.

———. [1962]. "The Significance and Value of the Overland Journal." In *Probing the American West: Papers from the Santa Fe Conference*, ed. K. Ross Toole et al. Santa Fe: Museum of New Mexico Press.

———, ed. 1963. *Overland in 1846: Diaries and Letters of the California-Oregon Trail*. Vol. 1. Lincoln: Univ. of Nebraska Press.

———. 2013. "The Significance and Value of the Overland Journal." *Overland Journal* 31, no. 2 (Summer): 75–80.

Morse, Jedidiah. 1822. *A Report to the Secretary of War of the United States, on Indian Affairs*. Washington, DC: Davis & Davis.

Mowry, Sylvester. 1965. "Lt. Sylvester Mowry's Report on His March in 1855 from Salt Lake City to Fort Tejon." Edited by Lynn R. Bailey. *Arizona and the West, A Quarterly Journal of History* 7, no. 4: 329–46. This edited version of the report does not have Mowry's "List of Camps" table.

Mukherjee, Siddhartha. 2016. *The Gene: An Intimate History*. New York: Scribner.

Munro-Fraser, J. P., ed. 1881. *History of Santa Clara County, California; Including Its Geography, Geology, Topography, Climatography and Description*. San Francisco: Alley, Bowen & Co.

National Park Service. 2001. *National Historic Trail Feasibility Study and Environmental Assessment: Old Spanish Trail*. [Washington, DC]: U.S. Government Printing Office.

Neiburger, E. J. 1986. "Debunking a Myth: The American Bison." *Central States Archaeological Journal* 33, no. 3 (July): 140–43.

Nevins, Allan. 1928. *Frémont: The West's Greatest Adventurer.* Vol. 2. New York: Harper & Brothers Publishers.

Newmark, Maurice H., and Marco R. Newmark. 1929. *Census of the City and County of Los Angeles, California for the Year 1850.* Los Angeles, CA: Times-Mirror Press.

New York City Marriage Notices, 1835–1880. Transcription. September 19, 2015. http://search.findmypast.com/record.

Oberly, James W. 1982. "Military Bounty Land Warrants of the Mexican War." *Prologue* 14, no. 1 (Spring): 25–34.

———. 1990. *Sixty Million Acres: American Veterans and the Public Lands before the Civil War.* Kent, OH: Kent State Univ. Press.

Ogle, Daniel G. 2006. "Indian Ricegrass." Plant Guide, USDA, Natural Resource Conservation Service, Idaho State Office, Boise.

Olmsted, Henry King, comp. 1912. *Genealogy of the Olmsted Family in America.* Revised and completed by Geo. K. Ward. New York: A. T. de la Mare Printing and Publishing Co., Ltd.

Ormsby, Calab N. 1850. "Letters from Dr. Ormsby." *Washtenaw Whig* (Ann Arbor, MI), June 26, 1850.

Orsak, Erik L. 2004. "Assessment of Environmental Contaminants in Muddy River Fishes, Clark County, Nevada." Final Report, USFWS, Southern Field Office. Report Number 200210008 (FFS #: 14320A–1130–1F38). Las Vegas, NV.

Osio, Antonio María. 1996. *The History of Alta California: A Memoir of Mexican California.* Translated, edited, and annotated by Rose Marie Beebe and Robert M. Senkewicz. Madison: Univ. of Wisconsin Press.

Owens, Kenneth N. 2004. *Gold Rush Saints: California Mormons and the Great Rush for Riches.* Vol. 7 of *Kingdom in the West: The Mormons and the American Frontier.* Spokane, WA: Arthur H. Clark Co.

PacifiCorp. 2010. "10-Year Anniversary of Final Dave Johnson Mine Coal Shipment." News release, Glenrock, WY, September 27, 2010.

Palmer, Brooks. 1950. *The Book of American Clocks.* New York: Macmillan Publishing Co.

Parke, Charles Ross. 1989. *Dreams to Dust: A Diary of the California Gold Rush, 1849–1850.* Edited by James E. Davis. Lincoln: Univ. of Nebraska Press.

Parks, Gregory S., and Shayne E. Jones. 2008. "Nigger: A Critical Race Realist Analysis of the N-word within Hate Crimes Law." *Journal of Criminal Law and Criminology* 98, no. 4 (Summer): 1305–52.

Pauley, Kenneth E., and Carol M. Pauley. 2005. *San Fernando, Rey De España: An Illustrated History.* Spokane, WA: Arthur H. Clark Co.

Paullin, Charles O. 1932. *Atlas of the Historical Geography of the United States.* Edited by John K. Wright. Carnegie Institution of Washington, Publication No. 401. Baltimore, MD: Carnegie Institution of Washington and American Geological Society of New York.

Peck, Washington. 2009. *On the Western Trails: The Overland Diaries of Washington Peck.* Edited by Susan M. Erb. Norman, OK: Arthur H. Clark Co.

Perkins, George E. 1947. *Pioneers of the Western Desert.* Los Angeles, CA: Wetzel Publishing Co.

Polk, James K. 1849. "Message of the President of the United States," December 5, 1848. *The Congressional Globe.* 30th Congress, 2nd Session, New Series No. 1, 3–13. City of Washington: Printed at the Office of Blair and Rives.

———. 1910. *The Diary of James K. Polk: During His Presidency 1845–1849.* Edited by Milo Milton Quaife. Vol. 4. Chicago: A. C. McClurg & Co.

Potter, David Morris, ed. 1945. *Trail to California: The Overland Journal of Vincent Geiger and Wakeman Bryarly.* New Haven, CT: Yale Univ. Press.

Pratt, Addison. 1990. *The Journals of Addison Pratt.* Edited by S. George Ellsworth. Salt Lake City: Univ. of Utah Press.

Pratt, Louisa Barnes. 1998. *The History of Louisa Barnes Pratt: Being the Autobiography of a Mormon Missionary Widow and Pioneer.* Edited by S. George Ellsworth. Logan: Utah State Univ. Press.

Pratt, Orson, and others. [1947]. *Exodus of Modern Israel.* Compiled by N. B. Lundwall. Independence, MO: Zion's Printing and Publishing Co.

Price, George R. 2002. "Hosea Easton: Forgotten Abolitionist 'Giant.'" In *The Human Tradition in America from the Colonial Era through Reconstruction*, edited by Charles W. Calhoun, 195–210. Wilmington, DE: Scholarly Resources.

Purdy, John H. 1850. To "Dear Brother." April 18. MSS 862, Harold B. Lee Library, Brigham Young Univ., Provo, UT.

Ramawat, K. G., ed. 2010. *Desert Plants: Biology and Biotechnology.* London: Springer-Verlag.

Rasmussen, Louis J. 1994. *California Wagon Train Lists.* Vol. 1, *April 5, 1849 to October 20, 1852.* Coloma, CA: San Francisco Historic Records.

Reid, John Phillip. 1980. *Law of the Elephant: Property and Social Behavior on the Overland Trail.* San Marino, CA: The Huntington Library.

"Report of the Commissioner of Patents for the Year 1854, Arts and Manufacturers. Vol. 1." 1855. House Ex. Doc. No. 59. 33rd Cong., 2nd sess. Washington, DC: A. O. P. Nicholson.

Ressler, Theodore C. 1964. *Trails Divided: A Dissertation on the Overland Journey from Iowa "Forty-Niners" of the "Sacramento Mining Company."* Williamsburg, IA: Privately printed.

Rhode, David. 2002. *Native Plants of Southern Nevada: An Ethnobotany.* Salt Lake City: Univ. of Utah Press.

Richard, Bernice C., comp. 1977. *1850 Federal Census of Henderson County, Illinois.* Chicago, IL: Frank Rademacher, Printer.

Ricketts, Norma Baldwin. 1996. *The Mormon Battalion: U.S. Army of the West, 1846–1848.* Logan: Utah State Univ. Press.

Robinson, John W. 2005. *Gateways to Southern California: Indian Footpaths, Horse Trails, Wagon Roads, Railroads, and Highways.* City of Industry, CA: Big Santa Anita Historical Society.

Rowley, Peter D., David B. Hacker, David J. Maxwell, Joshua D. Maxwell, and Jonathan T. Boswell. 2008. "Interim Geologic Map of the Utah Part of the Deer Lodge Canyon, Prohibition Flat, Uvada, and Pine Park Quadrangles, (East Part of the Caliente 30' X 60' Quadrangle), Iron and Washington Counties, Utah. Open-File Report 530, Utah Geological Survey. Salt Lake City: Utah Department of Natural Resources.

Runner, Meredith. 1995. "The '49 Gold Rush, Jayhawker Wagon #9, and the Bartholomew Bear." Typescript, 3 pages. In LeRoy Johnson files.

Russell, Carl P. 1957. *Guns on the Early Frontiers: A History of Black Powder Weapons from Colonial Times to the Mexican War.* New York: Barnes and Noble Books.

Sabin, Edwin L. 1995. *Kit Carson Days 1809–1868: "Adventures in the Path of Empire."* Rev. ed. Vol. 2. Lincoln: Univ. of Nebraska Press. First published 1935.

Sage, Rufus B. 1982. *Rocky Mountain Life; or, Startling Scenes and Perilous Adventures in the Far West, During an Expedition of Three Years.* Lincoln: Univ. of Nebraska Press. First published 1858.

Saunders, Richard L. 2016. "Lost in Time: Dale L. Morgan and the Forty-Niner Journal of William B. Lorton." *Historical Society of Southern California Quarterly* 98, no. 4: 457–86.

Schindler, Harold. 1966. *Orrin Porter Rockwell: Man of God, Son of Thunder.* Salt Lake City: Univ. of Utah Press.

Sessions, Gene A. 1982. *Mormon Thunder: A Documentary History of Jedediah Morgan Grant.* Urbana: Univ. of Illinois Press.

Seymour, H.M. 1849. To J.S. Swezy sent from Fort Laramie, June 5, 1849. Published in *Oquawka (IL) Spectato*r July 18, 1849.

Shaw, James H. 1995. "How Many Bison Originally Populated Western Rangelands?" *Rangelands* 17 no. 5 (October): 148–50.

Shomette, Donald G. 1998. "Heyday of the Horse Ferry: A Long-Forgotten Animal-Powered Craft Is Discovered on the Bottom of Lake Champlain." *National Geographic Magazine* 176, no. 4 (October): 548–66.

Shumate, Albert. 1969. *The Life of George Henry Goddard: Artist, Architect, Surveyor, and Map Maker.* Keepsake No. 17. Goddard's 1857 map of California in pocket. Berkeley, CA: Friends of The Bancroft Library, Univ. of California.

Shumway, Burgess. 1988. *California Ranchos: Patented Private Land Grants Listed by County.* San Bernardino: The Borgo Press, from Stokvis Studies in Historical Chronology and Thought, ISSN 0270–5338; No. 11, originally published in 1941–1942.

Shumway, George, Edward Durell, and Howard C. Frey. 1964. *Conestoga Wagon 1750–1850: Freight Carrier for 100 Years of America's Westward Expansion.* York, PA: Early American Industries Association and George Shumway.

Smith, Joseph. 1878. *The Pearl of Great Price: A Selection from the Revelations, Translations, and Narrations of Joseph Smith, First Prophet, Seer, and Revelator to The Church of Jesus Christ of Latter-day Saints.* Salt Lake City, UT: Printed at the Latter-day Saints' Printing and Publishing Establishment.

Smith, Joseph Fielding. 1979. *Essentials in Church History: A History of the Church from the Birth of Joseph Smith to the Present Time.* Salt Lake City, UT: Deseret Book Co.

Snow, John. 1849. *On the Mode of Communication of Cholera.* London: John Churchill, Princes Street, Soho.

Snowden, Frank M. 2006. *The Conquest of Malaria: Italy, 1900–1962.* New Haven, CT: Yale Univ. Press.

Snyder, Susan, ed. 2003. *Bear in Mind: The California Grizzly.* Berkeley, CA: Heyday Press.

Spencer, Thomas M. 2008. "Demand Nothing but What Is Strictly Right and Submit to Nothing That Is Wrong." *Missouri Historical Review* 103, no. 1 (October): 22–40.

Spurgeon, Terrence. 1996. "Wapato *(Sagittaria latifolia)* in Katzie Traditional Territory, Pitt Meadows, British Columbia." Master's thesis, Simon Fraser Univ., British Columbia, Canada.

Stansbury, Howard. 1988. *Exploration and Survey of the Valley of the Great Salt Lake of Utah.* Washington, DC: Smithsonian Institution Press. First published 1852.

Stathis, Stephen W. 1999. *Federal Holidays: Evolution and Application.* Congressional Research Service Report for Congress. Washington, DC: Congressional Research Service.

Statutes at Large. 1 Stat. 300. 1845. "An Act regulating foreign Coins, and for other purposes." February 9, 1793. *The Public Statutes at Large of the United States of America.* Vol. 1. Boston, MA: Charles C. Little and James Brown.

———. 2 Stat. 728. 1845. "An Act to provide for designating, surveying and granting the Military Bounty Lands.(a)." *The Public Statutes at Large of the United States of America.* Vol. 2. Boston, MA: Charles C. Little and James Brown.

———. 4 Stat. 729. 1846. "An Act to regulate Trade and intercourse with the Indian tribes, and to preserve peace on the frontiers." June 30, 1834. *The Public Statutes at Large of the United States of America.* Vol. 4. Boston, MA: Charles C. Little and James Brown.

———. 5 Stat. 352. 1856. "An Act to authorize the construction of a road from Dubuque, in the Territory of Iowa, to the northern boundary of the State of Missouri, and for other purposes." March 3, 1839. *The Public Statutes at Large of the United States of America.* Vol. 5. Boston, MA: Charles C. Little and James Brown.

———. 5 Stat. 453. 1846. "An Act to appropriate the proceeds of the sales of public lands." September 4, 1841. *The Public Statutes at Large of the United States of America.* Vol. 5. Boston, MA: Charles C. Little and James Brown.

———. 7 Stat. 448. 1846. "Made this ninth day of October, A.D. 1833, at the Grand Pawnee village, on the Platte River, between Henry L. Ellsworth, Commissioner in behalf of the United States, and the chiefs and head-men of the four confederate bands of Pawnees, viz.—Grand Pawnees, Pawnee Loups, Pawnee Republicans, and Pawnee Tappaye, residing on the Platte and the Loup fork." October 9, 1833. *The Public Statutes at Large of the United States of America.* Vol. 7. Boston, MA: Charles C. Little and James Brown.

———. 9 Stat. 123. 1862. "An Act to raise for a limited Time an additional military Force, and for other Purposes." February 11, 1847. [Commonly called the Ten Regiment Act.] *The Statutes at Large and Treaties of the United States of America from December 1, 1845 to March 3, 1851.* Vol. 9. Edited by George Minot. Boston, MA: Little, Brown and Company.

———. 9 Stat. 922. 1862. "Treaty of Peace, Friendship, Limits, and Settlement between the United States of America and the Mexican Republic." May 30, 1848. [Commonly called "Treaty of Guadalupe Hidalgo."] *The Statutes at Large and Treaties of the United States of America from December 1, 1845 to March 3, 1851, Arranged in Chronological Order.* Vol. 9. Edited by George Minot. Boston, MA: Little, Brown and Company.

———. 11 Stat. 163. 1859. "An Act relating to Foreign Coins and to the Coinage of Cents at the Mint of the United States." February 21, 1857. *The Statutes at Large and Treaties of the United States of America.* Vol. 11. Boston, MA: Charles C. Little and James Brown.

Steiner, Harold Austin. 1999. *The Old Spanish Trail, across the Mojave Desert: A History and Guide.* Las Vegas, NV: The Haldor Company.

Stephens, L[orenzo] Dow. 1916. *Life Sketches of a Jayhawker of '49: Actual Experiences of a Pioneer Told by Himself in His Own Way.* San Jose, CA: Nolta Bros.

Stewart, George R., ed. 1953. *The Opening of the California Trail.* Berkeley: Univ. of California Press.

——— 1960. *Ordeal by Hunger: The Story of the Donner Party.* Boston, MA: Houghton Mifflin Company. New edition with a supplement and three accounts by survivors.

———. 1962. *The California Trail: An Epic with Many Heroes.* New York: McGraw-Hill Company.

Stuart, Joseph A. 1895. *My Roving Life: A Diary of Travels and Adventures by Sea and Land, During Peace and War.* Vol. 1. 1849. Auburn, CA: By the author.

Sutak, Tom. 2010. "Jefferson Hunt: California's First Mormon Politician." *Journal of Mormon History* 36, no. 3 (Summer): 82–117.

———. 2012. *Into the Jaws of Hell, Jefferson Hunt: The Death Valley '49ers Wagon Train & His Adventures in California.* Danville, CA: Pine Park Publishing.

Swisher, John M. 1995. *Bits 'n' Pieces of the Mohave Desert's Weathered Past.* Hesperia, CA: Privately printed.

Tea, Roy D. 1999. *"The Southern Route" of the Forty-Niners: Salt Lake City South to Los Angeles.* Salt Lake City, UT: Oregon Trails Association, Utah Crossroads Chapter.

———. 2005a. "The Limitless Plain, Part 1." *Overland Journal* 23, no. 1 (Spring): 20–38.

———. 2005b. "The Limitless Plain, Part 2." *Overland Journal* 23, no. 2 (Summer): 61–89.

Thompson, David G. 1921. *Routes to Desert Watering Places in the Mohave Desert Region, California.* United States Geological Survey. Water-Supply Paper 490–B. Washington, DC: U.S. Government Printing Office.

Thompson, Gerald Eugene. 1978. "The Public Career of Edward Fitzgerald Beale, 1845–1893." PhD diss., Univ. of Arizona.

———. 1983. *Edward F. Beale & the American West.* Albuquerque: Univ. of New Mexico Press.

Thomson, Samuel. 1835. *New Guide to Health; or, Botanic Family Physician. Containing a Complete System of Practice, on a Plan Entirely New: With a Description of the Vegetables Made Use of, and Directions for Preparing and Administering Them, to Cure Disease. To Which Is Prefixed, A Narrative of the Life and Medical Discoveries of the Author.* Boston: J. Q. Adams.

———. 1849. *New Guide to Health; or, Botanic Family Physician: Containing a Complete System of Practice, on a Plan Entirely New: With a Description of the Vegetables Made Use of, and Directions for Preparing and Administering Them, to Cure Disease. To Which Is Added A Description of Several Cases of Diseases Attended by the Author with the Mode of Treatment and Cure.* London: Simpkin, Marshall & Co. New Edition.

Trennert, Robert A., Jr. 1972. "The Mormons and the Office of Indian Affairs: The Conflict over Winter Quarters, 1846–1848." *Nebraska History* 53: 381–400.

Tyler, Daniel. 2000. *A Concise History of the Mormon Battalion in the Mexican War: 1846–1847.* Heber City, UT: Archive Publishers. First published 1881.

"Underground Railroad Freedom Station: Galesburg Colony at Knox College." Knox College website. Online at http://www.knox.edu/x12131.xml.

Unruh, John D., Jr. 1979. *The Plains Across: The Overland Emigrants and the Trans-Mississippi West, 1840–60.* Urbana: Univ. of Illinois Press.

USDI. 1978. Entries in the National Register, Nevada Las Vegas Springs, Las Vegas, Clark County. National Register of Historic Places Inventory—Nomination Form, United States Department of Interior. Date entered, December 14, 1978.

Van Cott, John W., comp. 1990. *Utah Place Names.* Salt Lake City: Univ. of Utah Press.

Van der Zee, Jacob. 1914. "The Mormon Trails in Iowa." *Iowa Journal of History and Politics* 12, no. 1 (January): 3–16.

Van Wagoner, Richard S., and Steven Walker. 1982. "Joseph Smith: 'The Gift of Seeing.'" *Dialogue: A Journal of Mormon Thought* 15, no. 2 (Summer): 49–68.

Van Zandt, Franklin K. 1966. *Boundaries of the United States and the Several States.* Geological Survey Bulletin 1212. Washington, DC: U.S. Government Printing Office.

W. [Wood, Newton]. 1849. To Colonel from Fort Laramie, June 5, 1849. "For the Oquawka Spectator." Published in *Oquawka (IL) Spectator* August 8, 1849.

Wang, E., et al. 2004. "The Genetic Architecture of Selection at the Human Dopamine Receptor D4(DRD4) Gene Locus." *American Journal of Human Genetics* 74, no. 5 (May): 931–44.

Ware, Joseph E. 1972. *The Emigrants' Guide to California.* Edited by John Caughey. New York: Da Capo Press. First published 1849.

Waring, Gerald A. 1915. *Springs of California.* United States Geological Survey. Water-Supply Paper 338. Washington, DC: U.S. Government Printing Office.

Wasley, James. 1849. To "Dear Brother," October 21, 1849. Published in *Mineral Point (WI) Tribune,* March 1, 1850.

Watts, Martin. 1999. *Working Oxen.* Oxford, UK: Shire Publications Ltd.

Webster, Kimball. 1917. *The Gold Seekers of '49; A Personal Narrative of the Overland Trail and Adventures in California and Oregon from 1849 To 1854.* Manchester: N.H. Standard Book Company.

[Welch, Adonijah Strong]. 1849a. To "My Dear Friend, [mailed from] Fort Laramie, Camp of the Pioneers, June 28, 1849." Published in *Hillsdale (MI) Whig Standard* December 11, 1849.

———. 1849b. Journal fragment from west of Fort Bridger, August 2–3, 1849. Photocopy in The Bancroft Library, Berkeley, CA.

———. 1849c. Diary. In *Trails Divided*, edited by Theodore C. Ressler (1964), 255–74. Ressler attributed Welch's diary ("Log") to David Switzer.

———. 1959. Welch's March 1, 1850, letter to "Dear Fellow Friends." In "Three Gold Rush Letters of Adonijah Strong Welch." Edited by William H. Hermann. *Iowa Journal of History* 57, no. 1 (January): 61–73, and in Cumming 1985, 119–27.

Westervelt, Walter Tallman, comp. 1905. *Genealogy of the Westervelt Family*. Edited by Wharton Dickinson. New York: Press of Tobias A. Wright.

Wheat, Carl I. 1939. "The Forty-Niners in Death Valley (A Tentative Census)." *The Historical Society of Southern California Quarterly* 21, no. 4 (December): 102–17.

———. 1940. "The Jayhawkers at the Missouri: A Remarkable Discovery." *Historical Society of Southern California Quarterly* 22, no. 3 (September): 103–8.

———. 1956. "Mapping the American West: A Bibliographical Summary." *Papers of the Bibliographical Society of America* 50, no. 1: 1–16. Far Western Issue. New York, NY.

———. 1959. *Mapping the Transmississippi West, 1540–1861*. Vol. 3 of *From the Mexican War to the Boundary Surveys, 1846–1854*. San Francisco, CA: Institute of Historical Cartography.

Wheat, Carl I., and Dale L. Morgan. 1954. *Jedediah Smith and His Maps of the American West*. San Francisco: California Historical Society.

White, Richard. 1988. *The Roots of Dependency: Subsistence, Environment, and Social Change among the Choctaws, Pawnees, and Navajos*. Lincoln: Univ. of Nebraska Press.

White, William Wellington. 1927. "William Wellington White: An Autobiography." *Historical Society of Southern California Quarterly* 4, no. 4 (December): 202–16.

Whiteley, Lee. 1999. *The Cherokee Trail: Bent's Old Fort to Fort Bridger*. Boulder, CO: Johnson Printing.

Whitney, Horace K. 2018. *The Journey West: The Mormon Pioneer Journals of Horace K. Whitney with Insights by Helen Mar Kimball Whitney*. Edited by Richard E. Bennett. Provo, UT: Religious Studies Center, Brigham Young Univ.

Wiley, Nancy J. Haynes. n.d. "Story of the Jay-Hawkers of '49 from Accounts of Captain Asa Haynes." Written by his daughter, Nancy J. Haynes Wiley. Presumably handwritten. The 12-page typescript was "Typed by Nancy Cramer, June 28, 1937." Nancy Cramer is a granddaughter of Nancy Wiley. 987–3–1. Knox College Archives, Galesburg, IL.

Wilkins, James F. 1968. *An Artist on the Overland Trail: The 1849 Diary and Sketches of James F. Wilkins*. Edited by John Francis McDermott. San Marino, CA: The Huntington Library.

Williams, Stephen K., comp. 1958, reprint. R[oger] B. Taney, Chief Justice, U.S. Supreme Court. "The State of Missouri, Complainant v. The State of Iowa, Respondent. [and] The State of Iowa, Complainant v. The State of Missouri, Respondent." In *Cases Argued and Decided in the Supreme Court of the United States: 5, 6, 7, 8, Howard, Book 12, Lawyers' Edition*. January Term, 1849, pp. 657–80. Rochester, NY: The Lawyers Co-Operative Publishing Company, 1958.

Wright, Albert Hazen, and Anna Allen. 1957. *Handbook of Snakes of the United States and Canada*. 2 vols. Ithaca, NY: Comstock Publishing Associates.

Wright, Norman E. 1995. "Odometers: Distance Measurements on Western Emigrant Trails." *Overland Journal* 13, no. 3 (Fall): 14–24.

Yenne, Bill. 2004. *The Missions of California*. San Diego, CA: Thunder Bay Press.

Young, Brigham. 1997. *Manuscript History of Brigham Young, 1847–1850*. Edited by William S. Harwell. Salt Lake City, UT: Collier's Publishing.

Young, Sheldon. 1849a. March 18, 1849–December 15, 1850. "Diaries of His Trip to California, 1849–1850." MssHM 75663–75664, Western Historical Manuscripts. The Huntington Library, San Marino, CA. Surviving pages of the original Sheldon Young diary donated to the Huntington by his great-great-grandchildren David Duerr and Gretchen Forsyth, 2014.

———. 1849b. "Sheldon Youngs [*sic*] Log, 1849, Joliet Illinois to Rancho San Francisquito [San Francisco], California." Typescript of original diary, 1897. Title was added by John Colton. JA555, Jayhawkers of '49 Collection. The Huntington Library, San Marino, CA.

———. 1849c. Diary. Electronic scans made by David R. Duerr, Sheldon Young's great-great-grandson. In Johnson files. 2012.

Index

Names listed only in the Knox County Company Roster, in Appendix A, or only in other wagon lists and not elsewhere in the text are not listed in the Index. OST stands for Old Spanish Trail and SLC stands for Salt Lake City. Numbers in **bold** refer to figures or maps. Lorton's movements are listed chronologically, not alphabetically. Indian nations are listed under "Indians;" Forts are listed under "Forts."